The Educational Book Division of Prentice-Hall, Inc., is committed to the publication of outstanding textbooks. One important measure of a book's excellence is how well it communicates with its readers. To assure a highly readable book, the content for this text was selected, organized, and written at a level appropriate for the intended audience. The Dale-Chall readability formula was used to control readability level. An inviting and meaningful design was created to enhance the book's visual appeal as well as to facilitate the reading process. We are confident that the students for whom this book is intended will read it, comprehend it, and learn from it.

The following features were incorporated in the content and design of this text.

- A complete table of contents lists unit titles, chapter titles, and major section heads within each chapter.
- **All maps and charts in the text are listed on pages viii and ix, for student reference throughout their study of New York.**
- **Special features on important people, places, and events are built into the text and set off in boxes. A complete list of special features is on page ix.**
- A political map of New York State, located on page x, is a convenient and easy-to-find reference tool for students.
- Each unit begins with a time line of important events in New York history and in American history as well. New York dates are set off in color.
- Chapter objectives are listed at the opening of each chapter.
- Each chapter concludes with review questions, analysis questions, vocabulary, and a geography review.
- Important social studies concepts and terms are included in a glossary on page 364.

NEW YORK

THE EMPIRE STATE

NEW YORK

THE EMPIRE STATE

Fifth Edition

David M. Ellis

P.V. Rogers Professor of History
Hamilton College
Clinton, New York

James A. Frost

Executive Director
The Connecticut State Colleges
New Britain, Connecticut

William B. Fink

Professor of History and Social Science Education
State University College
Oneonta, New York

Prentice-Hall, Inc. Englewood Cliffs, New Jersey

SUPPLEMENTARY MATERIALS
Teacher's Manual and Tests

New York: The Empire State

Fifth Edition

David M. Ellis, James A. Frost, William B. Fink

ISBN 0-13-620419-8 10 9 8 7 6 5 4 3 2 1

Cover design, front and back matter, and unit and chapter opening design by Diane Irene Kachalsky

PRENTICE-HALL INTERNATIONAL, INC., London
PRENTICE-HALL OF AUSTRALIA, PTY. LTD., Sydney
PRENTICE-HALL OF CANADA, LTD., Toronto
PRENTICE-HALL OF INDIA PRIVATE LTD., New Delhi
PRENTICE-HALL OF JAPAN, INC., Tokyo
PRENTICE-HALL OF SOUTHEAST ASIA PTE. LTD., Singapore
WHITEHALL BOOKS LIMITED, Wellington, New Zealand

Photo Credits

Cover and Frontispiece photo: West Point Museum

Albright-Knox Gallery, 318 American Federation of Labor and Congress of Industrial Organizations, 259 American Telephone and Telegraph Company, 356 The Bettmann Archive, Inc., 68, 71, 111 Wil Blanche, 280 (bottom) The Bowne House Historical Society, 85 (top) Chase Manhattan Money Museum, 97, 168 Church of Jesus Christ of Latter-Day Saints (Mormon), 211 Colonial Williamsburg, 110 Colonie Center, 279 Columbia University, 191 Cross County Shopping Center, 278 Charles Phelps Cushing, 176 Laima Druskis/Editorial Photocolor Archives, 342 Editorial Photocolor Archives, 248, 342 (middle) Eastman Kodak Company, 243 General Electric Company, 257, 283 (bottom) Genesee County Department of History, 155 Harper's Weekly, 268, 357 Historical Pictures Service, Chicago, 76 Home Insurance Company, 209 International Ladies Garment Workers Union, 260 William Jacob, 140 Jane Latta, 104 Library of Congress, 230 (bottom), 231 Livingston Manor Chamber of Commerce, photo by H.B. Spriggs, 159 Macy's, New York, 152 Metropolitan Museum of Art: photo by Robert Gray, 281; Rogers Fund, 1925, 311; Given in memory of Jonathan Sturges by his Children, 1895, 221 Roger Moore, 328 Museum of the City of New York, 43, 87, 94, 106, 113, 171: The Edward W.C. Arnold Collection, 202; Byron Collection, 239, 240, 244; Harry T. Peters Collection, 187; Jacob Riis Collection, 265, 271 National Park Service and the Jamestown Foundation, 67 New York Convention and Visitors Bureau, 85 (bottom), 210, 308, 313, 316, 321 New York *Herald Tribune*, 229 New York Public Library, 42: Emmett Collection, 121, 139, 157, 216 (bottom); Schomburg Collection 228, 259; Stokes Collection, 82 New York State Department of Commerce, 8, 10, 11, 13, 27, 41, 44, 46, 61, 135, 141, 164, 287, 289, 300, 302, 327, 337 New York State Education Department, 120, 169, 217 New York State Executive Chamber, 305 New York State Historical Association, Cooperstown, 99, 143, 151, 153, 165, 189, 197, 199, 200, 218, 226, 230 (top), 347 New York State Mental Hygiene Photo, 336 New York State Museum, J.A. Glenn, photographer, 28 New York State Museum and Science Service, 40 New York Stock Exchange, 246 Office of General Affairs, Promotions & Public Affairs, 303 Office of the Governor, 304 Oswego *Palladium-Times*, 118 Palisade Interstate Park Commission, 5, 147 The Police Athletic League of New York, Inc. 362 Port of New York Authority, 241, 280 (top), 289, 292 Presbyterian Historical Society, 107 Chris Reeger, 277 Ringling Museum of Art, 45 Rochester Museum and Science Center, 30, 36 Rockefeller Center, Inc., 298 Hugh Rogers/Monkmeyer, 342 (top), 351 Franklin D. Roosevelt Library, 297 St. Mark's Church in the Bowery, photo by Paul Acton, 84 Sleepy Hollow Restorations, 86 South Street Seaport Museum, 196, 256 Standard Oil Company (N.J.), 9 Staten Island Institute of Arts and Sciences, 29 Syracuse University Library, 216 (top) United Nations, 358 University of Rochester, 208, 223 Utica Public Library, 144 West Point Museum, 37, 192 Westchester County Historical Society, 137 Xerox Corporation, 258 Yivo Institute for Jewish Research, 252, 254 George Zimbel/Monkmeyer, 351

Unit Openings:

Unit 1: Zimbel/Monkmeyer

Unit 2: New York Public Library Picture Collection

Unit 3: The New York Historical Society

Unit 4: The Granger Collection

Unit 5: The Granger Collection

Unit 6: Culver Pictures

Unit 7: The Granger Collection

Unit 8: New York State Department of Commerce

contents

Unit One: The Land and the Indians, 1

Unit Two: The Age of Discovery and Settlement, 49

Unit Three: Colonial Culture and Society, 89

maps

charts

special features

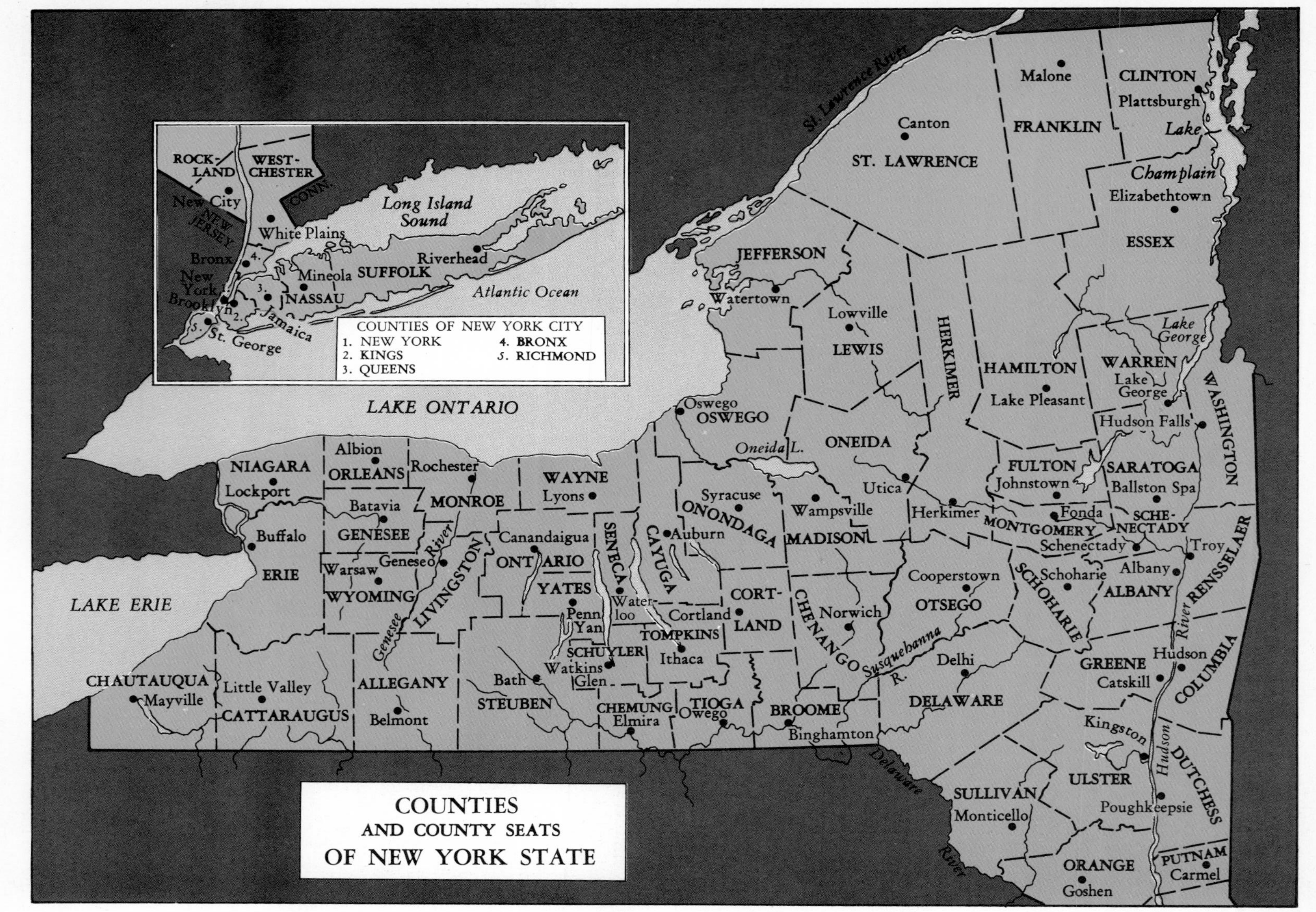
COUNTIES OF NEW YORK CITY
1. NEW YORK
2. KINGS
3. QUEENS
4. BRONX
5. RICHMOND
ROCKLAND
New City
WESTCHESTER
White Plains
CONN.
NEW JERSEY
Bronx
New York
Brooklyn
St. George
Jamaica
NASSAU
Mineola
SUFFOLK
Riverhead
Long Island Sound
Atlantic Ocean
LAKE ONTARIO
LAKE ERIE
St. Lawrence River
Lake Champlain
Lake George
Oneida L.
Genesee River
Susquehanna R.
Delaware River
Hudson River
CLINTON
Plattsburgh
FRANKLIN
Malone
ST. LAWRENCE
Canton
ESSEX
Elizabethtown
JEFFERSON
Watertown
LEWIS
Lowville
HERKIMER
Herkimer
HAMILTON
Lake Pleasant
WARREN
Lake George
WASHINGTON
Hudson Falls
OSWEGO
Oswego
ONEIDA
Utica
FULTON
Johnstown
SARATOGA
Ballston Spa
MONTGOMERY
Fonda
SCHENECTADY
Schenectady
RENSSELAER
Troy
ALBANY
Albany
SCHOHARIE
Schoharie
OTSEGO
Cooperstown
MADISON
Wampsville
ONONDAGA
Syracuse
CAYUGA
Auburn
SENECA
Waterloo
NIAGARA
Lockport
ORLEANS
Albion
MONROE
Rochester
WAYNE
Lyons
GENESEE
Batavia
ERIE
Buffalo
WYOMING
Warsaw
LIVINGSTON
Geneseo
ONTARIO
Canandaigua
YATES
Penn Yan
CORTLAND
Cortland
CHENANGO
Norwich
TOMPKINS
Ithaca
SCHUYLER
Watkins Glen
CHAUTAUQUA
Mayville
CATTARAUGUS
Little Valley
ALLEGANY
Belmont
STEUBEN
Bath
CHEMUNG
Elmira
TIOGA
Owego
BROOME
Binghamton
DELAWARE
Delhi
GREENE
Catskill
COLUMBIA
Hudson
ULSTER
Kingston
DUTCHESS
Poughkeepsie
SULLIVAN
Monticello
ORANGE
Goshen
PUTNAM
Carmel
COUNTIES
AND COUNTY SEATS
OF NEW YORK STATE

chapter 1: NATURE MOLDS NEW YORK and the WESTERN HEMISPHERE

chapter 2: INDIANS in AMERICA

chapter 3: The IROQUOIS RULE NEW YORK

unit one

The Land and the Indians

New York state history dates are shown in color.

c. 300-900 Height of Mayan civilization

1000 Algonquians are settled in New York

c. 1000-1532 Height of Inca civilization

1200-1521 Height of Aztec civilization

c. 1300 Iroquois conquer the Algonquians

1456 Movable type used for printing

1479 King Ferdinand and Queen Isabella unite their kingdoms in Spain

1521 Cortes conquers the Aztecs

1532 Pizarro topples the Incas

1570 Confederacy of the Five Nations is formed

1701 Iroquois and the French sign an alliance

1722 Tuscaroras join the Iroquois confederation of tribes

Visitors to New York have often noted many examples of people's ability to adjust to their environment. They admire the huge power plants at Niagara Falls and the St. Lawrence Seaway; they marvel at Manhattan skyscrapers; and they express admiration for the bridges over and the tunnels under the Hudson River. In few places in the world can one find so many good examples of human capacity to refashion the environment.

The natural environment—rivers, lakes, forests, mountains—controlled human actions for centuries. In fact, it still deeply affects the lives of most New Yorkers. The large lowland stretching from Utica to Buffalo has nourished the growth of many cities, and the excellent soils and climate provide an excellent region for raising crops and animals. Because of the splendid harbor at the mouth of the Hudson River and the Hudson-Mohawk route through the Appalachian barrier, a great metropolitan center has grown up, serving trade with Europe, Africa, South America, and Asia as well as with cities to the west. Nature formed soil and mineral resources, and left deposits of salt, talc, gypsum, and petroleum.

No group of New Yorkers exercised more power during New York's history than the Iroquois Indians in proportion to their numbers. Knowledge of the Iroquois way of life and culture will help us to understand not only them but also ourselves. We shall trace the origins of the Algonquian and Iroquois in New York, their response to European civilization, and their important role in the struggle for the fur trade and empire.

Chapter Objectives

To learn about

- the geography of New York
- the regions of the United States

chapter 1

NATURE MOLDS NEW YORK and the WESTERN HEMISPHERE

The Land Changes

The study of the history and structure of the earth is called geology. Only by examining geological changes can we understand the underlying natural resources upon which the economy and society of New Yorkers have developed. Millions of years ago, long before the appearance of humans on earth, whole ranges of mountains raised up. River valleys were cut deep into the hard rock below the surface of the land. Solid stone was ground into sand and gravel. From the hot depths, great quantities of melted rock and minerals were forced upward to the surface. Our study of the Empire State begins with these changes.

For countless ages large sections of New York lay beneath broad oceans. At other times the ocean floor was raised up high above the sea and became dry land. At other times great sheets of ice lay over the land, remaining there for thousands of years. Over the millions of years the highlands were worn down by wind and water and ice. This is still happening—we call it erosion—but it goes on too slowly for us to notice. How many ice ages have come and gone? How many mountain ranges have reared up, only to disappear? How many times have ancient seas covered the Empire State? Nobody knows.

We do know that a number of seas came into being only to disappear. Some have been named. One of these was the Grenville Ocean, which covered the state about two billion years ago. Into the Grenville Ocean washed pieces of stone and mud eroded from the surrounding land. The bits and pieces settled to the ocean floor and became beds of solid rock. These are called Grenville rocks and are among the oldest rocks found anywhere on earth. Today they still may be seen in many parts of New York. Once they were thousands of feet thick. Can you imagine how long it must have taken for them to form on the bottom of the Grenville Ocean?

The Hudson River Palisades across from New York City. These spectacular cliffs rise more than 500 feet above the river. They were formed of magma.

Sometimes great quantities of steam and gases rose from the hot depths of the earth. These left deposits of zinc, iron, and talc on the surface of the land. Today these deposits are mined and bring wealth to New Yorkers. Sometimes the surface of the earth broke and hot *lava* flowed out. Lava is melted rock from far under the earth's surface. When it cools, it becomes very hard. While lava is still below ground, it is called *magma.* Sometimes the magma pushing upward was trapped beneath the surface in pockets formed by other rocks. Ages later, when the surrounding rock crumbled and eroded away, the cooled and hardened magma was uncovered. The Palisades of the Hudson River are formed by a great sheet of magma. For several miles this hard rock forms a cliff along the edge of the river. It is so hard that the river has not yet been able to wear it away.

At times in the past, nearly all of the state was covered with great sheets of ice. In the northern part of the state, the ice was over two miles thick. Even the mountains were covered. Storms piled snow on top of the ice. The snow became squeezed into solid ice, too. Very slowly the great ice sheet, or *glacier,* flowed southward, carrying with it great boulders, mud, and small stones that were frozen into it. The warmer temperatures of the south melted the ice, and the materials that had been carried by the ice sheet piled up on the ground.

The southern limit of the ice sheet ran through the middle of Long Island from one end to the other. It did the same on Staten Island. On both islands are a series of hills made up of the materials deposited by the ice sheet. Such deposits are called *moraines.* The southern portion of Long Island is a low plain made up largely of fine particles of stone and other materials washed out from the moraines by the streams of water flowing from the melting ice.

As the climate became warmer, the edge of the ice sheet moved slowly northward. The melting ice dropped a layer of mud, sand, and gravel across the state. Piles of sand and gravel left by the ice are used today for making concrete and for other purposes. Some river valleys were dug deeper and made wider by the great ice mass which pushed through them. Sometimes the melting ice sheet deposited moraines across the valleys and formed dams. These valleys filled with water to create lakes. The Finger Lakes were formed in this manner. The largest of the Finger Lakes are Seneca Lake and Cayuga Lake. Find the

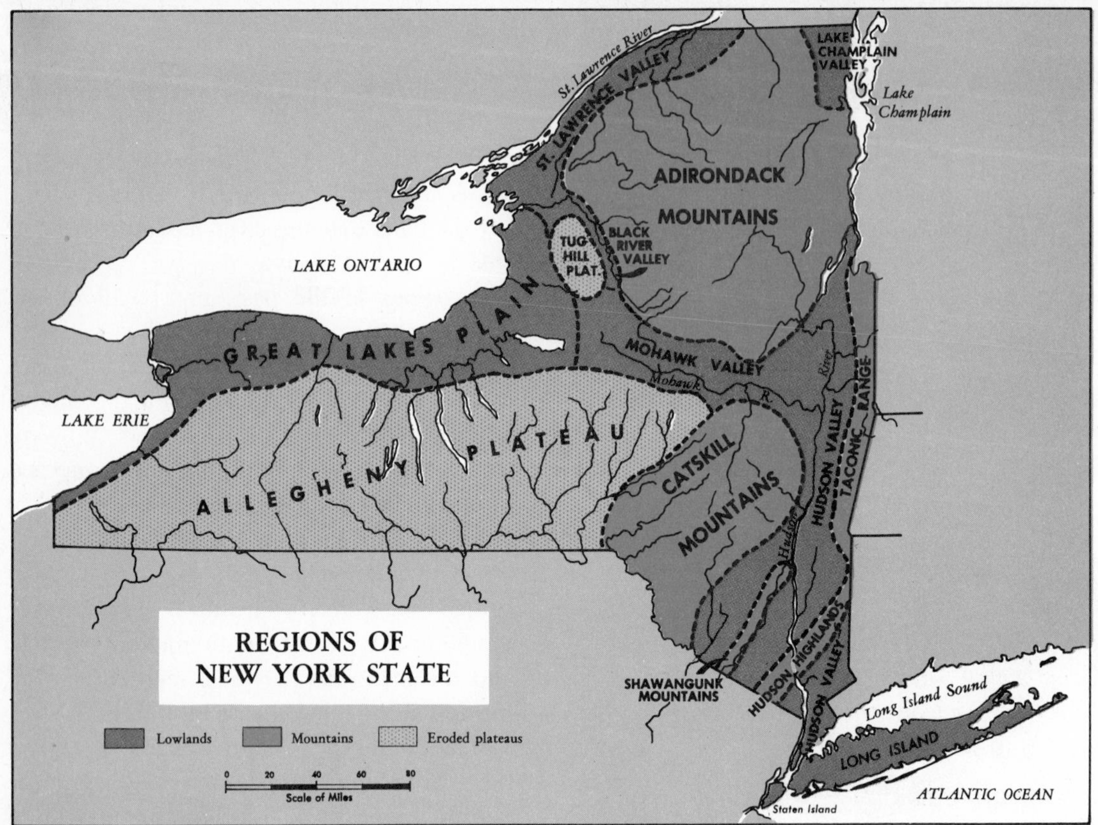

Map 1

Finger Lakes on Map 2, page 12. They are so long and narrow that they look like fingers.

The surface of New York has undergone many changes. The whole state has been slowly lifted and lowered. The channel of the Hudson River has been traced in the floor of the Atlantic Ocean for over 100 miles from the present shoreline. At one time this part of the ocean floor must have been dry land. Only if it had been above sea level could the river have flowed over it and cut the channel. As the land sank, the channel was covered by water.

It is fortunate that this sinking took place. When the land sank, the ocean water flowed in and formed Upper New York Bay and Long Island Sound. The long shoreline provides space for whole fleets of ships to load and unload. Boats can sail up the Hudson River to Albany and Troy. The East River joins Upper New York Bay with Long Island Sound. The Sound, about 90 miles long, furnishes a protected water route for trade with the New England States. It is also a fine place for general recreation.

The land surface of New York is divided equally among lowlands, mountains, and eroded *plateaus.* A plateau is an area of high flat land. The *eroded plateaus* have been worn away by streams and rivers, by wind and ice, so that they are no longer flat. They have been worn down to form hills and valleys. Look at Map 1. It will show you where the lowlands, mountains, and eroded plateaus are located.

The Lowlands

The lowlands include the low-lying level lands, especially those on the shores of the Great Lakes and the Atlantic Ocean and along the major waterways. The highest point on the lowlands is near Lake Erie where the altitude is about 900 feet above sea level. The lowlands can be divided into four sections. Locate them on Map 1.

1. The Great Lakes Plain.
2. The river valleys of the St. Lawrence, the Mohawk, and the Hudson.
3. The Lake Champlain Valley.
4. Long Island and Staten Island.

As the last ice age came to a close, the Great Lakes were much larger than they are now. Water covered the whole area of the Great Lakes Plain. The waves of the lakes wore the land down and flattened it. As it grew warmer, the ice melted in the Mohawk Valley. When this happened, the Great Lakes drained through the Mohawk Valley into the Hudson River. The flow of water was larger than that passing over Niagara Falls today. The roaring waters of this mighty river dug out the great Mohawk Valley.

As the earth grew warmer, the edge of the ice sheet moved farther north. In time the St. Lawrence Valley became free of ice in the region north of where Lake Champlain now lies, but the mouth of the St. Lawrence River remained frozen. When this happened, the Great Lakes stopped draining through the Mohawk Valley. Instead, the water flowed southward from the St. Lawrence into the Champlain Valley and then into the Hudson River. For unknown ages this great rush of water flowed through the Champlain Valley digging it deeper and flattening it. Finally all of the ice in the St. Lawrence Valley melted, and the waters of the Great Lakes began to drain through the St. Lawrence River.

The Mohawk and the Hudson river valleys together form the only level route through the wall of mountains that stretches from the St. Lawrence River in Canada to Alabama in southern United States. The Champlain Valley forms a passage for travel to Canada. As we shall see, both the Mohawk Valley and the Champlain Valley became important trade routes.

The Mountains and Plateaus

There are two great ranges of mountains in New York State. They are the Catskills and the Adirondacks. There are three smaller ranges: the Shawangunk Mountains, the Hudson Highlands, and the Taconic Mountains. Look at Map 1 to see where they are located. With the exception of the Adirondacks, all of these mountains form a part of the Appalachians.

The Adirondacks cover about one-fourth of the state. They are very old mountains. Hundreds of millions of years ago they were created by great pressure which burst the surface of the earth, forcing it upward into ridges thousands of feet high. These ridges are almost straight and run parallel to one another. The peaks of the Adirondacks are the high points of these parallel ridges. When the mountains were formed the area was covered with Grenville rock. From under the earth great quantities of hot melted stone pushed upward. The heat and pressure changed the Grenville rock. Much of it became marble and quartzite. Today the Adirondacks are a mixture of several types of very hard rock.

The peaks of the Adirondacks are from about 3,000 to 5,000 feet above sea level. The highest mountain in New York is Mount Marcy, 5,344 feet above sea level. When the Adirondacks were first formed, they were many thousands of feet higher than they are today. The tops have been eroded away by wind, water, and ice. The ice sheets formed many lakes in the Adirondacks by depositing moraines across river valleys. Among the most famous are Lake Placid, Lake George, and Saranac Lake.

The Catskill Mountains are very different from the Adirondacks. Hundreds of millions of years ago the region of the Catskills was a level plain. The plain was raised high above sea level. Wind, water, and ice eroded this plateau. Rivers formed and carried away great quantities of materials. What is left are rugged mountains of hard rock. The peaks of the Catskills do not run in parallel ridges as they do in the Adirondacks. They are scattered every which way. This is because the Catskills were formed by erosion rather than by pressure. The Catskill Mountains are not as high as the Adirondacks, but the peaks are usually over 3,000 feet above sea level. The highest, Slide Mountain, reaches an altitude of 4,024 feet. The Taconic Mountains are east of the Hudson River along the borders of Connecticut, Massachusetts, and Vermont. They include the Berkshire Hills in Massa-

Long Lake in the Adirondacks forms a ten-mile canoe route through the high peaks.

An eroded plateau section of New York near Index.

chusetts. Southeast of the Catskills lie the Shawangunk Mountains, a narrow ridge, rising at its highest point 2,289 feet above sea level.

The third range is called the Highlands of the Hudson. It runs northeast to southwest across the southeastern portion of the state and is cut by the Hudson River between Newburgh and Peekskill. Perhaps the best known of the peaks is Bear Mountain, one of the rugged Highland hills through which the mighty Hudson flows.

There are two eroded plateaus in New York. The Allegheny Plateau covers almost one-third of the state. It takes in nearly the whole southwestern part of New York. The Tug Hill Plateau is much smaller. It lies just north of the Mohawk Valley and west of the Adirondacks. Locate these two plateaus on Map 1.

The Drainage System

There are five major *drainage basins* in the Empire State. A drainage basin is an area from which all of the water flows by a single exit. For example, the Hudson Basin is made up of all the rivers and streams which flow into the Hudson, including the Hudson itself. A river that flows into another river is called a *tributary*. The Hudson River and its tributaries form the Hudson Basin. Map 2, page 12, shows the areas drained by each basin. You will need a large map of North America to trace the paths followed by the waters of each basin after they leave New York State. Your school will have such a map. Notice that the waters of the state enter the Atlantic at widely separated places.

The Great Lakes-St. Lawrence Basin. This basin drains a much larger section of the state than any other. About one-half of Lake Ontario is within the state. A much smaller part of Lake Erie belongs to New York. Lake Ontario is the smallest of the Great Lakes. It is 193 miles long and 53 miles wide and has an area of 7,540 square miles. The surface of Lake Ontario is 245 feet above sea level. The lake is 778 feet deep at its deepest point.

The Niagara River carries a vast quantity of water from Lake Erie to Lake Ontario. Although the Niagara is only about 34 miles long, the water drops 326 feet between Lake Erie and Lake Ontario. Niagara Falls is probably the best-known waterfall in the world. Here the river is divided into two sections by Goat Island. The section east of Goat Island is the American Falls. The American Falls are about 1,000 feet wide and about 165 feet high. The Canadian Falls (sometimes called the Horseshoe

Niagara Falls, the most famous waterfalls in the world. This is a view of the American Falls and down the gorge.

Falls) are west of the island. The Canadian Falls are about 2,500 feet wide and 155 feet high. Below the falls is a deep gorge through which the water rushes at a very rapid rate. The waters of the Niagara River are used to make electric power.

Three important rivers flow across New York into Lake Ontario. Locate them on Map 2 on page 12. The Genesee River begins in the highlands of Pennsylvania and enters the lake near Rochester. The Oswego River flows from the Finger Lakes, Lake Oneida, and part of the Tug Hill Plateau. Frontiersmen often used the Oswego River as a route of travel. To protect this route, a fort was built where the river reaches Lake Ontario. The Black River reaches deep into the southwestern part of the Adirondacks. On its way to Lake Ontario the Black River passes through the city of Watertown. The falls of the Black River provide power for many factories, especially those that make paper.

The St. Lawrence carries the waters of Lake Ontario to the Atlantic. It is a new river, formed after the last ice age. It has not had time to cut a deep valley. Between the New York and Canadian border, it passes over a ridge of hard rock. Many peaks of this ridge are above the surface of the river and form islands. There are so many of these that they are called the Thousand Islands.

Most rivers of northern New York drain into the St. Lawrence. Much of this water is caught in Lake Champlain. The Ausable River flows from the high ridges of the Adirondacks to Lake Champlain through a canyon or very deep gorge. Lake George also drains into Lake Champlain. The waters of Lake Champlain pass to the St. Lawrence through the Richelieu River. Notice the large area drained into the St. Lawrence through Lake Champlain. Note also there are rivers west of the lake which empty directly into the St. Lawrence. The most important of these is the Raquette River. The Raquette has its source in the heart of the Adirondacks.

The Hudson Basin. The Hudson is a mighty river, over 300 miles long. It begins in the Adirondacks and flows southward to the Atlantic in almost a straight line. Trace the Hudson River on Map 2. Notice the Mohawk River begins in the center of the state and flows eastward for 100 miles to the Hudson. A very large and important section of the state is drained by the Hudson River.

The Hudson passes through very rough country. To the east, the Taconic Mountains border the river valley for over half its length. Farther south are the Highlands of the Hudson. One would expect the river to twist and turn between the rocky hills but it does not. Why? When the river was first formed, there were no mountains in the way. It flowed over a flat plain in a straight line. The Hudson is also a deep river. Ocean-going ships can sail up the Hudson as far as Albany.

The Delaware Basin. For a considerable distance the Delaware River forms a part of the New York-Pennsylvania border. Water drains into it from the southwestern Catskills. Within New York the river is divided into the East and West Branches. The East Branch rises 1,886 feet above sea level. During the pioneer days, loads of logs, grain, furs, and other frontier products were floated down the river on rafts or canoes to the markets in New Jersey, Pennsylvania, and Delaware. Later the river was a source of waterpower for sawmills and grist mills. Today New York City pipes drinking water from the upper reaches of the Delaware.

The Susquehanna Basin. The Susquehanna and the rivers that flow into it drain a large part of the Allegheny Plateau. The northeastern edge of the plateau is made up of a wall of stone called the Helderberg Escarpment.

Trace the river on Map 2. The first major stream to join the Susquehanna is the Unadilla. Once the Unadilla marked the border between the white man's country and the Indian's. Farther down, the Chenango joins the river. Finally, the Susquehanna receives the waters of the Chemung. The Chemung

At Letchworth State Park, sometimes called the Grand Canyon of the East, are the Middle Falls of the Genesee River.

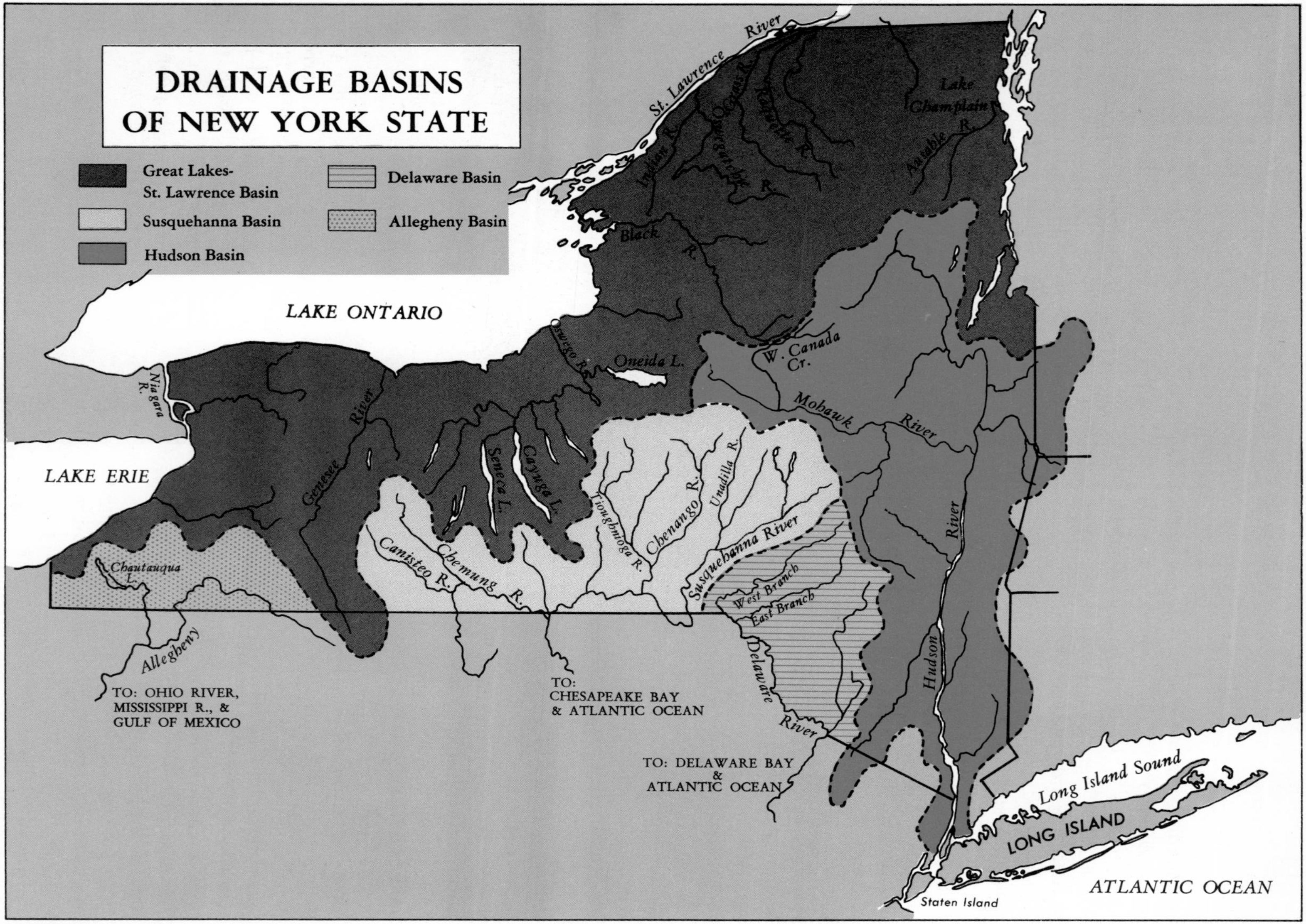

DRAINAGE BASINS OF NEW YORK STATE

- Great Lakes-St. Lawrence Basin
- Susquehanna Basin
- Hudson Basin
- Delaware Basin
- Allegheny Basin

LAKE ONTARIO
LAKE ERIE
St. Lawrence River
Indian R.
Oswegatchie R.
Grass R.
Raquette R.
Lake Champlain
Ausable R.
Black R.
W. Canada Cr.
Mohawk River
Oneida L.
Oswego R.
Niagara R.
Genesee River
Seneca L.
Cayuga L.
Tioughnioga R.
Chenango R.
Unadilla R.
Susquehanna River
West Branch
East Branch
Delaware River
Hudson River
Chautauqua L.
Canisteo R.
Chemung R.
Allegheny
TO: OHIO RIVER, MISSISSIPPI R., & GULF OF MEXICO
TO: CHESAPEAKE BAY & ATLANTIC OCEAN
TO: DELAWARE BAY & ATLANTIC OCEAN
Long Island Sound
LONG ISLAND
ATLANTIC OCEAN
Staten Island

Map 2

and the Canisteo, which flows into it, drain the area southwest of the Finger Lakes.

The Allegheny Basin. The western part of the Allegheny Plateau is drained by the Allegheny River. Look at Map 2. Note that the northern end of Lake Chautauqua is very near Lake Erie. You would expect Lake Chautauqua to drain into Lake Erie, but instead it drains into the Allegheny. Finally its waters reach the Gulf of Mexico many hundreds of miles to the south. Lake Chautauqua is a shallow lake formed when moraines blocked off river valleys after the last ice age.

The Western Hemisphere

Five hundred years ago the civilizations of Europe, Africa, and Asia had no knowledge of North and South America. They knew nothing of the great empires that rose and fell on these two large continents—empires with science, art, and architecture equal to those found elsewhere in the world. Yet, Europeans and Asians and, very possibly, Africans had reached the shores of this unknown world before the time of written history. The memory of these great adventures lived in song and story and in scraps of ancient writings.

Many scientists believe that 200 million years ago all the continents of earth formed a single land mass. Gradually this huge mass of land broke up. The continents began to drift slowly apart on the hot liquid rock that lies under the earth's surface. Today the continents of North and South America have moved far westward. They are separated from the other continents by the Atlantic and Pacific Oceans. (See Map 3, page 14.)

Watkins Glen, a major tourist attraction. Every year thousands of tourists marvel at the gorge and climb the trails.

The Isthmus of Panama links the two continents together. An *isthmus* is a narrow neck of land connecting two larger land masses. Northeast of the Isthmus and between the great land masses of North and South America is the Caribbean Sea. In the Caribbean are the West Indies, a group of islands. The best known of the West Indies are Puerto Rico and Cuba.

Nearly half-a-thousand years have passed since Columbus made his famous voyage to the New World, or Western Hemisphere. In all that time men have been unable to

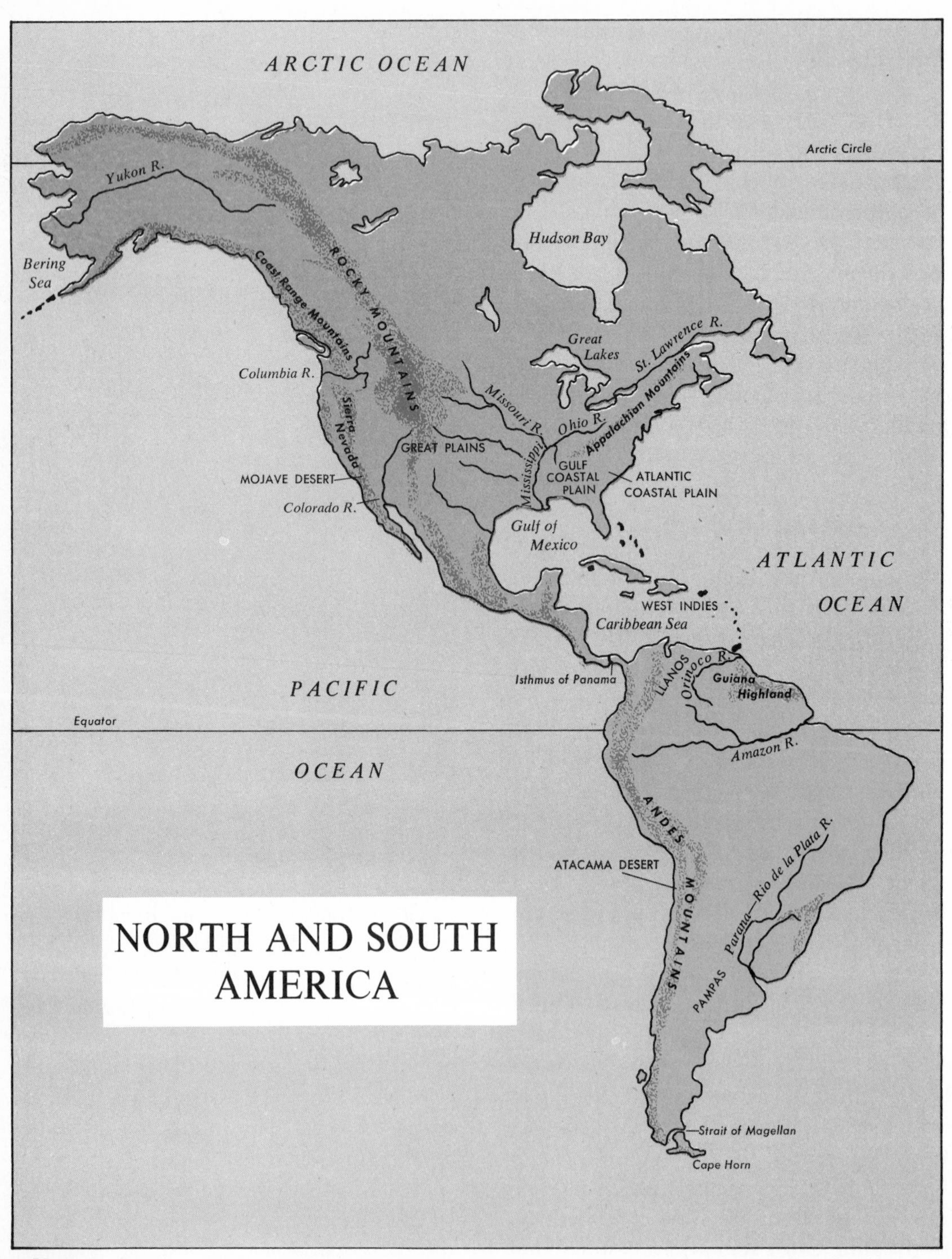
ARCTIC OCEAN
Arctic Circle
Yukon R.
Bering Sea
Hudson Bay
ROCKY MOUNTAINS
Coast Range Mountains
Great Lakes
St. Lawrence R.
Columbia R.
Missouri R.
Ohio R.
Appalachian Mountains
Sierra Nevada
GREAT PLAINS
Mississippi
GULF COASTAL PLAIN
ATLANTIC COASTAL PLAIN
MOJAVE DESERT
Colorado R.
Gulf of Mexico
ATLANTIC OCEAN
WEST INDIES
Caribbean Sea
Isthmus of Panama
LLANOS
Orinoco R.
Guiana Highland
PACIFIC OCEAN
Equator
Amazon R.
ANDES MOUNTAINS
ATACAMA DESERT
Rio de la Plata R.
Parana
PAMPAS
NORTH AND SOUTH AMERICA
Strait of Magellan
Cape Horn

Map 3

explore it fully and list all its riches. Its area is greater than that of Africa and Europe combined. The Great Lakes in North America form the largest body of fresh water in the world. The Amazon River of South America carries more water than any other river on earth. Ocean ships can travel it for a distance of 2,300 miles. Together the Amazon, Orinoco, and Paraná-Rio de la Plata of South America drain over 3,700,000 square miles, an area about the size of Europe. The great river of North America is the Mississippi, which drains 1,244,000 square miles—about 40 percent of the United States.

The Rocky Mountains of North America extend over 3,000 miles from northern Alaska, across Canada, to the middle of New Mexico. In South America the Andes Mountains run north and south—the length of the continent for a distance of 4,500 miles. Only the Himalayan Mountains of Asia have peaks higher than those of the Andes.

A prairie is a level or gently rolling land covered with grass but having no trees. The great prairies of the New World—the Great Plains of North America and the Pampas and Llanos of South America—are among the best regions in the world for raising cattle. The Pampas, most of which is in Argentina, covers an area of 250,000 square miles and is one of the richest farmlands on earth.

The Western Hemisphere has two great deserts. The Mojave of North America lies mostly in southern California. Death Valley, the lowest point in the United States, 282 feet below sea level, is in the Mojave. The rainfall in Death Valley averages about 2 inches per year. The Atacama Desert of South America is in northern Chile. No rainfall has ever been recorded there. (See Map 4, above.)

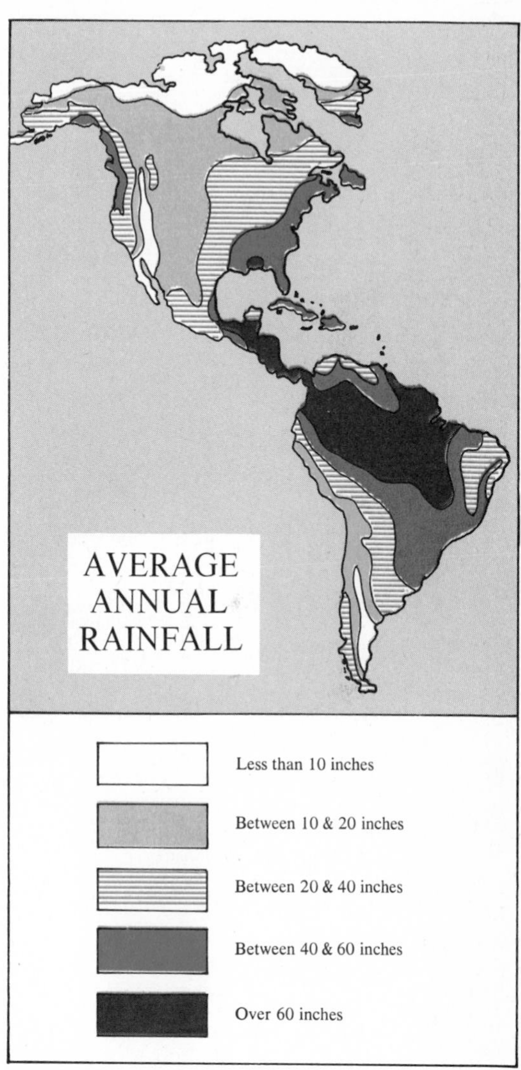

Map 4

Nearly all of North America lies between the Arctic Circle and the Tropics. Much of South America is in the tropics. It has a larger area of hot tropic lowlands than any other continent. South America extends farther south than any continent, except for Antarctica, and has a vast territory that lies

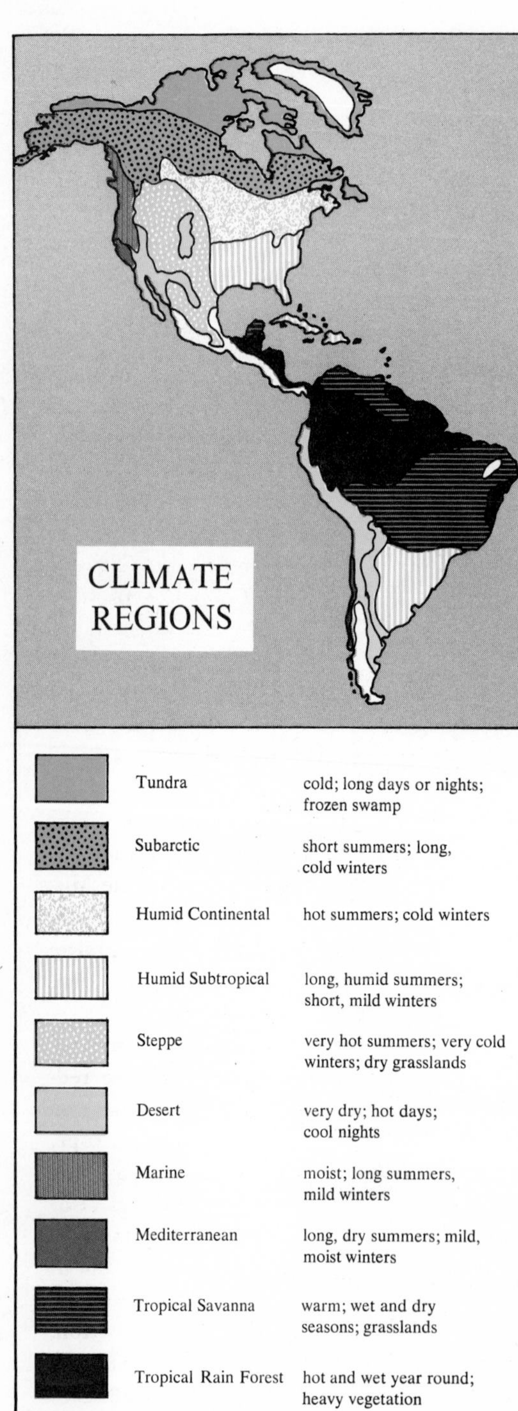

Map 5

in the temperate latitudes south of the equator.

The different climates and the size and variety of the lands in the Western Hemisphere offer great possibilities for ranching and for growing many kinds of agricultural crops. (See Map 5, at left.) Water power, navigable rivers, forests, and rich mineral deposits provide the natural resources needed for industry. The United States, stretching from the Atlantic to the Pacific across the center of the northern continent, possesses a richer concentration of natural resources than has been found in any other nation of the New World.

Animal life has a special history in the Western Hemisphere. Horses arrived with the Spaniard Cortes, who used mounted soldiers to overturn the Aztec kingdom. Soon horses carried Spanish soldiers into Texas and South America. When the Plains Indians learned how to ride horses, it changed their entire way of life. In North America bison by the millions thundered over the grasslands. After the Civil War, riflemen slaughtered them for their hides. Next the cattle kingdom sprang up, with millions of cattle being driven overland to the railheads.

The European settlers killed off the passenger pigeons, so numerous at first that they darkened the skies in their flight. The alligator and seal were hunted almost to extinction. Men and women today have taken legal steps to preserve wild game. Furthermore, certain species, such as deer, thrive in the underbrush, which has grown up after farmers stopped cultivating their fields. At present there are probably more deer in the Appalachian region than there were before the arrival of Columbus.

The Regions of the United States

Two states—Alaska and Hawaii—are separated from the others. Alaska, in the northwestern corner of North America, has many mountains. While the winters are mild in parts of Alaska, frigid weather dominates much of the state. Hawaii, a group of islands near the middle of the Pacific Ocean, has a semi-tropical climate.

The remaining 48 states are often called the Continental United States. They can be divided into six regions. (See Map 6, page 18.)

1. The Atlantic and Gulf of Mexico Coastal Plain. This land formation runs along the coasts of the Atlantic Ocean and the Gulf of Mexico. In the north it is narrow. In the south it becomes broad, taking in the whole state of Florida and reaching far inland. The coastal plain has many marshes but also gentle hills. The climate is cold in the north and subtropical in some parts of the south. The soils and the rainfall provide a good base for farming.

2. The Appalachian and Adirondack Mountains. The Appalachian Mountains begin in Alabama and run northeastward to Newfoundland. These mountains do not include the Adirondacks. For much of its length the Atlantic portion of the coastal plain is bounded on the west by the Appalachians.

3. The Interior Plains. This vast area reaches from the Appalachians to the Rockies in the west, a distance of over 1,000 miles. In the south the Interior Plains begin at the Gulf of Mexico Coastal Plain and extend northward to the Great Lakes in the east and up into Canada on the west. Nearly all of the Interior Plains is drained by the Mississippi River and its major tributaries, the Missouri and Ohio Rivers. The Interior

Plant Life in the New World

When Jacques Cartier, the French explorer who sailed up the St. Lawrence River in 1534, passed the site of Quebec, he noted "the magnificent trees of the same varieties as in France." Of course he could hardly have known that the Western Hemisphere had thousands of varieties unknown in France or in Europe. Consider the giant sequoia and redwood trees of California, the rubber trees of Brazil, the mahogany trees of Central America, and the Douglas fir of the Pacific Northwest.

If Cartier had pushed westward, he would have found a dense forest covering the eastern half of the continent. Beyond the Mississippi River the forest ended, gradually merging into the grasslands. Some prairie land occurred as far east as Indiana, where the Indians had burned the trees.

The white settlers changed their environment much more drastically than the redmen had done. They cleared the forests and brought in seeds and plants from Europe. Most of the crops grown in the United States today stem from imported seedlings. But probably the most important crop is corn, which the Indians of Central and South America had discovered. Among the other imported products were sugar cane, cotton, oranges, wheat, and sugar beets. The so-called Irish potato was originally an offshoot of a variety developed in the New World.

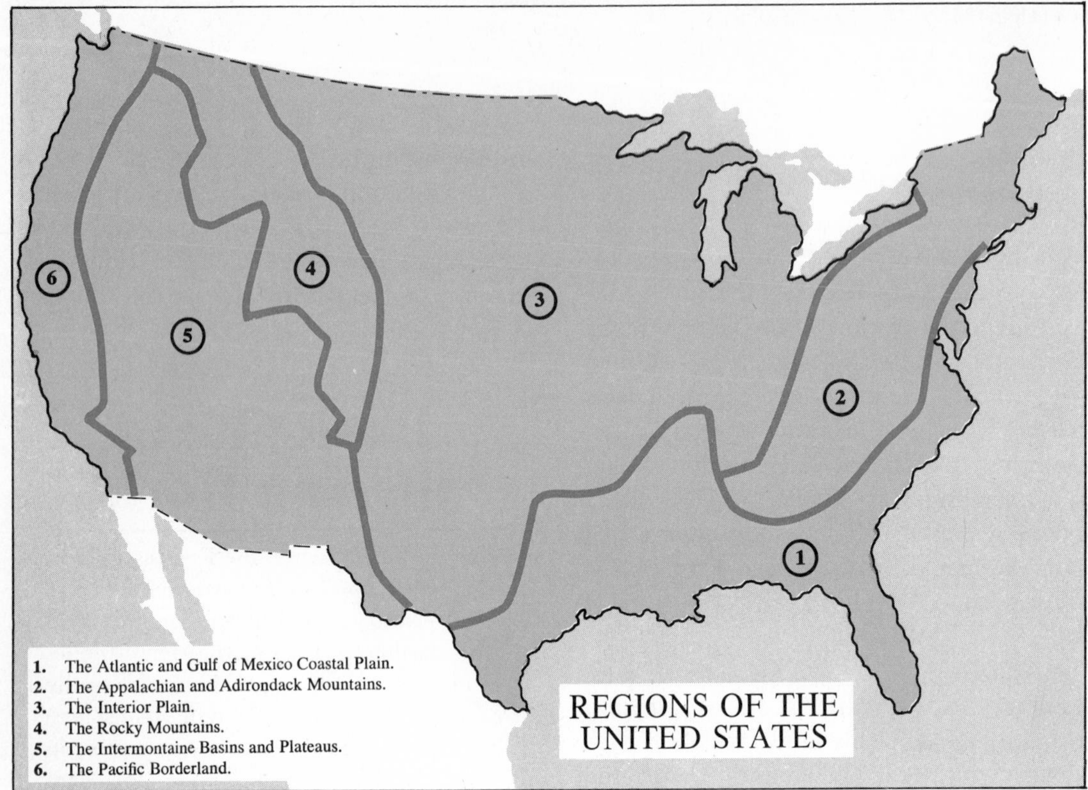

Map 6

Plains can be divided into two parts—the Central Lowlands and the Great Plains. The Central Lowlands begin at the Appalachians and extend to about 300 miles west of the Mississippi River. Originally they were covered by forest. The Central Lowlands have fertile soils and good rainfall. The Great Plains stretch westward from the Central Lowlands to the Rocky Mountains. They have an altitude of 2,000 feet in the east, sloping gently upward to 6,000 feet in the west. The Great Plains are a treeless grassland and suffer from a scarcity of rainfall. They are best used for raising cattle, but farmers also grow much wheat in this area.

4. The Rocky Mountains. This great mountain chain runs from north to south. It divides the eastern two thirds of the United States from the western third. The Rockies begin in Alaska, cross Canada, and reach southward in the United States into New Mexico. From this point other ranges connect the Rocky Mountains with the Sierra Madre Mountains of Mexico. The Rocky Mountains and the connecting ranges form a barrier across the entire United States.

5. The Intermontane Basins and Plateaus. Intermontane means between mountains. The Intermontane Basins and Plateaus lie between the Rocky Mountains on the east and the great ranges of the Pacific Borderland on the west. The best known of the latter mountains are the Cascade Mountains and the Sierra Nevadas.

The Intermontane Basins and Plateaus can be subdivided into three areas: the Columbia Plateau, the Colorado Plateau, and the Great Basin. Both the plateaus are eroded, or worn away by wind and water.

Drained by the Columbia River and by its tributary, the Snake River, the Columbia Plateau is a region of rocks and deep canyons. The Colorado Plateau is most famous for the Grand Canyon, which was formed by the Colorado River. Over 200,000 square miles is contained in the Great Basin. There is little rainfall; the area is used for ranching and for irrigated farming. Cut up by valleys and mountains, the Great Basin has no stream that reaches the sea. All water evaporates or is absorbed by the soil. Death Valley is in the Great Basin.

6. The Pacific Borderland. This is an area of mountains and valleys. Its eastern edge begins with the Cascade and Sierra Nevada Mountains, which include many towering peaks. West of the Cascades and Sierra Nevadas are other mountain ranges running roughly north and south and parallel to the Pacific Coast. There is almost no coastal plain in the western United States, and in many places the mountains extend to the sea. The rainfall is suitable for agriculture in most regions. Farming is carried on in the river valleys, with irrigation ditches used in some areas.

New York lies across two of the great land formations of the United States. Long Island, Staten Island, and the great harbor at New York City are in the Atlantic Coastal Plain. New York spreads northward and westward into the Appalachian and Adirondack Mountains. As we shall see, the lowland of the Mohawk Valley provided a way through the mountain barrier to the rich Interior Plains. This route and the harbor at the Hudson's mouth were to make New York a leader in trade. Another lesser route, but still important, followed the lowland of the Lake Champlain Valley into Canada.

Summary

The Western Hemisphere, sometimes called the New World, is made up of the North American continent, the South American continent, and the islands of the West Indies. The area is greater than that of Africa and Europe combined. It has vast areas of excellent farm lands, a wide variety of climates ranging from arctic to tropical, and great mineral wealth. The United States has the richest natural resources in the New World and, combined with Canada, the most valuable in the world. Most of the current crops and animals were brought to the Western Hemisphere by European settlers.

The 48 states of the continental United States are composed of six regions: the Atlantic and Gulf of Mexico Coastal Plain, the Appalachian and Adirondack Mountains, the Interior Plains, the Rocky Mountains, the Intermontane Basins and Plateaus, and the Pacific Borderland, with the towering Cascade and Sierra Nevada Mountains.

New York lies across the Atlantic Coastal Plain and stretches westward into the Appalachian and Adirondack Mountains. New York is divided almost evenly among lowlands, mountains, and eroded plateaus. The lowlands are best for transportation, agriculture, and industry.

In the mountain wall, stretching from Canada to Alabama, the Hudson-Mohawk valley forms the only level passage. The Adirondacks and the Catskills are the most important mountains. One-third of the state is covered by the Allegheny Plateau.

The most important drainage basins are the Hudson, the Great Lakes-St. Lawrence, and the Susquehanna. But water reaches the ocean at Delaware Bay via the Delaware river and the Gulf of Mexico via the Allegheny river which flows into the Ohio.

Checking the high points

1. What are Grenville rocks?

2. What did the ice sheets do to the surface of New York?

3. Do you live in a mountainous region, a lowland, or a plateau?

4. What are the chief lowland regions? Are they important?

5. Compare how nature formed the Adirondacks and Catskills.

6. What are the chief drainage basins of the Empire State?

7. What land is included in the Western Hemisphere?

8. Compare North and South America in regard to mountains, grasslands, deserts, climate.

9. What changes did the coming of Europeans make in the animal and plant life of the New World?

10. What are the major regions of the United States?

Think these over

1. Nature has given the United States the richest combination of resources of any nation. Compare this country with Brazil and Russia as to agricultural land, mineral resources, and transportation.

2. Did the changes the European settlers made in their environment result in a better life for the people?

3. Do you think that New York's location has given it an advantage over other areas of the Western Hemisphere?

Vocabulary building

Explain the means of these terms used in the chapter.

lava
magma
moraines
geology
highlands
plateau

drainage basin
continent
isthmus
intermontane
prairie
tributary

Checking locations

You used maps many times during your study of this chapter. You are now familiar with the main geographic features of New York State, the United States, and the Western Hemisphere. Try to locate these places quickly.

Long Island
Staten Island
Seneca Lake
Niagara Falls
Lake Champlain

Lake Ontario
Lake Erie
Adirondacks
Catskills
Oswego

Mexico
Rocky Mountains
Appalachian Mountains
Mississippi River
Great Lakes
Puerto Rico
Cuba
Colorado River

Brazil
West Indies
Isthmus of Panama
Hawaii
Alaska
Gulf of Mexico
Caribbean Sea
Columbia River

Chapter Objectives

To learn about

- Native American civilizations in America
- the Iroquois in New York

chapter 2

INDIANS in AMERICA

Asians Come to America

Scientists have discovered the first traces of human existence in Africa, Europe, and Asia. Humans had also reached the New World as early as 50,000 B.C. What is now the Bering Strait between Alaska and Siberia was once a grassy plain on which musk oxen, mammoths, and other animals grazed. Hunters from Asia tracked these animals and killed them. When the ice sheet retreated northward, the melting ice raised the level of the ocean and flooded over the land bridge between North America and Asia.

Gradually the hunters worked their way south, following the line of the Rocky Mountains. Some became cliff dwellers in Arizona; others crossed the plains and entered the eastern woodlands; others built boats and occupied the islands of the Caribbean Sea. Central and South America attracted still others who fanned out over the continent. Scholars have found traces of human life dating from 8,000 B.C. at the southern tip of South America.

These early people brought stone weapons and tools and a knowledge of how to use fire. About 10,000 years ago near what is now Folsom, New Mexico, people were fashioning beautiful stone spear points.

The Indians, or native Americans, were also farmers. At first they planted and harvested crops in a very crude fashion. They would set fire to the forest and then plant seeds around the charred stumps. They cultivated a wild grass which in time became known as maize, or Indian corn, by far the most useful crop in American history. Tobacco, a wild herb, was planted, and its use, ceremonial and recreational, spread rapidly. The natives discovered and cultivated potatoes, beans, tomatoes, and squash. In the warmer climates, they grew cotton from which they wove fine cloth.

The native Americans of Latin America developed advanced civilizations—the Mayas, Aztecs, and Incas. (See Map 7, page 23.) There were hundreds of other tribes, most of whom lived on a fairly primitive level.

The Mayas, who established the highest

civilization in pre-Columbian America, still remain a mystery. Although they developed a written language, not enough of their writings have survived to tell us much about their history. Their priests were great star-gazers and figured out a calendar more accurate than the one we use today. To make these calculations they learned a good deal about mathematics, including the concept of zero. Visitors to the jungles of Yucatan marvel at the remains of temples and cities lying within the jungle. These cities (the largest were built after A.D. 200) rival the splendors of ancient Rome. Apparently the cities were used largely for ceremonies. Only the priests and noblemen lived in the palaces surrounding the temple-topped pyramids, while the ordinary Mayans lived in huts on the edge of the jungle.

Mayan civilization, like most others, had peaks and declines. Perhaps the greatest mystery is why these people left their cities about A.D. 900. Somewhat later they rebuilt another series of cities which the invading Spanish easily conquered early in the sixteenth century.

Experts in Early Civilization

Not all detective work is done by policemen. There are hundreds of experts who put together the bits and pieces of information uncovered from ancient Indian campsites which help explain how early Americans lived.

Archaeologists dig in selected spots and study the relics or artifacts they find. They must take great care not to lose or damage important evidence as they sift through the dirt. Every piece of broken pottery or weaponry may tell a story about the early inhabitants of New York. For example, kernels of corn found in a campsite reveal that the former inhabitants were farmers.

Anthropologists are interested in the culture of primitive people. They trace the origins, the development, and the varieties of early civilization. By studying primitive peoples now living in Africa, South America, and Borneo, they hope to determine more precisely how Stone Age humans lived. Just as carefully, they study the tools, weapons, pots, and utensils of the Indian settlers of New York. They analyze the descriptions of travelers who saw the Indians in the period after the coming of the whites. Anthropologists observe the ceremonies of living Indians because these ceremonies have come down virtually unchanged for centuries. A New Yorker, Lewis Henry Morgan, was the father of anthropology. His book on the Iroquois, written in 1851, remains our best description of these people.

Other scientists also help us understand the history of primitive people. Physicists, for example, can determine the dates of past events within a few hundred years by estimating the rate of radioactivity of Carbon 14. Carbon exists in all plants and disintegrates at a constant rate. Half the "life" of Carbon 14 disappears in about 5600 years and another quarter vanishes in the next 5600 years. Given a sample which is three-fourths gone, physicists can judge it to be about 11,200 years old, plus or minus 250 years.

Amateurs have also helped to fill out the story. Pilots, for example, have discovered ruins from the air. Photographers can study pictures which show roads, the outlines of buildings, and village boundaries.

The Aztecs

The people of central Mexico have a long and complicated history. In the large basin around the present Mexico City, the city of Teotihuacán grew up with pyramids and buildings that covered an area more than three miles long by two miles wide. Its citizens raised corn and other food by irrigating the lowland near a lake. Teotihuacán collapsed about A.D. 900, probably due to crop failure. Today one can still visit the Pyramid of the Sun, which is almost the same size as the largest pyramid in Egypt.

Other cities rose and fell. Sometime after 1200, another tribe, later known as Aztecs, settled in the inland basin. They made their homes on a swampy island in Lake Texcoco, the site of today's Mexico City. The Aztecs claimed they were the Chosen People of the Sun God who had given them the right to rule over all other tribes. Ruthlessly they obeyed this command by waging war on their neighbors to the north and south. They built a large city called Tenochtitlan, which received its fresh water over an aqueduct. The city had more than 300,000 people in 1450, more than double that of London at that time. Tenochtitlan was a beautiful place with canals and floating gardens.

The Aztecs, like some of their rivals, believed in human sacrifice. Only if they made these sacrifices would the Sun God rise in the morning.

> Victims were lashed up as targets and shot full of arrows and darts so their dripping blood would fertilize the earth; children were sacrificed to the rain god, Tlaloc; victims were burned alive to celebrate the August heat of harvest.

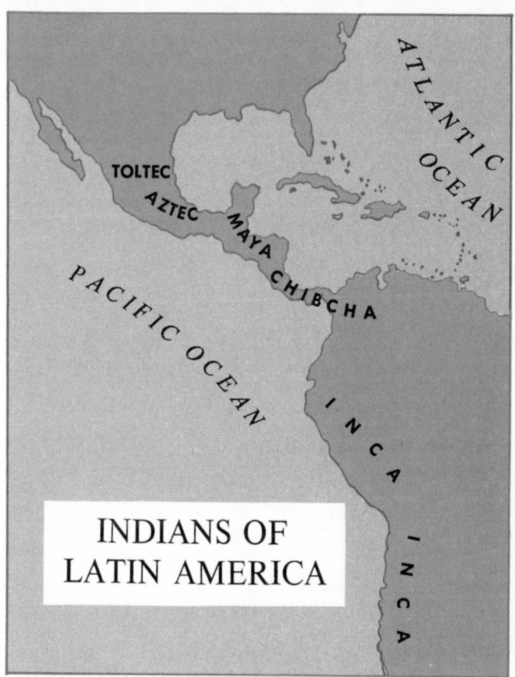

Map 7

The Aztecs built an empire on fear and terror, not on respect and justice. Naturally their neighbors hated these bloodthirsty Aztecs and willingly aided Cortes in 1521 in his triumphal march from the Gulf of Mexico to the Aztec capital.

The Mexicans of today take great pride in the achievements of their Indian forefathers. They preserve the great pyramids, and in Mexico City they have erected a National Museum. Here one can see splendid exhibits of pottery, weapons, and most impressive of all, the Aztec Calendar Stone.

Incas

Native Americans in Peru created an advanced civilization of large cities, textiles of beautiful designs, pottery, well-built roads, and impressive fortifications. They learned how to mine the metals hidden in the mountains. Today we can admire the design and workmanship of their gold and silver ornaments.

A small tribe of mountain people, known as Incas, settled in the Cuzco valley about the year 1200. This small tribe battled to keep alive by making alliances with other tribes and by conquering their rivals. Finally, in 1438, the Inca chieftain Pachacuti Inca Yupanqui came to power. During the next half-century this able but cruel chief and his son built a huge empire stretching over 2,000 miles and containing over 6,000,000 people.

The Incas were skilled engineers and showed great talent in organizing almost every aspect of life. They copied the features of the other tribes which they conquered. They assigned every family and tribe a job. Inca officials forced thousands of men to build roads over and around the mountains. They had considerable engineering skill, as is shown in their suspension bridges and irrigation ditches. Since there was not much good level land, the people had to build terraces, or level areas, on the mountain slopes. Here they raised cotton, corn, and other crops.

Inca civilization lasted hardly a century before it toppled before the armor-coated soldiers of Francisco Pizarro in 1531. The Spanish conquerors could hardly believe their eyes when they found tons of gold and silver in the Inca cities. For the average Indian the substitution of Spanish for Inca rule made little difference.

Indian Groups of North America

In 1492 over three million Indians were north of the Rio Grande River, which separates the United States from Mexico. Compare this thin and scattered population with the fifteen million native Americans living in Central and South America. The most striking thing about the Indians of North America was their great variety of living patterns. For example, over 200 dialects or languages were spoken among the hundreds of tribes.

Scholars have divided these tribes into certain groups: Southwestern, Californian, Plateau, Pacific Northwest, Plains, Southeastern, and Eastern Woodland. (See Map 8, page 25.)

The Southwestern Indians were a variety of peoples ranging from fairly advanced town dwellers to seed-gathering wanderers. The Pueblos began as primitive basketmakers who gradually built villages on the tops of cliffs for protection. They built houses out of sun-dried clay called adobe. Because there was not much rain, they brought water through irrigation ditches to their fields in the river valleys. Some of their neighboring tribes, such as the Apache and Navaho, remained hunters and raisers of sheep after 1700.

The dry and harsh area between the Rocky Mountains and the Pacific Ocean was the homeland of the Californian and Plateau Indians. Because their living patterns were quite similar, we will consider these two groups together. The men and women gathered seeds and nuts, while the men also hunted deer. A few in favored places planted crops and wove baskets. Much more advanced were the Indians of the Pacific Northwest, who were fine fishermen, sailors, and traders. Every spring they caught the salmon which swam up the Columbia and other rivers. Their dugout canoes, carved out of cedar trees, carried them along the waterways on their hunting and trading expeditions. They are most famous for their totem poles, which tell the history

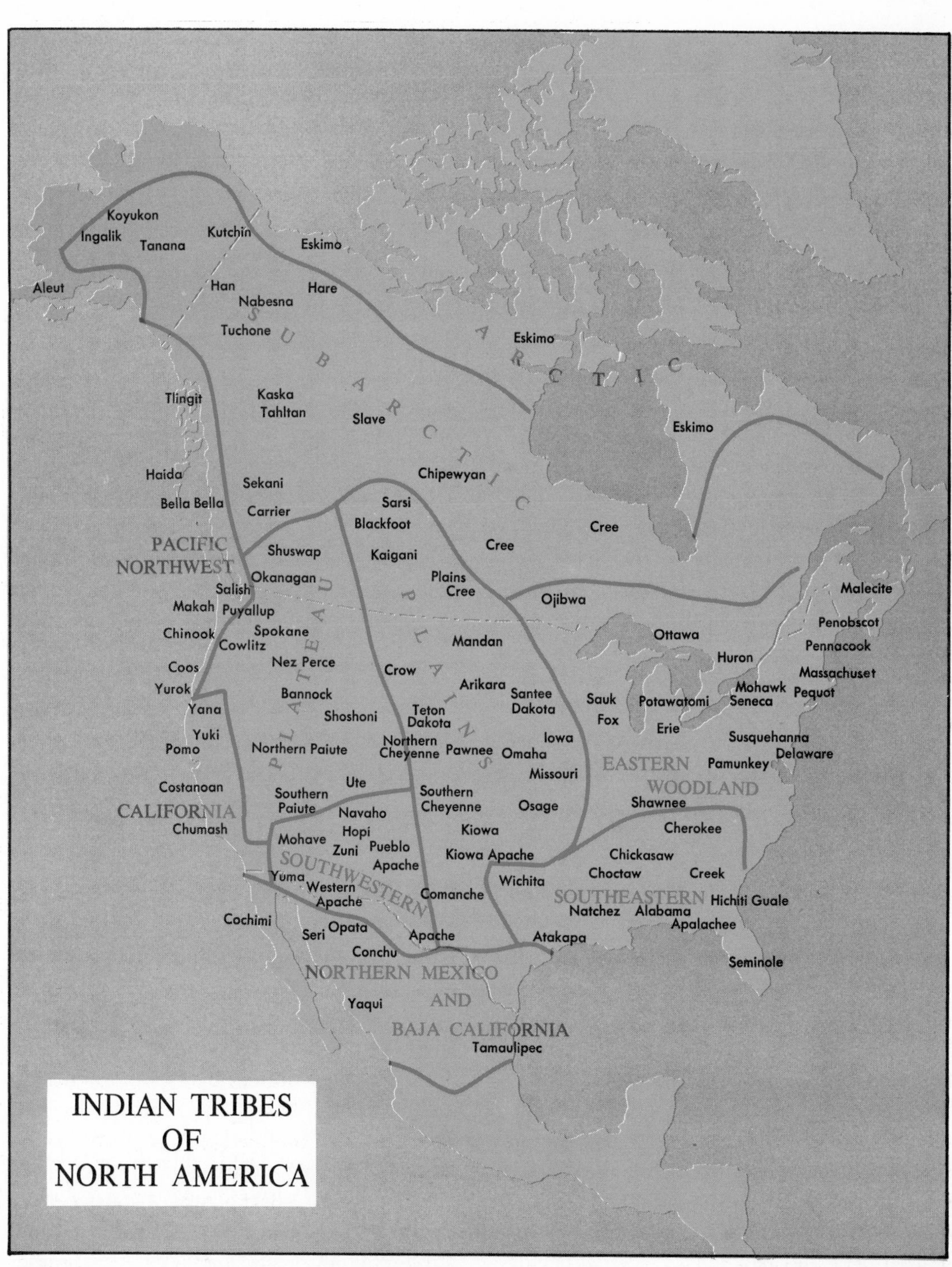
INDIAN TRIBES OF NORTH AMERICA
SUBARCTIC
ARCTIC
PACIFIC NORTHWEST
PLATEAU
PLAINS
CALIFORNIA
SOUTHWESTERN
EASTERN WOODLAND
SOUTHEASTERN
NORTHERN MEXICO AND BAJA CALIFORNIA
Koyukon
Ingalik
Tanana
Kutchin
Eskimo
Aleut
Han
Nabesna
Hare
Tuchone
Eskimo
Eskimo
Tlingit
Kaska
Tahltan
Slave
Haida
Sekani
Chipewyan
Bella Bella
Carrier
Sarsi
Blackfoot
Cree
Cree
Shuswap
Kaigani
Okanagan
Salish
Plains Cree
Ojibwa
Malecite
Makah
Puyallup
Penobscot
Chinook
Spokane
Cowlitz
Mandan
Ottawa
Pennacook
Nez Perce
Huron
Coos
Crow
Massachuset
Yurok
Bannock
Arikara
Santee Dakota
Sauk
Fox
Potawatomi
Mohawk
Seneca
Pequot
Yana
Shoshoni
Teton Dakota
Erie
Yuki
Pomo
Northern Paiute
Northern Cheyenne
Pawnee
Iowa
Omaha
Susquehanna
Delaware
Missouri
Pamunkey
Costanoan
Southern Paiute
Ute
Southern Cheyenne
Osage
Shawnee
Navaho
Chumash
Hopi
Kiowa
Cherokee
Mohave
Zuni
Pueblo
Apache
Kiowa Apache
Chickasaw
Choctaw
Creek
Yuma
Western Apache
Wichita
Comanche
Natchez
Alabama
Hichiti
Guale
Apalachee
Cochimi
Seri
Opata
Apache
Atakapa
Conchu
Seminole
Yaqui
Tamaulipec

Map 8

of families and tribes by brightly-colored carvings. The Haida and Chinook were keen traders who bought and sold houses, tools, and fishing stations.

Between the Mississippi River and the Rocky Mountains were the grasslands where a few thousand wandering tribesmen and their families made their homes. When they could, they killed the buffalo that roamed the plains. These Indians made their tepees and moccasins out of buffalo hide. Their lives were quiet and fairly peaceful for centuries until the arrival of the horse, brought in by the Spanish explorers. Once they had learned to ride, they became the most skilled horsemen and feared warriors on the continent. The Cheyenne, Sioux, Blackfeet, and Comanche for centuries held off the advancing whites—Spanish, French, English, Americans—until the railroad, the United States army, and cattlemen armed with six-shooters overwhelmed them in the years after the Civil War.

The Southeastern Indians—Cherokees and Creeks, to mention but two tribes—were good farmers and able politicians. They built strong confederacies for protection against their enemies. Their villages were made up of rectangular houses built of wooden poles and grass roofs.

The Eastern Woodlands contained dozens of tribes whose names have come down in the history books. Pocohantas, for example, belonged to the Powhatan confederacy that fought the settlers of Virginia. Probably the largest group was the Algonquian, that is, the tribes speaking varieties of the Algonquian languages. They occupied the Atlantic coastal region and occupied much of the territory north of the Great Lakes. The men hunted deer and paddled canoes, while the women planted corn, beans, and squash in the clearings. Their villages had wigwams—tents of poles covered with bark and skins. The Algonquians surrounded their villages with lines of tree trunks in order to protect themselves from their enemies, especially the Iroquois. The most famous Iroquois tribes were the Mohawks, Oneidas, Onondagas, Senecas, and Cayugas, who formed the Confederacy of the Five Nations.

The Indians Settle New York

The hunters, always on the move, were the first inhabitants to reach New York. They used stone weapons since they had no chance to develop better ones, such as bows and arrows. Gradually they acquired better weapons and tools made out of stone, wood, and bone. Some were developed by trial and error; others were borrowed from neighboring tribes or newcomers. In the 1920's archaeologists found a site in Schuyler County with over 10,000 bone and antler objects. Using Carbon 14 and other methods, they dated the find as 5,383 years old.

The Indians learned to fish with bone harpoons and to cultivate and grind corn. They began to cook their food in pots instead of roasting game over the open fire. Stone receptacles were first used but these were heavy and sometimes cracked when heated. Then the Indians found that soft clay would make good pots, which they fashioned, decorated inside and out with patterns, and baked hard. After they became farmers and had to stay in one place, they set up huts with bark and hides. Soon little villages sprang up. Later wooden stockades were built around their villages, for protection against attack.

The Algonquians included the Abnaki of

Owasco Indian Village on Emerson Lake at Auburn. Note the bark-covered longhouse and the stockade of saplings in the Iroquois manner.

Maine, the Wappingers and other tribes of southern New England, the Delawares, the Powhatan of Virginia, and several tribes in the Wisconsin-Minnesota region. These tribes invented the birch-bark canoe and snowshoes. The center of Algonquian strength was in the Delaware Valley, where the parent tribe, the Delawares, had several villages. The last Algonquians reached New York about 1000 A.D. They were conquered about 300 years later by the Iroquois.

The Iroquois, like hundreds of other Indian tribes, developed a distinctive *culture*, which is defined as the "total way of life of a people." Let us examine some of the Iroquois' institutions, such as the family, the role of women, and holidays or festivals—all of which differed sharply from those of Europeans.

The Iroquois Family, Clan, and Phratry

The basic social unit in America is the "nuclear family" composed of father, mother, and their children. Sometimes grandmother or grandfather appear but they are usually visitors, not really members of the unit. At Thanksgiving and perhaps at Christmas or other holidays, the family expands to include uncles, cousins, and aunts.

Like many Indians, the Iroquois developed the so-called "extended," or longhouse family which was headed by a woman, usually the oldest. Each Iroquois belonged to his mother's longhouse family. An Indian youngster thus regarded as his family not only his brothers, sisters, and mother, but also his mother's brothers, sisters, and the children of her sisters; his mother's mother, her brothers and sisters, and her sister's children. But his own father technically belonged to another longhouse family, even though he had come to live in the longhouse of his wife.

Each Iroquois thus had many brothers and sisters, some living outside his longhouse. He regarded the children of his

In the Onondaga Turtle Clan, the sachems discuss matters in the firekeeper's lodge. The matron of the clan here advises the young warriors who will carry her wishes to the council.

mother's sisters and of his father's brothers as brothers and sisters.

Marriages were arranged by the women of the longhouse. Women gave the family name to the children, owned the property, and directed the civilian activities such as planting and harvesting crops. With the men hunting and fighting, the continuity of the tribe was safer in the hands of the mothers.

A clan was composed of several longhouse families who believed that they had a common female ancestor. Clans took the names of animals or birds. Each of the Five Nations had at least three clans—Bear, Wolf, and Turtle. A member of the Mohawk's Bear Clan regarded members of the Seneca Bear Clan as brothers and sisters. Each clan had political as well as ceremonial functions. It adopted the captives taken in war. It paid the compensation owed another clan when a murder took place.

The clans in turn grouped themselves into larger units called *phratries*, a Greek word meaning a group of related families. Phratries had several functions in games, ceremonies, and funerals. Among the Onondagas, Cayugas, and the Senecas there were two phratries: one included the Bear, Wolf, Beaver, and Turtle clans; the other included the Hawk, Deer, Snipe, Heron, and Eel clans.

Every Iroquois thus felt related by blood or marriage to almost everyone in the village, the clan, and even beyond his tribe. This web of relationships gave him a strong feeling of belonging. He did not feel lonely and isolated. Furthermore, he felt a strong responsibility for all his relatives. In short, the group's welfare was more important than that of the individual.

Iroquois Time Patterns

Our culture places great emphasis on exact time. The Iroquois did not worry about specific time. For instance, they ate only one heavy meal a day, supplementing this with berries, fruit, and nuts, and by dipping into the simmering pot that always hung over the fire. Day and night marked the most important time division for them. Nature—the rhythm of the seasons, the phases of the moon, the sun's rise and setting—determined the way the Iroquois arranged time.

Furthermore, the Iroquois did not have as much sense of historical time as we have. To them the creation was only a few generations back. They tended to measure events in terms of "our fathers," "our grandfathers," "our great grandfathers," and so on. We, however, know that people have left records for thousands of years.

Americans in particular tend to think of time as moving forward. We tie it to the idea of progress, which assumes that things are improving as time passes. Iroquois, however, had little sense of progress. For them, life was a continuous round of duties tied to the seasons.

Festivals punctuated the seasons. In March the sap in the sugar maple begins to flow. The Iroquois tapped the trees, collected and boiled the sap, making it into sugar, as do many New York farmers today. In honor of the maple, the Iroquois held a festival which gave "Thanks to the Maple." In fact, it was a general period of Thanksgiving to the Creator not only for the maple but also for the renewal of life. After spring planting was over, a Planting Festival was held, marked by dancing, prayers, and burning of tobacco.

After the corn ripened in August or September, came the Green Corn Festival. At this time they named the children born since midwinter. They again gave thanks to the Creator. In the daytime their speeches and ceremonies were solemn, but at nighttime they danced and sang. After four days of celebrating, they set out to harvest the crops, and then they spent another four days in a Harvest Festival.

In the late fall and early winter, the braves set forth to hunt. As soon as they killed a deer or bear, the womenfolk skinned it and dried the meat. In February came the Midwinter Festival, the most important of the year. The people begged the Master of Life to restore life to the earth. Two heralds announced the beginning of the New Year. Dressed in bear skins and corn husks, "Our Two Uncles, the Bigheads," as they were called, directed the people to observe time-honored ceremonies of the tribe. They warned that if any person had a new dream, he must report it or else risk illness. Then one group tried to guess the dream of another group, which tried to disguise it in riddles. The persons who guessed a dream had to make for the dreamer a "charm," a miniature of the object mentioned in the dream.

Carved wooden masks like this were worn by the Iroquois when they danced to drive out demons. Representing supernatural beings, the masks and ceremonies "cured the ill."

Members of the Iroquois False Face Society wore wooden masks representing the "great rim faces" and the "common faces" of the forest spirits. These strange figures

Harvest time in the Seneca Tribe that lived around Rochester before A.D. 1600 meant house building, food preparation, storing corn and squash—and storytelling.

would dance around a sick person, rub hot ashes on his head, burn sacred tobacco, and sing weird songs in a tongue unknown to the rest of the tribe.

Was this method of treating disease as worthless as it seems to modern man accustomed to X-ray machines and miracle drugs? Obviously a good number of ill people recover under any kind of treatment. Furthermore, we know that the emotions have a great deal to do with recovery. No doubt the dramatic rituals convinced some of the patients that the spirits would help them get well. Because of their belief, they did get better. Some Indian herbs, moreover, were helpful for certain kinds of illnesses.

The White Dog Ceremony has special significance. On the first day of the festival the Indians strangled a dog in a way so that it did not shed any blood. Painting him white, they hung him on an eight-foot pole. At the end of the festival, they carried the dog's body to a blazing altar and burned it. Thus the dog began his trip to the Great Creator, who needed him for protection during the following year.

Death was mourned by the whole village. The Indians believed that the souls of the departed went to the land of the dead but that their ghosts remained in the neighborhood where they had lived.

Summary

The ancestors of the Indians, or native Americans, reached the New World from Asia as long ago as 50,000 B.C. Gradually these newcomers came to occupy the entire Western Hemisphere. Although hundreds of tribes lived on a primitive level, several groups, notably the Mayas in Central America, the Aztecs in Mexico, and the Incas in Peru, showed great skill and artistry in their buildings, jewelry, woven cloth, pottery, and weapons. The Spanish overturned these empires fairly easily in part because the Indian rulers had treated their subjects cruelly.

North America, north of Mexico, had over three million people scattered across the continent. This population was divided into hundreds of tribes with different customs, languages, and skills. In the Eastern Woodlands the two largest groups were the Algonquian and the Iroquoian language groups.

The Iroquois invaded New York about 1300, displacing the Algonquians who had arrived several hundred years earlier. The Iroquois had the longhouse, or extended family, headed by a woman. Each Indian belonged to a clan, a combination of longhouse families, and also to phratries, a still larger unit.

The rhythm of the seasons determined the time patterns of the Iroquois and their neighbors. They celebrated the major changes in the seasons with festivals such as the Green Corn Festival. Home for them was the longhouse, which lay in the small village surrounded by a few cleared fields.

Checking the high points

1. When and how did Asians settle the Western Hemisphere?

2. What crops did the Indians, or native Americans, develop?

3. Why is the Mayan civilization considered an advanced civilization?

4. What were the good and bad features of Aztec culture?

5. Why did Inca civilization collapse?

6. List five of the seven major Indian groups of North America. What tribe or way of life was found in each?

7. How did environment influence living patterns?

8. What was the role of the Algonquians and Iroquois in the settlement of New York area?

9. How did the longhouse family differ from our type of family?

10. What was the role of Iroquois women? What were their duties?

11. How did "time" figure in Iroquois life?

Think these over

1. Did women have more power in Iroquois society than in ours?

2. Did environment play a greater role in shaping Indian life than in our society? Explain.

3. Is Native American a better term than Indian? Why or why not?

Checking locations

Bering Strait
Arizona
Peru
Delaware Valley
Caribbean Sea
Mexico City
Schuyler County, New York
Alaska
Yucatan

Vocabulary building

nuclear family
clan
phratry
tepee
pyramids
dialect
wampum
primitive
terrace
adobe
classification
totem pole
confederacy
longhouse family
culture
archaeology
anthropologist
wigwam

Chapter Objectives

To learn about

- Iroquois culture
- the Iroquois Confederacy
- the effect of European civilization on the Iroquois

chapter 3

The IROQUOIS RULE NEW YORK

The Iroquois Religion Explains Creation

All peoples in all ages have tried to find some explanation for the beginnings of the world and the human race. These accounts become sacred and are handed down from one generation to another in poetical language. No doubt you are familiar with the story of Adam and Eve from the book of Genesis in the Bible.

The Iroquois had several variations of their Creation Myth, which for them was a true story of events. Outsiders should regard this account with the respect that they give to the sacred writings of their own religion. The following shortened form has skipped some of the original's rich detail.

In the beginning there was a great ocean filled with fish. High above it was the Sky-World, the home of the gods. A Great Tree with enormous roots grew in the center. A hungry wife talked her husband into taking bark from one of the roots of this sacred tree. In digging the hole, he broke through the cover of the sky. Full of curiosity, the woman looked down the hole and fell through. Some birds saw her peril and broke her fall by forming a cushion underneath her. She landed on the back of a great sea turtle.

The birds and sea creatures offered to help the woman, who was expecting a baby. The muskrat almost drowned by diving deep in the sea to secure some soil from its bottom. The woman took the earth and walked around it in the same direction that the sun goes. It grew and grew. She planted in it the roots which she had clutched from the Great Tree during her fall. Plants of many varieties sprang up. She built a hut and gave birth to a daughter who grew up to be a beautiful maiden.

One day a man appeared. The maiden fainted in fright. The man placed one sharp and one blunt arrow across her body and then slipped away. The maiden had twins; the right-handed one was born the usual way. His left-handed brother killed his mother by insisting on being born through her left armpit. Out of the body of the dead mother grew three sisters—

corn, beans, and squash. A tobacco plant sprang from her heart.

The twins hated each other and fought in various ways. The right-handed one told the truth and kept his word but the other twin told lies. When the first brother created the deer, the second created the mountain lion which hunted the deer. When the right-handed twin made the ground squirrel, the left-handed twin made the weasel which tried to kill all the squirrels. Finally the right-handed twin made man out of clay and baked him in a fire.

The twins were deadly rivals. When they gambled or played lacrosse, neither could beat the other. They dueled with clubs but neither won. Finally the right-handed twin picked up a deer antler and slew his brother. He threw the dead man over the edge of the world but the left-handed twin regained life and ruled this lower region. At night he came back to the earth and ruled although his brother ruled during daytime.

One day the right-handed twin quarreled with his grandmother when she called him a murderer. He flew into a rage and killed her by cutting off her head. He threw her head into the sky where it became the moon.

The Iroquois give thanks to the right-handed twin whom they call the Great Creator. At night, however, they dance and sing to the left-handed twin.

This Creation Myth has many meanings for its believers. First of all, it "explains" the origin of the world. It also tells why good and evil exist side by side. It points out that every creature, plant, and individual must carry out its duty. Thus men hunt animals while women gather food and plant crops.

Notice how all life was a matter of balance to the Iroquois. Thus the twins, each representing a different principle, battled each other for supremacy, neither winning a clearcut victory, one ruling at night while his brother ruled by day. Foreign travelers frequently noted the self-discipline of the Indians. This balance helped the Iroquois to remain calm and patient under pressure. At times, however, they "let off steam" by going on the warpath, hitting out with a lacrosse stick, and, after the white man came, drinking too much rum.

The Village in the Clearing

The women and children spent most of their time in the clearing surrounded by the dense, dark forest. In the center was the village, which numbered from 10 to 50 families, or from 50 to 250 persons. A few villages grew to over one thousand people. But the villages were not permanent settlements; every 10 years or so the chiefs decided to move—for a variety of reasons. The crops failed when the soil became worn out. The streams were fished out, and the game became scarce. Perhaps the piles of rubbish became too much of a nuisance.

The Iroquois constructed a stockade of pointed logs to surround their villages. To give added protection against sudden attack, sometimes they dug a trench along the outside wall or built on the edge of a steep slope.

Each settlement had a number of large houses, 50 to 150 feet long, about 20 feet wide, and 15 to 20 feet high. A longhouse had room for about 50 people. A carving of a bear, wolf, or turtle indicated which clan lived in the longhouse. The roofs were curved, supported by bent saplings and shingled with elm bark, with holes every 20 feet or so to let the smoke escape. Di-

Artist's sketch of a longhouse settlement. Note the random positioning of the houses. Observe the stockade and the cleared fields.

rectly below the holes were the fires over which the women cooked food. On each side of the longhouse were small compartments (about 13 feet by 6 feet) which was "home" for a fireside family, that is, father, mother, and children. These compartments rested on wooden platforms, a foot or so from the damp ground. Cornhusk mats on the floor served as beds, and the young children slept in bark-lined bunks. Besides the longhouses, there were some smaller, "single-fire" lodges with only two families.

The Indians were part-time farmers and hunters. While the women planted crops, the men trapped animals, hunted game, and caught fish. Both men and women had to work hard to get enough food for the family and clan.

Farming with rough tools was no simple matter. Each time a clan moved, the braves would have to clear new forestland. They would cut a band of bark from each tree trunk, causing it to die. Because the dead tree had no leaves, sunshine could reach the ground and crops could grow. Sometimes the Indians would burn the dead trees and form a clearing. The women planted corn, beans, and squash. The "mothers" of each family had their own plots, but they usually worked together on one another's fields. Using sharp sticks and pieces of bone to break the soil, they planted four to six kernels of corn in mounds about three feet apart.

Youngsters helped plant seeds and gather crops. The girls helped their mothers clean the house, cook the food, and work in the fields. The boys received training in hunting, fishing, and toolmaking from the men. All worked for the welfare of the family.

Discipline in the family was left to the mother. Infants created no problem; they were carried on cradleboards on the mother's back. When older children misbehaved, the mother threw water in their faces or sent very bad children into the dark night where masked figures scared them.

This life-size diorama at the Rochester Museum and Science Center shows an Iroquois family in its portion of a longhouse. The mother tends to the cooking, the young boy is learning to carve as his father does, and the papoose is snug in his cradleboard.

The diet centered around corn which, as the white pioneers discovered, could be served in many forms. Cornmeal mush and corn bread were the two most common ways. If the hunting party was successful, the family would feast on deer, bear, or fish. The Indians also ate berries, grapes, nuts, fruits, and roots.

Each village tried to grow or make everything it needed. Some men were highly skilled in making stone tools and weapons; others could carve wood. The women prepared skins to make into moccasins and clothing. They used a heavy piece of stone to chip flint to a sharp edge for arrows and knives. They twisted bark in such a way as to make canoes, storage barrels, and baskets. Sometimes, for ornament, they carved animal figures on the handles of spoons and on the sides of bowls. Out of bone they made fishhooks, picks, combs, and needles.

Travel and Trade

Despite all their efforts to make their own goods, the villagers often found it necessary to exchange goods with other tribes. Flints, dried fish, birch canoes, tobacco, furs, and skins were in greatest demand. The amount of trade between tribes grew rapidly, especially after the white men set up trading posts along the coast.

The Indians used paths and rivers as highways. The landform of New York lent itself well to this use. Silently, in single file, the warriors ran along the narrow paths which followed or connected the waterways. Many paths followed the ridges of the hills in order to avoid swamps and underbrush. Probably the most important trail in New York was the Iroquois trail, which began near Utica and ran westward to the Oneida and Onondaga villages. Thereafter it swung to the foot of Cayuga Lake, where the Cayuga nation had its main village. It also ran north of Seneca Lake, passing Canandaigua Lake, and going on to Niagara through the region of Avon and Geneseo. The most important crossroad was Tioga Point, near the state border, where runners coming down the Canisteo, Cohocton, and Chemung trails reached the Susquehanna trail.

Even more important than the trails were the excellent waterways, ideally suited for canoe travel. Indians found a low area near Rome over which they could carry or drag canoes from the Mohawk River to Wood Creek. This stream flowed into Oneida

This painting of Trout Fall Portage was done by Peter Rindinbacher, a Swiss who lived among the Indians when he was 16 and drew his scenes from life. While this picture was of the Indians in the Hudson Bay Country, the portage preparations are similar to those of the Iroquois.

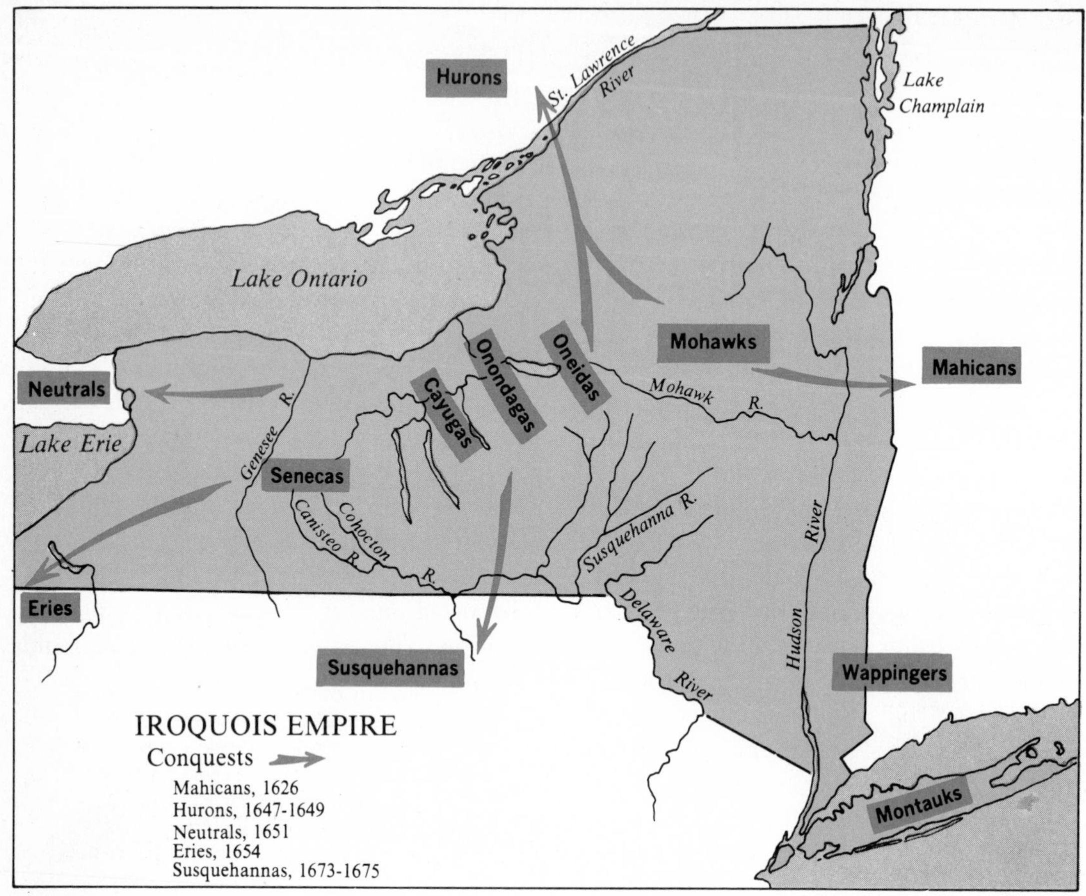

Map 9

Lake, which emptied its waters into Lake Ontario by the Oswego River. At Oswego the Indians could go westward along the shore of Lake Ontario to Niagara or eastward down the St. Lawrence. Other short "carries" connected the upper Hudson with Lake George and Lake Champlain.

The Iroquois Confederacy

"Not men—they are wolves"—so an Algonquian woman described the first Iroquois who invaded New York about the year 1300. Why did they come? The Iroquois had lived along the Mississippi River and its branches. Constant warfare and shortage of food drove them eastward in search of new hunting grounds. Slowly the Algonquians retreated before the Iroquois attacks. One group of Iroquois entered New York from south of Lake Erie and eventually formed the Seneca and Cayuga tribes. They built their villages in the hill country between the Genesee River and Skaneateles Lake. Meanwhile, other Iroquoian tribes swarmed into Canada north of Lakes Erie and Ontario. One band moved south into the neighborhood of Syracuse and became the Onondagas. Another band attacked the Algonquians near Quebec but met defeat. Retreating southward, they settled in the Mohawk Valley, which got its name from them. The Oneidas, an offshoot of the Mohawks, set up villages in the area near the present city of Oneida. Check these locations on Map 9, above.

In about 1570 the five Indian tribes of central and western New York formed a union called the Confederacy of the Five Nations. No one knows exactly how the Confederacy, or League, came into being, but legends and myths hint at the general course of events.

According to legend, Deganawidah was the originator of the Great Peace symbolized by the Great Tree of Peace. Born among the Hurons, Deganawidah set forth across the Ontario Lake and settled among the Mohawks, where he preached Good News of Peace and Power.

> The Word that I bring that all peoples shall love one another and live together in peace. This message has three parts: Righteousness and Health and Power.

Asked how these doctrines would be carried out, he replied:

> It will take the form of a longhouse in which there are many fires, one for each family, yet all live as one household under one chief mother. . . . They shall have one mind and live under one law.

Deganawidah met Hiawatha, a middle-aged Onondaga who accepted the message of peace and preached it to the various tribes. But Atotarho, the cruel and crippled chief of the Onondagas, mocked Hiawatha and rejected his pleas.

Deganawidah found the sad and lonely Hiawatha wandering in the forest. Together they worked out a code of laws. This code was based on the customs of the Iroquois but included methods of enforcing peace among the tribes. They won over the Mohawks, then the Oneidas and the Cayugas. All the Onondaga chieftains accepted the plan except the wily Atotarho. After the Senecas endorsed the Great Peace, Atotarho finally agreed to join if the Confederacy made him fire-keeper and the Onondagas the leading nation.

The Onondagas kept the sacred council fire which burned near Syracuse. The Mohawk nation became known as the Keeper of the Eastern Door; the Seneca nation, Keeper of the Western Door. The Oneidas and Cayuga were treated as "younger brothers" of the three more powerful nations. In about 1712 or 1714 the Five Nations added another member, the Tuscaroras, who were fleeing from their enemies in North Carolina.

The Confederacy was governed by 50 sachems, or chiefs, drawn from the five tribes. There were nine Mohawk, nine Oneida, fourteen Onondaga, ten Cayuga, and eight Seneca chiefs. Each chief was originally the head chief of his village. This is how he was chosen: the women of each clan (group of related families) met in council and selected the chief from a family which had traditionally inherited the honor of being noble. If the men meeting in council accepted their choice, then this man became ruling chief. Within each of the five tribes one of the clan chiefs became head chief.

The major idea behind the Confederacy was to set up a system of power and responsibility. Thus the Council of the League was divided into three groups: the older brothers (Mohawk and Seneca chiefs), the younger brothers (Cayuga and Oneida chiefs), and the fire-keepers (Onondaga chiefs).

The Onondagas called the meetings and presented the order of business that needed discussion and action. The Mohawks, however, had the most power, since no council could go ahead without their presence. After the Mohawks made a decision, they asked the Senecas to agree. If this was approved, they referred the question to the younger brothers, who in turn had to come to a unanimous agreement. Then the Mohawks informed the Onondagas of the positions taken by the two groups. If both had agreed, the Onondaga chiefs had to accept; if they disagreed, the Onondagas had the right to choose. Once the decision was reached, all the nations agreed to observe it.

Thus the Iroquois developed a complicated but workable method of balancing the rival interests of the various tribes. In addition they provided for a stable method of transferring power from one chief to another. Whenever a new chief was put into his office, they recited the Condolence Ceremony, which contained the message of Deganawidah to Hiawatha. The people sang the famous Peace Hymn which gave thanks for the Confederacy of the Five Nations. Part of it follows:

Hai Hai Hai
Hail Hail Hail
Once more we come to greet and thank the League;
Once more to greet and thank the nation's Peace.
Hai, hai, hai, hai, hai!
Hail, hail, hail, hail, hail!
Hail! Hail! Hail! that which our Forefathers accomplished!

Wampum

The Algonquians may have invented wampum, the strings of shell beads. Hard clams provided the most valuable beads because their lips had a purple color. Workmen cut, shaped, and polished the shells with stone tools. It took a long time for a stone drill to bore a hole in the shell. When the Dutch brought in metal drills, the work went faster. A good worker could manufacture about a hundred beads a day. A large ceremonial belt often had over a thousand beads in it. An ordinary one might have had about 350 beads.

Wampum had many uses. At first the natives probably collected pretty shells for ornamentation. Then wampum became a means of communication. One could string the beads in various patterns and convey a message: a proposal of marriage, a treaty, a payment. By 1600 wampum was often used as money.

The Iroquois used wampum in ceremonies. An agreement sealed by an exchange of wampum was considered unbreakable. A string of wampum served as a person's signature does in business affairs.

You see below an interesting example of wampum. It is called the Hiawatha Belt. The "Tree of Peace" in the center represents the Onondagas, the four squares the other nations in the Confederacy. In 1971 the New York legislature returned the sacred belt to the Iroquois.

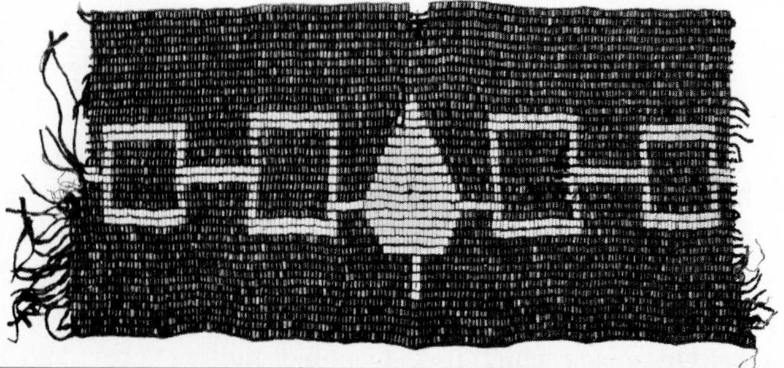

This monument to Samuel de Champlain was erected at Plattsburgh on the shore of the lake that bears his name.

Hail! Hail! Hail! the Law our Forefathers
established!
O listen to us, listen, continue to hear us,
our Grandsires!
O listen to us, listen, continue to hear us,
our Grandsires!

The Confederacy did not give up all war. It merely banned it among the Five Nations. In several instances member nations took up arms against each other but generally the tribes lived up to the Great Peace. Of course, each tribe kept the right to make war on outsiders. When other tribes refused to join the league, they suffered swift and terrible attack, with the Five Nations usually winning. There are several reasons for this: first, being centrally located on the waterways of New York permitted the Iroquois to strike rapidly in nearly every direction. Their warriors could paddle down the Hudson, Susquehanna, Delaware, and St. Lawrence rivers. Second, their chiefs were noted for courage and cunning. Their favorite method of attack was sudden and overwhelming force. Third, the Iroquois were among the first Indians to obtain guns from the Dutch. French, and English. Finally, the united confederacy gave them more strength than any had ever had as single tribes. As a result, the Iroquois were able to defeat their neighbors, one by one.

Contact with the White Men

The coming of the Dutch, the French, and the English meant the beginning of the end of Indian power and the Indian way of life. The white men had guns, knew how to organize expeditions, and kept increasing in number. The Iroquois, however, did not give up their homeland easily. They kept control of most of New York for over 150 years after the first white settlements had been made. To do this the Indians had to be not only brave fighters but skillful treaty-makers as well.

The French ran into trouble from the outset. Their great explorer, Samuel de Champlain, joined a Huron party in 1609 on its way south on Lake Champlain. The great enemies of the Five Nations were the tribes of the Huron Confederacy who lived in Canada between Lake Ontario and Lake Huron. Near Ticonderoga, Champlain and

A drawing of an Indian attack on Champlain, made by Champlain himself. He was an artist, writer, and mapmaker as well as an explorer.

the Huron braves met and fought a band of Iroquois. Read Champlain's account of this skirmish. Keep in mind that an arquebus was a kind of rifle.

> . . . each of us seized an arquebus and went ashore. Leaving their barricade the enemy, about two hundred strong and robust men, came towards us with a gravity and assurance that greatly pleased me. Our Indians told me that those who carried lofty plumes (probably deer antler), were the chiefs and that I should do what I could to kill them. When I saw them preparing to shoot their arrows at us. I raised my arquebus and, aiming directly at one of the chiefs, fired. Two of them fell dead at this shot and one of their companions received a wound from which he afterwards died. I had put four balls in my arquebus. The Indians were greatly surprised at seeing two of their men killed so suddenly, notwithstanding they were provided with arrow-proof armor of woven cotton thread and wood. Whilst I was reloading, one of my companions fired a shot which so astonished them anew that, seeing their leaders slain, others lost courage and fled into the forests whither I pursued them and killed some others.

Six years later Champlain led another party of Hurons deep into central New York and attacked an Oneida village. These attacks caused the Five Nations to hate the French. They regarded the Dutch and English as allies who sold them guns and helped them against the French.

Henry Hudson, exploring for the Dutch in 1609, welcomed the friendly Algonquians. Later the Dutch traders made friends with them on Long Island and in the Hudson Valley. However, Governor William Kieft mistreated the Indians and raided their villages. During the war that followed, the Dutch built a wall across the lower tip of Manhattan Island to protect themselves. Today Wall Street, center of American banking, marks the site of that wall. In spite of their warfare with the Algonquian Indians, the Dutch kept on good terms with the Iroquois because of the fur trade. The English also followed this Dutch policy of making friends with the Five Nations.

The Iroquois React to Christianity

The Indians worshiped nature in its various forms. Having no scientific knowledge, they did not understand what caused such things as rain, death, plant growth, and the changing seasons. They believed that spirits filled all the creatures and objects of the world. Above all, the Indians worshiped the Great Spirit, especially at the time of the Maple, Strawberry, and Green Corn festivals. They asked the Great Spirit to keep the evil spirits from destroying the crops and from helping their enemies.

After the white men arrived, Indian beliefs began to show the influence of Christian ideas. The French sent dozens of priests to convert the Iroquois to Christianity. One of these, Father Isaac Jogues, was the first Roman Catholic *martyr* in New York. [A martyr is one who dies for his beliefs.] Captured by the Mohawks, he described the torture which he suffered.

> They showered blows on me so that I fell under their number. I thought I must surely die on the rocky path leading to the hill under this frightful torture. . . . They burned one of my fingers and crushed another with their teeth. One of the Indians came up to me when I could hardly stand and, taking hold of my nose with one hand, prepared to cut it off with a knife.

Captain Henry Hudson Describes the Indians in 1609

"I sailed to the shore in one of their canoes, with an old man, who was the chief of the tribe consisting of forty men and seventeen women; these I saw there in a house well constructed of oak bark and circular in shape. On our coming into the house, two mats were spread out to sit upon, and immediately some food was served in well made red wooden bowls; two men were also dispatched at once with bows and arrows in quest of game, who soon after brought in a pair of pigeons. . . . They likewise killed a fat dog and skinned it in great haste with shells which they got out of the water. They supposed I would remain for the night, but I returned after a short time on board the ship. . . . The natives are a very good people; for, when they saw that I would not remain, they supposed that I was afraid of their bows, and taking the arrows, they broke them in pieces, and threw them into the fire. . . ."

Above, you see a model of Hudson's ship, the *Half Moon*.

Statue of Father Jogues at Lake George. Look at the right hand. Can you see signs of the torture Father Jogues suffered?

Father Jogues managed to escape to the Dutch forts on the Hudson, where he received a warm welcome. Later, the brave missionary returned to the Mohawk villages. Unfortunately, the Indians blamed him for a smallpox epidemic and killed him in 1648. Today a statue to his memory stands near the town of Auriesville.

The Dutch Reformed Church also sent missionaries to the Indians, as did the Church of England. The Presbyterians supported Samuel Kirkland, who made so many friends among the Oneidas that this tribe refused to fight for the British and against the patriots in the Revolutionary War.

In the years following the Revolutionary War, Handsome Lake, an elderly Seneca, preached a revival of the old Indian beliefs. He urged his followers to give up warfare and liquor and to take up agriculture. As a result, the religion of Hiawatha and Deganawidah is today the belief of at least one third of the Iroquois living in New York and Canada. Many of the Indians became Roman Catholics, while others belong to the Presbyterian and other Protestant churches.

The Fur Trade

The furs of America were especially valuable because gentlemen and noblemen in England and France liked to wear beaver hats. The traders of Albany and Montreal tried hard to control the fur trade in America. Their rivalry sometimes led to war between their nations and between the Indian tribes. The Mohawks, in 1626, defeated and drove away the Mahicans who had prospered by trading with the Dutch at Fort Orange (Albany). By 1640, most of the fur-bearing animals in central and western New York had been trapped by Iroquois hunters. No skins meant no guns, blankets, hatchets, not to mention whiskey and glass beads. Beaver were still plentiful in the region of the Great Lakes, but the Huron Indians controlled the trade with the tribes who trapped the beavers there.

The Five Nations asked the Hurons to grant them a share of their fur trade. When the Hurons refused this request, the Iroquois decided to destroy them. One thousand warriors struck the Huron villages in Canada. Terror-stricken, the Hurons fled into the forest, where many died.

The Iroquois then attacked other tribes accused of giving aid to Huron refugees and destroyed a Neutral village. The Eries became the next target, falling before the Iroquois in 1654. For a while after these tremendous victories the Five Nations were the only tribes enjoying the profitable trade with the interior.

The Decline of Iroquois Power

New threats, however, rose to challenge the Iroquois. To the south the Susquehannocks, with arms supplied by Maryland merchants, raided the Seneca country and made their bid for the western trade. But Maryland frontiersmen, who had suffered from Indian raids, struck the Susquehannocks a hard blow in 1675.

Meanwhile the French took steps to break the Iroquois blockade of the Ottawa River route to the interior. They found new Indian allies, and in the 1680's they began building forts on the upper Great Lakes. French raiding parties swept into the Mohawk and Seneca country in the 1680's, burning crops and destroying villages. These raids hurt the Iroquois so badly that they deserted their British alliance and signed a treaty of friendship with France (1701).

The Iroquois became involved in the fighting between England and France. They lost hundreds of their bravest warriors in four wars between these two nations. To offset these losses, they adopted hundreds of prisoners into their tribes and, as was noted earlier, admitted the Tuscaroras to the Confederation as the Sixth Nation. Probably disease took more Indian lives than war. Smallpox, tuberculosis, and influenza were deadly invaders of the villages.

The Revolutionary War between England and the American colonies destroyed the power of the Iroquois Confederacy for all time. The Iroquois, except for the Oneidas and Tuscaroras, remained loyal to the British King. During the War, George Washington sent an expedition under Generals John Sullivan and James Clinton into central and western New York to destroy the Senecas and their allies. The soldiers burned villages and destroyed cornfields. After the Revolution, many remaining Iroquois retreated to Canada. One Canadian area that they settled was the Grand River Valley, a few miles west of the Niagara River.

An Indian Trapper, painted by Frederick Remington, a New York artist, 1861–1909.

Not only the power of the Six Nations but also their way of life collapsed. New York State and the United States gave them small grants of money, but not enough to buy much food or clothing. Worst of all, the Iroquois lost almost all of their land to the state of New York. By 1800 all they had left were a dozen small reservations.

Present-Day New York Indians

Today there are only 8,000 to 9,000 Indians living on nine reservations. The Onondagas live south of Syracuse near their old council fire. The Cattaraugus reservation is near Gowanda; the Tonawanda near Akron; the Tuscarora near Niagara Falls. In the southwestern corner of the state is the Allegany reservation and north of the Adirondacks near the town of Hogansburg is the St. Regis reservation. Only a few

Present-day native Americans of the Tuscarora who live on the reservation in Lewiston examine some crafts of their ancestors.

Indians and Colonists

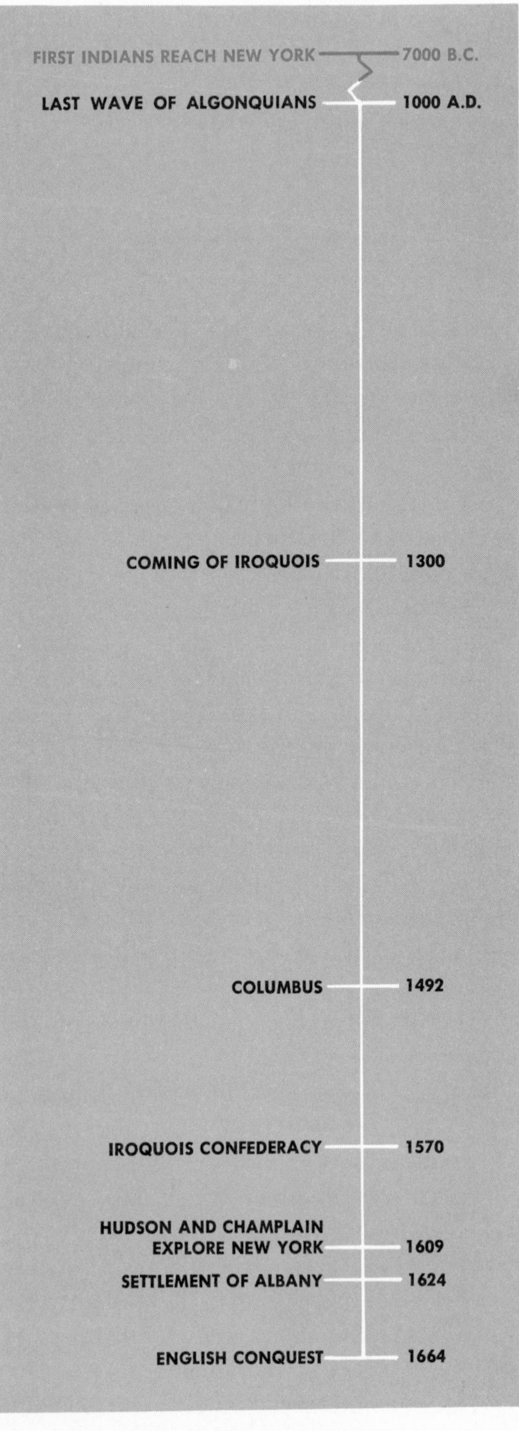

Indians live on the tracts for the Poosepatuck and Shinnecock tribes on Long Island. Other Indians have moved to the cities. In Brooklyn there is a colony of several hundred Mohawks who are skilled high-altitude construction workers. The state permits Indians on reservations to govern themselves by old tribal customs and grants them special privileges in hunting and fishing.

The New York State Department of Social Services has charge of the Indians; the state provides schools, clinics, welfare if needed, police protection, and other services. But the Indians still remain suspicious of the white men. They feel, and the record bears them out, that their white overlords have often cheated them of their lands and ignored their rights. For example, in 1962 the federal government took some 10,000 acres of Seneca land to build the Kinzua Dam in Pennsylvania. This flood control project also affected the Indians of the Allegany Reservation in New York. The Senecas received about fifteen million dollars and have used the money to build community halls and houses, to give college scholarships to Indian youths, and to encourage the development of local industry.

However, the Senecas still tend to distrust the white men, who have secured by purchase, trickery, and seizure over 99 percent of their holdings. They, like the other Iroquois, have a passionate love of the land. One put it this way: "The land is my mother. You cannot sell your mother."

Summary

The Iroquois worshipped nature as the giver and taker of life. Their creation myth explained the origins of the world and some of life's mysteries. The Iroquois lived in small villages surrounded by clearings and by the forest, which provided food, shelter, and fuel. Each village tried to make its own tools and clothing, and to raise its own foodstuffs.

The Iroquois, who conquered the Algonquins about the year 1300, became famous for their Confederacy and for their skill as warriors. They conquered most of their neighbors in their desire to get control of the fur trade. In the wars between England and France, they generally fought with the British.

Gradually, the civilization of the whites broke down that of the Indian, or native American. The Indian took over many of the good and bad points of European civilization. In turn, the white settlers gained many things from the Indians. From them they got corn, the most valuable crop of our farms today. They learned how to clear the forest and to live in the wilderness.

Checking the high points

1. What was the creation myth? Is it anything like our Bible story?

2. Describe life in the Iroquois village.

3. How did the Iroquois train their children?

4. Where did the Iroquois come from? How did they find their way into New York?

5. How did Deganawidah and Hiawatha bring about the Great Peace?

6. Why did the Dutch and the English try to be friends with the Iroquois?

7. Why did the Iroquois generally prefer the British to the French?

8. What impact did the white men have on the Iroquois religion?

9. Why did the Iroquois become weak?

10. What contributions did the Indians make to our life today?

11. Where do Indians live in New York today?

Think these over

1. Why did the Iroquois Confederacy, which was set up to bring about peace, lead to so many wars?

2. Do you see any ways in which the Iroquois Confederacy was like our government today?

3. What is most remarkable is not that Indian culture collapsed but that it lasted so long and had such influence on the white culture. Do you agree or disagree with this idea?

Vocabulary building

Do you know the meaning of these words which were used in the chapter?

confederacy
sachem
martyr
legend
arquebus
myth
condolence
council
unanimous
convert
missionary
monopoly
stockade

Checking locations

Check your ability to locate these places on the map.

St. Lawrence River
Lake Ontario
Quebec
Susquehanna River
Delaware River
Canandaigua Lake
Oneida Lake
Lake Erie
Cayuga Lake
Seneca Lake
Oswego River
Lake Champlain
Ottawa River

chapter 4: EUROPEANS DISCOVER and SETTLE the NEW WORLD

chapter 5: ENGLAND FOUNDS ITS NORTH AMERICAN COLONIES

chapter 6: DUTCH TRADERS and FARMERS SETTLE the HUDSON VALLEY

unit two

The Age of Discovery and Settlement

New York state history dates are shown in color.

c. 1000	Leif Ericson lands in North America
1095	Crusades begin
1271-1295	Marco Polo visits China
1492	Columbus discovers the Americas
1498	Vasco da Gama sails around Africa to India
1517	Protestant Reformation
1524	Verrazano sails into New York Harbor
1565	St. Augustine, Florida, is founded
1609	Henry Hudson explores the Hudson River
1619	First black people arrive in the colonies
1620	Pilgrims land at Plymouth
1624	Dutch establish Fort Orange
1626	Dutch purchase Manhattan Island from Indians
1630	Puritans settle Boston
1647	Peter Stuyvesant becomes governor of New Amsterdam
1664	English gain control of New Amsterdam

America's most famous lady—the 151-foot statue given to us by France as a centennial gift—stares out on upper New York Bay. *Liberty Enlightening the World*, her full title, has become the symbol of freedom to millions of immigrants. This statue is, of course, the Statue of Liberty.

The history of America is also the history of immigrants from other continents. Our twentieth century civilization is the result of contacts among several peoples: Indians whose ancestors migrated from Asia; black people from Africa; and white people from Europe. The achievements of the Indians, especially in Mexico and Central America, have long fascinated experts and tourists. The important contributions of blacks to all fields of endeavor have been notable in the development of America.

It was the Europeans, however, who put their stamp upon our language, laws, religion, and culture. Spain dominated the New World for more than a century after Columbus reached this hemisphere. Portugal found a water route around Africa to the wealth of the Indies, but had little impact on the New World, except in Brazil. Shortly after 1600, England, France, and the Netherlands made their first permanent settlements.

The drive for empire by the Europeans clashed with Indian society. The Indian way of life gave way before bullets, disease, and the superior tools and weapons of the Europeans. The efforts of whites to profit from raising sugar, tobacco, and other crops resulted in the harsh treatment of laborers—white, red, and black.

NOVUM AMSTERODAMUM

Chapter Objectives

To learn about

- European life and trade before 1492
- European discovery and settlement of the New World

chapter 4

EUROPEANS DISCOVER and SETTLE the NEW WORLD

Europe in the Middle Ages

Today Americans grant their loyalty or feelings of patriotism to the nation-state. But European peasants or farmers in the Middle Ages knew little of the world outside their local village. Serfs owed allegiance to their landlord and could not leave his soil. Part of their time was spent working on the lord's fields and part on their own plots, so they existed as neither fully free nor slave. Life for most was grim, with hunger, disease, and death as constant dangers.

But the Middle Ages was also a period of great cultural and commercial advances. Beautiful cathedrals and churches were built; universities were founded; cities grew and prospered because of the revival of trade. The Christian Church was the cement binding Europeans together with common beliefs. Unfortunately, the Christian ideal of love and peace did not prevent local warfare breaking out among lords. Each lord owed loyalty and fees to a higher lord. This system of land ownership and loyalties is sometimes called feudalism, or the feudal system.

Gradually a few of the lords won more and more power and took the title of kings. They became allies of wealthy merchants in the cities, who needed protection from robber barons and pirates. The kings cut down the power of the lesser lords and set up their own central courts. They laid taxes on the lords as well as on the city dwellers, and with the money they collected they formed standing armies. Wherever this happened, powerful nations appeared. Among them were Portugal, Spain, France, and England, which became the main colonizing powers.

The Norse Discoveries

Even before the movement to build strong nations got under way, the Norsemen who lived in Scandinavia were roving far from home in search of land and booty. Scandinavia includes Denmark, Norway, and

Sweden. In boats driven by sails and oars these warriors crossed the seas making settlements in Russia, Sicily in the Mediterranean, England, France, Iceland, and Greenland. About the year 1000 Leif Ericson landed in North America, which he called Vinland. A few years later Thorfinn Karlsefni established a colony in Vinland, but it disappeared in three years. The ruins of a Norse settlement have been found near L'Anse Au Meadow, a village in northern Newfoundland. Scientists believe that the Norsemen colonized this area about A.D. 1000. No one knows if this was Karlsefni's settlement, but it is proof that the Norse reached the Western Hemisphere about 500 years before Columbus made his famous voyage to America.

Icelandic sagas, or historical stories, give accounts of Norse voyages. America was first sighted by Bjorni Herjulfisson but he did not land. The sagas also tell of Leif Ericson's trips from Greenland and Iceland to Vinland over a 12-year period. Scientists today study ruins and old maps to uncover truths about these early voyages and discoveries.

European Trade with the Orient

In 1095 Pope Urban II preached a sermon calling for Christians to free Jerusalem and other Holy Places from the Moslem Turks and Arabs. As a result a series of wars took place during the next two centuries between Christian crusaders and the Moslems. Although the crusaders won temporary victories, even capturing Jerusalem, they failed to keep possession of the Holy Places. But the rough warriors learned much from their enemies. The Arabs had an advanced civilization of their own and were in contact with the Chinese, whose civilization had lasted for centuries. The Arabs taught the Europeans a good deal about science and art. The Europeans learned the value of spices—pepper, nutmeg, cinnamon, ginger, cloves, and mace. These flavorings helped preserve meat and improve the taste of food.

The Orient, that is, the countries of Asia, supplied colorful rugs and carpets to decorate the grim stone buildings of the nobles; silks and perfumes to clothe and scent their bodies; chinaware, fine glass, diamonds, pearls, and rubies to bring luxury and beauty to their lives. Also important were drugs—camphor, medicinal rhubarb, and opium, the only known pain-killer.

The only way Europeans could get these prized products was to trade with the Arabs. The Arabs controlled the Isthmus of Suez, thus blocking the traders of Europe from the Red Sea and the Indian Ocean. But the merchants of the Italian cities of Genoa and Venice visited the ports in the eastern Mediterranean, bought goods from the Arabs, and sold them back home. The gains from this trade brought prosperity to many Italian cities and encouraged the Italian Renaissance. The term "Renaissance" means rebirth. The Italian Renaissance, which began in the fourteenth century, expressed itself in paintings, sculpture, science, and literature. This flowering of culture, which included a revival of interest in ancient Greece and Rome, spread from Italy to other parts of Europe.

Other nations and cities envied the wealth of Venice and Genoa. Furthermore the report of Marco Polo, a Venetian who traveled to China and lived there for 17 years, stirred up much interest in the Orient and the best routes to get there.

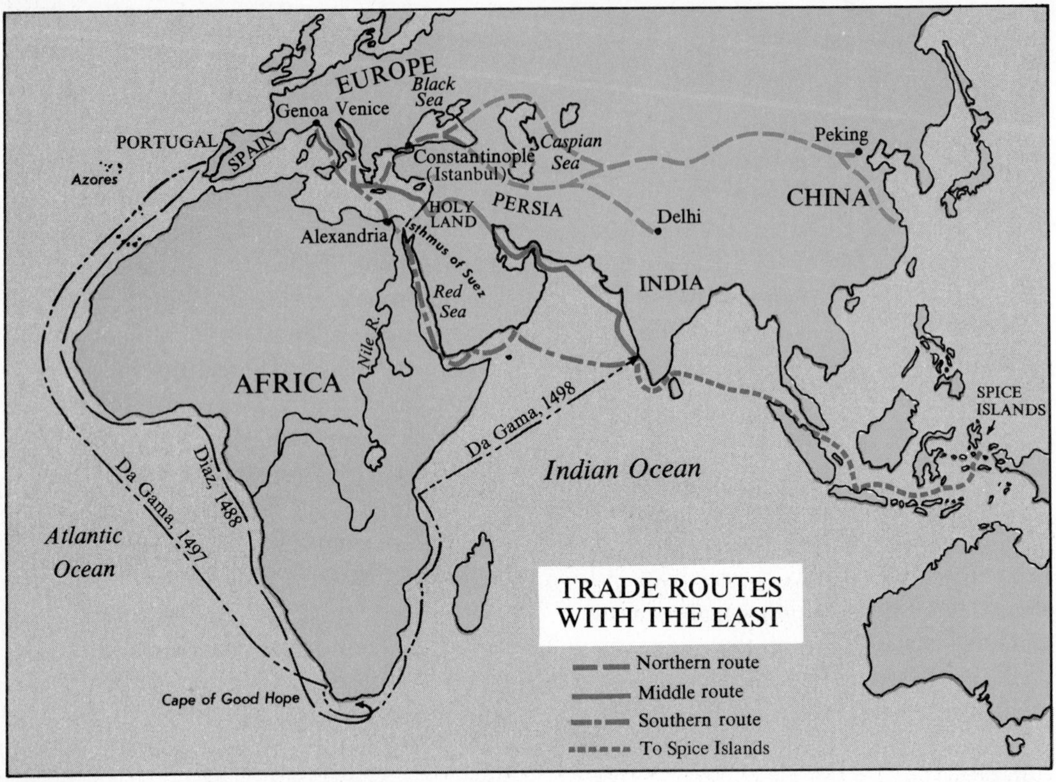
EUROPE
Black Sea
Genoa
Venice
PORTUGAL
SPAIN
Azores
Constantinople (Istanbul)
Caspian Sea
Peking
CHINA
PERSIA
Delhi
HOLY LAND
Alexandria
Isthmus of Suez
Red Sea
INDIA
Nile R.
AFRICA
SPICE ISLANDS
Da Gama, 1498
Indian Ocean
Diaz, 1488
Da Gama, 1497
Atlantic Ocean
TRADE ROUTES WITH THE EAST
Northern route
Middle route
Southern route
To Spice Islands
Cape of Good Hope

Map 10

Map 11

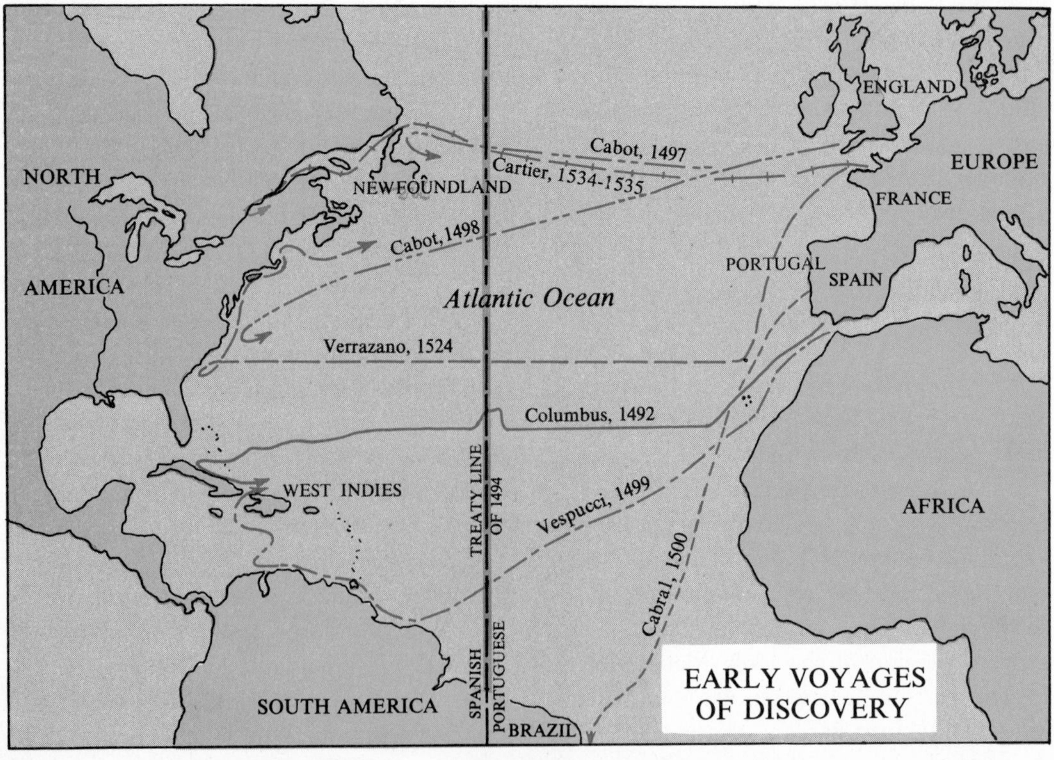
ENGLAND
EUROPE
Cabot, 1497
Cartier, 1534-1535
NORTH
NEWFOUNDLAND
FRANCE
Cabot, 1498
PORTUGAL
SPAIN
AMERICA
Atlantic Ocean
Verrazano, 1524
Columbus, 1492
WEST INDIES
TREATY LINE OF 1494
Vespucci, 1499
AFRICA
Cabral, 1500
SPANISH
PORTUGUESE
SOUTH AMERICA
BRAZIL
EARLY VOYAGES OF DISCOVERY

Spanish-Portuguese Rivalry

Prince Henry the Navigator (1394–1460) of Portugal established a school for seamen, where geography, navigation, and mathematics were studied. He also experimented in designing ships that could stand the rougher waters of the Atlantic. With his encouragement Portuguese explorers pushed southward, hugging the west coast of Africa. At various points they set up trading posts where the evil business of buying slaves began.

Meanwhile Christopher Columbus, an Italian-born sea captain, had been trying to convince European rulers that the Orient could be reached by sailing directly west. He finally persuaded Queen Isabella of Spain to finance his exploration. Columbus made two errors in calculation. First, he thought the land covered more of the earth's surface than it does. Second, he believed the earth to be smaller than it is. This combination of errors caused Columbus to estimate the distance from the Canary Islands to Japan at 2,400 nautical miles. The true distance is 10,600.

On September 6, 1492 Columbus' expedition of three small ships—Nina, Pinta, and Santa Maria—left the Canary Islands sailing due west. On October 12, 1492, an island was sighted. Columbus named it San Salvador. In those days the little-known countries of the Far East were referred to as "India" or "the Indies." Thinking he had reached the Orient, Columbus called the natives "Indians." The same error resulted in calling the Caribbean islands "the Indies." Today we refer to the Caribbean islands as the West Indies to distinguish them from the East Indies, islands off southeast Asia.

Columbus made three other voyages to the New World but never realized he had not reached the Orient. It was his skill and daring that opened the Western Hemisphere to Europeans, but the American continents are named in honor of another Italian—Amerigo Vespucci. An able navigator, Vespucci made voyages to Columbus' newfound land. He recognized that South America was an unknown continent and called it a new world. As a result, map makers began to call the new discovery America, in honor of Amerigo Vespucci.

The Portuguese became disturbed about Columbus' discovery. For many years they had been sailing south along the coast of Africa seeking a way around that continent to the Orient. The Portuguese insisted that whatever Columbus had found belonged to them. The Spanish disagreed. In the Treaty of Tordesillas (1494) the two nations agreed to divide the world along a line drawn 370 leagues west of the Cape Verde Islands. Non-Christian lands discovered west of the line were to belong to Spain, those east of it to Portugal. The kings of most other European nations refused to recognize this division but did not have the strength to challenge Spanish or Portuguese naval power. Because the coast of Brazil lay east of the treaty line, it was settled by the Portuguese. Today Spanish is the language of all South American countries except Brazil, where Portuguese is spoken.

Finally, in 1498, Vasco da Gama, a Portuguese sea captain, sailed around Africa and reached Calicut in India. The Portuguese were the first to discover a sea route to the Far East. They soon established a rich trade with the Orient.

In the years 1519–1522 Ferdinand Magellan, sailing for Spain, reached the Orient by going west as Columbus had proposed. Crossing the Atlantic he sailed southward along the coast of South America, through the Strait of Magellan (named in his honor) to the Pacific Ocean. After a terrible voyage the expedition reached the Philippine Islands, where Magellan was slain by natives. The expedition, reduced from five ships to one, sailed on westward across the Indian Ocean around Africa and northward up the African coast to Spain.

Magellan's voyage is important for several reasons: it proved that the earth is round; it revealed the great size of the New World; it showed that the Pacific was very wide; and it proved that the Orient could be reached by sailing west. Because Magellan had discovered the Philippines, Spain claimed ownership, even though they were clearly on the Portuguese side of the 1494 treaty line.

Spain in the New World

Spain had a free hand in the New World. Under the Treaty of Tordesillas, Portugal was restricted to Brazil. Besides, Portugal was so busy with the Far Eastern trade that its leaders had little energy left for the Western Hemisphere. The kings of England and France were interested in the new discoveries and in finding new trade routes to the Orient. But they did not dare to challenge the Spanish openly. Instead they sent expeditions of their own to the New World.

In 1497 an Italian-born seaman, John Cabot, went exploring for England. His idea was to sail west along a northerly route, which he hoped would carry him north of the newly discovered lands into the Pacific Ocean. Once he reached the Pacific, he could sail directly to the Orient. Over the years many others would seek such a route, which came to be called the Northwest Passage. The North American continent blocked Cabot, as it did those who followed him. It was not until 1906 that the first crossing of the arctic waters north of North America was made.

John Cabot made two voyages, one in 1497 and one in 1498. On his first voyage he discovered the rich fishing grounds off Newfoundland. Soon thousands of British and French seamen were sailing to these waters every year. The voyages trained many sailors and helped England and France become sea powers. English claims to North America were based on Cabot's discoveries.

Another Italian sea captain, Giovanni de Verrazano, entered the service of the king of France. Verrazano explored the coast of North America in 1524. He discovered the great harbor of present-day New York. Some years later the daring Italian lost his life while leading an expedition to the West Indies. The French king turned to Jacques Cartier who, starting in 1534, began a series of voyages. Cartier discovered and explored the St. Lawrence River, establishing France's claim to this part of the New World.

Meanwhile the Spanish were establishing themselves in America. Spain secured important bases on Hispaniola, Puerto Rico, and Cuba. The climate is sub-tropical and rainfall is abundant. Diseases, especially those carried by insects, threatened the settlers and killed many of them. Some gold was found, at least enough to stir up the greed of the explorers. The Spanish forced the native Indians to dig for gold. Later they set up sugar plantations, using black slaves imported from Africa.

The first permanent settlement was made on Hispaniola in 1496. Juan Ponce de Leon began the settlement of Puerto Rico a dozen years later. Soon Diego de Valazquez had established Spanish power in Cuba. From these West Indian bases Spain sent out expeditions to explore and settle North and South America.

Vasco Nunez de Balboa, who had gone bankrupt attempting to found a plantation on Hispaniola, took over the leadership of an expedition to the Isthmus of Panama. In 1513 he hacked his way through the jungle across the Isthmus to the Pacific Ocean. In this way the Spanish learned of the short overland route between the Atlantic and the Pacific.

The Spaniards called their military leaders in the New World "conquistadores," or conquerors. No man deserved this title more than Hernando Cortes. In 1519 he sailed from Cuba, landing at what is now Veracruz, Mexico. Aided by Indian allies, Cortes overthrew the Aztec Empire after three years of warfare. The great quantity of gold, silver, and jewels that the conquistador seized and sent home turned the attention of Spain from the Orient to the New World. Cortes pushed on to the Pacific Ocean and built a shipyard there. North of Mexico City the Spanish found rich gold and silver mines. By forcing the Indians to work the mines the Spaniards produced great wealth, and Mexico became a very important Spanish colony.

Another conquistador, Francisco Pizarro, crossed the Isthmus of Panama and sailed south along the coast of South America. In 1532 he landed in what is now Peru and moved through the Andes Mountains into the land held by the Incas. By pretending to be a friend, Pizarro seized Atahualpa, the Inca ruler. After receiving a huge ransom for Atahualpa's release, he killed the Inca. Warfare followed in which Pizarro won control of the Inca Empire and extended Spanish control over a large section of South America. Like Mexico, Peru supplied Spain with great quantities of gold and silver.

Spurred by the desire to find precious metals, the conquistadores explored much of what is now the United States. The first to do this was Juan Ponce de Leon, the governor of Puerto Rico. In 1513 de Leon landed near what is now St. Augustine, Florida, and made his way southward along the coast to Key West, where he turned north and sailed up the west coast. Eight years later he tried unsuccessfully to establish a settlement near what is the present city of Tampa.

Hernando de Soto who had fought with Pizarro in Peru, searched for similar riches in the southeastern United States. Landing

Map 12

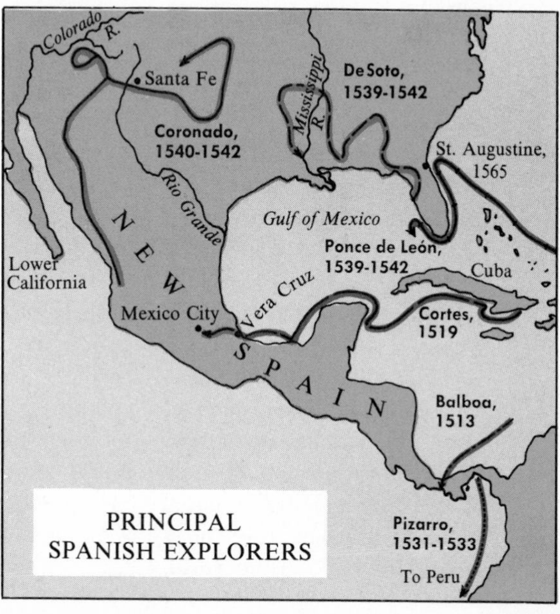

PRINCIPAL SPANISH EXPLORERS

near Tampa Bay in Florida, he enslaved Indians and with his expedition pressed northward through the territory that is now Georgia, South Carolina, and North Carolina. De Soto entered Tennessee and then turned south into Alabama. Moving westward, he crossed the Mississippi and continued up the Arkansas River into Oklahoma. The company then returned to the Mississippi River, where de Soto died. In one last attempt to find riches, the company moved westward into north Texas. Returning to the Mississippi empty handed, they went south along the river to the Gulf of Mexico. Finally, in 1543, after four years of wandering, the weary survivors arrived at Veracruz in Mexico. They brought with them some geographic knowledge but no treasure.

After hearing reports of great wealth to be found in what is now the southwestern United States, another expedition set out from Mexico in 1540 commanded by Francisco Vasquez de Coronado. Some members of the party moved along the Colorado River into what is now California. The main body marched into New Mexico, raiding the mud and stone villages of the Zuñi Indians. After discovering the Grand Canyon, Coronado went northeastward across parts of Texas and Oklahoma into Kansas. Two years later the weary Spaniards ceased their wanderings and returned to Mexico empty-handed.

Spanish ships sailed as far north as Newfoundland. On the Pacific coast they explored the western shores. All these voyages and expeditions provided much knowledge

The Horse

Montezuma and his Aztecs thought that Cortes and his sixteen mounted soldiers were very strange monsters. Without their horses the conquistadores could never have made such speedy conquests. In the New World these animals thrived and multiplied rapidly. By 1600, Spaniards were establishing ranches as far north as New Mexico.

Within fifty years the Plains Indians realized the value of horses. They caught and tamed the wild mustangs, and stole others. Before long, mounted Indians became the most skilled horsemen in the world.

By 1750, horses had spread across the Great Plains and as far north as Canada and as far west as California. They were introduced to the South Atlantic coast by the Spaniards who set up missions and towns such as St. Augustine in northeastern Florida.

New Englanders had also brought over horses and by 1650 were exporting them to the West Indian planters. The colonists used horses for riding, hunting, and racing, but preferred oxen as draft animals. Slower but stronger, the oxen were ideal for clearing away logs and brush. The German farmers of Pennsylvania, who had well-cleared fields, developed the Conestoga horse for farm purposes.

The horse played a tremendous role in the development of America. The pony served the trapper, miner, and hunter. The cattle kingdom relied upon the mounted cowboy. In transportation, stagecoaches, canal boats, and streetcars relied on horse power. The army used horses in its cavalry units and to position cannon. Horse racing was the leading form of recreation in colonial America and has continued to attract millions of followers.

about North America. The first permanent settlement within the present boundaries of the United States was made by the Spaniards at St. Augustine, Florida, in 1565. Here they began building a fortified base which would protect their treasure ships. These ships carried gold and silver from Peru and Mexico through the Straits of Florida on the way to Spain.

Although the conquistadores had found no treasure in Arizona and New Mexico, traders who bartered with the Indians found silver mines. In 1598 the first Spanish settlers entered New Mexico. The first settlement was at San Juan. In 1609 Santa Fe became the center of government. The Spanish colonization of southwestern United States went slowly. By 1700 Father Eusebio Francisco Kino had established a mission near Tucson, Arizona, and other missions began to appear in southern Texas. San Antonio de Valero, better known as the Alamo, was founded at San Antonio, Texas, in 1718.

Two Spanish pioneers opened California to settlement. In 1769 Father Junipero Serra built the mission of San Diego. Meanwhile Gaspar de Portolá pushed northward to establish a post at Monterey. Portolá discovered San Francisco Bay, one of the finest harbors on the West Coast. In 1776 a handful of settlers opened a post at San Francisco.

Long before the English colonized North America, the Spanish had built a successful empire. By 1574 about 160,000 Spaniards lived in nearly 200 cities and towns in the New World. They built hundreds of cathedrals and churches. They founded two universities: one at Mexico City, the other at Lima, Peru. They published books and gave prizes for good writing. This great empire was populated by millions of Indians and thousands of blacks, but it was ruled by only a few hundred officials and guarded by Spanish troops. Agriculture provided a livelihood for most people. Next in importance came the mining of silver.

Cities of the United States Founded by Spain

City	Year
St. Augustine, Florida	1565
Santa Fe, New Mexico	1609
El Paso, Texas	1659
Tucson, Arizona	1700
San Antonio, Texas	1718
San Diego, California	1769
Monterey, California	1770
San Francisco, California	1776
Los Angeles, California	1781

Note: San Juan, the capital of Puerto Rico, was founded by the Spanish in 1511.

The kings of Spain ruled the colonies first for their own benefit and second for the welfare of Spain. Little thought was given to the colonists. One-fifth of all gold and silver mined went to the crown. The king received taxes on all goods brought into or taken out of Spanish territories and on all goods sold within the colonies. Certain kinds of manufacturing were forbidden. There was no democracy. Local officials were appointed by the king or by the king's representatives.

All settlers were required to practice Roman Catholicism, the state religion of Spain. The Spanish kings believed it their duty to Christianize the Indians. This task they assigned to religious orders of the Roman Catholic Church, especially the Dominicans, Jesuits and Franciscans. The missionaries sought to improve the living conditions of the Indians. They taught not only Christianity but agriculture and crafts.

In frontier areas the Spaniards gathered the Indians together in villages called pueblos. Usually each pueblo had a mission and a garrison of soldiers. The military garrisons were called presidios. These three agencies—pueblo, mission, and presidio—were used to establish Spanish civilization on the frontier.

The lack of self-government and religious freedom, as well as the tax on trade, made Spanish America unattractive to settlers. Very few officials, soldiers, or craftsmen brought their wives with them. The missionaries did not marry. Consequently, the number of Spanish people remained small. Although the Spanish Empire covered a vast territory inhabited by millions of people, only a tiny proportion of them was pure Spanish.

English Expansion

English fishermen and merchants became more venturesome after 1500, especially under the Tudor kings, who encouraged trade and industry, Each year more ships left Bristol and other English ports for Spanish and Portuguese wharves. Money piled up in the hands of London merchants, who formed companies to trade with Russia, Africa, and the eastern Mediterranean. The most important groups, such as the British East India Company, received royal charters. These charters gave them the right to establish by force, if necessary, a monopoly of certain trades. Englishmen also invested in mining and manufacturing. Between 1575 and 1620 the output of coal, salt, iron and steel, ships, and glass increased more than five times. New industries—paper, brass, soap—sprang up, while clothmaking continued to prosper. Some refugees from European wars and religious persecution brought skills and some capital.

In addition to this vast economic growth, another important change was taking place: the rise of vigorous nationalism. After King Henry VIII broke with the Pope, setting up a separate church, England drifted toward war with Spain. Spain was trying to crush English Protestantism. English sailors began to seize Spanish ships and to raid Spain's colonies in the New World. These raiders, known as Sea Dogs, hoped to seize the famous treasure ships bringing gold and silver to Spain.

The most famous of the Sea Dogs was Sir Francis Drake. Sailing in his ship, the *Golden Hind,* Drake rounded South America and struck the unprotected Spanish settlements along the Pacific Coast. When the *Golden Hind* could hold no more treasure, Drake sailed north and beached the ship for repairs in California. These completed, he crossed the Pacific, bought spices in the East Indies, rounded Africa, and reached home in 1580. Queen Elizabeth I, who received a fortune as her share of Drake's treasure, knighted him.

Angered by the rise of English Protestantism and by the rise of the Sea Dogs, King Philip of Spain decided to conquer England. He built a great fleet, known as the Spanish Armada. When the Armada invaded English waters in 1588, war began. The English sent their small ships to dart in and around the huge Spanish ships and set them afire. They were aided by violent storms that destroyed many Spanish vessels and scattered the rest. Although this war lasted until 1604, the defeat of the Armada broke Spanish control of the sea. No longer could Spain prevent other nations from planting colonies in the New World.

Fort Sainte Marie de Gannentaha, north of Syracuse. This reproduction is typical of the French type of fort. The original was built in 1656 to protect French settlers.

French fishermen who stopped in Newfoundland to dry fish and secure water began to see the possibilities in fur trade with the Indians. Among them was Samuel de Champlain, a man of courage, endurance, and foresight. In 1608 Champlain founded the city of Quebec, on the St. Lawrence River. The next year he moved into what is now New York State and discovered the lake known as Lake Champlain. The colony was called New France, and Champlain devoted his life to it. Before he died in 1635, he had pushed exploration as far west as Wisconsin and had established fur-trading routes to the Indians in the Great Lakes region. Efforts by Champlain and others to promote farming and crafts in New France did not succeed. Furs remained the great source of profit.

Roman Catholic missionaries, seeking converts to Christianity, followed the traders to the interior. The Jesuits, who led this effort, suffered hardships and even torture to bring their message to the tribes. One of the greatest of the Jesuit explorers was Father Jacques Marquette. He spoke six Indian languages and worked among the Indians in the western Great Lakes. From the tribesmen Father Marquette heard of a mighty western river. He wondered if it flowed into the Pacific Ocean. If so, it might furnish a route to the Orient.

In 1673, accompanied by Louis Joliet, Father Marquette crossed Lake Michigan and traveled over the Fox and Wisconsin Rivers to the Mississippi. The two explorers floated down the Mississippi to the mouth of the Arkansas River, where de Soto had died more than a century earlier. Realizing that the Mississippi flowed into the Gulf of Mexico and not the Pacific, and fearing capture by the Spanish, the Frenchmen returned to Lake Michigan.

In 1682, another French party went down the Mississippi, this time as far as the Gulf of Mexico. The Mississippi Basin was claimed for France and named Louisiana in honor of the French king, Louis XIV. In 1718, the city of New Orleans was founded. By mid-century, rice, sugar, indigo (a blue dye), and tobacco were being grown in the lower Mississippi, and fig and orange trees had been planted. However, the population included only five thousand Europeans and two thousand Africans.

Cities of the United States That Were Founded by the French

City	*Year of Founding*
Biloxi, Mississippi	1699
Cahokia, Illinois	1699
Detroit, Michigan	1701
Vincennes, Indiana	1702
Mobile, Alabama	1710
Natchez, Mississippi	1716
New Orleans, Louisiana	1718
Pittsburgh, Pennsylvania*	1754
Saint Louis, Missouri	1764

*Colonists from Virginia were attempting to build a fort at what is now Pittsburgh when they were driven out by the French.

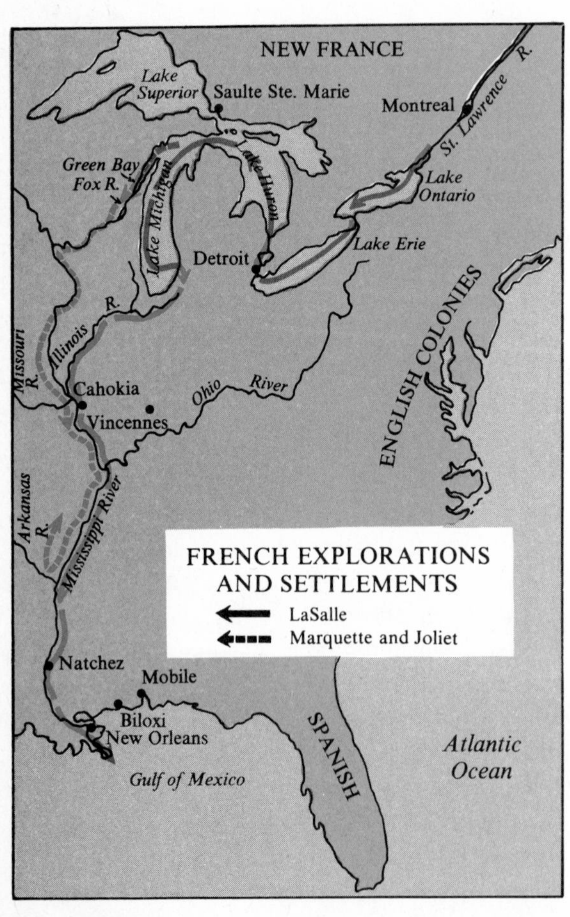

Map 13

The French holdings reached in a great curve from New Orleans on the Mississippi to Quebec on the St. Lawrence. These two fortress cities guarded the great waterways which provided transportation to the interior. They also controlled the commerce of the huge French Empire in North America. As a further defense forts were built at important points in the interior. Although there was some mining of copper and lead, as well as some farming, furs remained the chief source of income.

Like the Spaniards, the French tried to establish a feudal government in the New World. Land was given to nobles, called *Seigneurs*, who rented sections of their estates to farmers, called *habitants*. The scheme attracted few persons since they could make more money trading with the Indians. Three officials dominated New France: the governor, who commanded the military forces and ran the government; the intendant, who reported directly to the king and was in charge of finance; and the bishop, who managed the church. There was no religious toleration as we know it, and ordinary people had nothing to say about the government. These conditions made life in New France unattractive to settlers.

Summary

About A.D. 1000, the Norseman, Leif Ericson, landed in North America. Apparently other European nations had little knowledge of the Norse discoveries. The Crusades began in 1095 and continued for almost 200 years. During this struggle the Crusaders learned much from their Moslem enemies and began to trade with them for oriental goods. This oriental trade was controlled by two Italian cities, Venice and Genoa. Other nations, desiring to trade with the Far East, began to seek direct sea routes to the Orient. Columbus sailed west in search of such a route and opened the New World to Europeans in 1492. Six years later da Gama, a Portuguese, sailed around Africa to India, establishing a direct sea route to the Far East. In 1497 Cabot led an English expedition and discovered the Newfoundland fishing banks. The Magellan expedition sailed around the world in 1519–1522.

Using the West Indies as a base, Spaniards explored and settled much of South and North America. Cortes conquered the Aztecs in Mexico. Pizarro broke the power of the Incas and seized Peru. St. Augustine, Florida, founded by the Spaniards in 1565, is the first permanent settlement in the United States. The Spanish also set up posts in Texas, New Mexico, Arizona, and California. By 1600 Spain had a huge empire. Lack of religious and political freedom and heavy taxes made Spanish colonies unattractive to Europeans, who were greatly outnumbered by the Indians. The Spanish immigrants were officials, clergymen, and soldiers.

In 1588 the English defeated the Spanish Armada and ended Spain's superiority on the high seas. The Americas were now open to settlement by other nations. Led by Champlain, the French founded Quebec and took control of the St. Lawrence river. The French colonies exported furs and sugar, the latter from Louisiana and the French islands in the West Indies.

Checking the high points

1. How do we know the Norse reached the New World?

2. What effects did the Crusades have on Europe?

3. Why did Columbus call the people of the New World Indians?

4. Why do the people of Brazil speak Portuguese whereas most South Americans speak Spanish?

5. Explain the significance of the following: Prince Henry the Navigator, Amerigo Vespucci, Vasca da Gama, Ferdinand Magellan, John Cabot, Jacques Cartier.

6. How did Cortes and Pizarro expand the Spanish empire?

7. What was the Spanish influence on what became the United States? Note explorations and settlements.

8. What were the main features of the Spanish Empire in the New World?

9. Why was England ready for expansion by 1600?

10. Why was the defeat of the Spanish Armada so important?

11. Why was the French Empire so large but so lightly held?

Think these over

1. Explain this statement: The discovery of America is only a continuation of European expansion during the Middle Ages.

2. Do you agree with the statement that the United States is the child of Europe, not of England alone? Explain your answer.

Vocabulary building

Middle Ages	nobles
conquistador	Crusades
Renaissance	seigneur
habitants	serfs
feudalism	Orient

Checking locations

Scandinavia	St. Augustine
Indian Ocean	Santa Fe
Puerto Rico	Quebec
Orient	San Francisco
Red Sea	Isthmus of Suez
Far East	Isthmus of Panama
Indian Ocean	

Chapter Objectives

To learn about

- the three different types of British colonies in the New World
- the different ways of life that developed in the New England, Middle, and Southern colonies

chapter 5

ENGLAND FOUNDS ITS NORTH AMERICAN COLONIES

Over a century after Columbus' voyage, the English had not established a single permanent foothold in the Western Hemisphere. Nevertheless, by 1600 the fleet of Queen Elizabeth had smashed the Armada and raided the great Spanish port of Cadiz. Enterprising men had formed companies to trade in the far corners of the world. Within the next century England founded some 20 colonies with 350,000 inhabitants, stretching from Newfoundland on the North Atlantic to the island of Barbados in the southern Caribbean. Settlements had taken firm root and entered a stage of steady growth.

Three Types of British Colonies

The king was the official owner of all the land that England had acquired in the New World. To establish a colony it was necessary to get the king's approval, which came in the form of a charter. These charters stated how the colony was to be managed and listed the rights of Englishmen, including the right to trial by jury. Most charters required a representative assembly elected by the settlers. Voting was restricted to property owners or the members of a certain church. In most colonies a majority of white adult males had the right to vote. For those times the colonies were very democratic. In France, Spain, and other European countries the king ruled by divine right, and the ordinary people had no say in their government. In England itself only a handful of men had the right to vote for members of Parliament.

It took a great deal of money to start a colony and more to keep it going through the first difficult years. Sometimes a wealthy person would found a settlement. Sometimes church congregations migrated to the frontier where they could get away from the evils of society. The joint-stock company became the most useful method of raising money. Persons willing to risk their money

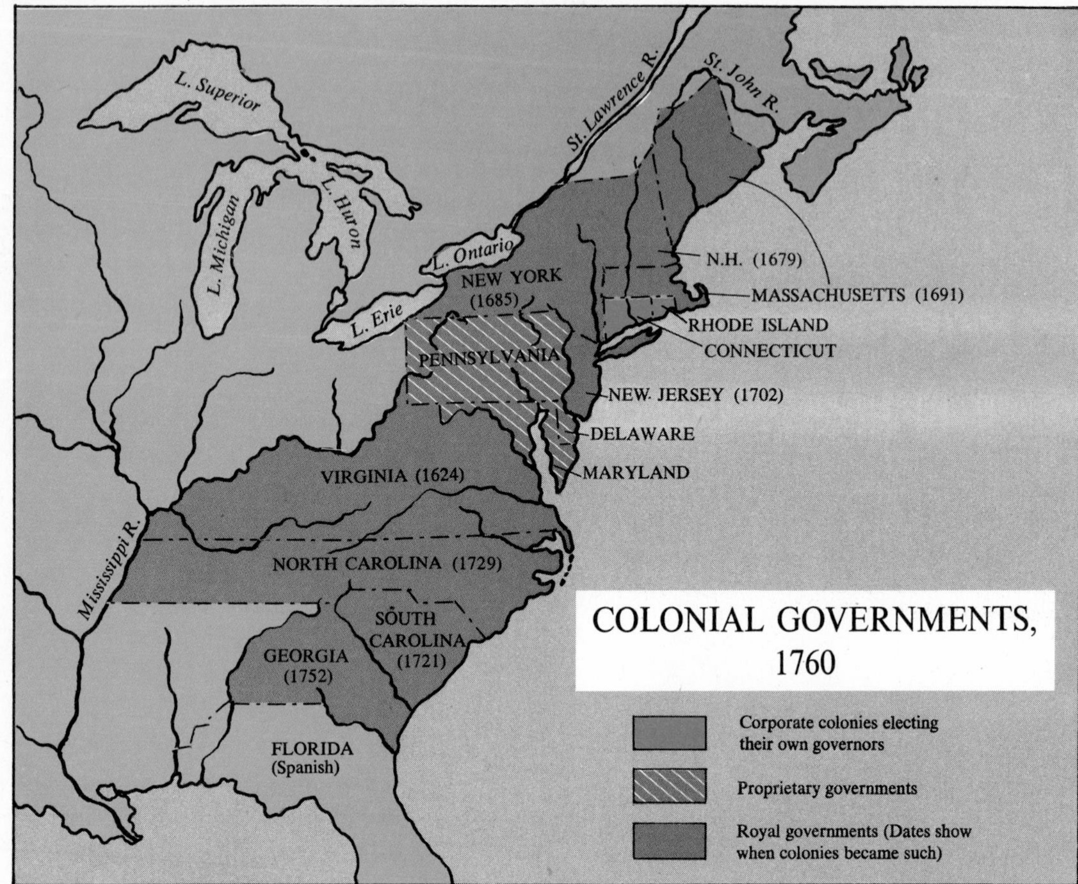

Map 14

bought shares of stock in the company. Each stockholder hoped to receive a share of the profits in proportion to the amount invested. Although joint-stock companies that tried to plant colonies in British North America did not make money, they did settle pioneers in many areas.

Three different types of colonies appeared: proprietary, self-governing, and royal. In proprietary colonies the king granted a charter to one or more proprietors who might or might not be organized as a company. Proprietor means owner. Self-governing colonies appeared when persons simply settled where they wanted to, and they ruled themselves. Later some colonies, especially those in New England, received a charter granting them the right to elect their own governors as well as members of the legislature. Royal colonies were those controlled and operated by a governor appointed by the king. Not one of the 13 colonies began as a royal colony; they became royal colonies later. The British government found that it was easier to control a colony if it could appoint a governor. By the time of the American Revolution, only three proprietary colonies (Pennsylvania, Delaware, and Maryland) and two self-governing colonies (Connecticut and Rhode Island) were left. Even in the royal colonies representative assemblies were elected and citizens enjoyed the rights of Englishmen, such as trial by jury.

Jamestown, 1607

The London Company, a joint-stock organization, received a charter to colonize Virginia. Three ships bearing 140 men and four boys set out from London in 1606. During the difficult passage, which lasted four months, 40 of the colonists died. On May 13, 1607, the survivors chose a peninsula in the James River on which to build their homes. They named the settlement Jamestown. The location was excellent for defense but it was unhealthful. Ocean tides made the James River salty, and there was no supply of good water. Further, the swampy ground around Jamestown bred disease-carrying mosquitoes.

Instead of planting crops and storing food, the settlers wasted valuable time searching for gold and silver and trying to find a water passage to the Far East. As winter approached they were weakened by hunger and fell prey to sickness and Indian attacks. By New Year's Day in 1608, a little over a year after the original band had left London, only 38 were still alive.

The arrival of two ships and the efforts of Captain John Smith, a brave and determined leader, saved Jamestown. Smith traded with the Indians for food and insisted that colonists plant crops and build fortifications. He was injured and had to go back to England. The colony returned to its old ways, and the winter of 1609–1610 became known as the "starving time." Of the 500 colonists alive in the fall, only 60 survived until spring. The settlers learned from their bitter experience. Large tracts of land were planted, and farm animals were bred. Fishing was begun on a large scale, producing much food.

John Rolfe successfully raised and cured a crop of tobacco in 1612. Soon large quantities of tobacco were being shipped to London and sold at a good price. So eager were the settlers to raise tobacco that it was planted in the streets of Jamestown and even between the graves in the cemetery. Tobacco put the colony on a good economic footing. However, it was a mixed blessing. The price of tobacco varied widely from year to year and so the colonists never knew how much income they would have. Further, tobacco wore out the soil, making it necessary to find new fields or face crop failure.

Archeologists and historians searching early colonial records have helped us get an idea what Jamestown looked like. There were 18 wattle-and-daub houses within a triangular palisade. This is artist Sidney E. King's conception of James Fort and the surrounding area.

The arrival of English women at Jamestown. The English arrived in families, unlike most French and Spanish colonists who came as missionaries, soldiers, and other single men.

Three events made 1619 an important year in the history of Jamestown: the arrival of the first group of blacks, the landing of the first large group of white women, and the establishment of the first representative assembly in North America. English law forbade the enslavement of Christians, so at first a few blacks came as indentured servants. They served a master for several years, usually seven. Unlike the thousands of white servants, blacks had to work for life. By 1640 Virginia set up slavery as a special condition for blacks.

There had been two white women in Jamestown as early as 1608. Twenty more arrived within the next three years. In 1619 ninety young women were brought to the settlement by the London Company. A bachelor who won the heart of one of these young ladies could marry her if he paid the cost of her transportation—120 pounds of tobacco for a bride.

The last of the historic events of 1619 was the founding of the House of Burgesses, the first representative assembly in America. On July 30 the elected delegates met in a church and passed a series of laws.

Unfortunately, ill will grew between the colonists and the Indians. In March 1622, the Indians made a surprise attack on the colony. It was a terrible blow, because about one-fourth of the colonists, including John Rolfe, lost their lives. Homes were burned, animals slaughtered or driven off. King James I used this massacre, poor management by company officials, and rumors of the sale of white servants as reasons for taking back the charter and turning Virginia into a royal colony.

For a time the House of Burgesses was discontinued, but it was restored by the king in 1628. Thus the custom of having a representative assembly in the royal colonies was established. In addition to the House of Burgesses elected by the colonists, Virginia had a governor and a governor's council. The governor and the members of the council were appointed by the king. This plan of government (elected assembly, a governor appointed by the king, and a governor's council appointed by the governor) was used in other royal colonies.

In Virginia the governor received his salary from a tax on tobacco, but the king usually took this money for other purposes. As a result the governor had to ask the House of Burgesses for money. If the governor failed to do what the House of Burgesses asked, he got no money. In this way the Virginia legislature influenced the governor. The pattern was repeated later in other colonies.

The New England Colonies

During the reign of Henry VIII the Church of England replaced the Roman Catholic Church as the official religion in England. The king became the head of the Church of England. John Calvin, a Frenchman, taught that each congregation should elect elders to rule the church and should select its own minister. The Calvinists did not believe in religious freedom, but they did call for democracy in church government. A powerful group of English Calvinists wanted to "purify" the Church of England by cutting down the power of bishops. They became known as Puritans. A few reformers refused to attend the Church of England and set up their own separate churches. They became known as Separatists, or later Congregationalists. The monarchs of England saw the Puritans and the Separatists as enemies.

A group of Separatists from Scrooby, England, fled to the Netherlands to escape persecution. After many difficulties the Separatists received permission to settle in Virginia and formed a joint-stock company with a group of London investors to raise money for the venture. On September 16, 1620, the colonists set out to sea in the *Mayflower*. Only 35 of the 101 passengers were Separatists; the others were colonists sent by the London investors. These two groups are known today as the Pilgrims.

After a long and terrible voyage the *Mayflower* arrived at Cape Cod, far north of its expected landing place and well outside the territory controlled by the Virginia Company. (The London Company that settled Jamestown came to be known as the Virginia Company.) The Pilgrims liked the region and decided to settle on the site of an abandoned Indian village that Captain John Smith had named Plymouth. Because Plymouth was outside the Virginia Company's territory, there was no government. Before landing, the Pilgrims signed the Mayflower Compact. In this agreement the Pilgrims declared themselves a political body with the power to pass laws. They also agreed to obey such laws. The Mayflower Compact is important because it established a government controlled by the people. Plymouth Colony never received a royal charter, and the Mayflower Compact served as its constitution.

On Christmas Day, 1620, the Pilgrims began building their homes in the wilderness. Like the settlers at Jamestown they went through a terrible winter in which half of their number died. Aided by Squanto, a kindly Indian, the Pilgrims raised North American plants—corn, beans, pumpkin, and squash. At their first harvest the colonists had a feast of Thanksgiving. Although the Pilgrims were not the first to declare a Thanksgiving holiday, it is from them that we have taken our Thanksgiving tradition. Plymouth Colony remained small. After 70 years of independence it was absorbed in 1691 by the Massachusetts Bay Colony—a colony founded by Puritans.

The Massachusetts Bay Company was formed in 1629. Its charter provided a government for the colony. Stockholders were called freemen and had the power to elect a governor, a deputy governor, and 18 assistants to the governor. The governor and his helpers enforced the law. The freemen together with the governor, deputy governor, and assistants made up the General Court, which could pass laws. The charter said that the freemen could appoint other freemen, who also could vote.

A group of wealthy Puritans bought up all the stock in the Massachusetts Bay Company. In 1630 they began settling Boston and nearby communities. The move was

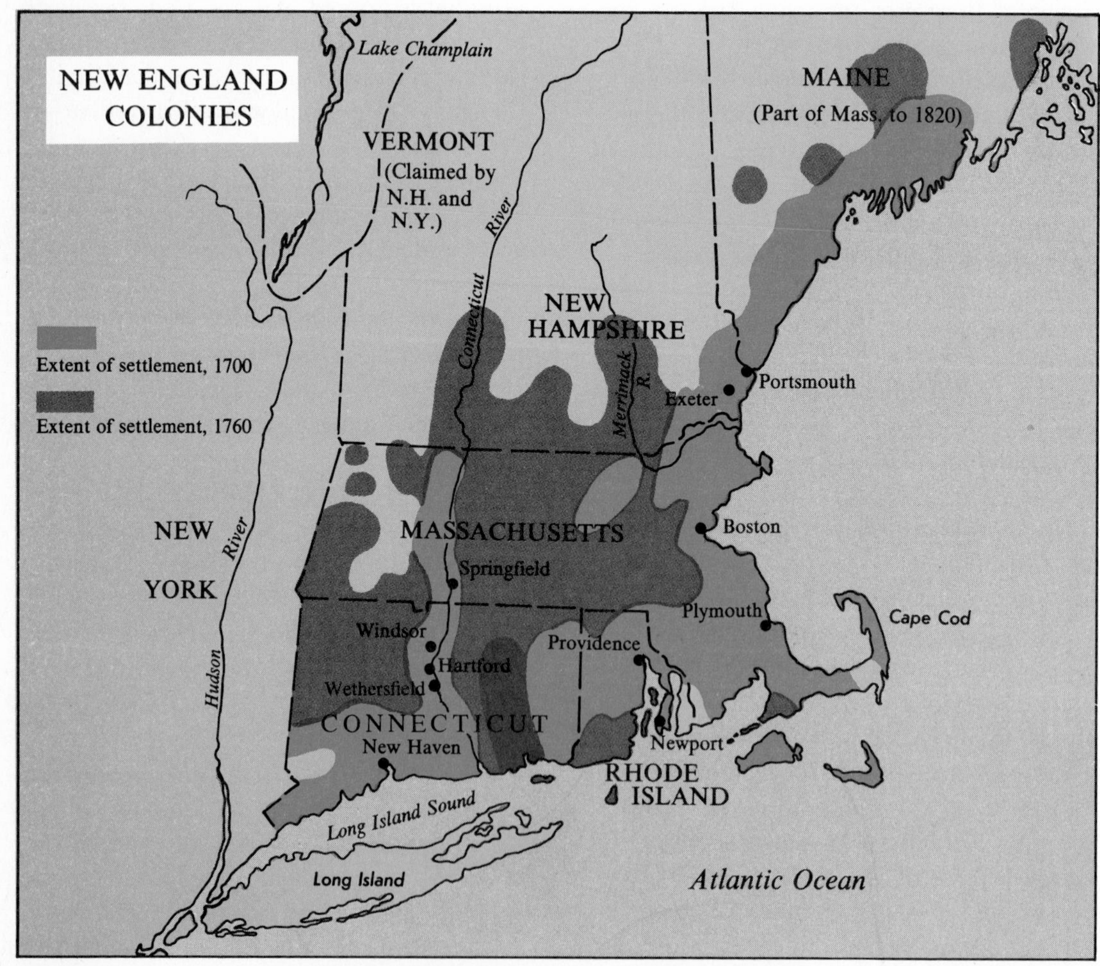

Map 15

carefully planned and there was no starving time. Among the first arrivals were fishermen, craftsmen, physicians, merchants, and clergymen. All of the stockholders in the company decided to migrate to the colony which meant local control of the government. By 1643 about 16,000 people were living in the colony.

Except for Plymouth, all of New England traces its origins to Massachusetts Bay. Two of the New England states did not appear until after the Revolution. Vermont became the 14th state in 1791 and Maine remained a part of Massachusetts until 1820.

Roger Williams, a Puritan minister, preached that every man should be free to worship God as he thought best. Williams said that men could have this religious freedom only if there was no official church supported by the state. Consequently, he called for a separation of the church and the state. The Puritan leaders did not believe in religious freedom, and they did not like what Williams was saying. They liked it even less when he said that the land did not belong to either the king or to the colony but to the Indians.

Banished from Massachusetts in 1636, Roger Williams fled to what is now Providence, Rhode Island. Here he purchased land from the Indians and, joined by others fleeing Massachusetts, began a settlement. It was the first American community with religious freedom for all. Other towns were founded by the followers of Mrs. Anne Hutchinson, who, like Williams, was banished by the Massachusetts Puritans. These settlements eventually joined together into Rhode Island. Religious freedom was so firmly established in Rhode Island that when it received a charter in 1663, the new charter guaranteed freedom of worship.

The Indians helped Roger Williams as he fled from Boston to Rhode Island.

In 1635 the Reverend Thomas Hooker received permission from the General Court in Massachusetts to settle in the Connecticut River Valley. People from the Bay Colony came to the valley and settled in three towns: Hartford, Windsor, and Wethersfield. In a famous election day sermon, Hooker said, "The foundation of authority is laid . . . in the free consent of the people . . ." The members of his congregation agreed with him. They had no intention of being ruled by Massachusetts. In 1639 the three Connecticut towns adopted the Fundamental Orders of Connecticut, the first written constitution in history to create a government. Under the Fundamental Orders all male members of the Puritan Church became freemen. Each year they elected a governor and six assistants. The General Court, which had the power to pass laws, was made up of the governor, the assistants, and four representatives from each town. In this way Connecticut governed itself even after it received a charter in 1662.

Meanwhile other pioneers from Massachusetts were moving into New Hampshire. Here they joined fur traders, fishermen, and settlers direct from England. Best known of the colonists from Massachusetts was Anne Hutchinson's brother-in-law, John Wheelwright, who had been banished from the Bay State. He founded the town of Exeter in 1638. Various groups claimed New Hampshire until 1679, when it was proclaimed a separate royal colony and given a charter.

The Middle Colonies

The Dutch West India Company established a colony called New Netherland in what is now New York, Delaware, and New Jersey. King Charles II of England gave the territory held by the Dutch to his brother, the Duke of York. In 1664 New Netherland surrendered to a British fleet.

The duke divided New Netherland, keeping what is now New York for himself and giving New Jersey to two of his friends—Sir George Carteret and Lord John Berkeley. In 1665 a representative assembly was established in New Jersey. Its acts had to be approved by the two proprietors. Freedom of religion was guaranteed and it was made easy to obtain land. These benefits attracted many people. Eventually Carteret and Berkeley sold their rights to a group of Quakers who proved to be poor managers. In 1702 New Jersey was made a royal colony.

The Society of Friends (better known as Quakers) had been founded about 1650 by George Fox, an Englishman. Members of this religious group refused military service because they believed that killing is sinful. They refused to bow or take off their hats before persons of high station because they reserved such signs of respect for God. These beliefs were considered dangerous, and the Quakers were often cruelly persecuted.

In 1681 William Penn, a noted Quaker, received a charter for the colony of Pennsylvania. He determined to make his colony a safe place for persons of all religious beliefs. To guarantee religious freedom to all those who believed in God, he drew up a Frame of Government. This sort of statement today would be called a constitution. It also gave the vote to all adult Christian men who owned 50 acres of land or property worth 50 pounds. (A pound is an English unit of money.) For its time Pennsylvania was a model of democracy. When the inhabitants of Delaware protested that they did not want to be governed from Pennsylvania, the proprietor granted them their own assembly. The first meeting of this assembly in 1704 marked Delaware as a separate colony.

Both regions prospered. Philadelphia, founded by Penn in 1682, became a major port. Settlers flocked in from the British Isles, Germany, the Netherlands, and Switzerland. Among the newcomers were Catholics, Jews, and persons belonging to a variety of Protestant sects. By 1715 more than 45,000 people were living in Pennsylvania and Delaware.

The Southern Colonies

Oddly, the very first and the very last British colonies were founded in the southern region. The first, of course, was Virginia, in 1607. The last was Georgia, in 1733. Meanwhile, Maryland and the Carolinas were settled.

George Calvert, better known as Lord Baltimore, was a Roman Catholic. The anti-Catholic laws in the British Isles were

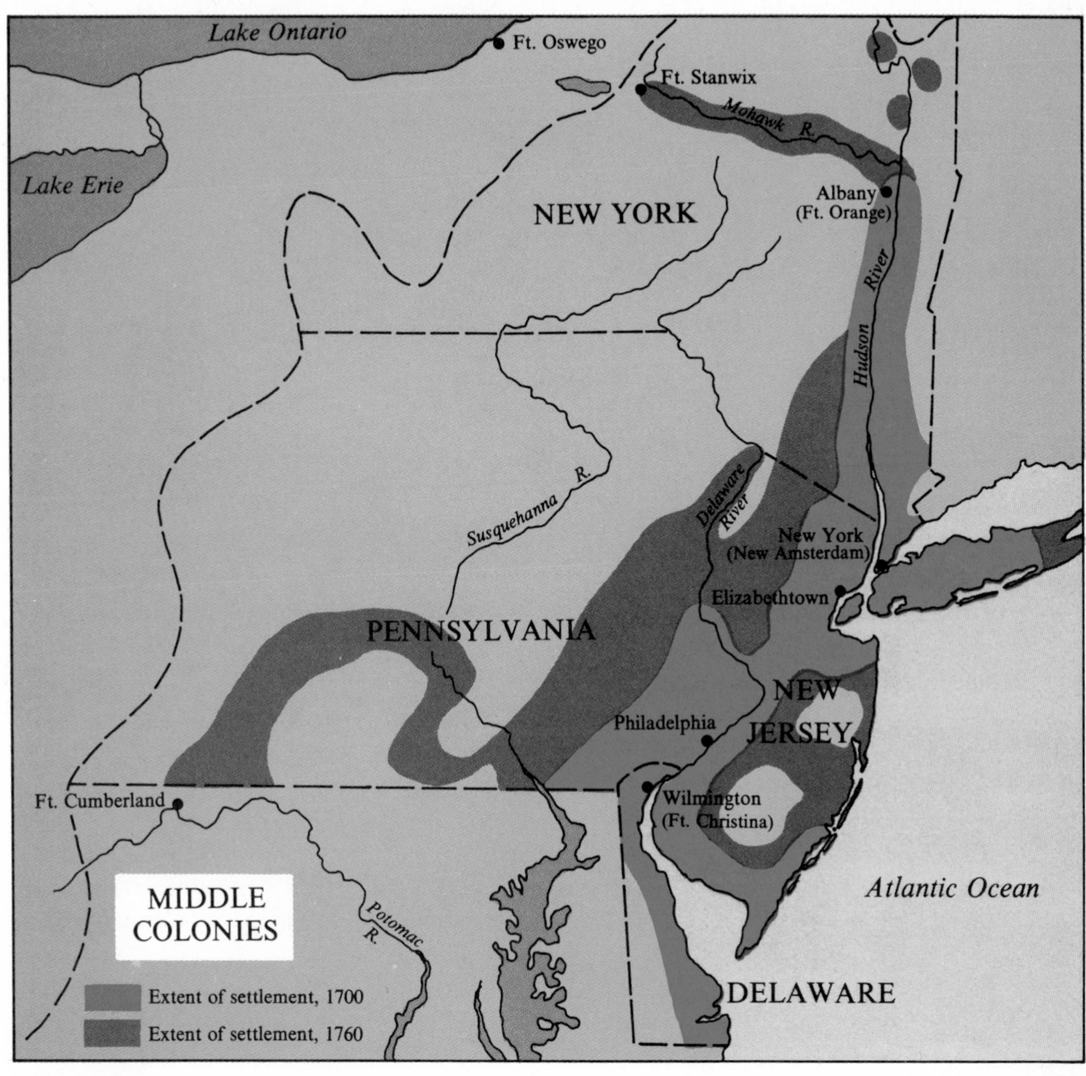

Map 16

very severe, and Lord Baltimore determined to establish a colony where Catholics could live undisturbed. With this in mind he persuaded King James I of England to give him a charter for Maryland. George Calvert died before he could carry out his plan. His elder son, Cecil Calvert, took up where his father left off.

In 1634 Leonard Calvert, Cecil's younger brother, founded St. Mary's on the Potomac River. The Calverts planned well, sending in skilled workmen to build their colony. A representative assembly was established, and in 1649 the Maryland Toleration Act was passed. Under it, religious freedom was granted to all Christians. Settlers came in

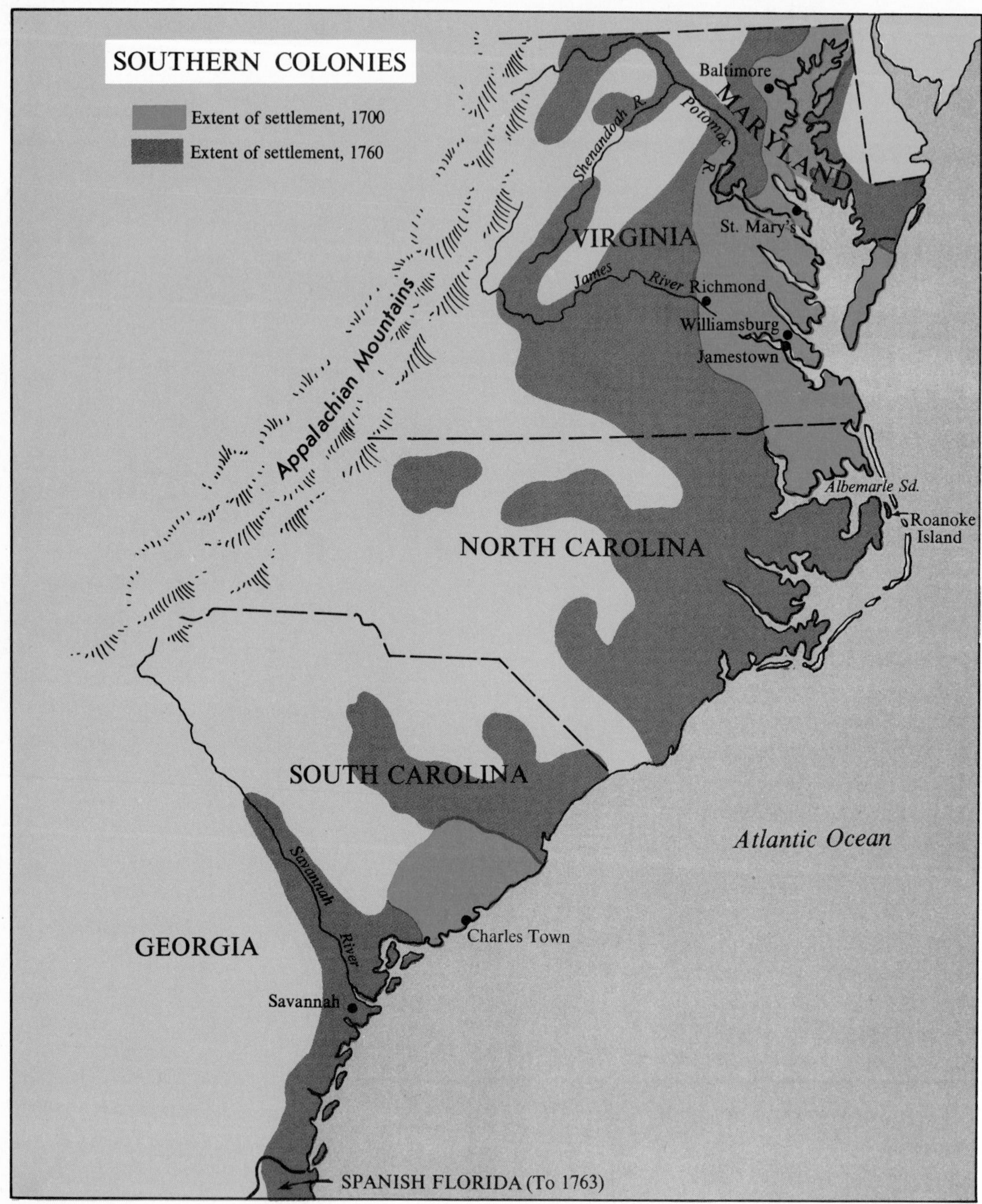

Map 17

large numbers. Tobacco growing became important, and with it, unfortunately, came slavery, since slaves were used to work the fields. In 1650 eight thousand people lived in Maryland. The Puritans won control of the Assembly in 1654 and repealed the Toleration Act. In 1691 Maryland became a Royal colony, but in 1715 the Calvert family regained its proprietary rights.

The first settlers in the Carolinas were

persons who could not find jobs or obtain farms in Virginia. They drifted southward and built homes near Albemarle Sound in what is now North Carolina, where they grew tobacco. Here they were joined by settlers from New England, the West Indies, and the British Isles. These colonists set up their own government with a representative assembly.

In 1663 King Charles gave eight of his nobles a charter for Carolina. The efforts of the proprietors to establish control over the Albemarle settlers failed. Finally, in 1712, the colony was divided into North Carolina and South Carolina. The north grew very slowly, but the south prospered. Charles Town (Charleston), South Carolina, was built in 1670, and it became an important trading center. The plantation style of agriculture, with its evil of slavery, became firmly fixed at an early date. Because the Spaniards regarded the South Carolina border as making inroads on their territory in Florida, they attacked South Carolina in an attempt to regain their land. However, their efforts were unsuccessful.

James Oglethorpe and his associates were given a charter to settle Georgia. Oglethorpe saw his colony as a place where debtors could start anew. The British government saw it as a haven for debtors, but more importantly as a barrier to the Spanish in Florida and the French in Louisiana. Money was contributed to the project, and the first settlement was made at Savannah in 1733. Oglethorpe's dream never came true. Only a few debtors arrived. Plantation agriculture began, and the laws prohibiting slavery and the importation of rum were overthrown. By 1760 about 9,000 people lived in Georgia, one-third of them as slaves.

The Colonial Way of Life

The different climates, soils, crops, and kinds of people under British rule led to the development of several different types of societies. Most of the 250,000 colonists in 1700 were of British stock. But in the southern colonies and in New York there were many blacks. For example, Virginia in 1708 had over 12,000 blacks, while the percentage in the Carolinas was almost one-half of the total population. In New York and New Jersey the Dutch minority still had its churches and schools. In Pennsylvania William Penn had attracted quite a number of Germans and several hundred Welsh Quakers before 1700.

The largest cities were Boston, New York, Philadelphia, and Charleston. As late as 1720, New York, with only 7,000 people, trailed behind Philadelphia's 10,000 and Boston's 12,000. Although these cities contained less than ten percent of the total population, they were the centers of economic, political, and intellectual life. Ships from Boston carried lumber, meat products, fish, and rum to the West Indies and down the coast. Wheat and flour were the largest items of export from New York and Philadelphia. From Charleston rice, indigo, and skins were exported to England. But Virginia, the largest and most populous colony, had practically no urban centers, largely because the tobacco planters often had their own wharves.

Most colonists were farmers who lived off the land. Because they desperately needed cash to buy necessities such as nails and salt, they located their farms near the coast or a navigable stream so that they could reach the markets more easily. In general,

Colonial cities were thriving centers almost from the beginning. Business was brisk, and craftsmen turned out products that equalled those of Europe.

farms were small in all the colonies, and the family supplied the labor. But in the southern colonies several hundred plantations had appeared by 1700. The planters were skillful farmers who added acres and slaves in order to increase their output of tobacco, rice, or indigo. The planter class had the leisure time in which to attend the annual sessions of the legislature and therefore dominated the government of the southern colonies.

Wheat did not do well in New England, but other grains were raised—barley for brewing beer, oats for feeding horses, and rye for making flour. Of course Indian corn remained the most useful crop on the farm. The Middle colonies grew so much wheat that they were known as the Bread Colonies. In the South, tobacco was by far the most important crop, especially in Virginia and Maryland. The fur trade continued to bring in considerable income in all the colonies.

By 1700 small farmers in Virginia and the Carolinas were moving into the Piedmont area, the hilly land between the broad coastal plain (known as the Tidewater) and the Appalachian Mountains. These backcountry farmers lived almost entirely off the fish and game in the neighborhood and the crops they grew in their small clearings.

The sea provided a living for thousands of Yankees, as the inhabitants of New England were called. Some built ships, using the fine stands of timber; others fished for cod or hunted whales; others carried goods to foreign markets.

The Yankees valued education highly because they believed everyone should read and study the Bible. In 1647 Massachusetts passed a law requiring each township of 50 or more families to set up an elementary school. The other New England colonies, with the exception of Rhode Island, passed similar laws. The law was not always obeyed, and the teaching and schoolbooks were often very poor. Nevertheless, New England led the world in education. Our tradition of public schools, open to all young people, comes from these early laws.

In the Middle colonies schooling lagged, and most children never saw the inside of a schoolroom. The Quakers did not particularly favor schools for ordinary folk. Because of the variety of churches, some with schools, parents avoided sending their chil-

Summary Chart of Economic and Social Features

Area	*Physical Conditions*	*Economic Patterns*	*Population*	*Religion, Education*
Quebec	St. Lawrence River—a route to interior. Forests. Harsh winters.	Fur trading dominated. Subsistence farming. Government regulation of trade.	French population about 60,000 in 1763. Fairly good relations with Indians.	R. Catholic Church government-supported Only Catholicism permitted. A few church schools
New England	Narrow coastal plain with submerged coast provided harbors. Pine forests. Thin soils. Rigorous climate.	Fishing and shipbuilding important. Trading with England, West Indies, and other colonies. Subsistence farming. Small farms for families.	Rapid growth. Largely English in origin. Boston, main center.	Intolerant Puritan founders; gradual growth of toleration led by Rhode Island. Emphasis on education with beginnings of public elementary education.
Middle Colonies (*N.Y., N.J., Pa., Del.*)	Wider fertile river valleys. Forests. Moderate climate.	Mixed farming, stressing wheat raising. Trading with England, West Indies, Africa, other colonies. Family-size farms dominated even in New York	Rapid growth after 1700. Mixed population, including English, Germans, Scotch-Irish, Dutch, Negroes. Two large cities: New York and Philadelphia.	Religious toleration, especially in Pa. Separation of church and state in almost all regions. Slow development of schools.

Summary Chart of Economic and Social Features (Continued)

Area	*Physical Conditions*	*Economic Patterns*	*Population*	*Religion, Education*
Southern Colonies (*Md., Va., N.C., S.C., Ga.*)	Broad coastal plain east of "fall line." Mild climate. Forests	Commercial farming, stressing tobacco and rice. Plantations, relying on slavery. Most numerous class were small subsistence farmers.	Rapid growth. White population largely English and Scotch-Irish. Large black population. Almost no cities except Charleston.	Church of England the state church. Other church members tolerated in practice. Little interest in education, except for sons of aristocrats.
Spanish Mexico	Great variety from highlands to tropical lowlands and dry deserts to lush lowlands. Warm climate.	Highlands used for mining and cattle-raising. Lowlands produce sugar. Plantation-type farming. Indians become "peons" on plantations.	Large Indian population. Spanish provide upper class. Many people of white and Indian blood. Cities develop early.	R. Catholic Church state-supported. Only Catholicism permitted. A few church schools for upper classes. Mission schools help Indians.

dren to schools where they might learn the "wrong" beliefs.

In the South, the scattered population made it extremely difficult to establish schools and churches. Only a few planters could afford to hire tutors for their children.

The Puritans tried to keep their faith pure by keeping out or expelling Quakers, Baptists, and others who did not accept their beliefs. Of course, most Puritans looked on Rhode Island as the "cesspool of New England" because of its tolerant attitude toward religion. As you have read, William Penn also preached and practiced toleration. The many different kinds of people in New York made it necessary for the government to permit people to worship as they pleased. Although the Church of England was the official church in all the colonies from Maryland to Georgia, it did not reach most people. There were not enough clergymen to minister to the population scattered up and down the rivers.

The way of life in the English colonies differed considerably from those in New France and New Spain. The following chart gives a quick summary of the major features of five regions of the New World. Climate, nearness to markets, natural resources, and differences in populations created still different societies in Cuba, Brazil, Peru, and other sections.

Summary

By 1700 the English colonies, containing over 250,000 inhabitants, were firmly established in the New World. Three types of colonies emerged: proprietary, self-governing, and royal. All colonies provided for the traditional rights of Englishmen and an assembly for which a good percentage of the people could vote. Jamestown, the first (1607) permanent settlement, became the starting point for Virginia. Tobacco assured the economic success of Virginia but also led to the plantation system and the evils of slavery. New England was founded by religious reformers who favored control of church government by the membership. The Pilgrims or Separatists were few in number, but the Puritans settled Boston and expanded into New Hampshire, Connecticut, and Rhode Island.

The conquest of New Netherland in 1664 led to the formation of New York, New Jersey, and Delaware. William Penn, the Quaker, acquired Delaware and received a charter for Pennsylvania, where he promoted religious freedom and democracy. Another proprietorship was granted to the Calvert family in Maryland. Settlers from Virginia drifted into Carolina, a colony granted to eight nobles in 1663. By 1712 it divided into North and South Carolina. The last colony formed (1733) was Georgia.

Most settlers came from the British Isles, although blacks, Germans, and Dutch were present outside of New England. The great majority of colonists were small farmers. But staple crops such as tobacco encouraged the formation of plantations which, by the last third of the century, came to rely upon slave labor. The main exports of the Middle colonies were wheat, flour, furs, and timber products. New England exported fish, timber, and meat products. The public schools in New England led those of the other colonies and indeed those of the world. Except for Maryland's Catholics, almost all the colonists were Protestants. In New England the Puritans were dominant and stressed the congregational form of church government. The Church of England was the official church in the Southern colonies and New York.

Checking the high points

1. Explain the different types of colonies. How much self-government was there?

2. Why was the joint-stock company useful?

3. What turned Virginia into a successful colony?

4. What part did religion play in the founding of New England?

5. How did the Puritans manage to secure self-government in the Massachusetts Bay colony?

6. Why was Roger Williams an important figure?

7. Trace the expansion of Puritans of Massachusetts Bay region to the rest of New England.

8. What were the origins of Maryland, the Carolinas, and Georgia?

9. Why did Pennsylvania grow so rapidly?

10. In 1700 what were the main nationality and racial groups in British North America?

11. Compare the New England, Middle, and Southern colonies as to crops, exports, educational and religious developments.

Think these over

1. The writing of the Mayflower Compact was an important precedent in the growth of American democracy. Comment.

2. The charters for the British colonies established a society and a form of government which differed markedly from that of New France and New Spain. Explain.

3. Some people claim that history books overemphasize the importance of New England in American history. Do you agree or disagree? Why?

Vocabulary building

proprietor
Puritan
Mayflower Compact
indigo
Tidewater
Piedmont
Separatist
House of Burgesses
Fundamental Orders of Connecticut
Penn's Frame of Government

Checking locations

Jamestown
Plymouth
Boston
Rhode Island
Connecticut
Maryland
New Hampshire
Pennsylvania
Savannah
New Jersey
Philadelphia
North Carolina
South Carolina
Maine
Delaware
Charleston
Albemarle Sound
Georgia
Virginia

Chapter Objectives

To learn about

- Dutch colonization of New Amsterdam
- the Dutch way of life and influence in the Hudson Valley
- Dutch withdrawal and the English takeover of New Amsterdam

chapter 6

DUTCH TRADERS and FARMERS SETTLE the HUDSON VALLEY

The Founding of New Netherland

As you read earlier, in 1609 the Dutch East India Company sent out Henry Hudson, an English navigator, to find a new water passage to the Far East. Hudson skirted the American coast looking for an opening. On September 2, 1609 he entered the harbor of New York, which Giovanni da Verrazano had discovered almost a century earlier. Verrazano, an Italian in the service of King Francis I of France, had observed the "very great river" and the natives "clothed with the feathers of birds of various colors," but he had not gone upstream. Hudson entered the river, sailing his small vessel past the Palisades and the Highlands to the region of Albany. Like Verrazano, he found the natives friendly and eager to trade. His men saw that the thick beaver and mink skins would bring a good price in Europe. Hudson's report of the country stirred up interest in Holland. As a result, many trading vessels visited the Hudson Valley. A temporary trading post, Fort Nassau, was erected on an island south of what is now Albany.

In 1621 the Dutch government granted a charter to the Dutch West India Company. This gave it the right to control all the trade by Dutchmen along the eastern coast of North and South America and the western coast of Africa. Small wonder, then, when we consider this tremendous grant, that the officers of the company paid little attention to the tiny colony that was established on the Hudson River.

The Dutch West India Company sent its first boatload of settlers in 1624—thirty families of French-speaking Protestants, who made, at Fort Orange (Albany), the first permanent settlement. The next year the company began to build Fort Amsterdam on the island of Manhattan as their headquarters. In a few years the company had fur posts on the Connecticut and Delaware rivers and at various points on the Hudson.

This map of New Netherland was attached to a memorial presented to the Dutch States-General in 1616. It is referred to in the document as showing the extent of discoveries of a small yacht named "Onrust" which was built in New Netherland.

The Weakness of New Netherland

When the English captured New Netherland in 1664, they found only 8,000 white settlers in the region between the Connecticut and Delaware rivers. Why was this so after 40 years of colonization and a still longer period of trading?

First of all, few Dutchmen wanted to leave their homeland, which was bursting with prosperity. If ambitious young men could make a good living at home, why should they go over 3,000 miles to risk the dangers of the wilderness? Furthermore, the Dutch enjoyed considerable religious toleration when most countries were persecuting those not belonging to the state church. Holland accepted refugess from religious persecution in Spain and Portugal, and later the Pilgrims fleeing England. In the Dutch Republic people had more freedom than in France or England, where the kings were trying to seize more power from Parliament.

Second, the Dutch West India Company's plans in the West Indies and Africa attracted much more attention than its few fur posts along the Hudson.

Third, the fur trade was favored over agriculture. Only a handful of men were needed to exchange guns and blankets for beaver pelts. Young men preferred to make money quickly in the fur trade rather than the long, hard job of clearing the forest and establishing farms. The company raised taxes to build and defend outposts and to pay for a costly expedition which conquered the Swedish settlements on the Delaware River. This also discouraged farmers.

Fourth, the Indians caused a great deal of trouble. At first, the Dutch got on well with both the Algonquians and the Iroquois. But when the Dutch sold guns to the Iroquois, but not to the Algonquians, the latter grew restless. Dutch farmers took some of the best flat land along the river. They harshly punished Indians caught stealing cattle and pigs. Finally, Governor William Kieft tried to lay a heavy tax on the Algonquians. When the Indians refused to pay, Kieft massacred over a hundred helpless natives. The Indians then almost wiped out the colony. Over a thousand Dutch settlers died in this war.

Fifth, the way the company sold land discouraged ordinary farmers from settling in the Hudson Valley. It gave a large piece of land, called a patroonship, to any of its members who would bring over 50 settlers. Several Dutch merchants planned to establish patroonships, but only one succeeded. It belonged to Killiaen Van Rensselaer, a diamond merchant, who had a huge tract of land on both sides of the Hudson near Albany. The farmers he brought in did not own their lands, but paid rent with part of their crops. He found it hard to get tenants. Why should anyone risk his life to cross the ocean just to become a tenant farmer? However, other Dutch farmers settled in New Netherland and cultivated their own farms. Did you know that the Bowery in New York City comes from the Dutch word for farm—"bouwerie"?

Last, New Netherland's government was undemocratic and inefficient. The main aim of the Dutch West India Company was income—not good government. The Company named the director general or governor and also the members of the council who helped him run the colony. It even chose local officials, clergymen, and school teachers. Most Dutch governors did not do a good job. Of course they had a very difficult task. Whereas the Company wanted profits, the settlers wanted low taxes, more freedom, and better protection against the Indians and white enemies. Within the colony the more important citizens often quarreled with the governor. Sometimes they even crossed the Atlantic Ocean to take their complaints to the officials of the company. Threatening the colony from outside were the British in New England, the French in Canada, and everywhere, the Indians.

In 1647 New Amsterdam acquired a new governor, Peter Stuyvesant, as famous for his hot temper as for his wooden leg. Stuyvesant organized an expedition of several ships which captured the Swedish settlements in the Delaware Valley. On the east he faced the stubborn New Englanders of Connecticut and Massachusetts. They drove the Dutch from the Connecticut Valley and forced Stuyvesant to give up most of Long Island east of Oyster Bay. Meanwhile, New Englanders were making settlements on Long Island and along the Sound. Since these Yankees had learned the value of self-government in their town meetings, they now demanded a share in running the government of New Netherland. In 1653 the people of Flushing and other towns protested against taxation without representation. These people were clearly ready for a change of government.

The Dutch Way of Life

Of the 8,000 people taken over by the English in 1664, probably not more than two out of three were Dutch. Hundreds of Yankees lived on Long Island; some had settled on Manhattan Island, along with Englishmen from the homeland. Germans, French, Swedes, Jews, blacks, and Scots were also present in small numbers. Governor Kieft wrote that over 18 languages were spoken on Manhattan Island.

A considerable number of its citizens lived in such centers as New Amsterdam, Beverwyck (Albany), and Wiltwyck (Kingston). Buying and selling was in the air as it was in Holland. The desire to make money filled the minds of almost everyone, from the directors of the company down to the small shopkeeper.

New Netherland, like the motherland became the home of persecuted groups, despite the opposition of the clergymen of the Dutch Reformed Church and Governor Stuyvesant. Stuyvesant disliked the Quakers in particular. He issued a proclamation that any person giving hospitality to a Quaker was to be fined. The people of Flushing on Long Island protested against this order. This Flushing Remonstrance of 1657 is the first declaration of religious tolerance by any group of citizens in American history.

On the whole, the church played a small role in the life of the colony as compared with the important position of the Puritan clergymen in Massachusetts and the Roman Catholic priests in Quebec. The Dutch were fairly easygoing. The people liked to go to the taverns for a good time. Governor Twiller was a notorious drinker. Governor Kieft had so little respect for one clergyman that he had cannon shot off and drums beaten during church services.

However, both the West India Company and the Dutch Reformed Church felt responsible for the religious welfare of the people. Clergymen were sent to serve the settlers. Some of them also worked with the Indians, attempting to convert them to Christianity. The clergy were interested in schools and helped to establish them. Governor Stuyvesant approved of education and gave his support to a secondary school. As a result of these efforts the Dutch Reformed Church was firmly established in the Hud-

Peter Stuyvesant

Peter Stuyvesant was recalled to Holland after the British conquered New Amsterdam. A year later he was allowed to return to his farm in Manhattan, where he died in 1672. He is buried in the Church of St. Marks-in-the-Bouwerie on Second Avenue and Tenth Street, New York City, only a few yards from where his residence used to stand. A stone table on the Church's outer wall marks his grave: "In this vault lies PETRUS STUYVESANT late

Captain General and Governor in Chief of Amsterdam in New Netherland now called New York and the Dutch West India Islands. Died A.D. 1671–1672. Aged 80 years, Rest in hope."

In 1915 Queen Wilhelmina of the Netherlands, a member of the House of Orange whose ancestors were ruling Holland during Stuyvesant's governorship, gave a bronze bust of Peter Stuyvesant to the people of New York. Today it stands in St. Marks' churchyard.

son Valley by the time the British conquered New Netherland.

A little Amsterdam grew up at the southern tip of Manhattan. Its waterfront, skyline, and buildings looked like the cities of Holland. In 1644 it had about 350 houses and 1,500 people. The walls of the fort had fallen apart almost as soon as built. Within these walls were the official offices of government and power: the governor's brick house; barracks for about 70 soldiers; company storehouses; a jail; and the Dutch Reformed Church. North and south of the fort were clusters of houses scattered about in no particular order. Governor Stuyvesant did succeed in laying out some streets and blocks. For example, Breede Weg (Broadway) ran north from the fort. Pigs, cows, and dogs wandered through the streets. There were many taverns filled with soldiers, sailors, and traders. The merchants had large brick houses with steep roofs and gables fronting on the street. Behind their houses lay spacious gardens and orchards.

The Dutch made tiny settlements around New York Bay, many of which are part of present day New York City. These old communities have given their names to sections of the city. Among these are Bushwick, Flatbush, Flushing, Gravesend, Harlem, Jamaica, and Williamsburg. Jonas Bronck, a Dane, acquired an estate on the mainland north of Manhattan. Today the region is called the Bronx. Staaten Eylandt (do you recognize it?) was raided several times by Indians. Brooklyn began in 1645 as Breuckelen, and its fame has gone over the world.

The Dutch left their mark on many aspects of New York life. They gave us crullers and cole slaw to eat. In our speech they left us such words as stoop and boss. In our

In 1662, for permitting Quakers to meet in the kitchen of his home, John Bowne was fined, imprisoned, and deported to Holland. There he successfully pled his case before the Dutch West India Company and was allowed to return two years later. Bowne House is today a national shrine to religious freedom in America.

The house of the Voorlezer (or schoolmaster and leader of church services). Built by the Dutch Congregation on Staten Island before 1696, this is the earliest known elementary school in the United States.

folklore they gave us figures such as Rip Van Winkle. At Christmas, the story of Santa Claus and the hanging of stockings at the fireplace remind us of Dutch customs. In politics, three presidents from New York—Martin Van Buren, Theodore Roosevelt, and Franklin D. Roosevelt—boasted of their Dutch origin.

The Dutch way of life did not end after the English conquest. Dutch continued to be spoken in many homes, churches, and schools for another century or more. Gradually, the young people picked up English habits and learned the English language. A Swedish traveler in 1749 noted that the "young people now speak principally English, and go only to the English church." These young people tried to introduce English into the services of the Reformed Church. The old people fought back for years but finally gave in. By 1805 all the Dutch Reformed churches in New York were using English in their services.

The English Conquest

The *Navigation Acts* were laws passed by England to control trade. Their aim was to keep foreign traders out of the British Empire and to secure for England certain goods produced in the colonies. The Dutch traders at the mouth of the Hudson were making it difficult for England to enforce its Navigation Acts. Traders operating out of Man-

Symbol Makers

Everybody looks at newspaper cartoons, because they can tell a story in one glance. For example, we all know that the donkey stands for the Democratic party and the elephant for the Republican party. We also recognize the tall man with a high hat and striped trousers as Uncle Sam. Some of us have also seen drawings of Father Knickerbocker—the pipe-smoking man who represents New York City.

Few know that New Yorkers started all these symbols or drawings. Thomas Nast, a newspaper man, fought dishonest government in New York City and gave us the donkey and the elephant. Samuel Wilson of Troy is supposed to have been the model for Uncle Sam. Wilson sold meat to the American Army during the War of 1812. He sent the meat to a man named Elbert Anderson at the army camp and marked each barrel "US-EA." This meant "United States-Elbert Anderson." The soldiers said that this meant "Uncle Sam" Wilson to Elbert Anderson. Before long they were calling other government property "Uncle Sam's."

Knickerbocker was a good old Dutch name which Washington Irving used when he wrote his humorous *History of New York*. Hiding behind the name of Diedrich Knickerbocker, Irving poked fun at the early Dutch settlers. He described them as lazy fat people who spent most of the time drinking, smoking, and sleeping. Do you think this was a true picture?

The original drawing for Father Knickerbocker as used in Irving's book appears above. The more simplified symbol developed over the years.

This diorama in the Museum of the City of New York shows Peter Stuyvesant defying the English when they demanded the surrender of New Amsterdam in 1664.

hattan could smuggle in goods to the English colonies. The Dutch colony also separated New England from Virginia and Maryland. King Charles II of England therefore decided to capture it.

Charles gave the entire region between the Connecticut River and the Delaware River to his brother, James, the Duke of York and Albany. James at once sent Colonel Richard Nicolls with four ships and 400 soldiers to seize the colony. Colonel Nicolls sent a letter to Stuyvesant demanding the surrender of the colony. The merchants begged Stuyvesant to give up, since an attack would destroy the city and cause many deaths. The peppery governor refused to let the letter be read to the people, and tore it to bits.

Stuyvesant awaited the approach of the English fleet. By his side was an artillery man holding a lighted match, ready to fire the cannon.

The Dutch pastor begged Stuyvesant not to resist. He said: "Do you not see that there is no help for us, either to the north or the south, the east or the west? What can our twenty guns do in the face of sixty-two pointed toward us on yonder frigates?"

A petition signed by 93 of the chief citizens then was presented to Stuyvesant, begging him to surrender. The governor replied, "I had rather be carried to my grave!" But at the last moment Stuyvesant gave in, and the white flag of surrender waved above the fort.

The terms of surrender were generous. Each man was given the choice of remaining in New York under English rule or of being loyal to the Dutch and leaving the colony. Most chose to stay. At first, the changes were few. In fact, many local officials stayed on in their posts. The main towns, however, received new names. New Amsterdam became New York; Beverwyck became Albany; Wiltwyck took the name of Kingston.

Summary

In 1609 Henry Hudson sailed the *Half Moon* as far north as present-day Albany. Other Dutch vessels visited the area and traded with the Indians. The Dutch West India Company sent the first permanent settlers in 1624.

At first the new colony grew slowly. Few Dutch families wished to emigrate; the fur trade required few workers; the Indians were a constant threat; and the government of New Netherland was undemocratic and inefficient. Peter Stuyvesant was the best of the governors. Although he conquered the Swedish settlements in the Delaware Valley, he had to give up most of the Dutch claims to Connecticut and Long Island.

The Dutch in New York

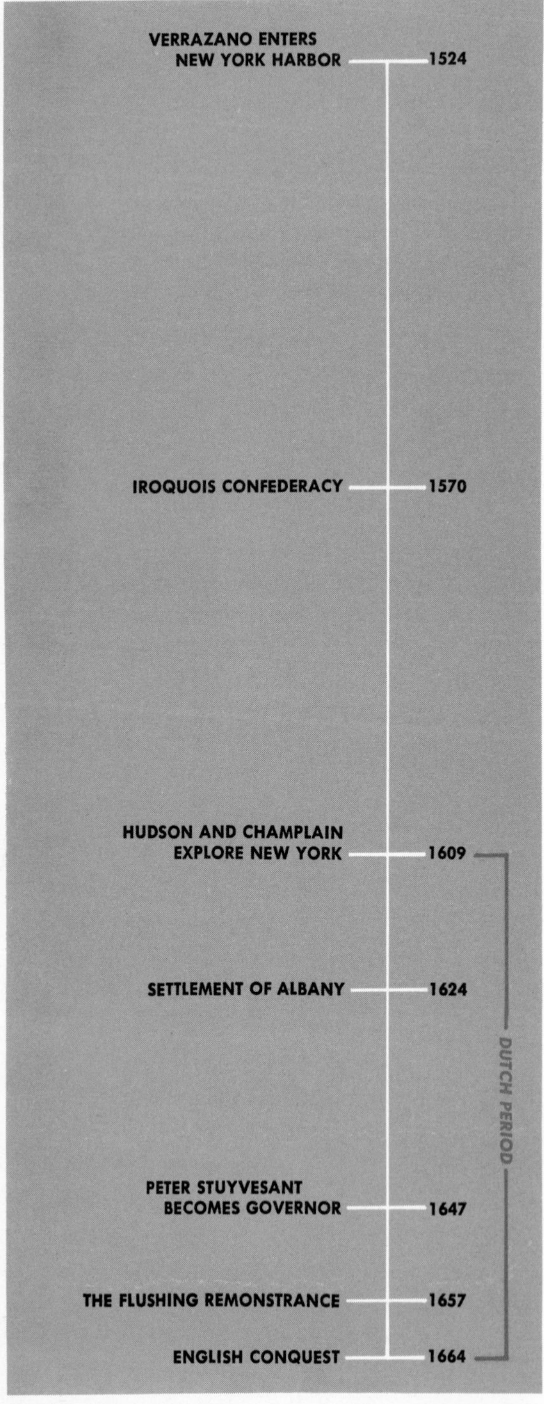

The Dutch brought over a few Dutch Reformed clergymen and set up some schools. Stuyvesant persecuted Quakers until checked by the officers of the Dutch West India Company and the protests of settlers.

In 1664 the English made a bloodless conquest of New Netherland. Dutch influence continued in the architecture, place names, and customs of New York.

Checking the high points

1. What dangers did the colony of New Netherland face?

2. Why was the patroon system unsuccessful?

3. How much influence did clergymen have in New Netherland?

4. Why did the Dutch have trouble with the Algonquian Indians?

5. Why were the people of New Netherland unwilling to fight the English?

Think these over

1. Was Peter Stuyvesant a good governor?

2. Did New Netherlanders practice freedom of religion?

Vocabulary building

Do you know the meaning of these words and expressions?

charter	bowery
persecution	toleration
patroon	remonstrance

Checking locations

Albany	Oyster Bay
Kingston	Connecticut River
Long Island	Delaware River

chapter 7: The COLONIES PROSPER WITHIN the BRITISH EMPIRE

chapter 8: A NEW SOCIETY is FORMED

chapter 9: The COLONIES LEARN SELF-GOVERNMENT

unit three

Colonial Culture and Society

New York state history dates are shown in color.

1647 Massachusetts law provides public schools

1654 First Jews arrive in New Amsterdam

1691 Massachusetts grants religious toleration to Protestants

1727 New Yorker Cadwallader Colden writes book on Iroquois

1733 Georgia, last of the thirteen colonies is founded

Molasses Act

1735 Editor Peter Zenger acquitted of criminal charges brought against him, a victory for freedom of the press

1754 Albany Plan of Union

1760 George III becomes King of England

1763 End of the English and French Wars; England wins North America

1765 Stamp Act passed

1767 Townshend Acts passed

1773 Tea Act

Boston Tea Party

1775 Battle of Lexington and Concord

Ticonderoga seized by Ethan Allen

1776 Declaration of Independence

By 1760 the American colonists had established a prosperous economy, representative government, and a vigorous culture with schools, churches, and newspapers. The population—about one million and a half—was growing rapidly and was beginning to push through the Appalachians. Distance (about six weeks by ship to England), wilderness, an abundance of good and cheap land, a mixed population, and a century of self-rule had changed Europeans into Americans.

Each of the thirteen colonies was proud of its special character. Many factors—the intentions and hopes of founders such as Pennsylvania's Quakers, crops such as tobacco, location and climate, churches, and a mixture of nationalities and races—made each colony different. New England bore the Puritan stamp as well as the Yankee interest in trade and education. Southern colonies (Maryland south to Georgia) developed a society based on tobacco, plantations, and the exploitation of slaves. A mixed economy of farmers, artisans, and traders along with many non-English immigrants marked the Middle colonies.

Most Americans seemed satisfied with life under king and parliament. Did they not, (always excepting black people) enjoy more freedoms than any other people in the world? Did they not have a high standard of living?

After 1763 when Britain tightened its control over trade and began to tax the colonists, many became alarmed. As proud British citizens they feared the loss of their liberties. In April 1775, the embattled farmers of Concord, Massachusetts "fired the shot heard round the world."

Chapter Objectives

To learn about

- labor, trade, and travel in the English colonies
- agriculture in the colonies
- fishing, forestry, manufacturing, and commerce in the colonies
- the mercantile system

chapter 7

The COLONIES PROSPER WITHIN the BRITISH EMPIRE

Labor: Free and Unfree

In America there was much work to do and few persons to do it. Families were large partly because many hands were needed to work on the farms and in the shops. To make the labor scarcity worse, laborers kept leaving their jobs to work on the land. Land was cheap and owning land was the most approved form of wealth. Employers kept complaining that they had to pay outrageous wages in order to get and keep help. As a result, the wage scale in the colonies was much higher than that of England.

To solve the problem, employers turned to two forms of bound labor—white and black servants and black slaves. Some workers were so eager to come to America that they sold themselves into a form of temporary service called indentured servitude. They agreed to work for a period of years (three to seven) in exchange for their passage and the promise of working tools and clothes at the end of term. Sometimes agents and captains would kidnap men in England and ship them to America. Criminals (over 50,000) were sent to serve their sentences as laborers for periods from seven to fourteen years. Some were dangerous men, and the colonists protested against this practice. Some were harmless debtors who had gone to jail for nonpayment of debts.

Parents sometimes bound their children to a craftsman who could teach them a trade. The apprentice agreed to obey the master's command, and the master agreed to provide "sufficient meat, drink, apparel, lodging, and washing" and to teach the skills of his craft.

Despite all these measures, labor remained in great demand. Planters in the tobacco colonies justified the use of African slaves on the ground that free labor was not available. By 1700 the colonies had adopted strict regulations concerning slavery, which was by then a regular feature of the colonial labor system. Blacks lost a good deal of their language, religion, customs, and traditions because of their capture and the break-up of their families. Slaves had little chance to do anything but work hard for their masters, and officials feared riots and uprisings. In New York, officials put down one revolt in 1712, and they hanged the leaders of another so-called conspiracy in 1741. Only the Quakers raised their voices against the shameful institution of slavery.

Domestic Trade and Travel

At first the merchants in colonial ports engaged in both wholesale and retail trade. They sold imported goods from their shops, which were often in their own homes. They also took the surplus goods of country storekeepers who exchanged farm products for sugar and manufactured products. Gradually some merchants found it profitable to specialize. Some sold only at retail to local customers; others sold only at wholesale. Still others concentrated on certain goods such as groceries, drygoods, and liquors. The town officials carefully regulated trade by permitting only licensed and local persons to buy and sell. In the South, where there were few cities and villages, the planters themselves were also traders. They piled their hogsheads of tobacco on their own wharves where ships were tied up. The ship captains bartered their imported goods for the tobacco.

Before 1700 most settlers lived near the ocean or navigable streams. In fact, for the next century most settlers found boats by far the best method of transport. The rivers carried a variety of craft, including sailboats, rowboats, canoes, and rafts. The colonists learned from the Indians how to portage, that is, to carry canoes or light boats around waterfalls and overland between streams. Sometimes settlements sprang up at portages and eventually became cities.

The colonists learned the value of Indian trails, which were about 18 inches wide and sometimes worn to a foot in depth. Men with light packs and pack animals found them useful because they were the easiest and often the shortest distance between settlements. The colonists widened the trails so they could use them for carts and wagons. But these roads were uniformly bad—muddy in spring, dusty in summer, and rough in all seasons. Sleds could travel these crude roads more easily than wheeled carts, so frontiersmen often took their goods to market in the wintertime. Rivers and streams were dangerous to cross, especially during spring floods. Communities had neither the money nor the knowledge to build bridges. At major crossings the ferryman with his boat carried passengers and sometimes a horse or two across the stream.

By 1732 travellers could buy a guidebook which described the roads from Boston to Providence, then on to New York, Philadelphia, and all the way to Jamestown. Most horsedrawn vehicles were owned and used locally. The first stagecoach line opened in 1732. Twenty-five years later one could go from New York to Philadelphia in three days, spending 18 hours each day in the coach. The driver would pull up at an inn at 10 P.M., where the weary passengers would alight and go to bed. At 3 A.M. a bugle would wake them up for another day of jolting travel.

In 1733 pioneers built a road west from Philadelphia to the Susquehanna Valley, where Scotch-Irish had settled. This roadway was extended to Harpers Ferry and then up the Shenandoah Valley. The "Old

New York City about 1717. Note the church within the walls of the old fort and the various types of ships in the harbor.

Wagon Road" opened up the heart of the Appalachian mountains to traders and frontiersmen. During the French and Indian War (1754–1763) military leaders, including Generals Forbes and Braddock, built roads through western Pennsylvania to the headwaters of the Ohio—the present site of Pittsburgh. In 1775 Daniel Boone cut the Wilderness Road through the Cumberland Gap down to the blue grass region of Kentucky.

A colonial post office was established in 1691, but it did not prosper at first. The rates were high; the service slow; the customers few. Mail was carried by anyone going in the right direction—ship captains, friends, travelers. The system improved somewhat after stagecoaches began to run. But it took Benjamin Franklin's appointment as deputy postmaster general in 1753 to achieve reforms. He speeded up delivery by improving the routes, marking the roads, and carrying mail by night as well as day. He lowered rates, which encouraged more use. He established fixed rates for newspapers, which meant that readers could subscribe to papers in distant cities. Political comment and editorials helped stir up resistance to British laws, such as the Stamp Act. (See p. 121)

Field and Forest

Agriculture was the most important economic activity supporting nine out of ten colonists. The types of farming varied in the different regions according to the soil, the nearness to market, the crop, and the kind of labor available. All farmers tried desperately to find a marketable product. How else could they pay for ammunition, salt, kettles, and other necessary products? How else could they secure silk, books, and other luxuries of life? At one extreme were farmers who remained largely self-sufficient. They were located in the hilly frontier region. At the other extreme were commercial farmers, especially southern planters, who spent most of their energies raising tobacco for the European market. In between were the great majority or ordinary farmers who grew as much as they could for the market but also provided most of their own fuel, foodstuff, and clothing.

People today often write about self-sufficient farming as a romantic period in which families were truly free and independent. This is largely untrue. Self-sufficiency chained pioneers to a life of grim poverty and endless drudgery. Pioneers accepted it as a necessary step toward a happier and more prosperous future.

Colonial farming was wasteful of soil and forest resources. Farmers planted crop after crop until the land "ran out." Then they cleared away more trees only to start the same process over again. George Washington in 1791 made a critical comment upon American farming:

> . . . . the aim of the farmers in this country, if they can be called farmers, is, not to make the most they can from the land, which, is, or has been cheap, but the most of their labour, which is dear; the consequence of which has been much ground has been scratched over and none cultivated or improved as it ought to have been: whereas a farmer in England, where land is dear, and labour cheap, finds it his interest to improve and cultivate highly . . .

In New England, long winters, short summers, stony soils, and hilly fields made farming difficult. But the Yankees managed to secure a decent living by hard work and thrift. Each township had its craftsmen who took food in exchange for tools, shoes, and other necessities. Even the preacher was paid in preserves, kindling wood, and free meals. Many farmers raised livestock partly for their own use but also for driving to the ports. There, butchers would prepare salt pork and barreled beef for the West Indian trade. Tapping the maple trees on his lot, the farmer secured sugar. He cut timber for firewood, fences, barns, and houses. He made barrel staves, which he could sell to West Indies planters for molasses. He collected the ashes after clearing his land and sold the potash, which always brought a fair price. He set traps hoping to secure the valuable beaver skins. He worked part-time in shipbuilding and fishing. The Yankee became noted as a "jack-of-all-trades."

The region west of the Hudson River and north of the Potomac River became the outstanding area for general farming. Wheat was the most important crop because flour was in great demand in the West Indies. Pennsylvania became the center of the livestock industry, and Philadelphia exported the bulk of colonial meats. The German farmers of eastern Pennsylvania had the reputation of being the best farmers because they spread manure over the fields and used lime on the land. They developed sturdy horses that were the best draft animals of the time. The Conestoga wagon, built in Conestoga, Pennsylvania, was the first of the famous covered wagons of future westward migration.

Southerners raised tobacco and other crops for the foreign market. The large planters were basically businessmen who secured loans from merchants in England and Scotland. Often they fell into debt because of their purchase of more land and more slaves. Planters in South Carolina began to cultivate rice in 1695. About 50 years later Eliza Pinckney experimented with indigo, a plant useful in making blue dyes.

The vast majority of farmers in the South had small farms and possessed no slaves. Some near waterways produced as much tobacco as their families could grow. Many had a low standard of living. The more fortunate had a cow or two, a horse, or a couple of oxen. The more ambitious and hardworking ones hoped for the day when they could become planters and thus join the groups that dominated political and social life.

Industries of the Sea and Forest

When a minister told his Boston congregation that their ancestors had come to America to worship God, a listener jumped up and stated, "Sir, you are mistaken . . . our main end was to catch fish." The legislature of Massachusetts selected the cod as the state symbol.

From the beginning, persons living near the coast looked seaward for their livelihood. Small boats moved offshore following the schools of fish. Gradually they joined the European fishing vessels catching cod and other fish off the Grand Banks of Newfoundland. When colonists saw a whale in shallow water, a crew of men chased the mammal and harpooned it. After the injured whale was exhausted, they towed it ashore and took out the oil and ground the bones. They used the oil to make candles. In 1760 Newport, Rhode Island, alone had 17 candle-making firms. Deep-sea whaling developed after 1700. Soon sailing vessels were pursuing whales to the polar oceans. When the lookout sighted a whale, the captain sent out small boats in pursuit. A harpooned whale, making desperate efforts to escape, would give his tormentors a wild ride called by sailors a "Nantucket sleigh ride." Yankee fishermen sold fish to the Catholic countries of southern Europe and to the planters of the West Indies. In return they bought wine, oranges, Spanish gold and silver, molasses, and sugar.

The forest supported a wide variety of activities. In fact most farmers were also part-time lumbermen, not to mention fishermen and hunters. The sawmill, often the first industry in a pioneer settlement, cut logs into boards for houses and fashioned timber for barns, tools, and fences. The barrel was the universal container for shipping commodities—Pennsylvania flour, Virginia tobacco, South Carolina rice, New England fish, West Indian molasses, and Spanish wine. The royal navy needed masts, yards, spars, and oars for ships. The white pine in the north and the yellow pine of the Carolinas furnished naval stores, pitch, tar, rosin, and turpentine. Ashes from burned trees provided another source of revenue for pioneers.

The forest was also the home of beaver, deer, and other game. Albany was an important center of the beaver trade, with the Iroquois securing many pelts from the Indians in the Great Lakes region. Charleston, the main center for deerskins, exported about 160,000 skins in 1748. Trains of mules, sometimes 80 animals long, carried skins to the seacoast and returned laden with goods for Cherokees, Creeks, and other Indians.

The great stands of timber close to waterways made it possible to build ships at a cost one-half to two-thirds that of England, even though colonial wages were higher. Shipyards sprang up along many ports and rivers, especially in New England and in New York harbor. At least one-third of all ships flying the British flag in 1776 were colonial-built. New Englanders owned over 2,000 ships, not counting fishing boats. About three-fourths of colonial commerce was carried in ships owned by colonists.

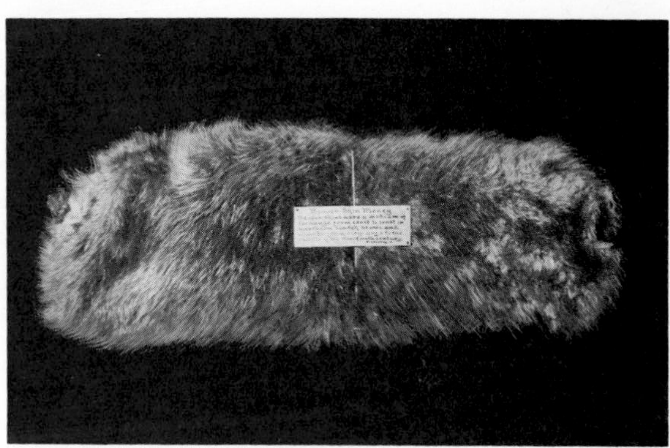

Goods sold to the Indians were priced in beaver skins. These skins were a medium of exchange in northern United States and Canada until the middle of the 1800's.

Manufactures

The iron industry was a growing business which had in 1775 more blast furnaces and forges than England and Wales. Indeed, the colonists produced about one-seventh of the world's iron. The British Parliament in 1750 prohibited colonists from making steel and other finished products. This law, however, was not enforced. Furthermore, it did not interfere with the making of nails and farm tools, the most important iron items in colonial America.

Hat making, concentrated in Rhode Island, New York, and Pennsylvania, angered English manufacturers; a law was passed in Parliament that forbade the colonists from exporting hats. Grist mills, often run as family enterprises, served the neighboring farmers. Some mills, especially those in Pennsylvania, were fairly large businesses. The colonists were heavy drinkers of beer, whisky, and rum. Rum became a valuable export from New England.

Compared with today, the amount of manufacturing was small, both in numbers of persons employed and the value of the product. Note that in the production of ships, lumber, and iron, the colonists ranked among the world's leaders. Colonial America developed a corps of skilled craftsmen—ironmasters, millwrights, shipbuilders—whose activities forecast the future manufacturing greatness of America.

Sea-borne Commerce

Boston kept its headstart over New York and Philadelphia as late as 1730. Its merchants were enterprising, and its shipyards gave it an edge. Boston had more than 150 warehouses for the storage of goods. The city was the major center for the collection of colonial products for shipment to Europe, and it was the major center for receiving English products. Over one thousand ships entered and left Boston harbor each year.

But Boston had handicaps that gradually slowed its growth. The surrounding territory provided few products as valuable as those grown in the neighborhood of Philadelphia and New York. Furthermore, shipbuilding in the Middle colonies expanded so that merchants could carry goods to Europe and the West Indies in their own ships. By the end of the colonial period, Philadelphia's population had grown to about 30,000 and New York's to about 22,000, while Boston trailed with 17,000 people.

To pay for manufactured goods from England which needed few products from New England, triangular trades grew up. Lumber and fish from New England or flour from the Middle colonies went to the West Indies in exchange for sugar or molasses. The sugar or molasses was then shipped to London; finally, English manufactures were sent to Boston, New York, and Philadelphia, completing the triangle. Perhaps most notorious is the triangular trade in which Yankee ships took rum and other products directly to West Africa. Here they traded their cargoes for gold, ivory, pepper, and slaves. The black captives were packed into dark and airless holds or chained on deck. The vessels recrossed the Atlantic to the West Indies, where the unhappy slaves were bartered for sugar or more molasses. These products were taken back to New England for manufacture into rum. There were many variations of these trades, based on the immoral business of bringing slaves to America. Fortunately, ordinary trade up and down the Atlantic coast carried much more tonnage than any of the trades to the West Indies and Africa.

Sea captains often called at the French West Indies because they could buy sugar more cheaply than in the British islands. Angered by this trade, the British sugar planters persuaded Parliament to pass the Molasses Act of 1733. It raised the tax so high on French products that it meant the end of profits. The Yankee traders, however, soon learned to get around this law, and trade with the French islands continued briskly. Actually the British government didn't object too much to this trade because Britain needed a healthy colonial shipbuilding and shipping industry at that time.

Colonial trade grew steadily, and merchants in the ports got rich. By 1763 the colonies were beginning to rival the mother country in commerce as well as manufacturing.

The Mercantile System

Mercantilism is an economic and political system based on the idea that wealth and military power go hand in hand. Wealth meant a nation could pay for armies and navies. Military power enabled a nation to hold colonies and to force favorable trade agreements, thus gaining more wealth. In colonial times many nations accepted mercantilism.

The control of sea-borne trade was part of the system of mercantilism. Not only did merchant ships earn money transporting goods, they could also serve as warships. They also trained sailors who could be used in the navy. In an effort to increase the size of the merchant fleet, Britain encouraged shipbuilding. She also passed laws restricting trade within the Empire to British-owned ships manned by British subjects. Vessels owned and manned by the colonists were naturally considered as British.

Under the mercantile system the wealth of a nation was measured by the amount of gold and silver it owned. The British had no gold or silver mines so they had to get these precious metals through trade. To bring gold and silver to the British Isles, Britain had to get more money for exports than it paid for imports. An inflow of gold

The Smith and Dimon shipyard, painted by James Pringle in 1833. Many fast clippers were built here. At this time New York City was the leading shipbuilding center in the United States.

and silver resulting from a nation getting more for goods it sells than it pays for goods it buys is known as a favorable balance of trade.

To enforce mercantilism throughout the Empire, the British government passed a series of trade laws based on four principles:

1. Trade within the Empire was to be in British ships manned by British sailors. This idea helped the New England shipbuilders and sea captains in their fight against Dutch rivals.
2. All European exports to the colonies were to pass through English ports before shipping to the colonies. The colonists didn't object to this because they preferred English manufactures. Furthermore, most English goods were the cheapest available.
3. Certain specified or "enumerated" products of the colonies had to go to England first. Gradually the British government added to the list all the major products: tobacco, rice, indigo, naval stores, beaver skins. By 1770 all but four percent of colonial exports had been listed. This regulation bothered colonists because they could not deal directly with foreign markets. Colonial products were taxed in English ports, and the English merchants made money handling the goods and re-exporting them to Europe.
4. Colonial manufacturing was held in check in order to prevent competition with English manufacturers. As we have seen, this goal did not prevent iron making, shipbuilding, and other industries from developing.

Because the Molasses Act of 1733 was often ignored, many historians have assumed that all the mercantilist regulations were also not enforced. This is not true. The acts had teeth, and the bite was sometimes painful. Naval officers and customs officials had considerable power to enforce these laws.

The colonists accepted the notion that the British government had the right to regulate trade. After all, they received great benefits from the royal navy, which protected colonial trade from pirates and enemies. The colonists also feared the Spanish and the French, who made claims to the land west of the Appalachian Mountains. Colonists realized that British soldiers protected them from Indian raids.

Most colonists seemed quite satisfied with the British Empire as of 1760. Its many benefits permitted them to prosper over more than a century. But when the British began to use trade regulations to secure tax income, and introduced taxes within the colonies, the colonists then protested vigorously.

Summary

Scarcity was the chief feature of colonial labor systems. Laborers in the colonies received higher wages than workingmen received in England.

Over half of the immigrants were not free people. A good number were indentured servants or apprentices. Most important were the black slaves, who formed almost a third of the population.

Most settlers tried to live near waterways so they could send their products to market. Roads gradually developed, often from old Indian trails. By 1750 travelers could go by stagecoach from Boston to Virginia, and follow primitive roads into the interior. Benjamin Franklin improved the postal service.

Agriculture was the main occupation of nine out of ten persons. Farmers sought for a marketable crop so that they could buy salt, ammunition, and other goods. New Englanders exported salted meats and fish; the Middle colonies exported wheat and flour; the South sent out tobacco and later rice and indigo.

The sea provided a living for many, especially New Englanders. Farmers everywhere looked to the forests for furs, ashes, naval supplies, fuel, and lumber products. Colonists developed important industries—iron making, shipbuilding, and lumbering. Boston at first led in commerce, especially with England and the West Indies. By 1750 New York and Philadelphia were challenging Boston's position in population and manufacturing. By 1763 the colonies were beginning to rival the mother country in commerce and in some fields of manufacturing. Great Britain established a series of laws often described as the mercantile system. These regulations did not prevent the colonies from developing a strong economic base, but some of the laws annoyed traders. Nevertheless, most colonists were quite happy in 1763 with their position in the British Empire and their relatively high standard of living.

Checking the high points

1. Why were wages in colonial America so high?

2. Compare three types of bound or non-free labor. Why did this kind of labor come about?

3. How did goods reach markets?

4. Plot a route from the upper Shenandoah Valley to Philadelphia and to Boston.

5. What improvements did Benjamin Franklin make in the postal service?

6. Were colonial farmers intelligent farmers? Explain.

7. Compare farming in New England, the Middle colonies and the South.

8. Why did New Englanders turn to the sea?

9. Show how two manufactures became important.

10. Why did triangular trades grow up?

11. What was the mercantile system and what were its goals?

Think these over

1. Why did colonial Americans look more to the sea and Europe than to the west and the forests of the frontier?

2. Is the statement true that the economy of New England was bound to clash with that of Old England? Explain.

3. It is as easy to say that America was born in forced labor as in freedom. How so?

4. Debate this statement: The colonists benefited as much from the mercantile system as they suffered from it.

Vocabulary building

indentured servant
portage
triangular trades
mercantilism
favorable balance of trade

Checking locations

West Africa
British West Indies
French West Indies
Harpers Ferry
Susquehanna Valley
Pittsburgh
Shenandoah River
South Carolina
Cumberland Gap

Chapter Objectives

To learn about

- population growth and ethnic diversity among the early colonists
- religion and education in colonial America
- social and cultural growth in the early colonies

chapter 8

A NEW SOCIETY is FORMED

A New Society

In 1700 most of the 294,000 people in the English colonies had English ancestry. The English had firmly planted their way of life and institutions. Language, literature, law, political forms, and even religious denominations were always to bear a heavy English stamp.

Population grew rapidly in the eighteenth century. In fact it shot up about 10 times by the time of the Revolution and over 20 times by 1800. People had large families, with an average family having between five to six children. In addition, large numbers of people immigrated to America.

The English kept coming, but other groups began to arrive in great numbers. The three most numerous groups were Germans, Scotch-Irish from northern Ireland, and blacks from Africa and the West Indies.

A breakdown of the population composition in 1790 shows the national origins and concentrations (see p. 103).

People of English stock remained the largest single group, forming about one-half of the population. English officials, soldiers, traders, servants, and craftsmen were among the immigrants. Almost all the New Englanders were of English descent, while a great majority of the white population in the Southern colonies were English. Approximately one-half of New Yorkers in 1775 had English blood. They occupied most of Long Island, the lower Hudson valley, and dominated the official and commercial life of New York City.

Population Growth

	1700	*1775*
New England colonies	130,000	589,000
Middle colonies	65,000	600,000
Southern colonies	99,000	1,015,000

Non-English Groups

Approximately 400,000 blacks lived in the colonies by the time of the American Revolution, most of them in the region south of

The slave market at the foot of Wall Street in New York City about 1730. By 1804, all states from New Jersey to Rhode Island had laws that children of slave mothers were to be freed upon reaching a certain age.

Pennsylvania. There were relatively few blacks before the 1680's, when, as you have read, planters imported them to plant and harvest their tobacco. The owners of rice and indigo plantations in South Carolina also used slaves. Although Georgia at first banned slavery, it lifted the ban when land owners decided to set up plantations.

New York had the largest number of slaves outside the South. In 1771 approximately 20,000 blacks lived in or near New York City. They worked on the wharves, served as field hands on the larger farms, and became house servants. Conditions were bad, but a few individuals, notably the Quakers, urged better treatment, and a handful even urged abolition. Through their efforts some black children in Philadelphia and New York received a bit of schooling. Some blacks bought or were given their freedom, and a few became owners of businesses.

The Irish immigrants, then and now, formed two distinct groups: those from

Population Composition in 1790

National Origins		*Places of Heaviest Concentration*
English	50%	All states, especially New England
Negroes	19%	Southern states and New York
Irish*	8%	Middle states
Scots	7%	Pennsylvania, North Carolina
Germans	7%	Pennsylvania, New York
Dutch	3%	New York, New Jersey
Others	6%	

*About half Scotch-Irish from Ulster, northern Ireland

southern Ireland, and those from Ulster in northern Ireland, who are often labelled Scotch-Irish because their ancestors came from Scotland. Most immigrants from Southern Ireland were indentured servants or small farmers. No doubt the most famous was William Johnson, who was later knighted by the King of England for his services as a military leader and Indian agent. Another, Governor Thomas Dongan, a Roman Catholic, called the first assembly elected by the freeholders of New York.

The Scotch-Irish left their Ulster region because of rising land rents, unfair taxes, and persecution—political and religious—by the British government. Over 300,000 migrated to the American colonies after 1700, and some became famous as Indian fighters. Most Americans have heard of Daniel Boone, Kit Carson, and Andrew Jackson. Rugged Scotch-Irish pioneers settled in the back country of Pennsylvania, the Carolinas, and Virginia. In New York they settled Cherry Valley in the 1740's.

A Pennsylvania Dutch barn. Most of these barns are decorated with elaborate and colorful "hex" signs like the ones seen here.

Governor George Clinton, of Scotch-Irish descent, led New York during the Revolutionary War.

Scots, direct from Scotland, found their way to the Middle and Southern colonies. With their near brothers, the Scotch-Irish, the Scots firmly established the Presbyterian Church.

Germans by the thousands arrived after 1707 and continued to come until the Revolution. In fact hundreds of German (Hessian) troops fighting for the British in the Revolutionary War liked America and remained here after the war. The region around Lancaster, Pennsylvania, had the greatest concentration of Germans, and is now know as the "Pennsylvania Dutch country." Visitors enjoy seeing their barns, their excellent farms, and their interesting folk art.

In 1710 ten ships carrying over 2,500 Germans sailed into New York harbor. These people were called Palatine Germans because they fled from the Palatinate, a district of Germany along the Rhine River. The armies of the French King had swept through their homeland and drove them out. The British government took them in and sent many to New York to make tar and pitch as well as to cut masts—all products needed by the Royal Navy.

This experiment on the lower Hudson failed because the Germans did not like to work in gangs under the orders of army officers. They also complained that the British government did not live up to its promises of free land and good food. Some stayed on as tenants near Rhinebeck in the Hudson valley. Over 100 German families marched through the winter snows to the Schoharie valley, which they claimed had been promised to them. Hardly had they laid out seven villages and built some rude huts before land speculators from Albany told them to pay for the land or get out. This demand angered the Germans, but they could not prevent the sheriffs from enforcing the land claims. Many families made the best deal they could with the speculators and stayed in the Schoharie valley. Others quit New York and went to Pennsylvania, which was welcoming Germans. Some accepted Governor Robert Hunter's offer of free land near Palatine and Stone Arabia, both in the Mohawk Valley. Other Palatines settled Herkimer, the westernmost settlement. When the Revolution came, these frontiersmen, led by General Nicholas Herkimer, held back the British advance in the famous battle of Oriskany.

Among the smaller groups were the Dutch, French, Swiss, Irish, Welsh, and Jews. As we have seen, Dutch influence remained strong but limited to the Hudson valley. The French were usually Protestant refugees, called Huguenots, who were fleeing from religious persecution. Several French families—the Jays and De Lanceys in New York, the Reveres in Massachusetts, and the Legares of South Carolina—provided outstanding leaders. New Paltz and New Rochelle were founded by French settlers.

There were Swiss settlers in North Carolina, Welsh around Philadelphia, and a few Jews in New York, Newport, and Philadelphia.

The Indian population kept dropping, especially after 1700. Many warriors died during the long wars with France and with other tribes. Smallpox, tuberculosis, scarlet fever, and other diseases killed thousands.

The mixed population of America, which was especially evident in Pennsylvania and New York, attracted much attention among foreigners. About 1770 a Frenchman, St. John de Crèvecoeur, wrote that out of this "melting pot" came a new man, an American, who was different from the Englishman, German, Irishman, or Jew. Crèvecoeur was partially right but actually more wrong than right. Most groups—Germans, French, Scotch-Irish—tried to keep their separate identities and resisted the pull of English customs, language, and institutions. Perhaps "mosaic" or "salad bowl" would be more accurate terms to describe the population.

Approximately nine out of ten persons lived on the land, but a fair number lived in cities, especially the main five: Boston, Newport (Rhode Island), New York, Philadelphia, and Charleston. Philadelphia, with about 40,000 people living in its vicinity, was the second largest city in the British Empire. These five cities were the centers of economic, political, and intellectual life. Here were located the powerful merchants, the artisan class, the courts of law, the legislatures, and the printers of newspapers. The cities funneled into America the ideas as well as the goods of Europe.

Churches

The Church of England (Anglican), having the largest number of churches in the colonies, was the established church of Virginia, Maryland, the Carolinas, Georgia, and four counties of New York. "Established" means that it was recognized and supported by the government. Despite this advantage, the Anglican Church did not succeed in enrolling a majority of the people in any colony. It lacked enough clergymen to fill its pulpits. It could not easily recruit more clergy-

This 1736 engraving shows the religious diversity of New York. The eight steeples, or cupolas, are from left to right: Trinity Church, the Lutheran Church, the new Dutch Reformed Church, L'eglise du St. Esprit (Huguenot), the City Hall, Old Dutch Church, the Secretary's office in Fort George, and the Church (Anglican) in the fort.

men because candidates had to sail all the way to London for ordination by a bishop. Theoretically, bishops and priests controlled the Church of England, but in America the laymen seized most of the power, largely because of the shortage of clergymen and the absence of a bishop. The Church of England sent more than 300 missionaries between 1701 and 1775 to help Indians, blacks, and poor whites.

The Congregational Church became the established church in Massachusetts, Connecticut, and New Hampshire where the Puritans had settled. Its members believed that when a group of true believers came together as a congregation, they could set up a church. The congregation elected a minister and a board of elders, who exercised strict control over the beliefs and morals of its members. Although the Puritans in the seventeenth century had persecuted Baptists and Quakers, they now had to grant religious toleration to all Protestants. The new royal charter of Massachusetts in 1691 granted toleration to all Protestants.

Many religions were practiced in the Middle colonies where the population was drawn from many different countries. In New York there were Dutch Reformed, Anglicans, Lutherans, Presbyterians, Quakers, and Congregationalists. In New Jersey and Pennsylvania the Quakers, though a small minority, remained very powerful. The influx of Germans brought in Lutherans and other German sects, while the immigrants from northern Ireland were mostly Presbyterian.

The Dutch Reformed Church grew slowly because it held on to the Dutch language, which many young people refused to learn.

Even so, it had the largest number of churches in New York as late as the Revolution. By contrast, the Presbyterian Church, which in 1700 had only a few scattered congregations, grew rapidly because of immigration from Scotland, northern Ireland, and New England. Many Yankee Congregationalists who settled in New York and New Jersey switched over to the Presbyterians, whose beliefs were quite similar.

The Quakers by 1700 had won much wealth, a large following, and a great deal of power in Pennsylvania, New Jersey, and even Rhode Island. But during the next century they grew slowly, losing many young people to the Church of England and other churches. The Quakers, or Friends, as they prefer to be called, gave up their preaching. Instead they turned their activities toward good works. The blacks, Indians, and the friendless had their most vigorous champions among the Quakers.

Meanwhile, persecuted groups such as the Mennonites, Moravians, Baptists, and even Presbyterians flocked to Pennsylvania, which offered toleration as well as good land. The Mennonites, like the Quakers, did not believe in bearing arms. The Moravians, another German sect, founded Bethlehem, Pennsylvania in 1740 and tried to help the neighboring Indians. Most German immigrants were Lutherans in background. By 1776 there were over 70 Lutheran churches in Pennsylvania and in other settlements such as the Schoharie valley and the Mohawk valley.

Few Roman Catholics settled in the English colonies before the Revolution. The largest number was concentrated in Maryland which was founded by Lord Baltimore, a Roman Catholic. America, however, was a great mission field for Catholic priests and friars such as the Jesuits and Franciscans. French Jesuits converted the Hurons to Christianity and sent dozens of missionaries to the Iroquois in New York. Along the Gulf of Mexico and in the Southwest, Spanish *padrés* set up missions among the Indians.

Beginning in 1720 a religious revival called the Great Awakening swept the colonies and reached peaks of enthusiasm in the 1730's and 1740's. George Whitefield, an English clergyman, made preaching tours along the Atlantic seaboard and called on the people to repent. Thousands accepted

A painting of Francis Makemie appearing before Governor Cornbury of New York. In 1707 the Governor arrested Makemie, a Presbyterian minister, for preaching without a license. A court freed Makemie and the Assembly came out for religious toleration.

his call. In the Connecticut valley Jonathan Edwards not only converted hundreds of people but wrote books which are still regarded as masterpieces of reasoning.

The Great Awakening led to the conversion of thousands in the countryside and in the cities. It also caused divisions in the churches because people quarreled over doctrine and the proper methods of conducting religious services. Many clergymen and elders did not like the excitement caused by the fiery sermons of the revivalists. They in turn were attacked as "cold" and not "saved." The revivals promoted a more democratic feeling because the "converted" often took control from the elders or organized new congregations. The Great Awakening gave the colonists a greater sense of unity since preachers visited various colonies and built up ties among the churches. It also led people into establishing hospitals and doing other good works. The newer churches, such as the Baptists and after 1760 the Methodists, made great gains on the frontier because they relied heavily on laymen. The revivals also led to the founding of colleges.

The Growth of Schools

In addition to founding colleges, the various religious groups were responsible for founding and supporting most of the schools. The church leaders felt that, in order to learn to read the Bible, the people needed schools. Furthermore, secondary schools (called grammar schools) prepared young men for colleges, which, in turn, trained them for the ministry and other professions. Since clergymen were usually fairly well educated, they were often hired to teach school.

Fewer than half of the children got the chance to attend school, except in New England. A Massachusetts law of 1647, which the other New England colonies copied in some form, required each township that had 50 or more families to appoint a person to "teach all such children as shall resort to him to write or reade." Each town with over 100 families was also required to provide a school where boys could be prepared for college. As a result most Yankees learned to read and write at a time when most people in Europe and elsewhere could

Colonial Colleges		
1636	Harvard (Massachusetts)	Congregational
1693	William and Mary (Virginia)	Church of England
1701	Yale (Connecticut)	Congregational
1746	Princeton (New Jersey)	Presbyterian
1754	Pennsylvania (Pennsylvania)	Non-demoninational
1754	Columbia (New York)	Church of England
1764	Brown (Rhode Island)	Baptist
1766	Rutgers (New Jersey)	Dutch Reformed
1769	Dartmouth (New Hampshire)	Congregational

do neither. After 1700 the New England school system declined, largely because of the scattering of the population. Gradually each neighborhood set up a school that was a district and not a town school. The district school often did a rather poor job of educating youngsters.

In contrast the Southern colonies did little to educate their young people. The wealthy continued to hire tutors to teach their children. Here and there leaders set up charity schools for poor whites and even a few for blacks and Indians. Well over half of the children never saw the inside of a schoolroom.

The Middle colonies offered a wide variety of schools, but these schools, too, reached less than half of the youngsters. The Germans often set up schools in their churches so that they could teach their children to read the Bible in German. The Dutch Reformed Church ran an elementary school in New York City that finally accepted English in 1772. Several charity schools were sponsored by the Anglican Church. Upper class parents hired tutors and sent their children to masters who had schools in their homes.

Secondary education was so exceptional that probably not one in a hundred youngsters studied Latin and the other subjects offered. Only in New England and in its larger towns did several good Latin grammar (secondary) schools thrive. In addition a very few private academies were founded to prepare boys for college. The South had the weakest education on the secondary as well as the primary and college levels. A handful of Anglican ministers set up a few grammar schools. New York was not much better because the citizens allowed the Latin grammar school of Dutch days to die. A few parents sent their boys to private schools. The Quakers of Philadelphia, however, supported several fine schools on both the elementary and secondary levels.

Only a very few men attended college. In fact, only 3,000 colonists had attended college at the time of the Revolution. New England led in higher education, with Harvard and Yale preparing young men for the ministry and other professions. William and Mary College in Virginia by mid-century was attracting a small but remarkable group of men such as Thomas Jefferson, James Madison, and John Marshall. These able men provided much of the leadership of the federal government. Because of the Great Awakening, most churches needed more clergymen and therefore set up their own colleges. Thus the Presbyterians established a college at Princeton, New Jersey, in 1746 and the Anglicans a few years later founded King's College (now Columbia University).

Girls received even less education than boys. The girl in an ordinary family learned how to cook, sew, and to care for children by watching her mother. Rich people hired tutors to teach their daughters good manners, dancing, and perhaps French, the language of high society. In spite of these handicaps, a few women became well educated. For instance, foreigners were impressed with the knowledge and ability of Abigail Adams, the wife of John Adams.

Newspapers Are Founded

The *Boston News-Letter,* which began in 1704, was the first regularly published newspaper in the British colonies. It managed to survive because it avoided controversy. Both in Boston and Philadelphia officials had closed down earlier papers which

In a print shop such as this one that has been restored in Williamsburg, Virginia, John Peter Zenger published the *New York Weekly Journal.*

criticized the government. James Franklin breathed fire into American journalism when he began publishing the *New England Courant* in 1721. His favorite targets were Harvard College and the Congregational clergy. Young Ben Franklin, who worked for his brother, left home to go to Philadelphia, where in time he made the *Pennsylvania Gazette* one of the most successful newspapers of the day.

Freedom of the press made some progress as a result of the jailing of John Peter Zenger, a New York printer, who had attacked a royal governor for corruption. Jailed for criminal libel in 1735, Zenger was able to hire Andrew Hamilton, an able lawyer from Philadelphia, to defend him. Hamilton convinced the jury that what Zenger had printed was true, therefore he could not be found guilty.

Colonial readers relied mostly on books and magazines published in England. A few had large collections. For example, George Washington had a library of over 900 volumes. The larger towns and cities had small public libraries. Benjamin Franklin organized the Library Company of Philadelphia in 1731. Members had to pay a small sum each year which gave them the right to take out books.

Culture and Science

Boston and Philadelphia led all other cities in music, drama, the arts, publishing, and other forms of culture. All colonials looked to London for the latest styles in dress and amusement as well as for their books, music, and plays. Colonial musicians, artists, and architects copied English and European models.

Music made small headway, although colonial society attended the concerts of visiting singers and performers. Philadelphia had a theater by 1724, and by mid-century English actors were performing in the colonies. John Copley painted fine portraits of John Hancock and other Boston people before he left for London. Another American, Benjamin West, had a studio in New York before he moved to London where he became President of the Royal Academy. Who does not know the portrait of George Washington by Gilbert Stuart which appears on the dollar bill? Most people are not aware that Paul Revere not only rode horses but also was a fine silversmith and engraver.

The New Englanders were the most active in writing from the very beginning. William Bradford's story of the first Thanksgiving can still inspire modern readers. An unusual writer was Phyllis

Wheatley, a former slave, who impressed Benjamin Franklin with her poems. George Washington invited her to meet him after she wrote a poem in his honor.

In science several Americans became well known in physics, chemistry, astronomy, botany, and medicine. Franklin's experiments were the most significant. Most school children are familiar with the story of how he flew a kite in a rainstorm in order to discover the nature of electricity. His friend, Cadwallader Colden of New York, wrote the first book on the Iroquois that described their customs in scientific fashion. Dr. Benjamin Rush of Philadelphia tried to find the cure for yellow fever and malaria, two dread diseases. He failed, but a century earlier Cotton Mather of Boston had shown that inoculation for smallpox protected people against that disease.

The Role of the Family

The family was and remains the basic unit of society. Most colonial families were "nuclear," consisting of mother, father, and children. Some were "extended" households where aged parents came to live with one of their children. The father was the head of the household. It was he who directed the work, owned the property, and represented the family in church and government. His wife shared the burdens of the home, and she might become the actual head if her husband died.

Parents taught children to accept the customs that held the community together. By what they did and what they said, they urged their children to obey the laws of God and society. A well-brought-up child was an obedient one who had the duty to pass on

Benjamin Franklin

Benjamin Franklin (1706–1790)—famed printer, inventor, writer, scientist, statesman, and philosopher—was the greatest figure in colonial America. At the age of ten he left school to aid his father, a soapmaker; at twelve he became an apprentice printer. Then at seventeen he ran away from Boston to Philadelphia, where he worked as a printer and finally published the *Pennsylvania Gazette* for over thirty years. Meanwhile he invented bifocal glasses, an improved stove, and carried out electrical experiments which won him in-

ternational fame. A dedicated civic leader, Franklin worked to improve the street lighting, pavements, fire fighting, and police system of Philadelphia. At the Albany Congress of 1754, he presented a plan for colonial union. As a member of the Second Continental Congress, he helped draft the Declaration of Independence. As a diplomat, he arranged the alliance with France and helped negotiate the peace treaty with Great Britain. His wisdom and advice smoothed the way for agreements among the delegates to the Constitution Convention. Franklin's *Poor Richard's Almanac* was immensely popular, while his *Autobiography* continues to win new readers.

his parent's values to his own children. In New England and in several other places church leaders enforced discipline on families whose members fell into drunkenness, immorality, quarreling, and the like. In the Southern colonies the isolation of families scattered over the wilderness prevented much discipline by the church or the community.

Fathers and mothers taught their children the skills with which to make a living, provide shelter, and avoid disease and death. Each farm, store, or craftsman's shop was in effect a school, training the young how to live.

Families were large. In America the age of marriage fell well below that of England and the continent of Europe. Young men who had cleared off the woods, who could live off the game and fish, also had confidence in their ability to make homes for themselves. Young women who had mastered the household arts wanted to have their own home. They did not have to wait long before getting married because all around them was space—endless acres awaiting the ax and the plow.

Children left the family homestead more often and more easily than their relatives did in Europe. Home for them, as for most generations of Americans, was a place to leave. Visitors have always noted the restlessness and migratory habits of Americans, which certainly have tended to prevent the formation of large family groups living in a neighborhood for a long time. A few nationalities, especially the German Mennonites, tried to stop the flight of the young from family control. They realized that the young on the frontier would not only lose the German language but might also forget the teachings of their religion. They were successful in keeping a good number at home, and the Pennsylvania Dutch society to some extent remains intact to the present day.

Social Classes

The England of 1600 took for granted that humanity was divided into higher and lower classes. Thus the King and the titled nobility enjoyed the highest honor and favors. Just below them were the untitled "gentlemen" who became high officials, army officers, and directors of the largest businesses. Below them were the "middling" class of farmers and tradesmen. At the bottom were common laborers, servants, and the poor.

American society, however, differed because it had no nobility and only a few "gentlemen" as settlers. An English observer in 1772 found rural New Englanders much alike:

> Nobody in these parts has the idea of a Superior or of a Gentleman, other than themselves. They seem to be a good substantial kind of farmers.

But in Boston and the other cities there was quite a gap between the rich merchants and the common laborers working on the wharves.

As you have read, well over half of all immigrants to the region south of New England were "bound labor," either indentured servants or black slaves. Benjamin Franklin stated as late as 1759 that labor "is performed chiefly by indentured servants brought from Great Britain, Ireland, and Germany." Although indentured servants usually did not receive good treatment, they at least had some hope of escaping their position after their period of servitude was over. Only a few ever secured enough funds to buy a farm.

Slaves stood at the bottom of the social ladder. Conditions under slavery were so bad that the threat of revolt was always present. As a result the various legislatures passed strict laws governing the conduct of slaves. In New York City in 1741 citizens blamed blacks for several mysterious fires. To put an end to the panic that followed, officials hanged 18 blacks, burned another 13, and banished 70 more from the colony. The slaves in New York and in the other colonies resisted as best they could the evil of slavery.

Social classes in the colonies were based largely on money. Because practically no one in America had a title, the nobility class did not exist. The rapid growth of the colonies and the ease by which persons could secure land created an "open society," one with less rigid class lines than in England. Able and ambitious young men often made their way to the top. An example is Robert Livingston, the son of a Scottish minister,

The Well-Dressed Man—Colonial Style

Did you know that in colonial days men of the upper classes spent as much time on their dress as did women? Arranging their wigs alone took a long time, because the gentlemen had their hair dressed everyday. Some of them used curling irons and put their curls up in papers at night. When an aristocrat selected a wig, he had a fancy collection of styles from which to choose. He could pick a pigeon's wing, the comet, the cauliflower, the rose, the long bob, the snail back, or several others. The barber sprinkled his choice with grey or blue powder, heavily scented.

The well-dressed man wore black velvet breeches. Where his silk stockings met the breeches were bright buckles.

His coat fitted tightly and reached to his shoes in the back. It was trimmed with lace and open from the neck to the waist to show the lace ruffles underneath. His sleeves had ruffles and buttons and braid. Underneath he wore a waistcoat (vest) with many buttons and flaps. He wore a sword and carried a cane, and on his head was a cocked beaver hat.

Remember that only the upper classes dressed this way. These were no clothes in which to do rough labor.

Social Classes in New York

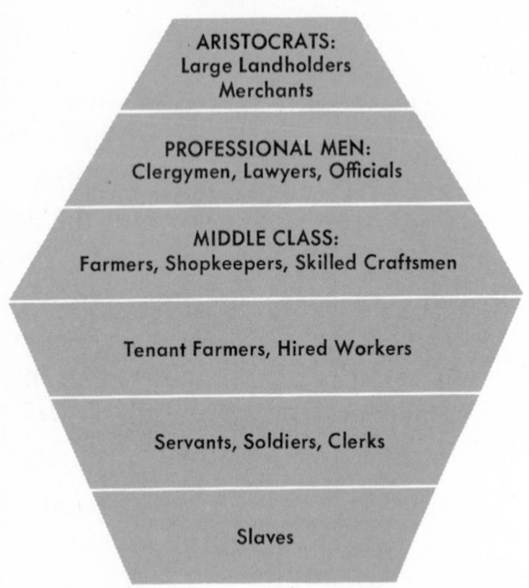

who acquired a large tract of land on the Hudson and married into the wealthy Van Rensselaer family.

In the eighteenth century it became harder for an unknown youth to break into the aristocracy of Boston, New York, Philadelphia, and the plantation South. But young men of drive and ability still continued to climb upward—for example, Benjamin Franklin in Philadelphia and Alexander Hamilton in New York. John Adams, from Boston, the son of a farmer, became President and founded one of America's great families. And on the frontier, especially, a person's rise in the world depended upon his or her energy and ability.

A French traveler found in 1772 that

> . . . the poorest laborer on the shore of the Delaware thinks himself entitled to deliver his sentiments in matters of religion or politics with as much freedom as the gentleman or scholar. Indeed, there is less distinction among the citizens of Philadelphia, than among those of any civilized city in the world. Riches give none. For every man expects one day or another to be upon a footing with his wealthiest neighbor.

Summary

Europeans became Americans under the influence of the wilderness as well as the immigration of various peoples. The English, forming about one-half of the population, dominated political and economic life and cultural patterns. But blacks, Scotch-Irish, Germans, Dutch, and others kept much of their separate identities while contributing to the formation of a common culture.

The immigrants brought with them their various churches: Church of England, Congregational, Presbyterian, Dutch Reformed, Lutheran, Quaker, and other sects. Between 1710 and 1740 the Great Awakening revived churches, stimulated colleges, and encouraged a feeling of unity.

Education made good gains, especially in New England, but elsewhere the majority of children never attended school. Newspapers sprang up in the cities, and freedom of the press received a step forward as a result of the Zenger Trial. Colonists generally imitated the art, music, plays, and science of England.

The family remained the center of life, both for educating the young and for earning a livelihood. In the colonies the rigid class system of England loosened up because of the opportunities for able young people. Indentured servants and slaves had little chance to escape their lowly status.

Checking the high points

1. What were the major nationality and racial groups in colonial America?

2. Compare the reasons of the Scotch-Irish and the Germans for coming to America.

3. What distinctive contribution did each make: English, blacks, Irish, Scotch-Irish, Germans?

4. What were the main churches and where were they strongest?

5. What problems faced the churches?

6. What were the results of the Great Awakening?

7. In what fields of culture did New Englanders lead?

8. Compare the education offered in the New England, Middle, and Southern colonies.

9. What advances did colonists make in arts, architecture, writing, and science?

10. What functions did the colonial family perform?

11. How did social classes in America differ from those of England?

12. Compare the situation of indentured servants and slaves.

Think these over

1. Is America more of a "salad bowl" than a "melting pot"? Discuss.

2. Are social classes inevitable? Are there any in America today?

3. By 1776 the American was more the product of local conditions than of European traditions. Comment.

Vocabulary building

religious toleration
Huguenot
Palatine
knighted
Pennsylvania Dutch
Anglican
established church
evangelism
sect
revival
indentured servant
Great Awakening
grammar school
aristocracy
tutor
melting pot
innoculation

Checking locations

Palatine, New York
Stone Arabia, New York
New Rochelle
Herkimer
Lancaster, Pennsylvania
Schoharie Valley
Bethlehem, Pennsylvania

Chapter Objectives

To learn about

- the trend toward increasing self-government in the colonies
- Britain's efforts to maintain control over its New World colonies
- colonial efforts to protest stricter British control
- the colonists' declaration of independence

chapter 9

The COLONIES LEARN SELF-GOVERNMENT

The Rise of the Assembly

The colonist regarded the government of his province as most important. True, King George was his sovereign and London was the seat of empire. The governors sent from England (in all but Connecticut and Rhode Island) were key men in the government structure. But the colonists believed that in an empire of many parts, the parts were more or less self-governing.

During the last third of the seventeenth century, officials in England tried to set up a stronger administration in London which could force the American colonists to obey the Acts of Trade and Navigation. Massachusetts lost its charter in 1684, and the next year James II combined all of New England into a single colony called the Dominion of New England. There was no representative assembly. Governor Edmund Andros and a council appointed by the king took command. In 1688 New York and New Jersey were added to the Dominion.

The colonists were frightened and angered by the loss of their charters. Furthermore, the new governor began to question the land titles of many colonists. Public unrest was increased by the raids of the French and the Indians against the frontier outposts. Then James II had trouble with Parliament, which removed him from the throne in 1688. The news of his downfall traveled rapidly overseas. In Boston the people rose up and put Andros in jail. The Dominion of New England vanished and the colonists quietly restored their old governments. In New York Jacob Leisler led a revolt and seized control. Although he was later hanged as a traitor, the assembly which he had established continued as a vital agency of government. William and Mary, the new sovereigns of Great Britain, refused to restore the old charter of Massachusetts under which the governor was elected. The new charter provided for a governor and a council appointed by the British Crown. The assembly, however, continued as before.

By 1750 the colonists had made great gains in self-government. Under English tradition the assemblies had to approve the spending of money and the levying of taxes. The assemblies used this power, sometimes called the "power of the purse," to strengthen their control. A governor who acted against the wishes of the assembly would sometimes find that no money was provided for his salary. By granting or withholding funds, the assemblies gained much control over the government. In 1754 the Board of Trade in England complained that the New York assembly

> have wrested from Your Majesty's governor, the nomination of all offices of government, the custody and direction of the public military stores, the mustering and direction of the troops raised for Your Majesty's service, and in short almost every other part of the executive government.

But the colonists continued to consider themselves part of the British Empire. In fact, they were proud of being English citizens. They recognized that the British government had the right to make laws controlling trade and usually found it profitable to obey such regulations. The Empire offered many advantages: trade, protection, and stability. The British navy protected colonial ships from pirates and foreign warships. British soldiers gave them protection against raiding Indians and French attacks.

The French and Indian Wars

Between 1689 and 1763 the colonies took part in four wars with France. Actually, these wars were only a small part of a worldwide struggle between the British and French empires. In truth North America was less important to Britain and France than was the capture or loss of territory in Europe or other parts of the world. For the colonists, of course, the struggle in the New World was of first importance. The fur trade was threatened by it, but worse by far was the continual dread of attack and massacre. On the night of February 8, 1690, a band of about 150 Frenchmen and 100 Indians crept through the snow and attacked Schenectady, New York. The howling invaders broke into houses, scalped their victims, and burned the settlement. Panic spread along the frontier, and families fled to Albany. Here the mayor of the city, the tough and able Peter Schuyler, took charge. He quieted the fearful and organized the defenses. The next year Schuyler led a successful attack against a French outpost.

Wars with France

King William's War	1689–1697
Queen Anne's War	1701–1713
King George's War	1744–1748
French and Indian War	1754–1763

The struggle reached its climax in the French and Indian War, which began in 1754 and lasted for nine years. The British and the colonists had two major Indian allies—the Iroquois, who lived west and north of the frontier settlements in New York, and the Cherokees, who occupied the area west of the settlements in the Southern colonies. Both of these Indian groups had advanced civilizations and were powerful fighting forces. Both were traditionally friends of the British and enemies of the French. At the start of the French and Indian War the Iroquois were angry because the colonists were settling on land in Indian

A modern view of Fort Ontario at Oswego. These ramparts were rebuilt by the British in 1759 and surrendered to the United States in 1796.

territory. The situation was so serious that the British government called a meeting at Albany, New York. Here representatives of seven colonies met with leaders of the Iroquois Confederation in what is known as the Albany Congress of 1754.

Chief Hendrick expressed the Iroquois worry:

> The governor of Virginia and the governor of Canada are both quarrelling about lands they think belong to us; and such a quarrel . . . may end in our destruction.

The Indians were given 30 wagonloads of presents, but they refused to make any promises. Throughout the war, however, most of the Iroquois tribes supported the British. Among those who fought against the French was Chief Hendrick, who paid for his loyalty with his life. He was slain in a battle at Lake George in 1755.

Benjamin Franklin attended the Albany Congress and proposed the Albany Plan of Union. The scheme called for the colonies to create a government uniting all the colonies and joining together all their military forces to provide better protection. Franklin's plan was not accepted. It was one of the first attempts to unite the colonies. While it did not succeed, the thinking it started may have made it easier to form a union during the Revolutionary times.

The war turned out badly for France. In 1758 General Jeffrey Amherst captured the French fortress of Louisbourg, which guarded the mouth of the St. Lawrence River. General John Forbes captured the French fort at what is now Pittsburgh. The next year General James Wolfe took Quebec; the French power in North America was broken. The war ended with the Treaty of Paris of 1763, in which all French territory east of the Mississippi was given to Britain except for New Orleans and two small islands in the mouth of the St. Lawrence.

For the colonists the situation was now changed. No longer did they have to rely on the British for defense against the French—a fact that made it easier for them to resist the laws laid down by the mother country.

Resistance to British Authority

At the war's end the British government faced two major problems, for which it was unable to find solutions that would not anger the colonists. The first was how to keep the Indians from going on the warpath, and the second was how to meet the cost of keeping troops in the colonies. The Indian problem appeared immediately.

The Indians were alarmed by the movement of white settlers into their hunting grounds and were resentful of fur traders who cheated them. The British knew that unless something was done to ease this situation, the Indians would attack. Should that happen, settlements would be destroyed and high taxes would be needed to pay for the additional soldiers. To calm the Indians, the British government issued the Proclamation of 1763, which said that no white settlement could be made west of the crest of the Appalachian Mountains. Furthermore, no person could trade with the Indians unless he had a *license.* As used here the word "license" means written permission. By issuing licenses only to persons who would agree to treat the Indians fairly, the British hoped to end cheating.

Three groups were made unhappy by the Proclamation. First were the fur traders, who did not want the government watching over their business dealings with the Indians. Second were the persons who had hoped to settle on Indian lands. The third and most powerful group was made up of wealthy *land speculators,* that is, men who bought up large areas cheaply and later sold them in small lots at higher prices.

The proclamation of 1763 did not keep colonists from settling on Indian lands. In an effort to calm the Indians, Sir William Johnson called a conference at Fort Stanwix (Rome, New York) in 1768. Over 2,000 Indians attended. A treaty was signed agreeing that the boundary between the whitemen's territory and that of the Indians would be a line running south from Fort Stanwix to the Unadilla River, down that stream to the Susquehanna River, and from that point south to the Delaware. (See Map 16.) New Yorkers did not keep their bargain and hundreds of settlers moved across the treaty line within a few years.

The problem of paying for the British troops stationed in the colonies caused even more trouble to the British government. Taxes within England were very high, so officials looked overseas for more revenues. Why not from the American colonies, which would get the benefit from troops stationed on the frontier? As a result Prime Minister George Grenville began to recognize the mercantile system, shifting from the older policy of regulating trade to a new policy of raising revenue.

You will recall that under the mercantile system colonies were supposed to send raw materials to England, to buy manufactured goods from England, and to use British ships. To enforce this system, the government had passed a number of laws known as the Navigation Acts.

These acts did not harm colonial manufacturers and merchants very much because the British government did not strictly enforce them. For example, the busy merchants of New York and Boston traded with the French and Spanish islands of the West Indies, where high prices were paid for wheat, lumber, and meat products. They did this even though the Molasses Act of 1733 placed a very high tax on molasses from these islands. Shipmasters seldom bothered to pay the tax, and British officials looked the other way. Colonial manufacturers not only made many products for use within the colonies but also exported raw iron and other goods to Great Britain itself.

Grenville tightened the enforcement of the Navigation Acts and imposed the Revenue Act of 1764, better known as the Sugar Act. This act was designed to raise money. If enforced, it would cut out the profitable trade with the French West Indies. The

Sir William Johnson (1715–1774)

Waraghiyaghey, meaning chief director of affairs, was the name the Iroquois warriors called Sir William Johnson. They loved the strong white man who danced their dances, played their games, spoke their language, and wore their clothing. Sir William respected the Iroquois and their customs. He was proud when they adopted him into their nation. When he was twenty-three years old, Johnson settled in the wilderness of the Mohawk Valley near what is now the city of Amsterdam. Here he began to trade with the Indians and to acquire large tracts of land. The Iroquois trusted Johnson because he did not cheat them.

When fighting broke out between the British and French in 1744, only Johnson kept the Iroquois from going over to the French. For this service the grateful British government made him a member of the Council of New York. When the French and Indian War began in 1754, he was made Superintendent of Indian Affairs. In the first battles, the British suffered defeats. But at the head of a group of colonists and Indians, Johnson defeated a French force near Lake George. For his services he was made a baronet. In 1759, an Army commanded by Sir William captured Niagara. The following year he was with General Jeffrey Amherst when Montreal was captured and the French control of Canada was broken.

Sir William was loyal to his Indian friends. He favored strict control of the fur trade to keep the Indians from being cheated. He tried to limit white settlement on Indian lands. In the Treaty of Fort Stanwix (1768) Johnson helped to draw a line beyond which the white men could not settle. He was also interested in educating the Indians. On July 11, 1774, Johnson made a two-hour speech to a group of Indians. A little later he became violently ill and died. Both Indians and white men mourned his passing for he was admired by all who knew him.

Above is a picture of Johnson Hall, home of Sir William. It was built in 1762 and is now a museum.

colonists challenged the act as illegal, claiming that only the colonial assemblies could levy taxes. In Massachusetts the fiery Sam Adams roared:

> If our Trade may be taxed why not our lands? Why not . . . everything we possess or make use of? This we apprehend annihilates our Charter Right to govern and tax ourselves . . . It strikes at our British Privileges.

Blind to this warning Grenville made more blunders. The Prime Minister believed the colonists should pay one-third the cost of the troops stationed in their territory. The Sugar Act did not bring in enough money to reach the one-third level. When the colonists failed to provide the difference, he got Parliament to enact the Stamp Act of 1765. This law had nothing to do with trade. It required that tax stamps be placed on all newspapers, legal documents, and official papers. The Stamp Tax struck the most influential groups in the colonies: publishers, lawyers, and merchants. Their reaction was quick and violent.

In Virginia the House of Burgesses, stung by the speech of Patrick Henry, passed a series of resolutions declaring that Parliament did not have the power to tax the colonies. The Sons of Liberty, an organization vigorously opposed to the Stamp Act, appeared in Connecticut and spread to other colonies. Rioting took place in the cities. In Massachusetts the General Court called for all the colonies to send delegates to New York City to consider further action. This meeting, attended by representatives from nine colonies, met in October 1765; it is known as the Stamp Act Congress.

The delegates declared that the colonists could be taxed only by representatives chosen by the colonists. What was equally important, by this meeting the majority of the colonies showed that they were able to unite to defend themselves against Parliament. The Stamp Act Congress and the violence in the cities disturbed the British leaders. When the merchants of New York agreed not to import British goods until the Stamp Act was repealed, they were joined by the Philadelphia merchants. The movement quickly spread to other cities. This *boycott* (refusal to buy) of British goods resulted in a loss of jobs for British workers and a loss of profit for British merchants. Because of these consequences Grenville fell from power. The hated Stamp Tax was repealed, and the colonies were swept by good feeling for the mother country. Toasts were drunk to King George III as the boycott vanished and trade was restored. Unnoticed in the joy of the hour was passage

This hated stamp was pressed onto legal documents when the particular tax was paid by the colonists.

by Parliament of the Declaratory Act of 1766. This act stated that, despite the repeal of the Stamp Act, the British government had complete control of the colonies, including the power of taxation.

The Coming of the Revolution

Charles Townshend, Chancellor of the Exchequer (Head of the Treasury Department), was a sly and clever man. He noticed that the colonists did not object to taxes that were intended to control trade. So, he decided to get Parliament to establish import taxes which apparently controlled trade but actually were meant to raise money. Townshend knew that the colonists were in the habit of avoiding import taxes; consequently, his plan would have to provide a means of enforcing collections. To carry out his scheme a series of laws known as the Townshend Acts were passed in 1767.

The Townshend Acts placed import taxes, or as they are usually known, *duties,* on a number of articles needed by Americans. Among the goods taxed were paper, glass, tea, white lead, and red lead. As time went on other products could be added to the tax list to provide a greater income. Other laws were passed to make sure that the duties were paid. A Board of Commissioners of Customs was set up in Boston to watch over the collection of duties. New courts were created to deal with cases of smuggling. Money from the import taxes was to be used to pay the salaries of tax collectors, governors, judges, and other officials, thus removing them from control by the colonial assemblies.

The colonists saw what Townshend was

The English in New York

trying to do and became very angry. Anger was increased when Parliament declared the New York assembly suspended, that is, stopped from doing business. The reason given was that the assembly had refused to provide enough sleeping quarters and provisions for the British troops stationed in the colony.

Once again the colonial merchants turned to the boycott. An agreement was made not to import goods taxed under the Townshend Acts. The Sons of Liberty reappeared in the northern cities and took over the job of enforcing the boycott. Alarmed by what was happening, British officials sent additional soldiers to Boston. The people of Boston became angrier than ever by the presence of so many troops. The Redcoats, or Lobsters, as the troops were called, were pelted with snowballs, seashells, stones, or anything at hand. Finally, on March 5, 1770, a small group of frightened soldiers fired on a Boston mob, killing five townspeople and wounding six. This unhappy event is known as the Boston Massacre.

On the very day the Massacre took place, Parliament began the repeal of the Townshend Acts. Only the tax on tea was kept in force. An uneasy peace settled over the colonies. In 1772 Samuel Adams persuaded a town meeting in Boston to establish a Committee of Correspondence to keep the other colonies informed of what was happening in Massachusetts. Other colonies set up their own committees, and soon a network bound the colonial leaders together. The committees were important in the movement toward independence. As times became more difficult and the committees reacted more strongly against the British government, those who favored milder treatment of the mother country dropped out. In this way the committees fell into the hands of those who favored forceful action.

The Tea Act of 1773 set into motion the events that resulted in armed conflict between the colonies and the mother country. The law authorized the British East India Company to ship tea directly from the Orient to the colonies, where it would be sold by company agents. This arrangement would lower the cost of tea in the colonies, even after the import duty remaining from the Townshend Acts was paid. Colonial merchants could not compete with the East India Company and considered the law unfair.

The Committees of Correspondence now proved their power. They urged a boycott of the Company's tea. Everywhere the colonists supported the boycott. In Charleston a shipment of tea was stored for three years before it was sold by Revolutionary leaders to raise money for their cause. Samuel Adams was not satisfied with the boycott. On December 16, 1773, a group of his followers, dressed as Indians, boarded three tea ships and dumped the cargo into Boston Harbor. The British government struck back savagely by passing the Intolerable Acts in 1774:

1. The Boston Port Act closed Boston harbor until the tea had been paid for.
2. The Massachusetts Government Act revised the colonial charter, giving the royal governor great powers, including greater control of the courts.
3. A new Quartering Act required that quarters for troops must be furnished immediately upon request or buildings would be seized for that purpose.
4. The Administration of Justice Act provided that officials accused of commit-

ting a crime while enforcing a law in Massachusetts could be tried outside that colony.

The Committees of Correspondence told everyone what was taking place in Massachusetts. All over the colonies people were upset because they realized that what was happening in Massachusetts could happen to them. Within Massachusetts feelings were bitter. General Gage, the British commander, found it necessary to keep his troops in Boston. Outside the city the Massachusetts legislature took control as local citizens banded together in militia units. Because they were to be ready at a moment's notice, these volunteers were known as Minutemen.

Under the influence of Patrick Henry, Thomas Jefferson, and Richard Henry Lee, the Virginia House of Burgesses called for a day of fasting and prayer when Boston harbor was closed. The Governor of Virginia, angered by this act, dissolved the legislature. Most of the members then gathered in a tavern and called for a congress of all the colonies. A few days later Massachusetts issued a similar call. As a result of these invitations, the First Continental Congress met in Philadelphia during September 1774. Only Georgia was not represented.

In an effort to force Parliament to repeal the Intolerable Acts, the First Continental Congress established the Association. This was an agreement not to import British goods until all colonial rights had been restored. The Congress then ordered every county, city, and town to elect a committee to enforce the Association. All across the colonies, elected committees arose to carry out these orders. In this way a Revolutionary government came into being. Before adjourning, the Continental Congress agreed to meet again in May if Parliament failed to meet its demands.

In Boston General Gage found his situation becoming more difficult as the Minutemen grew in numbers and continued to arm themselves. On the night of April 18, 1775, the British general sent a force of 800 Minutemen to destroy colonial military supplies stored at Concord. He also ordered them to arrest Samuel Adams and John Hancock, who were nearby at Lexington. General Gage's plans became known in Boston, and Paul Revere, William Dawes, and Samuel Prescott rode through the countryside spreading the alarm.

Early in the morning on April 19 the British entered Lexington and found themselves facing a band of Minutemen led by Captain John Parker. Firing broke out. The Minutemen withdrew, leaving eight dead. Samuel Adams and John Hancock escaped. The Redcoats pressed on to Concord and destroyed the military stores. Meanwhile, hundreds of Minutemen took positions and fired on the British column as it marched back to Boston. Seventy-three British soldiers were killed and over 200 were wounded or missing. Thousands of Minutemen swarmed around the city. The British were under seige in Boston. The Revolutionary War had begun.

The Colonists Declare Their Independence

Even as the Second Continental Congress met in Philadelphia on May 10, 1775, the Revolutionary War reached New York. On that day Ethan Allen captured Fort Ticonderoga. Two days later Seth Warner took

The Declaration of Independence

IN CONGRESS, JULY 4, 1776

The Unanimous Declaration of the Thirteen United States of America

When in the Course of human events it becomes necessary for one people to dissolve the political bands which have connected them with another, and to assume among the Powers of the earth, the separate and equal station to which the Laws of Nature and of Nature's God entitle them, a decent respect to the opinions of mankind requires that they should declare the causes which impel them to the separation.

We hold these truths to be self-evident, that all men are created equal, that they are endowed by their Creator with certain unalienable Rights, that among these are Life, Liberty and the pursuit of Happiness. —That to secure these rights, Governments are instituted among Men, deriving their just powers from the consent of the governed,—That whenever any Form of Government becomes destructive of these ends, it is the Right of the People to alter or to abolish it, and to institute new Government, laying its foundation on such principles and organizing its powers in such form, as to them shall seem most likely to effect their Safety and Happiness. Prudence, indeed, will dictate that Governments long established should not be changed for light and transient causes; and accordingly all experience hath shewn that mankind are more disposed to suffer, while evils are sufferable, than to right themselves by abolishing the forms to which they are accustomed. But when a long train of abuses and usurpations, pursuing invariably the same Object evinces a design to reduce them under absolute Despotism, it is their right, it is their duty, to throw off such Government, and to provide new Guards for their future security.—Such has been the patient sufferance of these Colonies; and such is now the necessity which constrains them to alter their former Systems of Government. The history of the present King of Great Britain is a history of repeated injuries and usurpations, all having in direct object the establishment of an absolute Tyranny over these States. To prove this, let Facts be submitted to a candid world.

He has refused his Assent to Laws, the most wholesome and necessary for the public good.

He has forbidden his Governors to pass Laws of immediate and pressing importance, unless suspended in their operation till his Assent should be obtained; and when so suspended, he has utterly neglected to attend to them.

He has refused to pass other Laws for the accommodation of large districts of people, unless those people would relinquish the right of Representation in the Legislature, a right inestimable to them and formidable to tyrants only.

He has called together legislative bodies at places unusual, uncomfortable, and distant from the depository of their Public Records, for the sole purpose of fatiguing them into compliance with his measures.

He has dissolved Representative Houses repeatedly, for opposing with manly firmness his invasions on the rights of the people.

He has refused for a long time, after such dissolutions, to cause others to be elected; whereby the Legislative Powers, incapable of Annihilation, have returned to the People at large for their exercise; the State remaining in the mean time exposed to all the dangers of invasion from without, and convulsions within.

He has endeavored to prevent the population of these States; for that purpose obstructing the Laws for Naturalization of Foreigners; refusing to pass others to encourage their migrations hither, and raising the conditions of new Appropriations of Lands.

He has obstructed the Administration of Justice, by refusing his Assent to Laws for establishing Judiciary Powers.

He has made Judges dependent on his Will alone, for the tenure of their offices, and the amount and payment of their salaries.

He has erected a multitude of New Offices, and sent hither swarms of Officers to harass our people, and eat out their substance.

He has kept among us, in times of peace, Standing Armies without the Consent of our legislatures.

He has affected to render the Military independent of and superior to the Civil Power.

He has combined with others to subject us to a jurisdiction foreign to our constitution, and unacknowledged by our laws; giving his Assent to their Acts of pretended Legislation.

For quartering large bodies of armed troops among us:

For protecting them, by a mock Trial, from Punishment for any Murders which they should commit on the Inhabitants of these States:

For cutting off our Trade with all parts of the world:

For imposing Taxes on us without our Consent:

For depriving us in many cases, of the benefits of Trial by Jury:

For transporting us beyond Seas to be tried for pretended offences:

For abolishing the free System of English Laws in a neighbouring Province, establishing therein an Arbitrary government, and enlarging its Boundaries so as to render it at once an example and fit instrument for introducing the same absolute rule into these Colonies:

For taking away our Charters, abolishing our most valuable Laws and altering fundamentally the Forms of our Governments:

For suspending our own Legislatures, and declaring themselves invested with power to legislate for us in all cases whatsoever.

He has abdicated Government here, by declaring us out of his Protection and waging War against us.

He has plundered our seas, ravaged our Coasts, burnt our towns, and destroyed the lives of our people.

He is at this time transporting large armies of foreign mercenaries to compleat the works of death, desolation and tyranny, already begun with circumstances of Cruelty & Perfidy scarcely paralleled in the most barbarous ages, and totally unworthy the Head of a civilized nation.

He has constrained our fellow Citizens taken Captive on the high Seas to bear Arms against their Country, to become the executioners of their friends and Brethren, or to fall themselves by their Hands.

He has excited domestic insurrections amongst us, and has endeavoured to bring on the inhabitants of our frontiers, the merciless Indian Savages, whose known rule of warfare, is an undistinguished destruction of all ages, sexes and conditions.

In every stage of these Oppressions We have Petitioned for Redress in the most humble terms: Our repeated Petitions have been answered only by repeated injury. A Prince, whose character is thus marked by every act which may define a Tyrant, is unfit to be the ruler of a free people.

Nor have We been wanting in attentions to our British brethren. We have warned them from time to time of attempts by their legislature to extend an unwarrantable jurisdiction over us. We have reminded them of the circumstances of our emigration and settlement here. We have appealed to their native justice and magnanimity, and we have conjured them by the ties of our common kindred to disavow these usurpations, which would inevitably interrupt our connections and correspondence. They too have been deaf to the voice of justice and of consanguinity. We must, therefore, acquiesce in the necessity, which denounces our Separation, and hold them, as we hold the rest of mankind, Enemies in War, in Peace Friends.

We therefore, the Representatives of the United States of America, in General Congress, Assembled, appealing to the Supreme Judge of the world for the rectitude of our intentions, do, in the Name, and by Authority of the good People of these Colonies, solemnly publish and declare, That these United Colonies are, and of Right ought to be Free and Independent States; that they are Absolved from all Allegiance to the British Crown, and that all political connection between them and the State of Great Britain, is and ought to be totally dissolved; and that as Free and Independent States, they have full Power to levy War, conclude Peace, contract Alliances, establish Commerce, and to do all other Acts and Things which Independent States may of right do.—And for the support of this Declaration, with a firm reliance on the protection of Divine Providence, we mutually pledge to each other our Lives, our Fortunes and our sacred Honor.

John Hancock (MASS.)

Josiah Bartlett (N.H.)

Philip Livingston (N.Y.)

Robert T. Pain (MASS.)

William Floyd (N.Y.)

John Adams (MASS.)

Francis Lewis (N.Y.)

George Walton (GA.)

Samuel Adams (MASS.)

Richard Stockton (N.J.)

Samuel Huntington (CONN.)

Stephen Hopkins (R.I.)

John Hart (N.J.)

Abraham Clark (N.J.)

Lewis Morris (N.Y.)

John Morton (PA.)

Francis Lightfoot Lee (VA.)

John Penn (N.C.)

Roger Sherman (CONN.)

William Whipple (N.H.)

John Witherspoon (N.J.)

William Ellery (R.I.)

William Hooper (N.C.)

Robert Morris (PA.)

Benjamin Harrison (VA.)

William Williams (CONN.)

Benjamin Franklin (PA.)

William Paca (MD.)

Francis Hopkinson (N.J.)

Thomas Stone (MD.)

Charles Carroll (MD.)

Thomas Jefferson (VA.)

George Taylor (PA.)

Edward Rutledge (S.C.)

Joseph Hewes (N.C.)

James Smith (PA.)

George Ross (PA.)

George Clymer (PA.)

Thomas Heyward, Jr. (S.C.)

Button Gwinnett (GA.)

George Read (DEL.)

James Wilson (PA.)

Thomas Lynch, Jr. (S.C.)

Samuel Chase (MD.)

Carter Braxton (VA.)

Benjamin Rush (PA.)

Lyman Hall (GA.)

Caesar Rodney (DEL.)

Thomas Nelson (VA.)

Arthur Middleton (S.C.)

Crown Point. The Continental Congress immediately took charge of the colonial militia surrounding Boston and named George Washington commander-in-chief of the Continental forces.

The cannon taken at Ticonderoga and Crown Point were sent to General Washington. He made good use of them. Seizing a position overlooking Boston, the American general placed his cannon in a position to bombard the British positions within the city. General Howe, who had replaced Gage as the British commander, realized that his situation was hopeless. On March 12, 1776 he sailed from Boston with his troops, leaving the city in the hands of the Continental Army.

From the French and Indian War to the Revolution

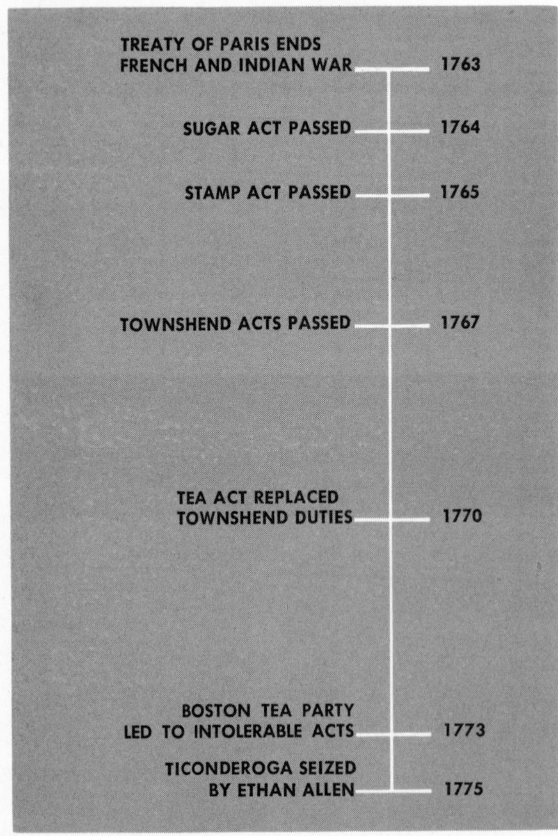

By this time many colonists were beginning to think of independence. Thomas Paine did much to win support for the idea in his pamphlet *Common Sense.* He pointed out the advantages to be gained by separation from the British Empire: freedom to trade anywhere in the world; an end to dealing with a Parliament located some 3,000 miles away; no more trials at British courts; and no involvement in European Wars. Finally, the Continental Congress appointed a committee to draw up a declaration of independence. The members of the committee were John Adams of Massachusetts, Benjamin Franklin of Pennsylvania, Thomas Jefferson of Virginia, Robert R. Livingston of New York, and Roger Sherman of Connecticut. Jefferson did the writing. On July 4, 1776 the Continental Congress approved the Declaration of Independence.

Summary

In all but the self-governing colonies of Connecticut and Rhode Island, a struggle took place between elected assemblies and the governors appointed by the king or the proprietor. Gradually the assemblies won power. They did this by controlling the spending of money.

A series of struggles between the British and French Empires took place between 1689 and 1763. The American colonies were involved and suffered heavy damage from attacks made by the French and their Indian allies. In the Treaty of Paris (1763),

France surrendered to Britain its territory east of the Mississippi except for New Orleans and two small islands. After this the colonists no longer needed British protection against the French.

The Proclamation of 1763 angered fur traders, persons who wished to settle on Indian lands, and land speculators. To raise money to pay for the troops stationed in the colonies, Parliament passed the Sugar Act of 1764 and the Stamp Act of 1765. The colonists felt that Parliament could control trade but should not have the right to tax it. A boycott of British goods resulted in repeal of the Stamp Act.

Parliament now turned to the Townshend Acts to raise revenue by taxing certain imports and by preventing smuggling. The colonial merchants agreed to boycott goods taxed by the Townshend Acts. Parliament then repealed the Acts except for a tax on tea. The Tea Act of 1773 gave the British East India Company control of the tea trade. The Committees of Correspondence then called for a boycott of tea. In Boston the cargoes of tea ships were dumped in the sea. Parliament reacted by passing the Intolerable Acts of 1774, closing Boston harbor until the tea was paid for and reducing the power of the Massachusetts assembly. The First Continental Congress met in Philadelphia and established the Association—an agreement not to buy British goods until colonial rights were restored. When the British sent troops to destroy colonial supplies at Concord, fighting broke out at Lexington, beginning the Revolutionary War.

The Second Continental Congress met in May 1775 and took control of the colonial militia surrounding Boston. George Washington was named commander-in-chief of the Continental forces and drove the British from Boston. Thomas Paine in his pamphlet *Common Sense* argued for independence. On July 4, 1776 the Second Continental Congress approved the Declaration of Independence.

Checking the high points

1. How might the following people have felt about the Proclamation of 1763?

a. an Iroquois Indian

b. a white fur trader

c. a land speculator

d. a member of Parliament

2. Did the colonists have reason to be concerned over the creation of the Dominion of New England? Why? Should colonists in New York have been concerned? In Virginia?

3. What advantage did the assemblies have in their struggle with the governors? How did they use this advantage?

4. Why did the British government call the Albany Congress of 1754? Was it successful?

5. Why is the Treaty of Paris of 1763 important to Americans?

6. How did the Sugar Act of 1764 differ from the Molasses Act of 1733?

7. In what ways did the Stamp Act of 1765 unite the colonies in their opposition to control by the motherland? Why was the boycott so effective a weapon?

8. What were the main provisions of the Townshend Acts?

9. Why were the Intolerable Acts passed? What were their major provisions?

10. What circumstances led to the Battle of Lexington?

11. What were the most important accomplishments of the First Continental Congress?

12. What were Thomas Paine's reasons for favoring independence?

13. What democratic ideals are stated in the Declaration of Independence?

Think these over

1. Did Parliament have a right to expect the colonies to pay part of the cost of keeping troops in the colonies?

2. The defeat of the French in 1763 made it certain that the colonies would become independent. Do you agree or disagree? Why?

3. The colonists said they were fighting for "no taxation without representation" but what they really wanted was freedom to trade wherever and with whomever they wished. Do you agree or disagree? Why?

4. The Declaration of Independence states "all men are created equal." Did the signers really believe this? Do you? Explain.

Vocabulary building

Sons of Liberty
Minutemen
boycott
Committee of Correspondence
Navigation Acts
license
land speculator
duty

Checking locations

Louisbourg
Pittsburgh
Fort Ticonderoga
Dominion of New England
Lexington
Concord
Crown Point

chapter 10: NEW YORKERS FIGHT in the REVOLUTIONARY WAR

chapter 11: NEW YORK BECOMES the EMPIRE STATE

chapter 12: NEW YORK MOVES TOWARD DEMOCRACY

unit four

New York in the Emerging Nation

New York state history dates are shown in color.

1776 Revolutionary War begins
1777 British defeated at Saratoga
N.Y. adopts its first state constitution
1781 British surrender at Yorktown, marking end of Revolutionary War
1785-1789 New York City is the nation's capital
1788 New York ratifies U.S. Constitution and becomes the 11th state
1789 George Washington is elected President
1791 Bill of Rights becomes part of the Constitution
1797 Albany chosen as state capital
1800 Washington, D.C. becomes the nation's capital
1808 Congress outlaws the importation of slaves
1812 War of 1812
1818 New York legislature ends slavery as of 1827
1823 Monroe Doctrine
1825 Erie Canal opens

No state suffered greater losses in property and population than New York during the Revolutionary War. Thousands of New Yorkers fought for each side. About one third of all battles and skirmishes took place on New York soil and waterways.

Both British and American leaders realized the importance of controlling New York harbor, the Hudson Valley, and Lake Champlain. When Britain sent General Burgoyne to capture Albany, the Patriots forced his surrender at Saratoga. This victory, the most important of the war, brought in France as an American ally.

After the war, New York became first in population, agriculture, commerce, transportation, finance, and manufacturing. Citizens from all walks of life—frontier families, merchants, ship captains, speculators, manufacturers, and workers—helped create the Empire State. Able young men, including George Clinton, Alexander Hamilton, and John Jay, came forward to direct the new state government and to serve President George Washington.

New Yorkers formed political parties and joined the movement to secure more democracy. By 1822 New York granted the right to vote to almost all adult white males. De Witt Clinton and other leaders planned, financed, and constructed the Erie Canal, which tightened New York's influence over domestic and foreign trade. This silver streak through three hundred miles of wilderness expressed the boundless energy and daring vision of New Yorkers.

Chapter Objectives

To learn about

- New York's role in the Revolutionary War
- the important Revolutionary War battles fought in New York

chapter 10

NEW YORKERS FIGHT in the REVOLUTIONARY WAR

New York Declares Its Independence

New Yorkers followed the example of Massachusetts in resisting the British government's efforts to impose taxes. As we have seen, the Sons of Liberty arose to protest the Stamp Act and later the Townshend Act. Although most members were small shopkeepers and artisans, the leaders were usually men of some wealth and influence. When the British passed the Tea Act in 1773, the merchants promptly joined hands with the Sons of Liberty. They resented this act which gave the British East India Company the right to sell tea in the American colonies. A document entitled "The Association of the Sons of Liberty" called for the boycott of anyone accepting tea from the hated company. The first tea ship to reach New York returned to England without unloading. When the second ship arrived, angry New Yorkers boarded it and dumped the tea into the harbor.

As you have read, when Boston had its famous "Tea Party," the British government punished Massachusetts by passing a series of laws called the Intolerable Acts. One law closed Boston harbor until the tea was paid for. New Yorkers were worried that the British would strike at New York with similar laws. In New York City a committee was created to deal with the problem. Meanwhile, the colonists sent delegates to the First Continental Congress, which met in Philadelphia to discuss a boycott against Great Britain. The New York delegates voted against the plan.

Congress called upon each county, city, and town to elect committees to enforce the boycott. Within a year local committees were formed in most parts of the colony.

The New York Assembly, still run by Loyalists, refused to approve the Association. It also refused to send delegates to the Second Continental Congress. When this happened, the Sons of Liberty set up a Provincial Congress, representing all New York. The Provincial Congress selected delegates to the Second Continental Congress.

At Fort Ticonderoga, a guide in a uniform of the Colonial period shows how the old cannon were fired. Note the national flag of 1777 flying over this strategic fort that has been held by the French, the British, the Colonial Patriots, and the Americans.

The foundations of the Revolutionary government were now laid. At the top was the Continental Congress, which could pass orders to the Provincial Congress, which, in turn, could direct the activities of the town, city, and county committees. As the feeling between Great Britain and the colonists grew more bitter, these organizations took on more and more power until they became the government.

When news of the Battle of Lexington reached New York City, the local citizens seized about 600 British muskets and formed bands to protect the colony. Upstate, the same thing was happening.

There was still no demand for independence. For many reasons, the people did not want to break with the Empire. After all, for over a century they had been loyal to the British government. Many farmers in the frontier region were afraid the Indians would burn their farms if British soldiers left the area. New York merchants needed the protection of the British fleet on the high seas. They also needed the right to buy and sell within the Empire. Many of the well-to-do merchants and landlords were worried about the democratic beliefs of the Sons of Liberty. They feared that a revolutionary government might take away their privileges and perhaps their wealth. Probably there was a higher percentage of Loyalists in New York than in any other state. In any case, over 30,000 Loyalists left New York when the Revolution ended.

During the winter and spring of 1775–1776 the arguments over independence grew hotter. The fighting at Boston and the news that Great Britain had decided to use force to crush the colonies made many think that independence was the only answer. A number of well-known New Yorkers called for independence. Among these were Isaac Sears, John Lamb, and Alexander McDougall—the fiery leaders of the Sons of Liberty. Also favoring independence were George Clinton, who would soon become the first governor of New York State; John Jay, who was to become a governor of New York and first Chief Justice of the United States; and Alexander Hamilton, who would make a fine record as the first Secretary of the Treasury of the United States. On the other hand, many New Yorkers hesitated. When the Second Continental Congress adopted the Declaration of Independence on July 4, 1776, the delegates from New York did not sign it.

On October 19, 1775, the British representative, Acting Governor Tryon, fled from New York City to a British warship anchored in the harbor. The Provincial Congress declared that this action left the colony without a government. It therefore called for the establishment of a new government. A newly elected Provincial Congress met in the courthouse at White Plains on July 9, 1776. It approved the Declaration of Independence, which was then signed by New York's delegates to the Continental Congress. With this act, New York became an independent state. Later it was to join with the other colonies to form the United States of America. On July 10, the Provincial Congress changed its name to the Convention of the Representatives of the State of New York.

The Conquest of New York City

As we have seen, fighting between the American colonies and Great Britain broke out in April, 1775, over a year before New York declared her independence from the mother country. When Paul Revere brought news of the fighting in Massachusetts, New Yorkers prepared for the struggle. Blacksmiths worked night and day to make gun barrels and bayonets. Carpenters dropped their saws and clerks shut their record books to pick up muskets and train for war. Loyalists found it safer to keep off the streets. President Myles Cooper of King's College had to flee from his bed to escape a band of Patriots. The Provincial Congress seized power from the dying Assembly, and New Yorkers were now very much in the Revolution.

Thrilled with the victory at Boston, the Americans decided to attack Canada. In the fall of 1775 Richard Montgomery, a New

United Empire Loyalists

The American Revolution created an independent New York State and led to the establishment of the United States of America. It also created British North America.

Thousands of colonists, especially those in New York, remained loyal to the British Empire. The great majority were tradesmen, farmers, storekeepers, and people of ordinary means as well as some large landholders and professional men. Since most American communities were spiteful toward the Loyalists, approximately 50,000 decided to leave. In 1783, large numbers took ship for Nova Scotia, where about two-thirds finally settled. The next year several thousand settled in Quebec and along the upper St. Lawrence River and the northeastern shores of Lake Ontario.

The Loyalists underwent many hardships, since most of them lost their possessions. Some fled across Lake Ontario in small boats. Others paddled down the Richelieu River. When they arrived in Nova Scotia or Quebec, they had to live through the winter in tents or makeshift cabins. To be sure, the British government made generous gifts for their support as well as donations of land, farm tools, and livestock. Nevertheless, the first years were difficult ones before the little clearings yielded crops enough for their needs. It was very hard to start a new settlement.

Governor Guy Carleton gave the Loyalists the right to put the initials U.E.L., for the United Empire Loyalists, after their names as a title of honor. Canadians today pay tribute to the U.E.L. for their courage in pioneering, their share in establishing a parliamentary system of government, and their loyalty to Britain. New Yorkers are interested in knowing that many of the New York Tories such as John Johnson and Joseph Brant played an honorable role in building Canada.

Reading the Declaration of Independence at White Plains, New York, July 11, 1776. The Court House here pictured was destroyed by fire the following November. This painting is now in the County Trust Company in Yonkers.

Yorker, moved northward on Lake Champlain with about 1200 men and captured Montreal. Pushing on down the St. Lawrence River, he joined forces with an expedition from Maine led by Benedict Arnold. They attacked Quebec in a blinding snowstorm. Montgomery was killed in the battle. New Yorkers later named a county after him. The Americans slowly retreated to Lake Champlain.

The British wanted to take New York City as a first step in putting down the Revolution. The docks, housing, and storage space made the city a good place to land an army with its supplies. From New York City the fleet could attack cities along the Atlantic Coast and could *blockade* the colonies. A blockade is the use of military force to cut off supplies.

Knowing these facts, New Yorkers in the spring of 1776 were worried. They had good reason, for Indians and Loyalists, led by Sir John Johnson, Guy Johnson, John Butler, and Walter Butler, were raiding the northern frontier. A seaborne attack on New York City was expected.

On April 13 General George Washington arrived in New York City to prepare its defenses. At the end of June, Sir William Howe landed on Staten Island. General Howe had an army of 31,000 men, who were fully equipped, well trained, and experienced in warfare. In addition, he could get help from the British fleet commanded by his brother, Admiral Sir Richard Howe. Against this powerful enemy General Washington had 28,000 poorly trained and poorly supplied soldiers, many of whom were ill. Nor could General Washington give all his attention to General Howe, because, in Canada, Sir Guy Carleton, another British general, was preparing an invasion. Howe was to seize the mouth of the Hudson while Carleton took the upper Hudson Valley; then the two would join forces near Albany.

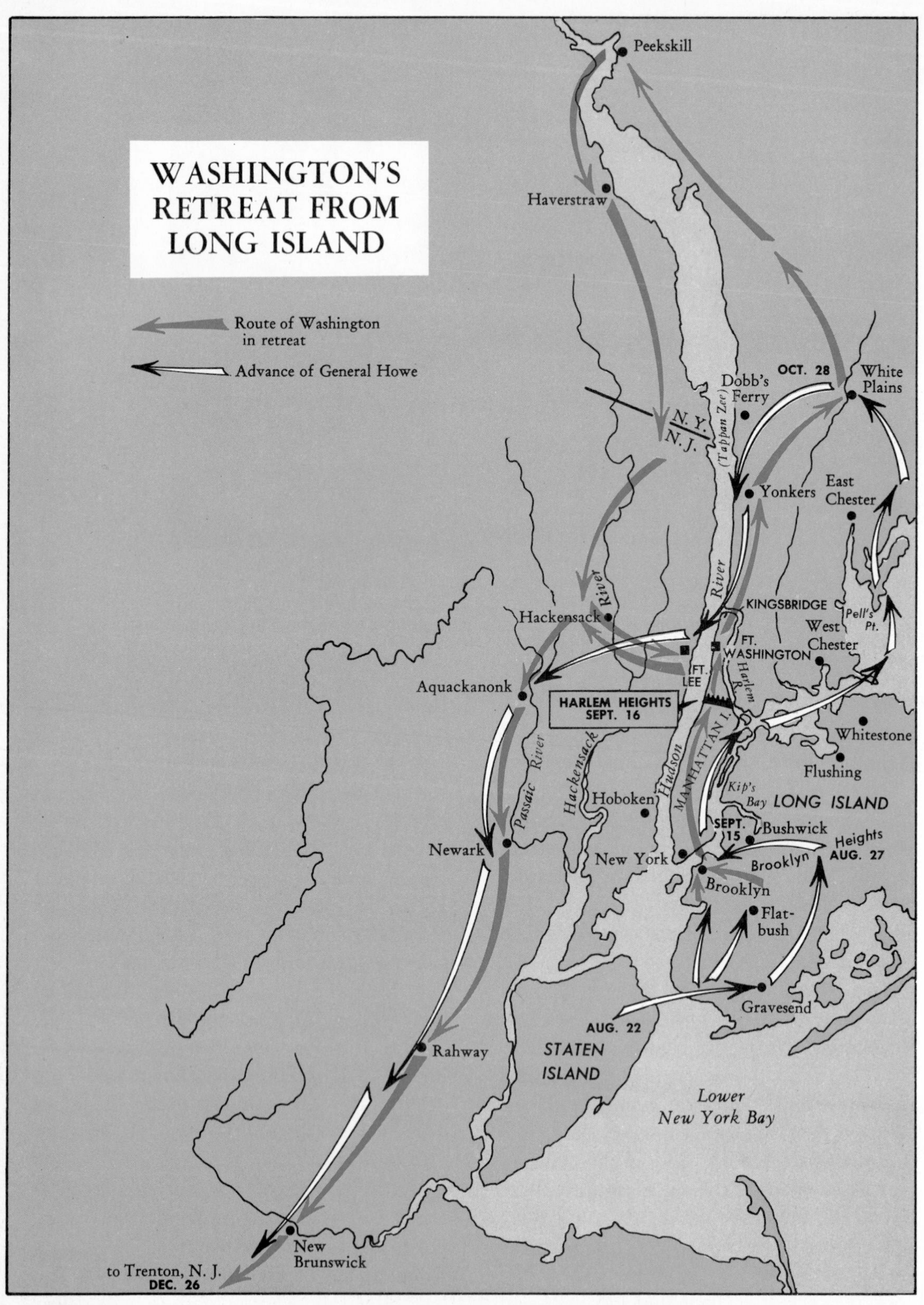

WASHINGTON'S RETREAT FROM LONG ISLAND
Route of Washington in retreat
Advance of General Howe
Peekskill
Haverstraw
OCT. 28
White Plains
Dobb's Ferry
(Tappan Zee)
N. Y.
N. J.
Yonkers
East Chester
River
River
KINGSBRIDGE
Pell's Pt.
West Chester
Hackensack
FT. WASHINGTON
FT. LEE
Harlem R.
Aquackanonk
HARLEM HEIGHTS SEPT. 16
MANHATTAN I.
Whitestone
Flushing
Hackensack
Passaic River
Hudson
Kip's Bay
LONG ISLAND
Hoboken
SEPT. 15
Bushwick
Heights
Newark
New York
Brooklyn
AUG. 27
Brooklyn
Flatbush
Gravesend
AUG. 22
STATEN ISLAND
Rahway
Lower New York Bay
New Brunswick
to Trenton, N. J.
DEC. 26

Map 18

General Howe moved part of his army to Long Island and attacked the Patriots, who were behind fortifications at Brooklyn Heights. The British attack was successful. General Washington rushed to the scene to find his troops thoroughly defeated and confused. With great courage and calmness he reorganized them and brought them safely across the East River to Manhattan. He did this in the dead of night and under the nose of the British fleet. General Howe awoke the next morning to find the American army gone. No wonder the British began to call General Washington the Old Fox. Map 18, page 138, shows the movements of the British and American forces in the struggle for New York City.

On September 15, General Howe captured New York City (which then included only the southern tip of Manhattan), and Washington moved his forces northward. The next day the British attacked the Patriots, who had fortified the upper part of Manhattan. This is known as the Battle of Harlem Heights. The British were driven back. The victory encouraged the Americans. A short time later Captain Nathan Hale, who had been sent to spy on the British, was captured and hanged. The brave way the young officer met death increased the determination of the Patriots.

General Howe began moving his army up the East River. If you will look at Map 18, you can see why he did this. If he could

This painting by Alonzo Chappel caught the feeling of the disorderly retreat of some American troops during the battle of Long Island.

New Windsor Cantonment, near Vail's Gate, was the site of the final encampment of the Revolutionary forces in the winter of 1782–83. This officer's hut is the only existing original building built and used by Washington's soldiers. Others usually seen in historic spots are reconstructions.

get the British army behind the Americans—that is, north of them—he could drive them southward to the bay. There they would be trapped. The Old Fox was too wise to be caught by this trick. Keeping ahead of the enemy, he moved his forces northward, leaving a garrison of about 3,000 troops in Fort Washington on the upper end of Manhattan Island. Since he could not get behind the Patriots, General Howe attacked them at White Plains. The Americans were driven back, but the British suffered heavy losses. By this time Fort Washington was deep in enemy territory and had to surrender. About 2,800 men were captured, together with a large amount of military supplies.

The struggle between General Washington and General Howe now shifted to New Jersey and Pennsylvania. The battle for New York City had lasted three months. The Patriots had lost most of their cannon. Four thousand of their soldiers were prisoners. Six hundred of their men were dead, and a large number were wounded. Fortunately, these defeats around New York City were balanced by a victory in the north.

The Patriots Check Invasion

The British plans in 1776 called for Sir Guy Carleton to invade the upper Hudson Valley. Knowing that the British had more men and better weapons than the Patriots, General Benedict Arnold, in command of the Patriots, decided to try to slow down the advance of the enemy. He hoped that winter weather would force General Carleton to withdraw to Canada. With great effort, the Patriots built a small fleet of fighting ships on Lake Champlain. As a result, the British could not move their men and supplies over the lake. In turn, Carleton stopped to build a fleet to attack the American warships. It took the entire summer to do this. Finally, on October 11, 1776, the two fleets met in battle off Valcour Island, near Plattsburgh. The American warships were destroyed after a fierce fight in which the British suffered heavy damage.

Following his victory at Valcour Island, General Carleton recaptured Crown Point. By then it was almost winter and he was afraid to try to take Fort Ticonderoga, which was defended by 9,000 Patriots. For this reason Carleton returned to Canada. With courage and skill, Benedict Arnold had delayed the British and had forced them to retreat to Canada to avoid a winter campaign in the Lake Champlain area.

In 1777 the British planned three moves. General John Burgoyne, known as Gentleman Johnny, was to move up the Richelieu River, over Lakes Champlain and George, and overland to the upper Hudson Valley. He was to accomplish what Carleton had failed to do. Colonel Barry St. Leger was to advance up the Oswego River, and march to the Mohawk River and down that river to the Hudson. Sir William Howe was to send forces up the Hudson to meet St. Leger and Burgoyne. If you look at Map 19, page 142, you will see that this was a good plan, which, if successful, would capture New York.

On July 5, 1777, General Burgoyne appeared before Fort Ticonderoga. The Patriots abandoned the fort when Burgoyne placed cannon on nearby Mt. Defiance.

General Philip Schuyler realized that he could not risk an open battle with the British. Therefore, he decided to delay the advance of the enemy. He had his men set up log blockades, by cutting down huge trees along the route. This clever plan was very successful against Gentleman Johnny, who was trying to move many cannon and military supplies through the forests. While General Burgoyne struggled through the tangle, local citizens drove off their farm animals and burned their fields. Not until July 30 did General Burgoyne reach Fort Edward, at the bend of the Hudson River. It took the British army over three weeks to move almost 22 miles from Skenesboro (Whitehall) to Fort Edward—a distance that we can travel today in less than one hour by automobile.

General Burgoyne soon found his food supply low. On August 13 he sent some of his soldiers to capture American supplies at Bennington, Vermont. Three days later this band of raiders was badly defeated by two groups of Patriots under the command of Seth Warner and John Stark at Walloomsac, New York. The fight is known as the Battle of Bennington. This victory encouraged the Americans, and they flocked from the villages and countryside to join the army under General Horatio Gates. A few days later the Patriots were further encouraged by good news from the Mohawk Valley.

You will remember that Colonel Barry St. Leger was to advance along the Mohawk to join Burgoyne and Howe. He was accompanied by Loyalists led by Sir John Johnson and Colonel John Butler, and by Indians under Joseph Brant, a Mohawk chief. On August 3 this force appeared outside Fort Stanwix. The defenders were badly outnumbered. Realizing the seriousness of the situation, General Nicholas Herkimer moved toward Fort Stanwix with reinforcements. While on the march, General Herkimer was surprised near Oriskany. Here neighbor fought neighbor, because many of Johnson's and Butler's men were Loyalists who had come from the Mohawk

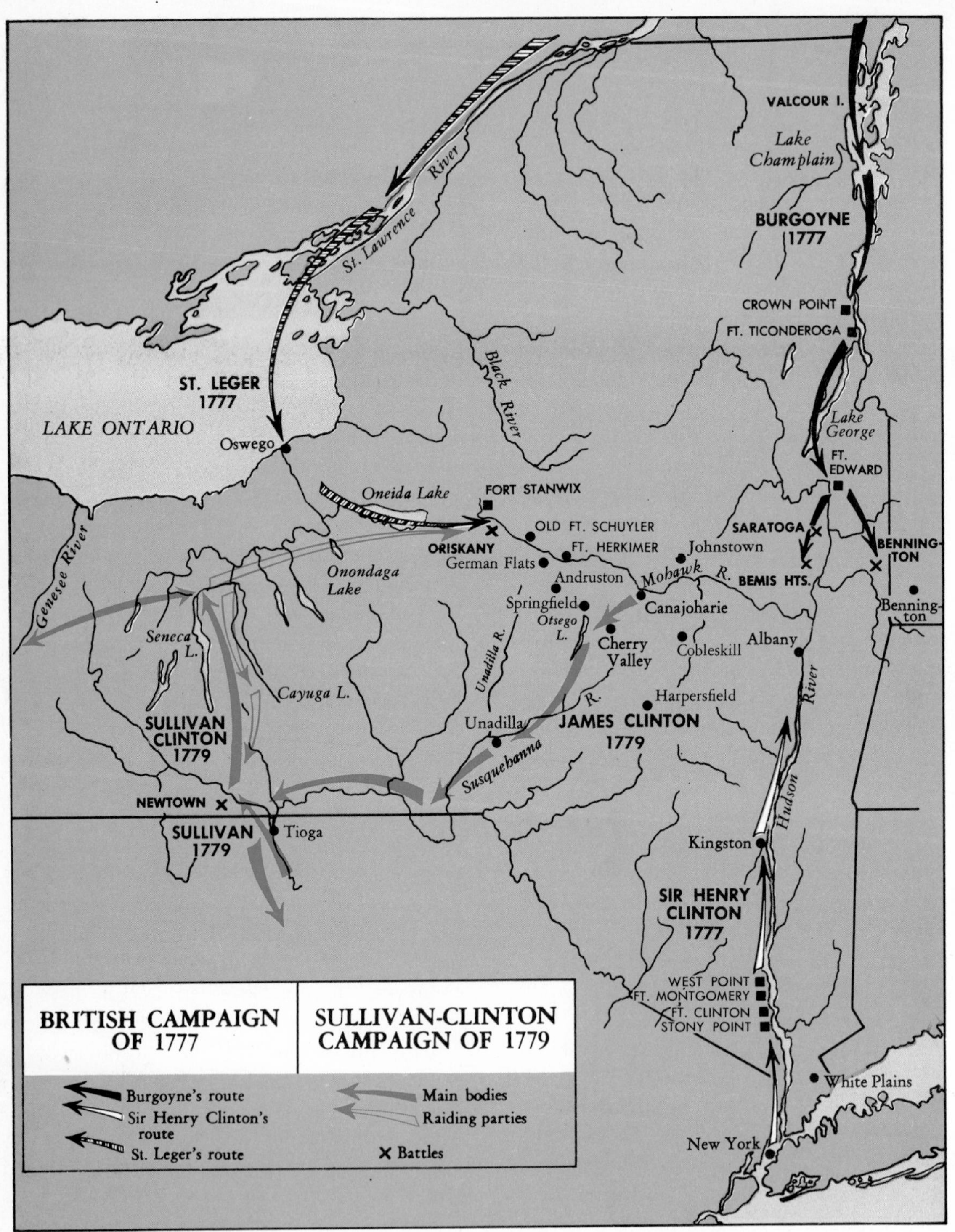
VALCOUR I.
Lake Champlain
BURGOYNE 1777
CROWN POINT
FT. TICONDEROGA
Lake George
FT. EDWARD
SARATOGA
BENNINGTON
BEMIS HTS.
Bennington
St. Lawrence River
ST. LEGER 1777
LAKE ONTARIO
Oswego
Black River
Oneida Lake
FORT STANWIX
ORISKANY
OLD FT. SCHUYLER
FT. HERKIMER
German Flats
Johnstown
Andruston
Mohawk R.
Springfield
Otsego L.
Canajoharie
Cherry Valley
Cobleskill
Albany
Genesee River
Onondaga Lake
Seneca L.
Cayuga L.
Unadilla R.
Harpersfield
Unadilla
JAMES CLINTON 1779
Susquehanna R.
SULLIVAN CLINTON 1779
NEWTOWN
SULLIVAN 1779
Tioga
Hudson River
Kingston
SIR HENRY CLINTON 1777
WEST POINT
FT. MONTGOMERY
FT. CLINTON
STONY POINT
White Plains
New York
BRITISH CAMPAIGN OF 1777
SULLIVAN-CLINTON CAMPAIGN OF 1779
Burgoyne's route
Sir Henry Clinton's route
St. Leger's route
Main bodies
Raiding parties
Battles

Map 19

region. Early in the struggle, General Herkimer's leg was smashed, and his horse killed. The courageous general then sat at the base of a beech tree and directed the fight, as he calmly smoked his pipe. Herkimer noticed that the Indians would wait for one of the Patriots to shoot and then would rush in to tomahawk him before he could reload. He reorganized his defenses by putting two men in each position. When an Indian ran in to kill a Patriot who had just fired his gun, he would be shot by the second American. Discouraged by this deadly treatment, the Indians broke off the attack. Many of them deserted Colonel St. Leger and vanished into the forest. A few days later, General Benedict Arnold arrived with more Americans, and the British fled, leaving much equipment behind.

In the middle of September, General Burgoyne crossed the Hudson at old Saratoga (now Schuylerville) and began his advance down the river. The struggle which followed is known as the Battle of Saratoga. General Gates placed his army behind fortifications at Bemis Heights and waited for the British attack. Twice Burgoyne tried to break through the American lines only to lose hundreds of men. On October 9 Burgoyne began to retreat. By now, Gentleman Johnny was in serious trouble. There was no sign of General Howe's army, which, he hoped, would move up the Hudson and attack the Americans from behind. Burgoyne's supplies were running low, and many of his soldiers were ill or wounded. By October 12 the Americans had over 17,000 men, while the British had fewer than 5,000 fit for fighting. Five days later, General Burgoyne surrendered.

This victory not only saved New York from being divided or defeated, but it also encouraged George Washington and all the Patriots in the other states. Furthermore, it caused the French government to enter into an alliance with the rebellious Americans. The French, smarting from their loss of Canada in 1763, were eager to get revenge. Perhaps, too, they might be able to secure the American trade and regain their former territories. As a result, the French king decided to ally his country with the Americans. French soldiers, sailors, and money played an important part in the final victory.

This picture of Joseph Brant, the Mohawk chief, was painted in 1786 by the famous American artist, Gilbert Stuart.

We do not know why the British failed to cooperate better. But we know that Howe decided to attack Philadelphia, where the Continental Congress was meeting. Sir

General Herkimer directs his troops at the battle of Oriskany.

Henry Clinton, whom Howe had left at New York City with eight or nine thousand men, moved up the Hudson with a part of that force. He captured several forts and burned Kingston, the meeting place of the Provincial Congress, on October 16. But his weak force could advance no further even though he learned that Burgoyne's situation was desperate. Not wishing to face the large Patriot army under Gates, Clinton retreated to New York City.

With courage and skill, the Americans had crushed a major British offensive. It is interesting to see that this entire action took place within the boundaries of New York State, although many of the defenders came from other states.

The Frontier War

In 1778 the British attacked the frontier settlements. These raids were carried out chiefly by Indians and Loyalists, many of whom were frontiersmen. The raiders had able leaders, such as Colonel John Butler, his son Walter Butler, and the Mohawk chief, Joseph Brant. Although the attacking forces were small, they were made up of men who were wise in the ways of the wilderness. Bands of such men moved quickly and struck hard before the Patriots could gather men for defense. Even though Joseph Brant and the British officers usually tried to protect them, all too often defenseless women and children were abused or killed by the attacking Indians.

The British burned Cobleskill in May. They destroyed Springfield in June. In July, Andrustown, near the present city of Herkimer, was burned. All these attacks were much like the raid on German Flats which took place on September 13. A scout had warned the Patriots that the raiders were coming. The inhabitants left their homes and went to three fortified buildings. The attacking Loyalists and Indians paid no attention to the defenders in these fortifications, but swept down on the village. They drove off the cattle, carried away anything they wanted, and burned all the buildings.

Fortunately, few lives were lost. A similar raid was carried out against Cherry Valley. Here the raiders surprised several people outside the blockhouse and killed or captured them.

The purpose of the British raids was to weaken the fighting power of the Patriots. Food and horses for the American armies came from the frontier settlements. Raiding parties destroyed these supplies. The Patriots also had to weaken their forces in other parts of the state to defend the frontier. So the frontier attacks served several military purposes.

General Washington realized that the British attacks were a serious drain on New York. He knew that many of the raiders were Indians and that Loyalist raiders obtained food and shelter at Indian villages. For these reasons he planned an attack against the Iroquois in central and western New York. The campaign began in April 1779, and lasted until October. Map 19 shows the paths of the Patriot war parties.

Schoharie's Old Stone Fort is one of the few remaining Revolutionary War forts in existence. Erected as a church in 1772, the building was fortified during the Revolution, and is now a history museum.

The Clintons

Four men who shared the name Clinton are important in the early history of New York State. Three of them were related.

Sir Henry Clinton. **A British general who fought against the Patriots in the Revolutionary War.**

George Clinton. **The first governor of New York State and a leader in the revolt against Great Britain.**

James Clinton. **A brother of George Clinton and a general in the Patriotic army. A leader of the Sullivan-Clinton campaign.**

De Witt Clinton. **The son of James Clinton and the nephew of George Clinton. He became governor of New York State and is known for his successful effort to have the Erie Canal built.**

General Washington ordered General James Clinton to begin the campaign. First, Clinton sent a party from Fort Stanwix to the region of Onondaga Lake. Here, Indian villages and supplies were burned. Next, Clinton moved his troops and supplies to Lake Otsego. The outlet of the lake was dammed at the present location of Cooperstown, and the water level raised two feet. When all was ready the dam was broken, and the soldiers floated their supplies down the flooded waters of the Susquehanna River in boats. They destroyed the Indian settlements along the way. Clinton joined forces with General John Sullivan at Tioga, near Waverly. Their combined forces numbered about 3,500 men. The Patriots advanced to Newtown, near what is now the city of Elmira. Here a small and poorly equipped band of Indians and Loyalists under John Butler tried to stop them. Twelve of Butler's men were killed and three of Sullivan's. Not much of a battle, you may say. Yet the Battle of Newtown was a very serious effort to stop the Patriot forces.

The Sullivan-Clinton expedition traveled to the valley of the Genesee River and back. It passed through the heart of the Seneca country, burning villages, destroying orchards, and killing cattle. It weakened the power of the Indians to raid the frontier, and meant that the British now had to furnish food and supplies to their Indian allies.

However, the Sullivan-Clinton campaign did not end the frontier raids. Joseph Brant destroyed Minisink in 1779, even while the attacks against the Iroquois were going on. In the following year Harpersfield, Johnstown, Canajoharie, and German Flats were attacked. Nevertheless, the raids did become fewer. The last battle of the Revolutionary War to be fought on New York soil was against raiders near Johnstown in 1781. Here 400 Patriots forced some 600 British, Loyalists, and Indians to retreat. Fighting to protect the rear of his force from the hotly pursuing Patriots, Walter Butler was shot and killed. The Patriots were so happy at the death of the famous raider that they sent his scalp to Albany.

In the meantime, one of the most daring deeds in all American history took place in New York: the capture of Stony Point on July 16, 1779 by a chosen body of Patriots led by General "Mad" Anthony Wayne. The British believed that their strong position at Stony Point could not be taken. On land sticking out a half mile into the Hudson River and rising 150 feet above the water, the fort was surrounded by the river on three sides. On the land side it was protected by a marsh. The central part of the fortress was behind two rows of sharpened wooden stakes placed in back of the marsh to hold off invaders.

Major Military Campaigns Fought in New York During the Revolution

Campaigns of 1776

August-November. Sir William Howe took New York City.

September-October. Sir Guy Carleton attempted an invasion across Lake Champlain. Delayed by American resistance, the British withdrew to Canada. The major engagement was the Battle of Valcour Island.

Campaigns of 1777

June-October. General John Burgoyne invaded the upper Hudson Valley. The British Army surrendered at Saratoga on October 17.

July-August. Colonel Barry St. Leger invaded the Upper Mohawk Valley by way of Oswego. Checked by General Herkimer at the Battle of Oriskany, the British retreated to Canada.

October. General Sir Henry Clinton led a British Army up the Hudson. Clinton returned to New York City after he had burned Kingston.

Clinton-Sullivan Campaign of 1779

April-October. An army of Patriots led by Generals John Sullivan and James Clinton destroyed Iroquois villages in western New York.

Frontier Raids

In 1778, 1779, 1780, and 1781, a series of destructive raids on the frontier were carried out by British and Indians.

Blacks and the Revolution

The Revolutionary War provided opportunities for some blacks to escape slavery, and they seized every chance. When wealthy Loyalists fled, they often had to leave their slaves behind. These blacks became free. In 1784 the New York Legislature freed all slaves belonging to Loyalists. In addition, the British played a part in freeing slaves. Sir Henry Clinton, commander-in-chief of the British forces, declared in 1779 that all slaves who fled to British lines would become freemen. He wanted to deprive the Patriots of forced labor, but he also hoped to hire ex-slaves to work for his army, and to enlist some of them as soldiers. As a result a large number of blacks did accept Clinton's promises.

Few blacks fought on the Patriot side. Why should they support a revolutionary cause which clearly had no intention of ending slavery? Nevertheless some did fight, and with distinction. The state legislature in 1781 granted freedom to any slave who served three years in the Patriot army. Because a slave needed the permission of his owner, the legislature granted the owner 500 acres of public land for each slave he allowed to join the Patriots.

Meanwhile some New Yorkers, including John Jay and Alexander Hamilton, were beginning to attack slavery on moral grounds.

Some steps were taken to reduce slavery. A state law in 1799 declared that all male children born to a slave woman after July 4, 1799 would be free at the age of 28. But New Yorkers still treated their black countrymen as different and inferior. For example, black men had to meet higher standards to vote than those set for white men. Clearly the failure of whites to grant equality to blacks represented a great injustice, not to mention a vast loss of talents and abilities.

General Wayne's force, divided into three groups, attacked at night. One group was to pretend to attack the center of the British line by keeping up a rapid fire. Meanwhile, the other two groups were to enter the fortifications on the right and left. At the head of each of these two groups were 150 brave men carrying axes to cut through the wooden stakes. With both groups of axmen was a "forlorn hope," or what today we would call a suicide squad.

The Patriots' plan worked very well. The British were drawn to the center by the shooting in that area. Meanwhile, the axmen cut through the two lines of stakes. The American right and left, led by the forlorn hope and using only bayonets and knives, charged into the fortress shouting "The fort's our own!" In the darkness the attackers identified each other by pieces of white paper worn in their hats.

The speed and courage of the Patriots overwhelmed the confused defenders. The British lost 15 pieces of artillery and a large quantity of military supplies. Five hundred and forty-three British soldiers were captured, over 70 were wounded, and 63 were killed. The American losses were 80 wounded, one of whom was General Wayne, and 15 killed. All through the nation the Patriots cheered the success of this daring attack. There is now a state park at Stony Point. You will find it an interesting place to visit.

In September of 1780, Major John Andre, a British officer who was carrying messages from General Benedict Arnold to Sir Henry Clinton, was captured near Tarrytown. As a result, Arnold's treason came to light.

Arnold had written to General Sir Henry Clinton, the Commander of the British

Army in New York City, saying that he was ready to change sides and turn against the Patriots. Arnold commanded the garrison at West Point and agreed to surrender it. If West Point were turned over to the enemy, Sir Henry Clinton could move up the Hudson, join forces with other British troops coming southward, and could cut off all of New England. The Patriots in the Mohawk Valley were too busy fighting raiders to stop Clinton. Fortunately, the plan was unsuccessful. Arnold fled to the British lines. Major Andre, although he was well liked by both the Americans and the British, was hanged as a spy near Tappan.

Benedict Arnold's treason was the last serious threat to New York. The British General Cornwallis surrendered at Yorktown, Virginia on October 19, 1781. There was little fighting after that date. Finally, on September 3, 1783, a treaty was signed in which the British government recognized the independence of her former colonies.

Waves of excitement swept New York City on November 25. British soldiers rowed into the harbor and climbed aboard warships, which carried them out to sea. A parade started with General Washington and Governor Clinton in the lead. Behind them marched Patriot troops followed by citizens on horseback and on foot. Cheers rose from the crowds as General Washington came into view. Here was the man who had outfought the British and who had kept the cause of freedom alive in the darkest hours.

Over Fort George waved the Stars and Stripes—a warning to the kings of Europe, and a promise of freedom for America. New Yorkers turned their backs on their heavy losses and began to build the Empire State.

Summary

New York played a very important part in the Revolutionary War. New Yorkers were not united. Some remained loyal to Great Britain, while others joined the Continental army. Gradually the Provincial Congress took control of New York and on July 9, 1776 approved the Declaration of Independence.

In the fighting that followed, the British gained control of New York City. However, the Patriots stopped an invasion of New York at the Battle of Valcour Island. No state suffered greater damage than New York. Nearly one-third of all the battles fought in the war took place on New York soil, of which the most important was the Battle of Saratoga. General Burgoyne was forced to surrender there.

The war on the frontier was particularly bloody because the British and their Indian allies raided poorly defended Patriot villages. The Sullivan-Clinton expedition carried the war to the Senecas. Finally, in 1781 the British surrendered at Yorktown, Virginia, in the last important battle of the Revolution. The treaty of peace, in 1783, which was signed at Paris, gave the American colonies their independence.

Checking the high points

1. If you had been a New York merchant would you have supported the Association of the Sons of Liberty? Why? If you had been a New Yorker, but not a merchant, would you have supported it? Why?

2. What were the most important developments in the struggle against Britain in 1775 and 1776?

3. Why did the Intolerable Acts worry New Yorkers?

4. Why is the Battle of Saratoga sometimes called the turning point of the Revolution?

5. Was the British plan of attack in 1777—the St. Leger-Burgoyne-Howe campaign—a good one? Why?

6. You are a Patriot in the Mohawk Valley. What is your opinion of the following?

a. Walter Butler
b. Nicholas Herkimer
c. Joseph Brant

7. Was the Sullivan-Clinton campaign successful? Why?

8. What military advantages did the British get from the frontier raids?

9. Why was the attack at Stony Point important?

Think these over

1. Were Loyalists traitors?

2. Was Benedict Arnold really a traitor? Do you think his good points balanced his bad?

3. New Yorkers often think that their state did more to win the Revolutionary War than other states. What do you think about this point of view?

4. Why is George Washington considered a great general?

Checking locations

To understand this chapter you needed to turn to the map on page 138. Are you sure you know the location of these places? Check yourself.

White Plains	Harlem Heights
Peekskill	Fort Lee
Brooklyn Heights	Pell's Point

Vocabulary building

Give the meaning of these words in the chapter.

Loyalist	garrison
Patriot	blockade
Tory	treason
aristocracy	assault
ambush	prosperity
"forlorn hope"	cantonment
strategic	"suicide squad"

Chapter Objectives

To learn about

- the influx of colonial settlers into New York in the late 18th and early 19th centuries
- how improved transportation affected the growth and expansion of New York
- how pioneers lived and farmed in New York

chapter 11

NEW YORK BECOMES the EMPIRE STATE

The Yankee Invasion

The New England migration to New York is a thrilling story. The Yankees came by land and by sea, in winter and in summer, in groups and as individuals. Ships sailed up the Hudson laden with the household goods of families. Sleighs and ox carts came overland through the steep hills fringing the state border. During a three-day period in 1795, about 1200 sleighs passed through Albany on the way to the Genesee country. During the summer, settlers often used boats, which rivermen poled up the Mohawk. Others preferred to take one of the roads pointing westward from Catskill, Kingston, or Albany. Wagons carried only the absolute necessities—pots, pans, beds, and farm tools. The young, the old, and sick rode; the ablebodied men and women walked. The two or three cows and scraggly sheep were driven ahead of the wagons by the young men and boys.

Even before the Revolution, Yankees had made important settlements within New York. Practically all of Long Island east of Brooklyn and the eastern townships of Westchester and Dutchess counties were settled by New Englanders. After the Revolution a tidal wave of settlers moved westward from Connecticut, Massachusetts, and Vermont to New York. By 1820 about two out of every three residents of New York had Yankee ancestors.

The chief reason the Yankees migrated to New York was to find new farms. In Massachusetts high taxes and falling prices ruined thousands of farmers. The soil of much of southern New England was worn out by poor methods of farming.

Families were large in those days. People married young and had many children. Because of the large families, some of the young people had to leave home and seek new land. Still other Yankees disliked the special privileges of the Congregational Church which received money from the taxpayers. For all these reasons, but especially because they wanted land, thousands of people were eager to leave the New England states.

Restless Yankees knew from the reports of missionaries and from the veterans of General Sullivan's army that New York's soil would be fine for farming. The first pioneers wrote back enthusiastic letters, urging their relatives and neighbors to come to New York. Hugh White of Whitestown (near Utica) sent back to his friends his tallest stalks of corn, his largest potatoes and onions. Land agents handed out handbills offering new farms at low prices with payment over a long period of time.

The Yankees swept into the valleys and villages of almost every section of New York. The small Dutch settlements in the Hudson Valley and the German settlements along the Mohawk and Schoharie rivers were almost swamped by the flood of newcomers. The North Country, the region lying between Lake Champlain and Lake Ontario and south from the St. Lawrence River to the Adirondacks, became almost a colony of Vermont. New Englanders overran the region drained by the Delaware and Susquehanna rivers. They outnumbered the trickle of Pennsylvanians, New Jerseymen, and even Marylanders who were working their way up these rivers. The story is told that the town of Penn Yan on Keuka Lake got its name as a result of a deal between settlers from *Penn*sylvania and *Yan*keeland.

Central New York by 1800 was almost an extension of Connecticut. The story of western New York is much the same, for almost every town had its quota of settlers from New England.

The effect of the New Englanders upon New York's business, politics, religion, and culture was tremendous. Axes swung by Yankees cleared most of the forests. Accounts kept by Yankee clerks for Yankee businessmen recorded most of the growing trade of New York City and of the upstate cities and towns. Some of the founders of textile factories came from Rhode Island. Many of the clergymen, lawyers, physicians, and school teachers came from the academies and colleges of New England.

In New York City the shipyards, counting houses, and stores swarmed with craftsmen and businessmen from New England. In fact, a new aristocracy of Yankee businessmen came to dominate much of the business life of New York City. One of these men was R. H. Macy, who came from Nantucket Island to begin his famous store on Manhattan. Shrewd Yankees also ran most of the business activities of the growing cities along the Erie Canal.

Many men of New England stock went into New York politics. In religion, the New Englanders brought with them their piety

Early plows with which New York's pioneer farms were tilled.

and faith. The Yankees had much to do with establishing free public schools in New York. Gideon Hawley from New England directed the first successful system of state-aided neighborhood schools. Other Yankees set up academies (high schools) throughout the state. The first colleges drew most of their teachers from New England. Hamilton College, established in 1793, got six of its first seven presidents from Connecticut.

Landlords and Farmers in Eastern New York

Eastern New York was the first part of the state to show growth after the Revolution. It had much to offer newcomers. Land was available not only in the valleys but also on the hills. New Englanders liked this region because they could reach it quickly and easily. Furthermore, they could ship goods on the magnificent Hudson River to the growing cities on its banks.

The Revolution, as we have seen, loosened the grip of the aristocratic landholders, who had done little to develop their tracts. The Tories lost their lands during the war. In many cases, speculators bought up their estates from the New York government and sold the land in small pieces to former tenants. Westchester County, once six manors, now was tilled by landowning farmers.

Landholders who backed the American side held on to their estates. After the Revolution they developed them. William Cooper advised the landlords to sell and not to lease their land, because a farmer as an owner would work harder than as a tenant. Most landholders agreed with Cooper. Furthermore, the incoming Yankees did not like to rent land, for back in New England they had owned their farms.

Some large owners, however, decided to rent out their land. Stephen Van Rensselaer, in 1785, surveyed his holdings and

R. H. Macy opened his first store in 1858 on Sixth Avenue near 14th Street in New York City. This is a replica of the original building.

Albany at Church and Market Streets looked like this in 1805. Notice the hitching posts on the left, the cobblestones, and the Dutch door. The large building behind the hay wagon is the Dutch Reformed Church.

advertised for tenants. His terms were quite liberal. A tenant would receive free rent for seven years, after which he would pay each year 14 bushels of wheat for each hundred acres of land, plus four fat fowl, and a day's work with a team. If a tenant should sell or transfer his farm to someone else, he would have to pay one-fourth of the price he received to the Van Rensselaer family.

Other landholders followed the same system. On Livingston Manor in Columbia County, tenants could keep their farms during the lives of two persons named in the lease. After the death of the second person, the Livingston family got back the farm. In general, the leasehold idea did not spread outside the Hudson-Mohawk Valley. The main exceptions were Delaware County, and the Genesee Valley, where the Wadsworth family leased land to many tenants.

The tenancy system did not work out very well. The average American wanted to own his own farm. Tenants did little to improve their fields or buildings because the landlord would get the most benefit. Most tenants thought that it was wrong for free Americans to pay rent to aristocrats, who lived in a big house and had a great number of servants. Again and again, the tenant farmers banded together to stop rent collections. With the aid of the law, however, the landlords were successful in beating down these uprisings. In the 1840's the greatest of all tenant revolts took place. This time the tenants won and destroyed the hated land system.

Central and Western New York Are Opened Up to Settlement

The forest lands of central, western, and northern New York attracted speculators and settlers. But no great migration took place until the problem of the Indians and the ownership of the land was decided. Between 1784 and 1790, various tribes sold most of their hunting grounds between Rome and the Genesee River. In another ten years, the Iroquois had given up their land west of the Genesee River and north of the Mohawk River.

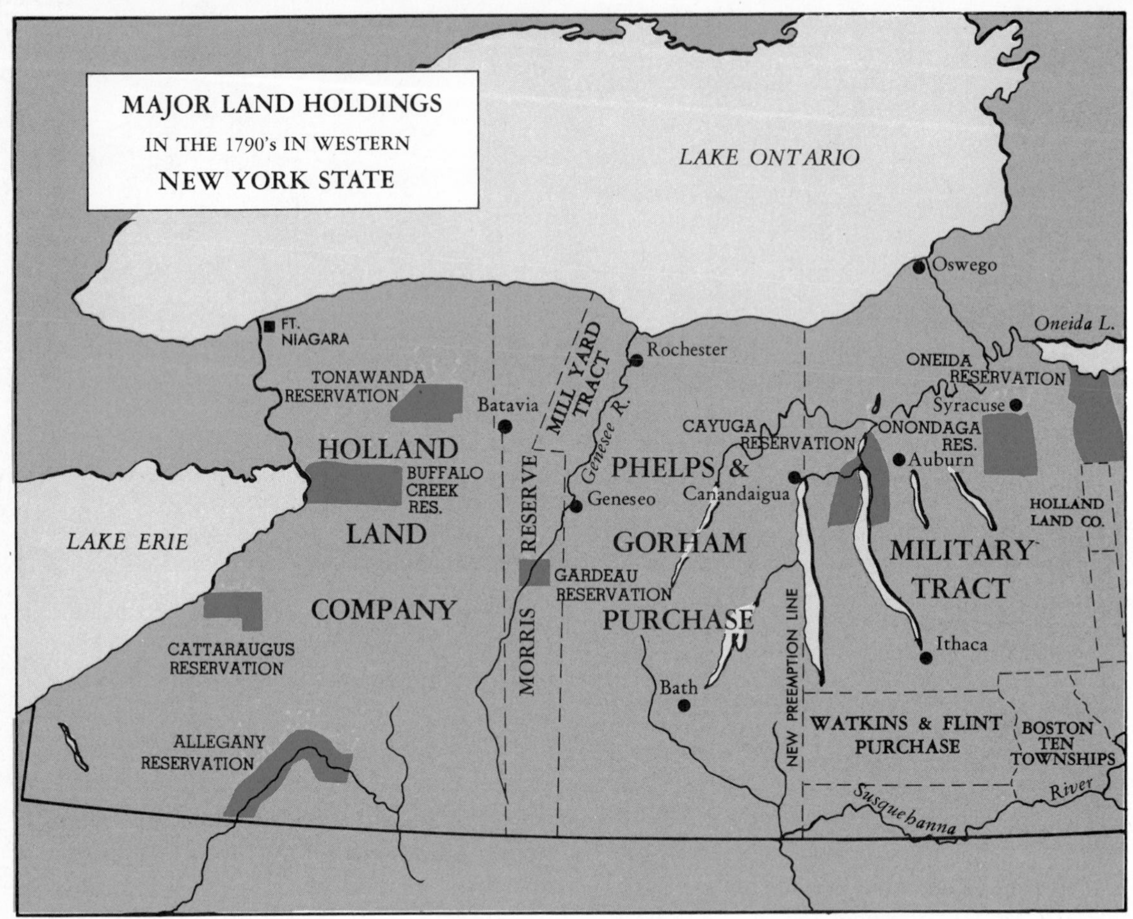

Map 20

The lands of central and western New York fell into the hands of many different people. During the Revolutionary War the New York state government promised every volunteer 600 acres of land. The state reserved some land, known as the Military Tract, to make good its promise to the war veterans. Other land was bought by New England speculators. Englishmen and Dutchmen acquired millions of acres in western New York. They hoped to sell the land and make a good profit on it. Map 20 will show you how complicated the land ownership of western New York was.

William Cooper, the father of the novelist James Fenimore Cooper, bought many acres in Otsego County and founded the village of Cooperstown. In 1785 Cooper visited the land he had purchased. At the time it was nothing but wilderness. In the spring of the next year he put on sale 40,000 acres of land, and within 16 days settlers had bought it all.

The settlers were poor, but Cooper was a kind man. He believed in charging a moderate price and allowing the people a long time in which to pay. He built a storehouse and filled it with grain, so there would be food during the winter months. Even so, in the winter of 1788–89 a number of his settlers nearly starved to death. Many lived on the roots of the wild leek, which is a plant something like an onion. Others lived on milk from their few cows, or drank a syrup made of maple sugar and water. Fortunately, in the early spring the

The Holland Land Office at Batavia was built in 1815. Here the settlers on the three-million-acre tract made their payments to the company. The phrase "doing a land office business" is said to have started here.

settlers were able to net thousands of fish in the Susquehanna River. This, with 1700 bushels of corn provided by the state legislature, saved the settlement.

Gradually the village of Cooperstown grew, and the settlers in the surrounding country prospered. Cooper himself moved his family to Cooperstown and built a large brick house, which he called Otsego Hall. Here he entertained many important visitors and became famous for his hospitality. Before his death in 1809, he wrote with pride that his entire settlement then numbered 8,000 people and had schools, academies, churches, meetinghouses, roads, and a market town. The settlers produced wheat and other grain, pork, and vegetables.

In western New York a Dutch company called the Holland Land Company bought a tremendous tract of land—about 3,300,000 acres. The company did not want to spend a lot of money developing its land, so it decided to provide only the bare necessities for settlers. The Dutch investors appointed Joseph Ellicott to survey and manage their lands. Ellicott built several roads to make it easier to enter the area. When he sold farms, he required only small down payments, because the early settlers had very little cash. Nevertheless, sometimes the settlers found it hard to pay the installments on their land. Some farmers complained that the Holland Land Company was squeezing them. Finally, in 1835 a mob of angry settlers looted the office of a company agent in Mayville. When the Dutch company realized that the farmers would not pay, they sold out their interests to American speculators.

The land of northern New York was also gobbled up by speculators. However, poor soil, mountains, cold climate, and few roads made it difficult to attract settlers. Only two sections—the hill country along the Black River and the Lake Ontario shore, and the woodlands along the St. Lawrence—appealed to pioneers. Because most of the settlers north of the Adirondacks came from

Vermont, this region was sometimes named "New Vermont" on old maps. Only a few thousand people were willing to risk the climate of the North Country. Most of the Adirondack area remained a wilderness until well after the Civil War.

The land agents did a great deal to develop New York. They surveyed and divided the large tracts. Their advertisements in New England and European papers attracted thousands of home seekers. Their roads, mills, and taverns helped make the first years of pioneering more bearable. By allowing the settlers to pay for their lands gradually, they made it possible for many to become owners. Naturally, they hoped to make good profits, but the great amount of land that was available kept them from overcharging the settler.

Natural Waterways

Cheap transportation was the key to the growth of the Empire State. Settlers wanted ways to get to the fertile lands of the West. Farmers needed ways to get their crops to market.

New York was blessed with a fine system of waterways. From the earliest days New Yorkers were quick to take advantage of three important types of trade: the transatlantic trade, the trade along the coast, and that with the interior. New Yorkers were among the first to use steamships and clipper ships on the high seas. This gave them a leading position in the Atlantic and coastal trades. To capture the trade of the interior, they constructed the great Erie Canal.

The natural waterways—the Atlantic Ocean, New York Bay, Long Island Sound, the Hudson and Mohawk Rivers, Lake Champlain, Lake Ontario, Lake Erie, and the Finger Lakes—remained until the Civil War the most important means of transporting goods and people within and outside New York. Such names as the New York & Erie Railroad and the Delaware and Hudson Canal show clearly that most canals and railroads were built to connect rivers and lakes.

The Hudson River continued to carry a great amount of traffic. Small sloops sailed up and down the slow-moving waters. In August 1807 a steamboat chugged up the Hudson River to Albany in 32 hours. Robert Fulton, who developed this first practical steamboat, said:

> The morning I left New York, there were not perhaps thirty persons in the city who believed that the boat would move one mile an hour or be of the least utility.

Crowds watched the steamboat with mixed feeling. Some hailed it as a great step forward in transportation. One spectator wrote:

> . . . Fishermen became terrified, and rode homewards, and they saw nothing but destruction devastating their fishing grounds, whilst the wreaths of black vapor and rushing noise of the paddle wheels, foaming with the stirred up water, produced great excitement. . .

Robert Fulton and his company got a monopoly to navigate the waters of the state with steam vessels. They charged high rates and ran only a few boats. But in 1824 the Supreme Court of the United States said that New York State did not have the right to control navigable waters since that right belonged to the United States Congress.

After this decision, many individuals operated steamboats, and rates fell to low levels. Captains often raced their boats, sometimes tying down the safety valve on their boilers to get more pressure and thus more speed. After 80 people had lost their lives in the burning of the *Henry Clay* in 1852, the legislature passed a strict Steamboat Inspection Act. The substitution of coal for wood also cut the fire risk.

Upstate lakes boasted of their steamboats. Lake Champlain had its first steamship in 1809, and huge rafts of lumber towed by steamboats became a common sight. The Canadians put the first steamer on Lake Ontario, but the Americans were first on Lake Erie when they launched the *Walk-in-the-Water* in 1818. After the opening of the Erie Canal, the number of steamboats on Lake Erie grew rapidly, and Buffalo became a major port. Steamboats took immigrants and manufactured goods west. Coming east they brought lumber, wheat, and, much later, iron ore.

Gradually, steamboat captains dared to take their vessels out on the ocean, although they kept within sheltered waters as much as they could. Regular service between New York and the cities on Long Island Sound was established. In 1847 the Fall River Line began its service. This enabled people to travel between New York and Boston in a short time.

The "commodore" of the steamboats was Cornelius Vanderbilt. He began his career rowing passengers from his home in Staten Island to Manhattan. As business increased, he took people and cargo all over New York harbor. Gradually his activities expanded. His ships, sail- and steam-driven, called at

This drawing appeared in France some years after the first steamship made its initial voyage. Notice the name Clermont at the stern.

many ports. They ferried many men on their way to Nicaragua and Panama, and then to the gold fields of California. By 1860 Vanderbilt had won the title of Commodore and had made more than $20,000,000. In the next 20 years he tripled his fortune in the railroad business.

Roads and Turnpikes

Farmers and townsmen had to use the country roads leading back from the rivers. These roads were little more than broad paths through the forest. Ruts, mudholes, stumps, and stones made wagons lurch crazily and teamsters swear. Logs were laid side by side to form corduroy roads across swampy places. Travelers had to ford streams or use ferries.

Elkanah Watson, the same man who helped bring about improvements in farming, stated in 1791, "The present road system is disgraceful to this fine state. . . ." Why was this so? First of all, the pioneer farmers did not need all-weather roads as do our modern farmers, who take their milk each morning to the creamery. In those early days the farmers went to market only a few times a year. Quite often they would keep their wheat and potash until the snow had fallen and then use sleighs. Secondly, little was done to take care of the roads. Each year the overseer of highways in a town would call upon all able-bodied men to put in a few days' work on the road. Neither the overseer nor the men knew much about road building, so little was accomplished.

As more and more people moved westward, the need for better roads became greater. The state legislature built a few highways, such as the Genesee Road, which ran from Utica to the Genesee Valley. But businessmen and farmers in all sections kept demanding more roads at once. To meet this demand, the state permitted private individuals to organize companies which could construct roads and charge tolls.

Waterfalls in the Mohawk River made it necessary to unload cargo boats at Schenectady, which therefore became the logical place for a road terminal. In 1797 the first turnpike company built a hard-surfaced road from Albany to Schenectady. Albany was the leading turnpike center in New York. Eight turnpikes thrust outward from the city like spokes in a wheel. The main highway from the east approached the city from New Lebanon. To the west were two main roads, one passing up the Mohawk Valley via Schenectady, the other following the present Route 20. Other turnpikes ran

Captain Dean

Who has heard of Captain Stewart Dean of Albany, captain of the 80-ton sloop, the *Experiment?* Captain Dean, in 1785, left Albany with a crew of eight men and two boys. In the hold were ginseng (a root from which Chinese made medicine), furs, spirits, and snuff. Dean took his tiny ship around the tip of South America, across the west Pacific to the Chinese city of Canton. Late in April 1787, Dean brought his ship home. He had traded New York ginseng and furs for a cargo of fine tea, silks, satins, and taffetas.

Albany's citizens gave Dean a hero's welcome, and named a street after him. Dean sailed off to China seven more times before he retired.

west from Newburgh and Catskill. Both the Newburgh and Cochocton and the Susquehanna Turnpike, the latter ending in Wattles Ferry (near Unadilla), had western branches which permitted travelers to reach Ithaca and Bath. On the eastern bank of the Hudson the advancing roads of the New England network met roads from Albany, Hudson, and Poughkeepsie. By 1821 about 4000 miles of turnpiked roads were serving the people of New York.

The turnpikes gradually declined in importance after the Erie Canal was built, and especially after railroads were constructed. But they had had a tremendous effect upon New York. Regions that were not near navigable rivers were opened up to settlement. The cost of freighting was cut. Passenger travel became faster. Scores of stagecoach companies sprang up to carry the passengers, but travel in one of these coaches could be very uncomfortable. Let Captain Barclay, a British officer, describe a stagecoach he traveled in during 1841.

> The American stage-coach is a most ungainly vehicle, carrying nine inside, three on a front seat, three on a back seat, and three on a bench hung in the middle; instead of panels, it has oil-skin curtains to shut down at night; its body is something in the form of a boat, resting on strong leather slings instead of steel springs, which indeed would not stand a mile on their roads; it consequently dances in the air like a balloon, giving a certain kind of variety to the monotony of a journey. The coachman sits on a bench, considerably lower than the top of the coach, and lower even than the horses, and there being no pad-terrets the reins dangle loose and afford no command of the horses, . . . Each man drives a twelve or fifteen mile stage, and what much surprised me, pulls up every four or five miles and gives his horses an . . . dose of water. Including the long delays in changing horses, dining, breakfasting, etc. the average speed does not exceed four miles an hour.

Shortly before 1850 many companies began constructing plank roads. They were about eight feet wide and were constructed of four-inch planks laid crosswise. At first the plank roads seemed ideal. They were cheap, easy to build, and useful in any kind of weather. Soon, however, travelers discovered that plank roads were far from perfect. The lumber rotted and horses were hurt when they put their legs in the spaces between the planks. By 1860 there were few plank road companies still operating in New York State.

Bridge building also made great progress. In 1800 most bridges were little more than planks laid over stone piers. Later, covered bridges were constructed; several are still

Vantran's Bridge in Livingston Manor has been in continuous use for well over 100 years. It is 98 feet long, all wood, and features "Towne" trusses. The safety signs are a modern feature.

The junction of the Erie and Champlain Canals in 1830. Note the type of boat and the hotel by the waterside.

standing. In 1855 John A. Roebling astonished the country by building a suspension bridge across the Niagara Gorge. It had a span of 821 feet. The upper level was used by railroad trains. On the lower level ordinary traffic passed between the United States and Canada.

The Erie Canal

The turnpikes did not solve the problem of cheap transportation for heavy freight. Farmers in central and western New York had to use roundabout or poor routes to get their goods to market. Farmers in the upper Genesee Valley floated their wheat, potash, and meat products on rafts from Arkport down the Canisteo, the Chemung, and the Susquehanna to Baltimore. Others used the Finger Lakes, the Oswego River, Lake Oneida, and the Mohawk River. The best outlet was down the Genesee River to the falls (near present day Rochester) and then to Lake Ontario, where there was water transportation to Montreal. Most of the settlers along Lake Champlain, the St. Lawrence River, and Lake Ontario found Montreal their best market.

Meanwhile the national government was building a National Road from Cumberland, Maryland, to Wheeling on the Ohio River. The merchants of New York City feared that the trade of the interior would enrich the traders of Baltimore and Philadelphia. Furthermore, the steamboat permitted the merchants of New Orleans to send goods up the Mississippi and Ohio rivers. If New York City was to get a share of this western trade, it would need a cheap water route to the west.

The state should build a canal to connect Lake Erie with the Hudson. So said De Witt Clinton and others. At first, most people scoffed at the idea. Where could the state find engineers to direct the work? Who would dig the ditch, 40 feet wide and 4 feet deep, for over 364 miles through forest and swamp? How could New Yorkers (fewer than one million) pay for such a huge project?

De Witt Clinton toured up and down the state, answering these questions. Finally, he won over a majority of the people, and the legislature voted to go ahead. On July 4, 1817 the first spadeful of dirt was turned over at Rome. The people cheered, but many wondered whether the project would make or break the state.

Thousands of persons had a hand in building the canal. Many farmers along the route became contractors and built a section of the bed. The first job was to open up a path through the forest. This task was not too hard for the skilled frontiersmen. Someone invented a plow equipped with knives to cut through brush. Axmen chopped down trees. They received help from a new machine which pulled down trees with a cable. Another machine yanked out the stumps of big trees.

The farmers and workmen fell behind schedule. Then the contractors had the fine idea of importing Irishmen to help, especially in building the canal through the Montezuma Swamp, a five-mile-wide marsh at the head of Cayuga Lake. Here the ground was so soft that the mud kept filling in the canal bed. The banks turned into mud. The Irish sang a song:

> We are digging the Ditch through the mire:
> Through the mire right up to our neck, by Heck!

Worse than the mud were the mosquitoes which swarmed down on the men working ankle-deep in the water and mud. Some men were bitten so many times that they could hardly open their eyes. Soon most of the men got the "shakes" or the "fever," which we know today was malaria. The sick men lay in their bunkhouses without proper care or food. Many died. Others ran away. Work came to a halt.

But cold weather saved the day. It drove away the mosquitoes, and the men got better. They put on gloves and dug a channel through the frozen mud. When spring came, boats could pass through the Montezuma Swamp.

Other problems faced the canal builders. At Lockport and Little Falls they had to cut through solid rock. They had to carry the canal over river gorges by means of raised wooden troughs, or aqueducts. You can see the ruins of some of these aqueducts in several parts of the state.

New Yorkers have never shown more courage and determination than they did in those years. By 1825 the channel was open from Albany to Buffalo. For good measure, the Champlain Canal, connecting the upper Hudson River with Lake Champlain, was also built. The people celebrated the opening with pageants, firing of cannon, and the drinking of toasts. At the head of a procession of boats, De Witt Clinton led the way from Buffalo to Albany, and then down the Hudson to New York Harbor.

The Erie Canal was a spectacular success as a carrier of freight and as a money-maker for New York State. Freight rates dropped over 90 percent between Buffalo and Albany. Farmers in western New York could send their wheat and lumber products to market. Within ten years the state had to enlarge and deepen the canal in order to take care of the increasing amount of canal traffic.

Pioneer Society

The pioneers in the Genesee Valley, the Finger Lake region, and the Ontario region faced the same difficulties as the pioneers of colonial times. Of course, conditions varied from farm to farm. Let us look at the stages of pioneering in a typical frontier region, the Genesee Valley.

The farmer, tired of his worn-out farm in New England or eastern New York, often set out in autumn, on foot or horseback, to see the famed Genesee country. After looking at the land maps and talking with land agents, he inspected the lots. He wanted a good water supply and nearness to a road or a river. He usually preferred the rolling hill country to the flat open spaces along the river. The lowlands were swampy and fever-ridden. Today we know that malaria was the disease known as the "Genesee fever" of pioneer days. Floods and dense underbrush kept some settlers from the lowlands. Furthermore, practically all upland was relatively fertile because of the thick layer of plant matter laid down through the centuries. For these reasons, many of the first settlements took place on the hills back from the valley.

The farmers' main task was to clear off the forest either by girdling or by chopping down the trees. This job usually lasted a lifetime. In fact, New Yorkers were still clearing land until after the Civil War.

Do you envy the pioneer living in a log cabin? He had few of the comforts to which

Mrs. John Young, Pioneer Wife

"My husband having the year before been out and purchased his land upon the Holland Purchase, in the fall of 1804, we started from our home in Virginia on horseback, for our new location. We came through Maryland, crossing the Susquehanna at Milton; then via Tioga Point, and the then usual route.

"In crossing the Alleghany mountains, night came upon us, the horses became frightened by wild beasts and refused to proceed. We wrapped ourselves in our cloaks and horse blankets, and attempted to get some rest, but had a disturbed night of it. Panthers came near us, often giving terrific screams, the frightened horses snorted and stamped upon the rocks.

"Arriving at our destination, a family by the name of Clark, had preceded us in the neighborhood. Myself and husband, and the family named, were the first settlers on the Oak Orchard road—or in fact, north of Batavia. Mr. Clark was kind enough to give us a shelter for a few days until my husband built a shanty. It was about ten feet square, flat roofed, covered with split ash basswood; no chimney; a blanket answered the purpose of a door for a while, until my husband got time to make a door of split plank. We needed no window; the light came in where the smoke went out. So much for the shanty, and now for the furniture:—For chairs, we had benches made by splitting logs and setting the sections upon legs. A bedstead was made by boring holes in the side of the shanty, inserting pieces of timber, which rested upon two upright posts in front; a side piece completing the structure; pealed basswood bark, answering the place of a cord. . . . Buying a little iron ware, crockery, and a few knives and forks, we were soon under way, house or shanty keeping."

we are accustomed. Here is a description of an early cabin in New York:

> The house was about 20 by 60 feet, constructed of round log chinked with pieces of split logs, and plastered on the outside with clay. The floors were made of split logs with the flat side up; the doors, of thin pieces of the same. The windows were holes, unprotected by glass or sash; the fireplace was made of stone, and the chimney of sticks and clay.

The pioneer family in the Genesee Valley tried to provide all its own food, fuel, and clothing. Food was not always plentiful. Sometimes the fish did not bite. Still more often the deer hid themselves in the thickets. The settler depended on corn to feed his family and his animals. To make the johnnycakes go down more easily, maple sugar or molasses was used. Wild berries were eagerly gathered by the children. Clothing was largely homemade out of wool, flax, or animal skins.

Pioneer families often joined together to do big jobs in a hurry. Neighbors for miles around brought their oxen and chains to logging "bees." Settlers got together to build barns and houses. These affairs were called "raisings." At harvest time several families would gather the crops. After the work was done, the young people danced and played games while the old people talked. The host supplied cider, rum, or whiskey, while the womenfolk brought huge quantities of food.

First some trees were felled and a cabin built, then fields were planted, and, as the family prospered, more farmland was cleared and a better home could be had.

Agricultural Improvements

The pioneers immediately looked around for some product which they could sell. They needed cash to pay for land, necessities, and some luxuries. The forest around them provided the first crop. Settlers chopped down the trees, rolled them together, and burned them. They took the ashes and made potash, which was used in fertilizers and dyes.

Pioneers turned to wheat as their first field crop. Farmers in eastern New York, especially those near the waterways, got a head start because they could get the bulky product to market. After the canal was built, farmers in the other sections, such as the remote Genesee Valley, grew and shipped large quantities of wheat. Wheat

A farm near Saugerties. This area was settled by many Germans.

continued to be the most important cash crop until about 1850, when dairy products took first place.

Corn, oats, barley, rye, and hay were also important crops. The demand for oats and hay rose higher as stagecoach operators, canalboat owners, and contractors acquired more horses. Corn, the most important single crop, was mainly used on the farm to feed cattle and hogs. New York led the nation in the production of barley, flax, and hops. Hops are used in the manufacture of beer. "Hop money" built many of the fine farmhouses in the region between Waterville and Cooperstown in central New York.

Farmers gradually turned to *animal husbandry*, that is, the raising of animals. The well-watered hillsides provided fine pasture land for sheep and cattle. Cattle dealers would visit the farms and buy cattle. After they had bought a herd, they would drive it overland to Albany or New York City slaughterhouses. By 1840 New York was packing more beef than any other state. In the 1850's cattle raised on the western prairies and transported over the railroads began to reach New York slaughter houses.

At first, most farmers raised only enough sheep to furnish wool for their own use. Shortly after 1800 a craze for Merino sheep swept the northeastern part of the United States. Many hill farmers in New York found more profit in raising sheep than in wheat. Between 1830 and 1845 the sheep industry reached its peak in this state. New woolen mills in New York and New England used more and more wool. After 1845 New York's sheep industry rapidly declined. Low-priced wool from abroad and cheap Ohio wool made it unprofitable to raise sheep in most parts of New York.

Very few farmers before 1800 knew anything about scientific agriculture. Most farmers "skinned their land," planting the same crop year after year until nothing came up. Their cattle ran wild, and no effort was made to improve the breeds. A few gentlemen farmers such as Robert Livingston and John Jay experimented with new methods, but the dirt farmers paid little attention. Why, they argued, should they conserve the soil, when plenty of other land was available?

Slowly improvements in farming came about. One man stood out as the leader in this. He was Elkanah Watson, a New Englander who spent most of his life in New York. During the Revolution, Watson, who was only 21 years of age, carried secret messages to Benjamin Franklin, our ambassador in Paris.

Watson settled in Albany in 1789. He supported all kinds of improvements, from banks to schools. He was one of the first to urge the construction of a canal to Lake Erie. In 1807 Watson decided to "show Americans how to farm." He bought two sheep and tied them to a tree in the public square, thus starting America's first fair. Three years later Watson put on a real fair in Pittsfield, Massachusetts. Listen to his description:

> It was as splendid, novel, and imposing, beyond anything of the kind ever exhibited in America. . . . In this procession were 69 oxen, connected by chains, drawing a plough held by the oldest man in the county: a band of music—the society, bearing appropriate ensigns [flags], and each member decorated with a badge of wheat in his hat.

Watson's fair carried the country by storm. Farmers in New York asked him to come and organize county fairs. Watson gave them all the help he could. Soon, people by the thousands were admiring the best specimens of cows, horses, poultry, and pigs. The women competed for prizes for handicrafts. In this way the average farm family learned better methods of farming.

Elkanah Watson, the "father" of the agricultural fair. This is a painting by Samuel F. B. Morse.

Summary

New York's population soared to first place by 1820. From New England came tens of thousands of land-hungry settlers, who influenced the business, cultural, and political life of the state. In eastern New York farmers bought land from landowners, although a few tried to keep the old tenant system alive. Speculators bought up the tracts of central, western, and northern New York and sold them off in small tracts to settlers.

Fulton's steamboat speeded up transportation on inland waterways. Private companies secured public and private money to construct turnpikes which ended at the waterways. Turnpikes enabled stagecoaches to speed passenger traffic, but they did not provide cheap transportation for freight. That came from the Erie Canal, the result of De Witt Clinton's foresight and energy.

The pioneer farmers had to clear the forest and provide most of their own food, fuel, shelter, and clothing. They needed a cash crop, and turned to wheat and potash. In time they undertook animal husbandry. Farmers were slow to use scientific agriculture, although new breeds of sheep and new tools gradually appeared on the farms.

Checking the high points

1. Why did the Yankees come to New York?

2. What was the impact of the Yankees on New York?

3. What kind of land system grew up in eastern, central, and western New York?

4. Why were these individuals important: William Cooper? Joseph Ellicott? Elkanah Watson?

5. How did the steamboat help New York grow?

6. What was a turnpike of the 1800's? Were these turnpikes successful?

7. What difficulties faced the promoters of the Erie Canal?

8. What were the chief jobs of a pioneer?

9. What crops did the pioneer farmer raise?

Think these over

1. Would you rather own or rent your home? Explain your reasons.

2. Was pioneering a glorious adventure or unending drudgery?

3. Were pioneers good farmers, considering their circumstances?

Checking locations

Catskill
Kingston
Schoharie River
Delaware River
Susquehanna River
North Country
Keuka Lake
Otsego County
Genesee Valley
Black River
Cooperstown
Syracuse

Vocabulary building

migration
emigration
immigration
ledger
speculator
leasehold
tenancy
creditors
scientific agriculture
scythe
girdling
malaria

Chapter Objectives

To learn about

- the establishment of a state government in New York
- the role played by New Yorkers in the creation of our federal government
- New York and the War of 1812
- the growth of democracy in New York

chapter 12

NEW YORK MOVES TOWARD DEMOCRACY

Setting up a State Government

When George Clinton was elected the first governor of New York in 1777, Philip Schuyler said in a letter to John Jay that while Clinton was honest, brave, and intelligent, he was not entitled to the governorship because he came from the common people. Ordinary people, however, hailed Clinton's victory over the hated aristocrats. Frontier farmers felt that they and their spokesmen were fully qualified to handle state affairs. Workers and shopkeepers in New York City demanded more power for the people. These folk—carpenters, shoemakers, butchers, and other workmen—had formed the main body of the Sons of Liberty. They had seized the hated stamps, enforced the boycott against British goods, and dumped tea into the harbor.

New Yorkers by 1770 had developed much skill in the art of politics. Politicians used many modern techniques: slogans, mass meetings, campaign literature, and banners. Their papers and speakers discussed issues as well as personalities.

On July 9, 1776 General Washington drew up his army on a field in New York City to hear the Declaration of Independence. Hardly had the reading finished when soldiers ran to the statue of King George III and pulled it down. The ideas of the Declaration burned in the minds of New Yorkers—all men are equal, the government gets its powers from the people it rules. Surely this meant all men should have a voice in the government. So important did New Yorkers consider the Declaration of Independence, that they included it in their first constitution in 1777. Yet the government established by the first constitution was far from being democratic.

John Jay was a Patriot but also an aristocrat. He had a major part in writing the first constitution, which was approved by Provincial Convention. The government it set up was not very different from the gov-

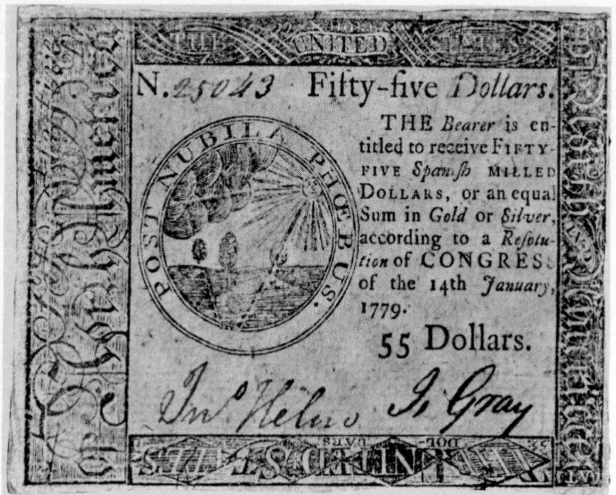

Here is a Continental note for $55 printed in 1779. Not only state-issued money but all paper money was held in low esteem, from which came the phrase, "Not worth a Continental."

ernment of colonial New York. It had an elected legislature with an Assembly and Senate. The governor, who had less power than the royal governors, had the duty to enforce the laws passed by the legislature. The courts decided whether the laws had been broken and punished law breakers.

Compared with foreign countries, the qualifications for voting and holding office were extremely democratic. Nevertheless, in order to vote for an assemblyman, a man had to own a certain amount of property or pay a certain amount of rent. To vote for state senator or governor one had to possess even more property. About one-third of adult white men could vote for governor and about two-thirds for assemblymen and congressmen. Women could neither vote nor hold office.

The first constitution did protect some of the rights of the people. It guaranteed trial by jury and freedom of religion. It stated that no religious group could receive money from the state government.

In September 1777 the state legislature met for the first time at Kingston. Soon it fled from the British army under Henry Clinton, who burned the town. Fortunately, Governor George Clinton was an able leader. He got the new government working, organized a strong militia, and collected supplies.

The common people loved Clinton because he fought for their rights, gave them honest government, and believed firmly in democracy. Many important people, including George Washington, also respected this able leader. New Yorkers elected George Clinton to the governorship five times in a row.

The large number of Loyalists in New York was a difficult problem for the new state government. Local committees of Patriots rode around to the homes of Tories and removed their weapons. They generally did not bother the families of Tories who took no active part in the war. But they tarred and feathered Loyalists they thought were giving supplies or information to the British.

The scarcity of money was critical, and the state could not pay its soldiers. In desperation it printed its own money, promising to redeem it with gold and silver after the war. Would the government of New York last? With the British army in New York City and Indian raids on the frontier, most people had doubts. Because of this lack of faith, the paper money rapidly lost most of its value.

But New York did collect revenue. It sold land taken away from the Loyalists and the British government. It also placed taxes or tariff duties on goods brought into the state. After the war the state paid off most of its debts and took some of the paper money out of circulation.

Changes during the Revolutionary period made life more democratic. Because many

The first session of the State Senate was held in this stone house in Kingston in 1777.

aristocrats had joined the Loyalists, they fled to Canada or Britain after the war. One result was that more common people found it easier to move into positions of leadership. The number of land-owning farmers was increased by the sale of Tory lands. One Loyalist estate near New York City, for example, was divided among 250 people. The increase in farm ownership meant that more farmers could meet the qualifications for voting.

It took many years, however, before the greater democracy resulted in legislation that corrected the evils of the time. For example, the laws of colonial New York called for cruel punishments of lawbreakers. Both George Clinton and John Jay protested, and finally the legislature reduced the number of crimes punishable by death to three: murder, treason, and robbing a church.

Slavery, the worst evil of those days, also came under attack. The legislature prohibited bringing in any more slaves. In 1799 a new law provided for the gradual ending of slavery. Finally, in 1818, the legislature fixed July 4, 1827 as the date for the end of slavery in New York State. Actually, most slaves were set free years before this date.

New Yorkers Help Start the United States

During the Revolution, New Yorkers regarded themselves as citizens only of their state. They looked upon the Continental Congress as a weak body with no real powers; and they were correct. The Articles of Confederation could not stop states from quarreling and could not win the respect for American rights from foreign governments.

In 1787 delegates from 12 of the 13 states met in Philadelphia to revise the Articles of Confederation. George Washington

The Bill of Rights

New Yorkers fought hard for the Bill of Rights. We should know what these rights are, because they protect us today even more than they protected the people in George Washington's times. If you do not understand some of them, ask your teacher or your parents. Here are fifteen rights which are guaranteed in the first ten amendments to the United States Constitution. Note that these amendments regulated the relations of the citizens with the *federal government only*. To protect themselves from misgovernment by their state, citizens had to look for rights in their state constitution. This is true in New York State as well as for all others.

1. Congress may not interfere with your freedom to worship as you please.
2. Congress may not interfere with your freedom of speech.
3. Congress may not prohibit the freedom of the press.
4. You have the right to hold meetings to discuss questions.
5. You have the right of petition. For instance, you can ask Congress to pass or reject a law. Or, you can write to members of Congress, the President, and other government officials telling them what you think should be done.
6. You have the right to keep and carry arms. Of course, the government may make necessary regulations.
7. Congress may not put soldiers in your home without your consent, except in time of war. Even in wartime it can be done only by making a new law.
8. Your house and property cannot be searched and you cannot be arrested unless there is good reason to believe that you have done something illegal.
9. You have a right to a fair trial before being punished.
10. You have the right to a trial by jury.
11. You must be indicted before you can be tried for a major crime. That means, there must be enough evidence against you to justify a trial.
12. Congress may not take your property without fair payment.
13. If you are accused of a crime:
    a. You do not have to testify against yourself.
    b. You must be tried as soon as possible in the district where the crime was committed. It must be a public trial before a fair jury.
    c. You must be told what crime you are accused of.
    d. You can cross-examine witnesses against you.
    e. You can force witnesses to appear in court.
    f. You can have a lawyer to defend you.
    g. You cannot be tried twice for the same crime.
14. The federal government cannot impose on you excessive bail, excessive fines, or cruel or unusual punishments.
15. The listing of these rights does not mean that your other rights may be taken away.

was chairman of the meeting. New York sent three representatives—Robert Yates, John Lansing, and Alexander Hamilton. Yates and Lansing did not want a strong national government. They soon returned home, saying that the delegates at Philadelphia had no power to write a new constitution for the country. Hamilton disagreed. While he had little to do with the writing of the constitution, he made several speeches urging a stronger federal government.

The constitution that was written at Philadelphia in 1787 called for a powerful federal government. Control of both foreign trade and trade among the states was given to the national government. The government also received the power to tax. The powers of the states were limited by the new constitution. States could not issue money. They could not make treaties with foreign countries. They could not interfere with foreign trade or with trade between states. These were to be federal matters.

You would expect New Yorkers to be in favor of the new constitution. Strangely enough, most of them were against it. Why? For one thing, New York collected a great deal of money from its tax on imported goods. Under the new constitution it would lose this tax. Many New Yorkers were afraid a strong central government, American or British, might levy taxes and regulate trade. Also, some people were worried because the constitution had no *Bill of Rights.* As used here, "bill" means list. A Bill of Rights is a list of the rights of the people.

New York called a convention to decide whether to accept the new form of government. All free men were eligible to vote for delegates to the convention. The Federalists, led by Alexander Hamilton, wanted the constitution. The Anti-Federalists, led by

This diorama in the Museum of the City of New York shows the inauguration of George Washington at Federal Hall. The man in the long robe is Robert R. Livingston, an important New Yorker.

George Clinton, were against it and elected 46 delegates to the convention at Poughkeepsie. The Federalists elected only 19 delegates.

The Anti-Federalists had the support of many ordinary people—farmers, shopkeepers, craftsmen. These people had great faith in George Clinton and looked to the state government to protect their rights. Since Anti-Federalists controlled the convention, you would expect them to turn down the constitution. But, unexpectedly, they accepted it. Why?

The Federalists had several able men at the convention, among them Hamilton, Jay, and Robert Livingston. They admitted the need for a Bill of Rights and promised to work for one. Even more important was the adoption of the constitution by New Hampshire, the ninth state, on June 21. After nine states accepted it, the constitution would go into effect, leaving New York outside the United States. Were this to happen, the new nation might refuse to trade with New York. On June 26, 1788 the Poughkeepsie Convention voted to ratify the constitution. New York thus became the 11th state to ratify.

On April 30, 1789, the day on which General Washington became President, crowds filled the streets of New York City. Soldiers and important citizens paraded through the city to Federal Hall. A short time later the first president took the oath of office. All day and all night the people crowded the streets, talking excitedly. Cannon were fired from time to time and fireworks were set off. It was a joyous and important occasion.

President Washington chose Alexander Hamilton to be the Secretary of the Treasury, and John Jay was given the important job of Chief Justice of the United States. As Secretary of the Treasury, Hamilton worked out a plan to pay the debts of the United States. The success of the new government was due, in large measure, to Hamilton's fine work.

The Anti-Federalists

The farmers, who formed over 80 percent of the population, usually joined the Anti-Federalists led by George Clinton. Had he not led them to victory? Had he not punished the Tories and whipped the aristocracy? Most farmers feared that a strong national government would tax them and perhaps take away their liberties.

Hamilton opposed strenuously any steps which might get us into war with England, which was then at war with France. Such a war would ruin his financial program. President Washington also saw that the United States needed a period of peace. Therefore, in 1793 he declared that the United States would remain neutral, despite the fact that France had been our ally since 1777. But neutrality itself caused problems. Edmond Genêt, France's ambassador to this country, tried to stir up the people to support France. Washington, angered and disturbed, asked the French government to recall Genêt.

Meanwhile, England was violating our neutral rights by interfering with our trade with the French West Indies. Furthermore, they *impressed* American sailors; that is, took them off American ships and put them to work in the British navy. New Yorkers were particularly irritated with Great Britain because of her failure to give up five forts within our borders. After Britain had seized almost 300 ships, many Americans demanded war.

To straighten out these difficulties, Washington sent Jay to England. Jay signed a compromise treaty which did secure the forts. But the British refused to stop the impressment of our sailors or to permit our ships to trade freely with the British West Indies. When the Anti-Federalists heard about this, they denounced Jay as selling out to the British.

The Anti-Federalists united behind Thomas Jefferson and helped him to victory over John Adams in the Presidential election of 1800. The next year the Anti-Federalists, who now called themselves Democratic-Republicans, put George Clinton back into the governor's office in New York. However, they fell to quarreling among themselves.

The most famous political feud was between Alexander Hamilton and Aaron Burr. Burr was an ambitious young man with considerable ability and charm who built a strong political machine in New York City. In 1800 the Anti-Federalists ran Jefferson for President and selected Burr as his run-

Alexander Hamilton (1755–1804)

Aaron Burr took aim at Alexander Hamilton and pulled the trigger. Hamilton fell forward, firing into the ground. The next day Hamilton died in agony. Thus ended the most famous two-man gun fight in American history. Burr blamed Hamilton for thwarting all his political ambitions and wanted his enemy dead. Thereafter, New Yorkers would have nothing to do with Aaron Burr. After completing his term as Vice-President, Burr engaged in a plot to seize land from Spain. He died in disgrace.

Hamilton was one of the most remarkable New Yorkers of all time. He was born on the Island of Nevis in the British West Indies. He was doing a man's work by the time he was age 14. In his spare time he studied by himself because he had little chance for schooling. At 16, Alexander was managing his employer's store and writing newspaper articles. His ability won him friends who sent him to school. In 1773 he entered King's College (now Columbia University) in New York City, but he gave up his studies before graduation to join the struggle against British policies.

Hamilton strongly favored the colonies, and at 21, he

became a captain in the Revolutionary Army and took part in the battle for New York City. He also fought in the battles of White Plains, Trenton, and Princeton.

In 1777 Alexander Hamilton was made a lieutenant colonel and was placed on General Washington's staff, where he served for four years. General Washington was very impressed with Hamilton and gave him a number of important jobs. One of these took him to Albany, where he met his future wife, Elizabeth Schuyler, the daughter of General Philip Schuyler.

After the war, Hamilton served for a time in Congress, and then began to practice law in New York City. He was a very successful lawyer, but he kept worrying about the federation of states. He saw that the Articles of Confederation did not provide for a strong enough national government. Hamilton worked hard to have the federal constitution adopted. He, together with John Jay and James Madison of Virginia, wrote *The Federalist.* This was a series of newspaper articles supporting the constitution. Most of them were written by Hamilton.

President Washington appointed Alexander Hamilton to the most important position in his cabinet—Secretary of the Treasury. He established confidence in the nation's credit by paying off the debts in systematic fashion and by collecting taxes on imports and whiskey.

In 1795 he returned to the practice of law in New York City. He remained active in politics, and in 1798 took command of the army under Washington's direction. On July 11, 1804 the man who had escaped British bullets during eight years of war was shot down in a peaceful field at Weehawken, New Jersey. His untimely death did much to end the foolish practice of dueling.

ning mate in order to carry New York. Burr and Jefferson received the same number of electoral votes. The Constitution at that time stated that the person with the highest number of votes should be President. Burr tried to move into the top spot by making deals with enemies of Jefferson. Hamilton disliked Jefferson but he detested Burr. He persuaded some of his Federalist friends to vote for Jefferson, and the Virginian was elected President of the United States with Burr as Vice-President.

Shortly afterward, Burr quarreled with his fellow Republicans and ran for the governorship with some Federalist support. Hamilton campaigned against Burr and helped defeat him. Claiming that Hamilton had blackened his character, Burr then challenged him to a duel. Hamilton felt that he had to fight, even though he did not approve of dueling. His own son had been killed in a duel a short time before. Near Weehawken, New Jersey, on July 11, 1804, Burr shot Hamilton.

Daniel D. Tompkins (1774–1825) painted by John Wesley Jarvis in 1820.

Governor Tompkins and the War of 1812

Meanwhile, a new political leader was rising. He was Daniel Tompkins, sometimes called the "First Farmer Governor." A strong follower of Jefferson, Tompkins believed in fighting for American rights on the high seas. He became Governor in 1807 and won re-election three years later.

Relations between the United States and Great Britain were going from bad to worse. Britain, which was fighting desperately against the French under Napoleon, paid little attention to American rights. Congressmen from the western sections of the country claimed that Britain was stirring up the Indians to attack frontier settlements. American frontiersmen also had their eyes on the fertile lands of Canada on which they hoped to settle if they could capture them. Some New Yorkers, however, opposed a war with Britain. For example, many of the merchants and shipowners of New York City believed that war would ruin commerce and bring a depression. Moreover, they felt that Napoleon—not Britain—was the real enemy of the United States. President James Madison, however, favored war and asked Congress to declare war in order to protect American rights.

Governor Tompkins tried very hard to get New Yorkers to work for victory. He had to overcome many problems. The state militia was poorly trained and poorly led. The frontier forts were undermanned. The Federalists in control of the Assembly did not want to pay higher taxes to support the war effort.

The Americans planned a grand invasion of Canada with two thrusts from New York. Major General Stephen Van Rensselaer was to attack Niagara, while General Henry Dearborn was to strike north from Plattsburgh and take Montreal. Van Rensselaer threw a force of men across the Niagara River in the hope of capturing the heights surrounding the British fort at Queenston. About 600 men climbed up the cliff and at the top they were attacked by a strong British force. They were at last pushed over the cliff down to the rushing waters of the Niagara. There they surrendered. Equally discouraging was the American failure on Lake Champlain where Dearborn had trained 5,000 of his troops. In mid-November he marched north toward Canada, but the militia refused to fight outside the state.

The next spring Dearborn assembled 4,000 men at Sacket's Harbor on Lake Ontario. He sent an expedition across the lake to York (now Toronto). It burned down the public buildings of the Canadian government. Meanwhile the British struck back at Sacket's Harbor, which had too few defenders. When the news spread that a British fleet was offshore, the farmers in the region rallied behind their able leader,

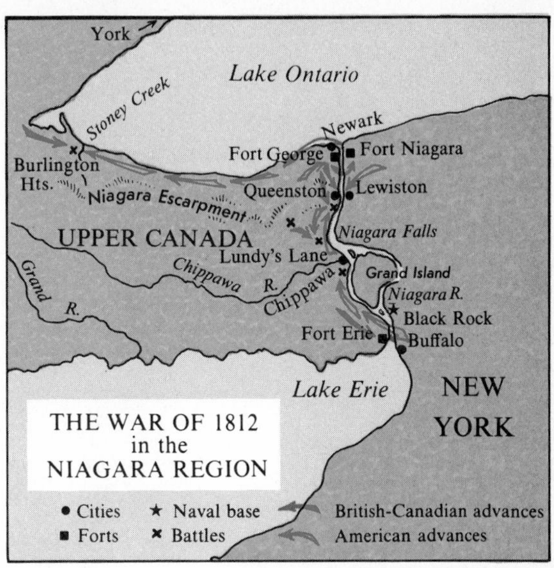

Map 21

Jacob Brown. Brown's men fought well against the British regulars, who failed to capture the fort.

The Christmas season of 1813 was not a happy one for New Yorkers. A British force recaptured Fort Niagara and then set fire to Buffalo. Offsetting these defeats, however, was the stirring victory of Oliver Perry at Put-in-Bay in September. Perry won control of Lake Erie and thrilled all Americans with his message, "We have met the enemy and they are ours."

In 1814 the British prepared to invade the United States from three directions—Chesapeake Bay, the mouth of the Mississippi, and Lake Champlain. The British no longer had to worry about Napoleon, who was in exile on the island of Elba. They had tens of thousands of veteran troops who had fought in Europe. But the American armies had also improved a great deal. Young vigorous officers had taken the place of old and incompetent ones, and the soldiers had become battle-hardened. As a result the American forces succeeded in throwing back each of the three British invasions.

An artist's view of the naval battle of Plattsburgh. Who do you think the officer in the center of the picture is?

New Yorkers played an important part in holding off the British attack. Jacob Brown crossed the Niagara River in July and inflicted heavy losses on the enemy at Chippawa and Lundy's Lane. The militia fought bravely and skillfully. Jacob Brown wrote proudly to Governor Tompkins that "the militia of New York have redeemed their character—they behaved gallantly."

The scene now shifted to Lake Champlain. A British army, 10,000 strong, marched southward to the outskirts of Plattsburgh. To oppose this force was an American army of only 1,500 men. But in Plattsburgh Bay there was also a fleet of 14 gunboats under the command of Captain Thomas Macdonough. Knowing that the British fleet had more ships and more guns, Macdonough tried to add to his firepower. He provided his anchored ships with devices so that they could swing around quickly. After a ship had fired a broadside, its crew could swing it around and then fire another broadside from the cannon on the other side. This move proved to be the deciding factor. After several hours of bloody fighting, the main British ships surrendered. Shortly thereafter the British army retreated to Montreal.

Democracy Makes Progress

Many people were saying in 1815 that De Witt Clinton's career was ended. His enemies—and they were many—had forced the governor to fire him from his job as mayor of New York City. But Clinton soon found the issue upon which he would make a great come-back. As you read earlier, he demanded the construction of a canal to Lake Erie and one to Lake Champlain. Earlier

Clinton had studied the best route through the wilderness, but the War of 1812 had caused the people to put aside the project. When peace came, the legislature formed a canal commission which picked De Witt Clinton as its head.

De Witt Clinton became so popular that he won the governorship in 1817 with 95 percent of the vote. Unfortunately, by 1822 Clinton had lost so much popularity that he did not dare to run again. Martin Van Buren and his friends had an easy time electing their candidate for governor. Their next move was to fire De Witt Clinton from the Canal Board, on which he had served without pay for many years. This ungrateful act shocked the people. Up and down the state, public meetings passed resolutions praising Clinton's work on the Canal Board. As a result, Clinton decided to run again for governor, and he won the election by a large margin. It was only right that Clinton was governor when, in 1825, the canal was finally opened for traffic.

New York, in less than half a century, had developed from a colony controlled by British governors and a small aristocracy, to a government controlled by the people. Gradually, more and more people were coming to believe in the principles of the Declaration of Independence. After the War of 1812 a wave of democratic feeling swept across the northern states.

In 1821 the most distinguished citizens of New York met in Albany to revise the state constitution. Heading the small but brilliant Federalist delegation were Judge James Kent, a firm believer in aristocracy, and Stephen Van Rensselaer, the great landlord. Facing them were the more democratic forces led by Daniel Tompkins and Martin Van Buren.

This picture of De Witt Clinton was painted about 1825 when Clinton was 56 years old. It was done in the year the Erie Canal was opened.

The convention gave the governor the power to veto laws but allowed the legislature, by means of a two-thirds vote of both houses, to override his veto. The governor was given the power to make appointments, although he had to get the consent of the Senate for the more important offices.

A handful of diehard Federalists led by Chancellor James Kent opposed any extension of the vote. On the other side, a small group of "radical democrats" favored the granting of the vote to all adult white males. Between them stood Martin Van Buren, who warned about the dangers of a wholly unrestricted suffrage. Manhood suffrage, he asserted, would give too much power to New York City and "to the very worst population." Nevertheless he wanted to give the owners of "personal property" and "householders" the same voting rights enjoyed by freeholders. As a result of his position 84 percent of adult white males were eligible to vote for governor. Blacks, however, had to meet higher property qualifications than white men, so few could vote.

Summary

The state constitution, adopted in 1777, established a government made up of a legislature, a governor, and courts. It extended the right to vote to a majority of adult

How New York Lost Vermont

Did you know that all Vermont, as well as western Massachusetts and western Connecticut, were once a part of New York? The charter King Charles II gave to his brother, the Duke of York, said the eastern boundary of the colony was the west side of the Connecticut River. Because the people of Massachusetts and Connecticut moved into the region west of the Connecticut River, New York agreed to set the western boundaries of these two colonies along a line drawn 20 miles east of the Hudson River.

In 1741 Benning Wentworth became governor of New Hampshire. Wentworth maintained that the western boundary of New Hampshire was similar to that of Massachusetts and Connecticut. On this basis he granted title to the lands lying west of the Connecticut River. By 1764 there were 131 New Hampshire townships in this region. Governor Wentworth set aside some millions of acres for himself and his friends.

Naturally, New York did not recognize persons holding claims from New Hampshire as being the true owners of the land. New York also gave title to land in the disputed area. When the New York owners tried to move into the region, they were driven out by New Englanders who had settled on the "New Hampshire Grants." But the New Englanders were worried over whether they could hold their land in the face of the claims made by New York.

The Allen brothers—Heman, Ira, and Ethan—saw a chance to make a fortune. Together with Remember Baker they formed the Onion River Company, which bought up New Hampshire titles from discouraged holders at low prices. If the New Hampshire titles could be made to hold, the Onion River Company would make a great profit. The Allen brothers organized the New England settlers into a military force known as the "Green Mountain Boys," which successfully fought off the authority of New York.

In 1777 while New York was involved in the Revolution, the local inhabitants declared themselves the independent State of Vermont and drew up a constitution. The next year the first General Assembly of Vermont met at Windsor. Thomas Chittenden was elected governor and Ira Allen became treasurer. Laws were made and an armed force was established. For all practical purposes the State of Vermont had come into being.

Governor George Clinton of New York stubbornly refused to recognize Vermont. Unconcerned, the Vermonters continued their independent way, coining money, setting up roads, establishing post offices. After the Revolution, Vermont even negotiated treaties with the British. Finally, New York could hold out no longer. Commissioners from the two states met and agreed that Vermont would pay New York $30,000 for land claims and that New York would acknowledge the independence of Vermont. On March 4, 1791 Vermont was admitted to the Union as the fourteenth state.

males. George Clinton became the first governor, a position which he held for seven terms. He helped fight the British in the Revolutionary War, and the democratic forces rallied behind him.

George Clinton (1739-1812) was elected the first governor of New York in 1777. He was vice president of the United States from 1805 to 1812.

New Yorkers distrusted the new federal constitution but accepted it after the Federalists promised to add a Bill of Rights. Hamilton, Jay, and other citizens aided Washington when he organized the new government. Two political parties emerged. The Federalists, led by Hamilton and Jay, favored a strong central government and neutrality in foreign affairs. The Anti-Federalists, led by George Clinton, disliked Hamilton's economic program. Quarreling was common within as well as between parties, the most shocking example of which was the Burr-Hamilton duel.

In 1812 the United States fought England again, and once again New York soil saw much fighting. Governor Daniel D. Tompkins was an able war governor. After the war New Yorkers sought to make their government more democratic by simplifying the structure of the government and extending the vote to almost all white adult males.

Checking the high points

1. Was the first state constitution of 1777 a good constitution? Why?

2. What democratic reforms resulted from the Revolutionary period?

3. What were George Clinton's claims to the title "the father of New York State"?

4. How do you explain the fact that although most New Yorkers were against the federal constitution, the Poughkeepsie Convention voted for it?

5. What part did New Yorkers play in starting the Government of the United States?

6. What groups of people supported the Federalists? the Anti-Federalists? Why?

7. Why did Aaron Burr hate Alexander Hamilton?

Think these over

1. Who do you think did the more for New York State—George Clinton or Alexander Hamilton? Explain.

2. Did the Revolutionary War result in more democracy in New York State?

3. Should people be allowed to criticize the President or the Congress of the United States?

4. Should Hamilton have refused to fight Burr?

Vocabulary building

These widely used words appear in the chapter. Are you sure of their meaning?

constitution
Bill of Rights
depression
Confederation
capital
federal
ratification
alien
sedition
impressment
qualifications
paper money
undermanned
delegation
fraternity
broadside

Checking locations

Weehawken, New Jersey
Plattsburgh
Toronto, Canada
Sacket's Harbor
Buffalo
Kingston, Ontario
Kinderhook

chapter 13: NEW YORKERS IMPROVE AGRICULTURE and TRANSPORTATION

chapter 14: NEW YORKERS EXPAND THEIR BUSINESS EMPIRE

chapter 15: NEW YORKERS MAKE SOCIAL PROGRESS

chapter 16: ISSUES DIVIDE NEW YORKERS

unit five

The Age of Homespun

New York state history dates are shown in color.

1817 New York Stock Exchange opens
1820 Compromise of 1820
1831 New York's first railroad begins Albany to Schenectady service
1832 First horse-drawn streetcar in New York City
1836 New Yorker Martin van Buren elected President
1839 New Yorker Abner Doubleday set down rules of baseball
1844 New Yorker Samuel Morse invents telegraph
1848 Telegraph communication set up between New York and Chicago
Potato famine in Ireland causes many to immigrate to U.S.
Political turmoil causes large-scale German immigration to U.S.
New Yorker Millard Fillmore elected Vice President
1850 Millard Fillmore succeeds to the presidency
Fugitive Slave Law
Compromise of 1850
1854 Kansas-Nebraska Act
1855 Castle Garden leased by U.S. as receiving center for immigrants
1860 Abraham Lincoln elected President
1861 Civil War erupts

Visitors love to see reconstructed villages such as those at Cooperstown, Mumford, and Old Bethpage. How peaceful, how close to nature, how calm life seemed before the Civil War, in a time known as the Age of Homespun.

Actually change—constant, sweeping, uprooting—marked the Age of Homespun as it has every generation of New Yorkers. The Erie Canal spurred trade, revolutionized farming, and stimulated cities along its route. Railroads linked farms with cities and New York City with the West. Immigrants, pouring in from New England, Ireland, and Germany, came to dominate city life. By 1860 about one out of two New Yorkers was living in or near cities. Home manufacturing almost died as it moved to the slope of artisans. Tailors, shoemakers, and other craftsmen in turn began to feel the competition of factory-made goods.

Change brought more wealth and an increasing standard of living. Although New Yorkers were criticized for their devotion to earning money, they worked hard to improve society. Many campaigned for free public schools, temperance, and better treatment of women. They also opposed the expansion of slavery in the West.

Politics absorbed their attention more than in most periods. New Yorkers debated a wide range of issues; they made government more democratic; they formed new parties. In the 1850s two burning issues—the status of immigrants and slavery expansion—destroyed old parties and created new ones. The Civil War brought about even more basic changes, perhaps more than any other single development in state history. Postwar New York was a different society in which cities, factories, and banks overshadowed farms, villages, and crafts.

Chapter Objectives

To learn about

- the Age of Homespun
- family patterns and lifestyles during the Age of Homespun
- the rise of the dairy industry in New York
- 19th century developments in water and land travel in New York
- the development of New York as an important shipping and railroad center

chapter 13

NEW YORKERS IMPROVE AGRICULTURE and TRANSPORTATION

Family Patterns

Wherever one goes in the world or searches back in history, one finds that most people live in family groups. Families feed and shelter their members. Children are taught the customary ways of living, the difference between right and wrong, and basic skills such as speech. Each culture expects a certain kind of behavior of the father, the mother, and the children. The work of men usually differs from the tasks of women. Even boys and girls may have special chores assigned to them.

American families have usually been *patrilineal;* that is, the name and property of the family come down through the father. You will recall that the Iroquois society had *matrilineal* families, with the name and property descending through the mother.

During the Age of Homespun the most common type of family was *nuclear,* which means the household included a father, mother, and children. After pioneers grew older and their children married, the family might become an *extended* family; that is, grandparents also lived within or close to the household. Many frontiersmen bought more land than they needed in order to have room for their children to live with or near them. Families were thus clusters of relatives with aunts, uncles, grandparents, and cousins all sharing their joys and concerns. One may still see this type of family today among many of the Italian, Polish, and Oriental people.

Work and Space

Society in the Age of Homespun defined the jobs of men and women more sharply than today. Certain jobs, for example, cooking and sewing, were called women's work. Everyone knew that the woman of the house ruled the kitchen. On the other hand, men did most of the "outside" work in the forests, fields, and outbuildings. The barn belonged to the menfolk, although the womenfolk earned the name of dairymaids by milking the cows.

The seasons—spring, summer, fall, and winter—set the pattern of life. In the following reading Anne G. Sneller recalls her childhood days on a farm near Cicero in central New York. Compare her childhood experiences with your own.

> Well time passed on, on a farm the days are nearly all the same, nothing changes but the seasons. In the early morning, before the sun was up, I would dress and build the fire, and put on the tea kettle for hot water, go out to the hen house, feed and water the chickens, come in and get breakfast, calling all hands to the table. By this time the men have finished the milking, and the horses have been curried and fed, ready for work. Coffee and hot cakes are all ready, now we have breakfast. Then for five to six long hours in the field and in the house. Then a good dinner and back to work again till sun down, then supper and the milking; and then with some there would be a reading of a chapter in the Bible and a prayer, then to bed till another day.
>
> Life was a sort of routine. Monday washday, Tuesday ironing and mending, Wednesday baking and cleaning, Thursday sewing, Friday sewing and odd jobs, such as working in the garden or with the flowers. We did all of our own sewing, cleaning, papering, painting—we were thrifty farmers. In the spring, there were the maple trees to be tapped, so as to have syrup and sugar, then to boil up a barrel of soft soap to last the year through. And now house cleaning time comes on, and before that is finished, it is time to gather small fruit; in between, the housework must be kept up. All this is supposed to be cared for by the women and children. Then there is more or less sickness in a large family, but no doctor unless death comes stalking in your door, we depended on home nursing.
>
> Then in the spring after the corn was planted, and a circus came to town, the boys would have a day off for recreation. The girls had to wait for summer picnics. Later there would be fairs for older people. And farmers and their wives were supposed to furnish produce for the fair.
>
> And thus it was from year to year.*

Dairy Farming

The rise of the dairy industry was the most important development in New York's agricultural history. The rolling countryside provided excellent pasturage. The ever increasing number of people living in the cities from Buffalo to New York City demanded more and more cheese, butter, and milk. Dairying often engaged the energies of the entire farm family. Women and children helped in milking the cows and churning the butter. Canals and, later, the railroads and trucks made it easy for the farmers to market butter, cheese, and milk.

Butter was the main dairy product before the Civil War. Although many farmers in all parts of the state made butter, Orange County for a long time had the reputation for the best butter. Cheese-making centered in and around Herkimer County, which is still famous for its cheese. By securing better breeds of cattle and by taking better care of their cows and pastures, the cheesemakers were able to keep up with the great demand. Cheese factories sprang up, especially in central New York. Skilled managers were now able to turn out a better product.

*Anne G. Sneller, *A Vanished World* (Syracuse University Press)

The milk industry was small because milk could not be taken to market rapidly. Before 1855 most milk in New York City came from cows that were fed only the waste products from the manufacture of liquor. This milk had practically no food value. In fact, doctors blamed milk for many deaths among babies and children. After the railroads were built, fresh country milk reached New York City.

The agricultural fair movement was revived during the 1840's after a temporary setback. In fact, the state legislature set up a state fair. It finally selected Syracuse as the permanent place for the fair. Every year since then large crowds have visited the fair grounds to see the exhibits.

Farm papers were more important than fairs in spreading knowledge of crop rotation, deep plowing, draining, breeding of livestock, fertilizers, and farm machinery. Jesse Buel was an outstanding farm journalist. His *Cultivator* kept preaching the value of better methods. The *Rural New-Yorker* and the *American Agriculturist* were also important farm papers.

New York farmers were willing to try new machinery and tools. In 1819 Jethro Wood perfected a plow made of iron parts bolted together. This plow was a big improvement over the crude wooden plows, since it permitted deeper plowing with fewer horses. The horse-drawn mowing machine made easier the task of cutting hay. The grain grower needed machinery because he had only a few days to cut, bind, and gather the wheat. After 1800 the scythe and the cradle gradually replaced the sickle, which had been used since the days of Moses. With the scythe the farmer could cut a much wider swath. The cradle, a scythe fitted with forklike prongs, permitted the harvester to cut and then leave the grain in neat piles. After 1850 some farmers bought horse-drawn reapers Cyrus McCormick was then manufacturing.

Clipper Ships and Canal Boats

On the high seas the wooden sailing vessels remained supreme, although the iron steamship began to provide some competition after 1848. Most sailing vessels were tramps, that is, ships that followed no fixed route or regular schedule. After the War of 1812 another group of ships became important, the regular traders, which followed a fixed route between the important ports. The passenger and mail business fell into their hands because they tried to keep to a time schedule. Monthly service to Liverpool from New York started in 1817. By the middle of the 1840's there were 52 transatlantic *packets* (ships that carry passengers and goods regularly on a fixed route) sailing from New York. Other square-rigged packets sailed between New York and the cotton ports in the South.

Another important change was the ever increasing size of ships. Sloops, small craft with one mast, continued to carry much of the trade on Long Island Sound and the Hudson River until the steamboat took over. But two-masted schooners, which were larger than sloops, carried goods along the Atlantic Coast. For the longer voyages there were square-rigged vessels, two-masted brigs, and three-masted ships. The full-rigged (at least three masts) ships were the pride of the American merchant marine in the golden age of sailing. The East River yards turned out larger and larger vessels. In 1856 the *Ocean Monarch* of 2,145 tons,

It took the clipper ship "Dreadnought" 13 days to cross the Atlantic. How long does it take to cross that ocean today by ship? By air?

the largest of the wooden ships, was launched.

The greatest achievement of the New York and Yankee ship builders was the clipper ship, which had speed, beauty, and grace. As its huge sails filled, its sharp bow and narrow hull cut through the water like a knife. These clippers set speed records never surpassed by other sailing vessels. The clipper ships reached their peak about 1850, when the demand for goods by the California gold-rushers made fortunes for ship owners. Sometimes a ship owner could pay for his ship by selling the cargo from only one voyage.

Shortly after 1855 the clipper era came to an end. The building of too many ships led to low rates, which meant losses for the owners. The iron steamship began to offer cheaper rates and better service. The shipyards, after some delay, improved the engines and adopted such improvements as the screw propeller. Unfortunately, Americans held on to the wooden sailing vessel much too long. As a result, the British who turned to iron steamships early were able to control the best trade routes.

The Erie Canal became the main freight route between the Atlantic coast and the Great Lakes. It played a big part in developing such states as Ohio, Michigan, and Illinois. Thousands of settlers coming from New England or from Europe used the canal boats to transport their goods to new farms in the Middle West. The wheat from middle western farms helped to build up Buffalo and New York City. On the other hand, wheat farmers in eastern New York were forced into dairying because they could not produce wheat as cheaply as the western farmers. Along the canal route, villages sprang up and some became important cities. Canal centers—Buffalo, Rochester, Syracuse, Utica—quickly exceeded in population the turnpike centers—Geneva, Auburn, Canandaigua, Bath—which lost much of their profitable freight business to the canal which moved goods more cheaply.

People in other parts of New York also wanted canals. They could see how population increased, business boomed, and land

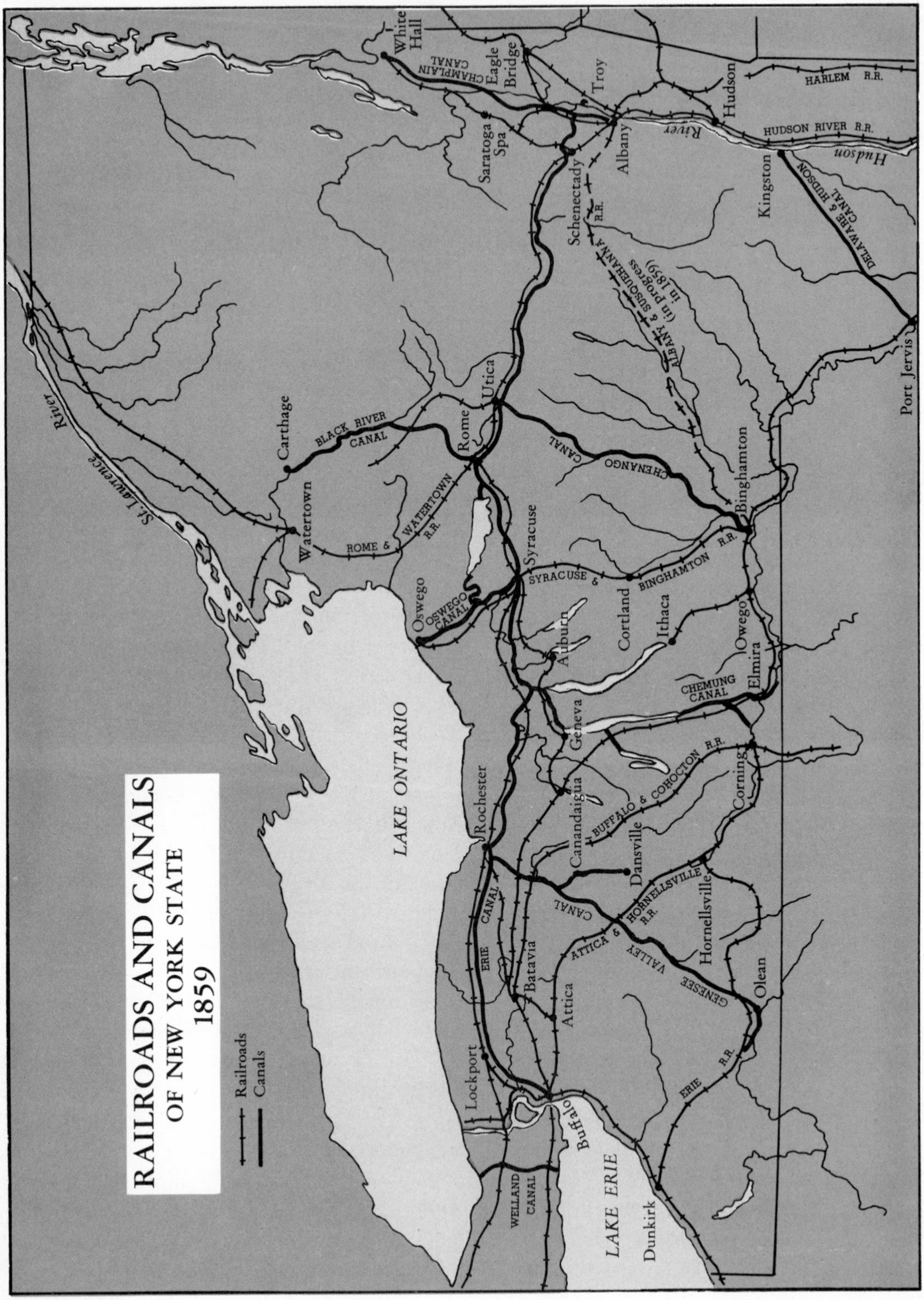

RAILROADS AND CANALS
OF NEW YORK STATE
1859

Railroads
Canals

St. Lawrence River
LAKE ONTARIO
LAKE ERIE
Watertown
Carthage
BLACK RIVER CANAL
ROME & WATERTOWN R.R.
Oswego
OSWEGO CANAL
Rome
Utica
White Hall
CHAMPLAIN CANAL
Saratoga Spa
Eagle Bridge
Lockport
Rochester
ERIE CANAL
WELLAND CANAL
Buffalo
Batavia
Attica
Syracuse
SYRACUSE & BINGHAMTON R.R.
Auburn
Geneva
Canandaigua
Dansville
ATTICA & HORNELLSVILLE R.R.
GENESEE VALLEY CANAL
BUFFALO & COHOCTON R.R.
Schenectady
Troy
Albany
ALBANY & SUSQUEHANNA R.R. (in progress in 1859)
Cortland
CHENANGO CANAL
Ithaca
Dunkirk
ERIE R.R.
Hornellsville
Olean
Corning
CHEMUNG CANAL
Elmira
Owego
Binghamton
Hudson
Kingston
DELAWARE & HUDSON CANAL
Hudson River
HUDSON RIVER R.R.
HARLEM R.R.
Port Jervis

Map 22

prices rose along the Erie route. The state, therefore, built several shorter canals. The Chenango Canal linked Utica with Binghamton on the Susquehanna River. It brought coal from the Pennsylvania coal fields to the industries of the Mohawk Valley. The Genesee Valley Canal, running from Rochester to Olean on the Allegheny River, was a failure and never did enough business to meet the costs of operation. Another set of short canals connected the Erie Canal with Cayuga Lake, Lake Seneca, Keuka Lake, and the Chemung River.

The Oswego Canal from Syracuse to Oswego was the most successful branch. Oswego became an important milling center and much flour was brought down the canal toward New York City. Less successful was the Black River Canal which extended north from Rome to Carthage, and which carried some lumber.

The Delaware and Hudson Canal was the only important canal in New York owned by a private company. It ran from Kingston to Port Jervis and then by the Delaware River to Honesdale, Pennsylvania. Enlarged several times, it carried a tremendous amount of hard coal to New York and New England cities. The profitable company later became the Delaware and Hudson Railroad Company. The Canadians also became canal enthusiasts. They opened the Welland Canal in 1833, which enabled ships to bypass the falls of the Niagara River.

Most canals branching off the Erie did not pay their way. In the 1870's the people of New York voted to keep in operation only the Erie, Oswego, Cayuga, Seneca, Black River, and Champlain canals. The rest were abandoned.

Let us follow Thomas L. McKenney on a packet trip over the Erie Canal in June 1826:

> The boat is drawn . . . by three horses, connected to it by means of a rope about eighty feet long. These horses trot along the *tow path*, as it is called, and which is immediately on the border of the canal, and at the rate, generally, of four miles the hour. . . . The hindmost horse is rode

Travelers in this picture are enjoying the comforts of an Erie Canal boat. There is a "low bridge" ahead. Do you think these people can remain seated?

> by a "lad," as they call him, with a rusty white hat with a large rim, and a crown that fits his own to a shaving. The horses are relieved every ten miles, or fifteen, when the driver is changed also; . . .
>
> I was most agreeably surprised, however, on going into the cabin, to find such a show of accommodation and comfort. Around the sides are settees, some moveable and some stationary, and in the floor, for the accommodation of those who may want to read, or write, are tables, whilst the walls, if I may so call them, . . . are nicely painted, and ornamented with mirrors, etc. etc. . . .
>
> I have lived as much as I could to-day upon the top of this box, called a deck, and which inclines every way from the middle to let the water off, I suppose, but around which are no railings or net work. But this is done at the risk of being scraped off by the bridges, many of which are so low as to leave scarcely room enough between the deck and their sleepers for my body, though I extend it along the deck and spread myself out upon it as flat as a lizard. . . .The bridges appear to me to average at least one for every quarter of a mile. . . .

No wonder that one of the favorite songs was:

> Low bridge! Everybody down!
> Low bridge! We're coming to a town!

Railroads

The first railroad company incorporated in America was the Mohawk and Hudson. It was built to save time for the people traveling between Albany and Schenectady. It took more than a day for canalboats to make the trip between the two cities.

This railroad did not parallel the canal because the legislature did not want anything to hurt the Erie Canal. In fact, the legislature would not permit any railroads paralleling the canal to carry freight except in the winter season. It did this because the state received money from the canal tolls. During the 1840's New Yorkers began to point out the advantages of railroads: speed, dependability, and all-year-round service. When businessmen in other cities on the Atlantic coast, such as Philadelphia, Baltimore, and Boston, started railroads to the west, New Yorkers took fright. Would not these businessmen get the trade of the people living across the Appalachian Mountains? As a result, they put their money behind New York's railroads.

August 9, 1831 was a great day in Albany and in American history. On that day the tiny locomotive, *DeWitt Clinton,* drawing three coaches, started its first run to Schenectady. Thus began the craze for railroads that was to sweep all sections of New York State during the 1830's. Every town believed that good rail connections would make it a great city in the same way that the Erie Canal had built up the cities along its route.

Troy, for example, decided to elbow Albany aside as the main transportation center of eastern New York. First of all, the citizens of Troy built a railroad line to Ballston Spa in order to capture the passenger traffic going to Saratoga Springs. The government of Troy then spent $500,000 to build a railroad to Schenectady, because they wanted to attract passengers from the Albany-Schenectady line. The fact that Troy had a bridge across the Hudson gave it a great advantage over Albany, where passengers had to cross the river by boat. Troy

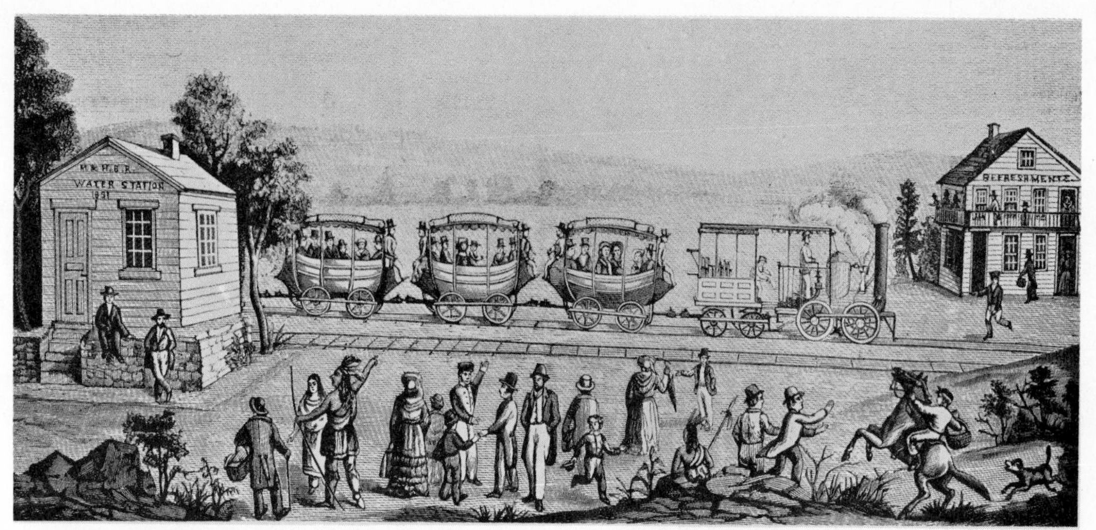

A trial trip by the "De Witt Clinton." Why do you think this locomotive was named thus? Note that the cars are built like stagecoaches. Would you have enjoyed riding this train?

businessmen also tried to get control of the railroads coming from Boston and from New York City. They did not succeed. Meanwhile, citizens of Albany were lending money to a railroad running from Rensselaer to West Stockbridge in Massachusetts. In 1841 this line was completed, and Albany had a connection with Boston.

This achievement shook the businessmen of New York City to the tips of their boots. Boston merchants would take away much of the western trade, especially during the winter months. To stop this, the merchants of New York City began to show more interest in railroads. Two weak companies pushing up the east bank of the Hudson toward Rensselaer received more support. The two railroads reached Rensselaer in 1851. The Albany-Troy feud, however, did not end. Albany tried to get the right to build a bridge, but Troy politicians blocked it for several years. Albany, in turn, blocked Troy from making connections with the Hudson River Railroad at Rensselaer. Finally, Albany secured its bridge. Since that time most of the through railroad traffic has passed through Albany.

Businessmen in other cities demanded railroad service. In a short time a chain of railroads stretched across New York, following the Mohawk Route. In 1836 the Utica and Schenectady began to run cars along its route, the longest one in the world at the time. Three years later the Syracuse and Utica began operations. Other links were opened up: Auburn and Syracuse, Auburn and Rochester, the Tonawanda from Rochester to Batavia to Attica, and the Attica and Buffalo.

Making this chain did not solve all problems. Passengers grew angry because they had to change cars in every city. The companies reluctantly agreed to run through trains. The state in 1851 ended its ban on freight carried by canal-side railroads. After that, the railroads were able to attract practically all of the freight except the bulky lumber and wheat products. In 1853 Erastus Corning combined the short lines and their branches into the New York Central.

Cornelius Vanderbilt, after making a tremendous fortune in steamboats and sailing vessels, became interested in railroads. First, he acquired railroads running from

A Hudson River Railroad locomotive. Note the changes and improvements made since the "De Witt Clinton."

New York to Albany. Next, he got control of the New York Central. Then, he added to his empire the Lake Shore and Southern, which permitted him to run trains all the way from New York City to Chicago.

Farmers and businessmen in all sections of the state demanded railroads. People in the Southern Tier, as the counties west of the Catskills and bordering Pennsylvania are called, were particularly eager for a railroad. In 1832 some New York merchants and enthusiasts decided to build a railroad through this section in spite of the obstacles presented by steep hills, winding valleys, and many gorges. Only a few thousand people lived in these counties. Few people wanted to invest any money in this doubtful and costly venture. As a result, the promoters went to the state legislature and finally secured a loan (never paid back) of over $3,000,000. Construction was slow. The Erie, as this new railroad was called, reached Binghamton in 1848, Corning in 1849, and Dunkirk in 1851. President Millard Fillmore and Daniel Webster rode on the first train which ran from Piermont on the Hudson to Dunkirk, the longest continuous railroad line in the world.

The Erie Railroad had many troubles. At first its terminals were poorly located. The six-foot-wide track used by the Erie required special equipment and cars and prevented the company from making good connections with railroads using the standard width of track. To add to its troubles, a group of dishonest men got hold of the company and ruined its financial standing.

But the Erie survived these troubles and became an important carrier. It acquired connections to Jersey City and to Buffalo. Later, it changed its track to the standard gauge. The citizens of the Southern Tier were thankful to the Erie for bringing them closer to the great markets of the east coast.

During the 1850's several attempts were made to connect the New York Central and the Erie railroads. From Buffalo, Rochester, Syracuse, Utica, and Albany, railroad companies pushed their steel prongs southward. The most important railroad was the line (now part of the Delaware and Hudson Railroad) which finally reached Binghamton from Albany after the Civil War.

Improvements kept step with the growth of the railroad network. Solid iron T-shaped rails replaced the earlier wooden rails capped with an iron strap. These straps often worked loose, poked up through the floor, and injured passengers. In 1847 the New York legislature required all railroads to install the T rail. The first roadbeds of heavy granite block had no "give" and shook cars to pieces. After much experimentation, engineers found that wooden cross ties imbedded in gravel provided a better roadway. Locomotives became more powerful and much more dependable.

Passengers complained loudly about the soot, hard seats, continual jolting, and long delays. At first, each car had a hand brake which meant sharp jolts as each car was stopped. George Westinghouse of Schenectady developed the air brake, which permitted the engineer to apply pressure evenly on each car, and in that way to stop much of the jolting. Fences to keep animals off the track, heavier rails, and improved cars and wheels helped to cut down the number of accidents. One of the most important changes was using the telegraph to dispatch trains. Superintendents would wire ahead their position. As a result, engineers on trains coming from the opposite direction knew when to pull over to the siding or speed forward. Another improvement was the sleeping car. Three New Yorkers—George Pullman, Webster Wagner, and Theodore Woodruff—were responsible for developing the sleeping car, parlor car, and diner.

Summary

During the Age of Homespun most New York families consisted of a husband, wife, and children, all of whom had special tasks. The seasons largely determined the type of work the families performed. Pioneer farmers tended to be self-sufficient but tried to find a cash crop, with dairying bringing in the greatest income. Improvements slowly reached the farmers through farm papers, fairs, and the efforts of reformers. The wooden sailing vessels were supreme on the high seas, with the clipper ship reaching its peak about 1850. The Erie Canal was such a smashing success that it set off a canal boom in other parts of the state and throughout the Northeast. The Erie Canal cut freight rates, gave life to old and new cities, and linked the Midwest to New York City. Railroads during the 1850's carried most of the traffic. Cornelius Vanderbilt acquired lines that ran from New York to Chicago. New Yorkers had a good deal to do with making rail travel more safe and more comfortable.

Checking the high points

1. What kind of families existed in the Age of Homespun?

2. How did the seasons determine the pattern of life?

3. What skills did people have in the countryside and villages?

4. Why did dairying spread?

5. How did information about agricultural improvements reach the farmers?

6. Why did clipper ships rise and decline?

7. What was the effect of Erie Canal within and beyond New York State?

8. What railroads were built before 1860?

9. How did New Yorkers make railroad travel safer and more comfortable?

Think these over

1. Certain jobs should be assigned to men and others to women. Explain why you agree or disagree.

2. True or false: Change, not stability, was the main feature of life in the Age of Homespun. Give examples to support your answer.

3. Do you believe that government should support canals, railroads, and bus lines even if they do not make a profit and even lose money? Why or why not?

Checking locations

Geneva
Auburn
Binghamton
Olean
Port Jervis
Carthage
Ballston Spa
Saratoga Springs
Rensselaer
Southern Tier
Dunkirk

Vocabulary building

patrilineal
matrilineal
nuclear family
extended family
homespun
cradle
scythe
packets
clipper ships
tow path
tramp steamer
full-rigged ship
aqueduct
railroad terminal

Chapter Objectives

To learn about

- the growth of cities in New York in the first half of the 19th century
- the importance of trade and industry in pre-Civil War New York
- early attempts at organizing unions

chapter 14

NEW YORKERS EXPAND THEIR BUSINESS EMPIRE

New York City: The Nation's Largest City

Shortly after the War of 1812 New York City took the lead in population from Philadelphia and Boston, which in colonial times had usually had more people. This it has never given up.

Many things account for the rise of New York City: (1) Its merchants gained control of the important trade routes. New York got most of the trade across the Atlantic partly because of its fine harbor, but largely because of intelligent action. (2) Right after the War of 1812 many British manufacturers shipped their surplus textile goods to New York to get what they could for them. (3) A New York law said that all goods offered for sale at an *auction* had to be sold for whatever they would bring. (An auction is a sale where goods are sold to the highest bidder.) Sometimes goods sold for practically nothing. (4) New York also was the key port for most of the passenger traffic between the United States and Europe. In 1817 the Black Ball Line began service on a regular schedule with Liverpool, England. Businessmen and immigrants liked this arrangement because they knew when the ships would leave and arrive. In 1825 and for the next hundred years, one-half of all goods imported to the United States came through New York Harbor.

New Yorkers also got a big share of the trade passing up and down the Atlantic and Gulf coasts. They even captured the cotton trade, the largest export business of the United States. Ships, carrying manufactured goods, would leave for southern ports and pick up a cargo of cotton. Sometimes they would return to New York filled with cotton. More frequently they would go directly to Liverpool or other European ports. Then the ship would bring back to New York manufactured goods and immigrants. This trade system was known as the Cotton Triangle.

Everybody knows how much New York

South Street in Manhattan in 1857. The building with the five chimneys is still standing. This gives an idea of how much activity there was at the waterfront.

owes to the Erie Canal, but let us not forget that even before this canal was started New York City had become the largest city in the country. The Erie Canal gave New York the best route to the interior of the United States, which was growing at a tremendous rate. From the interior came a flood of wheat, flour, and lumber. In return, the merchants of New York sent manufactured goods, sugar, spices, and other products which the country storekeepers ordered for their customers.

The railroads also contributed to the commercial greatness of New York. By the time of the Civil War, New York had rail connections with all the important cities. Its links to the west—the New York Central and the Erie railroads—were beginning to rival the Erie Canal in bringing to Manhattan the products of the territory west of the Appalachian Mountains.

All these things encouraged the growth of manufacturing in New York City. Businessmen who wanted to set up factories found plenty of money in the banks. Labor of every kind was plentiful. The market kept increasing with the growing population of the city, state, and nation. A network of canalboats, steamboats, railroad cars, tramp sailing vessels, and packet lines fed the city with cheap raw materials and carried away finished products.

New York outranked Boston and Philadelphia as the financial center of the United States. A large number of banks were established in New York City. The New York Stock Exchange, organized in 1817, became the place where brokers bought and sold stocks and bonds. Manufacturers and railroad promoters who needed money for business came to New York to borrow it.

For all these reasons, the businessmen of New York City became the richest and most important in the country. White collar workers, clerks, and skilled craftsmen also found plenty of jobs. Even the poor found it possible to work their way up the ladder to better jobs.

Upstate Trading Centers

New York today has cities of all sizes, ranging from New York City, which has 8,000,000 people, to Sherrill, which has about 2,000 residents. Practically all of the cities were founded before the Civil War, although they grew most rapidly after that war. Let us see why cities began at certain places. The waterways of New York played the most important part in deciding the location of our major cities, but some cities grew up near natural resources. Syracuse, for example, is near the salt wells, and Rochester is at the Genesee Falls. Before the coming of factories, the size of upstate cities depended on the number of farmers and lumbermen in the surrounding countryside who would come to the city to trade.

The first cities of New York clung to the banks of the Hudson River. New York City was the transfer point between ocean and river shipping. Albany was at the head of navigation on the Hudson. The small village of Schenectady grew up at the place where goods floating down the Mohawk River had to be taken overland to Albany.

After the Revolution more cities sprang up along the Hudson, especially after thousands of farmers began to settle land back from the river. Six miles to the north of Albany some Yankees founded Troy. Its merchants served the growing farm population of western Vermont and the upper Hudson. The city of Hudson had a rather

The busy harbor at Oswego about 1850. Note the different types of vessels. Can you find a paddle wheeler? A propellor-driven steamboat? A raft?

unusual origin. It was founded by some whalers from Nantucket Island, who had suffered severely from the British raids during the Revolutionary War and had decided to move to a safer place. Whaling vessels left Hudson for long trips on the high seas for over 40 years, bringing back to the Hudson Valley their cargoes of whale oil. However, whales were used for more than their valuable oil.

New Yorkers could not decide for many years where the state capital should be. During the Revolution the legislature wandered from town to town, partly to escape British raids. After the British had left, the legislature moved to New York City. But the farmers wanted the representatives nearer the farms and out of the "wicked city," which was controlled by the Federalist merchants. In 1797 the legislature voted to make Albany the permanent capital.

Almost all the cities founded after 1800 were located along waterways. Buffalo, at the foot of Lake Erie, was at the southern end of the portage around the falls of the Niagara River. Binghamton was built where the Chenango joined the Susquehanna rivers. Ogdensburg grew up at the junction of the Oswegatchie and St. Lawrence rivers. A town usually grew up at the head and the foot of each of the larger Finger Lakes. Note the location of Geneva, Ithaca, and Canandaigua.

Turnpikes, too, fixed the location of cities and villages, since settlements grew at the point where turnpikes crossed or reached important waterways. Turnpikes also increased the business and the size of Albany, Troy, Catskill, Kingston, and other ports that had grown up beside the Hudson River.

Let us examine one city to see how many factors helped its growth. Utica was at the head of boat navigation on the Mohawk. A ford made it easy to cross the river there. The state road, called the Great Genesee Road, ran west from Utica to the Genesee Valley. Later the Erie Canal, and still later, the railroad gave a big boost to the growth of Utica. In the 1840's Utica became an industrial city as well as a commercial center. Businessmen built textile factories, using coal brought from Pennsylvania over the Chenango Canal, which ran from Binghamton to Utica.

The Erie Canal had a very important effect upon the location and growth of the larger upstate cities. Syracuse, hardly more than a cluster of houses around salt springs, grew rapidly after the canal reached central

Saratoga Springs

Saratoga Springs has a very unusual history, quite unlike that of any other city in New York. Animals were the first to find the mineral springs bubbling out of the rocks. The Indians regarded the region as one of their favorite hunting grounds. White men heard about the springs even before the Revolution and bathed in the waters, which were supposed to cure many ailments. In 1802 Gideon Putnam built the first large hotel and Saratoga became one of the first resort cities in the United States. To attract still more visitors, the leaders of Saratoga began to offer all kinds of entertainment, especially horse racing, dancing, and card playing. The rich and the famous flocked to Saratoga in order to have a good time. It is said that the excellent chefs at Saratoga discovered how to make "potato chips."

New York. Rochester's population more than tripled in the first 10 years after the canal was opened. Flour mills multiplied along the river banks, and hundreds of men built canalboats. Buffalo shot upward in population, since it was the place where cargoes from the Great Lakes were transferred to the Erie Canal. The canal probably checked the growth of older turnpike centers, such as Auburn, Geneva, and Canandaigua, since the heavy freight no longer passed over the turnpikes. The Erie Canal had much the same effect upon the Cherry Valley Turnpike that the Thomas E. Dewey Thruway had upon Route 20 over a hundred years later. Look up the Thruway and Route 20 on a road map. Do you understand why Route 20 has lost traffic since the Thruway was built?

Early manufacturers relied upon waterpower to turn the wheels in mills and factories. The falls on the Oswego and the Genesee rivers attracted millers who needed power to turn the huge wheels for grinding wheat into flour. The textile mills at Cohoes used the power in the falls of the Mohawk. During the 1830's and 1840's factory owners found that coal provided a more reliable source of power than water. As a result, factories using steam power sprang up along the route of the canals and the railroads.

The railroads did not create many new cities in New York. They generally served cities already in existence. The Erie Railroad, however, gave a boost to the small villages in the Southern Tier. Binghamton, at the southern end of the Chenango Canal, enjoyed, after 1848, direct rail connections with New York City and shortly thereafter with Buffalo. The city, however, remained small. Elmira and Corning were very small towns before the Civil War.

Country Storekeepers

The country storekeeper was an important man in his community. He bought goods from farmers and sold them to merchants in the large cities. He imported hardware, cloth, and other necessities used by farm families. Usually the storekeeper was active in political and community affairs.

If you have seen the country store at the Farmers' Museum in Cooperstown, you have a good idea of how a country store looked and smelled a hundred years ago. What a difference from the well-lighted and clean supermarkets with colorful packages, canned goods, and bins of fresh vegetables! Imagine a rather gloomy room with only one or two lanterns. The storekeeper often stood behind glass cases where he kept jewelry, candy, or small articles of clothing. Under the counter were bins full of dry beans, rice, tea, and coffee. On the shelves

The interior of the Old Country Store in Cooperstown at the Farmers' Museum.

were tins containing spices. Other shelves had bolts of silk, gingham, and calico, which the housewives admired and fingered. In the back of the store or in the cellar were barrels of vinegar, molasses, salt pork, chests of tea, bags of coffee, boxes of cheese, and kegs of codfish or mackerel. From the rafters hung clothes for men along with slabs of bacon and smoked ham. A heavy, rich odor hung over the entire store.

The center of the store had a stove which gave off much heat and some light. It was the job of the storekeeper's boy to keep the fire going and to run errands. The clerk waited on customers and sometimes delivered goods with his wagon. During the day many men wandered into the store, not only to buy goods, but also to swap stories and to talk politics. Every store had a couple of old-timers who played endless games of checkers. They often reached into the nearby cracker barrel.

A trip to the store was something special for most farm families. After all, the roads were rough and travel was slow. Then, too, most families tried to raise much of their own foodstuffs and make their own clothes. Farmers usually visited the country store about once a month—perhaps more often in the fall when they had goods to sell. The farmer filled his wagon with wheat, butter, and meat while the housewife brought along some eggs. At the store they argued with the storekeeper over the price of farm goods. Then the farmer ordered some hardware, salt, and other supplies. Meanwhile his wife bought some coffee, tea, and perhaps a couple yards of calico. Little cash changed hands. The storekeeper copied down in his big ledger what the farmer ordered and then he gave him credit for the goods brought in.

When the storekeeper had enough wheat, meat, or butter to fill his wagon, he sent it eastward to the Hudson Valley markets. His wagon would bring back goods needed in the store. These goods he bought on credit from the large merchants in Albany or New York City.

Manufacturing Moves From Home To Factory

The work of the world was done with hand tools before 1800. Power came from human and animal muscle or from the harnessing of running water or wind. Since 1800, machines have gradually supplied an increasing share of power. This shift from hand tools to power machinery is what we mean by the term, *Industrial Revolution.*

In 1800 the average family produced most of its own food and almost all of its clothing, shoes, and household and farm tools. As the farmers sold more and more

You don't see any power tools on this Cooperstown carpenter's bench. The Industrial Revolution brought many changes.

wheat, potash, and meat products, they came to rely upon the craftsmen and the storekeepers. They bought goods from the millers, shoemakers, blacksmiths, weavers, sawmill operators, and tanners who set up their shops in the new villages. Some of these craftsmen hired more helpers and supplied not only their local customers, but also sent their flour, leather, cloth, and lumber to outside markets.

Americans followed the example of Great Britain in turning to factory production. Heavy equipment required the construction of larger buildings called mills or factories. Improvements in spinning led to the manufacturing of extra yarn. This, in turn, led inventors to improve looms for weaving cloth. Gradually the power loom, driven by water, then by steam engine, was developed. Power increased production.

Soon, businessmen bought machines and put up factories. They hired workers and managers to run the machines. The output was sold to merchants far and wide.

The making of goods in factories caused great changes. These, however, came rather slowly. As late as 1850 most goods were still made by hand in homes and shops. Only a small fraction of the people worked in factories. Fewer than 10,000 New Yorkers were working in factories in 1820, and most of these worked in the small textile mills of Oneida, Columbia, and Dutchess counties. The textile industry got its start when the War of 1812 made it hard for citizens to import British textiles. The first mills sometimes completed only part of the process of making cloth. Housewives often wove on hand looms the yarn they got from the local factories. Gradually the mills became larger and finally took over the whole job of manufacturing cloth. This meant that cheap cloth was available everywhere. Railway trains and canal boats took it even into the less settled parts of New York. As a result, housewives stopped spinning and weaving.

The manufacture of clothing was begun before the Civil War. Since then, more people have worked in the clothing industry than in any other industry in New York. At first, master tailors made suits on order for their customers. Today most people wear ready-made clothes. What caused the change? For one thing, the invention of the sewing machine made it possible to hire semi-skilled women instead of highly skilled tailors. Secondly, most Americans were willing to buy clothes that were ready-to-wear because they were less expensive than tailor-made clothes. New York City and Rochester were among the first cities to manufacture large amounts of clothing.

The forges and furnaces of the colonial iron industry were tiny compared with the furnaces in use by the time of the Civil War. Henry Burden of Troy was a leader in iron-making, and invented a machine which made a horseshoe every second. Iron also went into railroad rails, freight cars, locomotives, bridges, plows, steam engines, and stoves. Although lagging far behind Pittsburgh and other Pennsylvania cities, New York City and Troy turned out a large quantity of iron products.

New York became the greatest leather-producing state. Tanneries, where hides were made into leather, sprang up in all parts of the state. In the Catskills several large tanneries were built near the large stands of hemlock trees, the bark of which was used to make tanning fluid. The hides tanned in the Catskill tanneries went into shoes, luggage, and other leather goods.

A detailed engraving of an iron foundry in the 1840's.

Before the Civil War, New York was the leading salt producer. After the Revolution, the state government bought from the Onondaga Indians the salt springs near Syracuse. The state leased lots to salt makers, who paid a tax of four cents on each bushel of salt they produced. Salt water flowed into huge kettles under which wood fires were begun. After the water had boiled off, men collected the salt, put it in barrels, and shipped it to every part of the United States. Salt water is still being pumped and converted to salt.

The industries preparing foodstuffs and beverages—slaughterhouses, breweries, distilleries, flour mills—flourished. In Rochester, and later in Buffalo and Oswego, large mills ground out the flour which was grown in the neighborhood or which came from the West.

Along the East River in New York City there grew up the nation's largest shipyards, managed by many of the ablest shipbuilders. The 1840's and 1850's was the golden age of the wooden ships. Builders turned out large numbers of packets, clippers, warships, steamships, schooners, and rivercraft.

After the Revolution the lumbering industry grew rapidly until New York rivaled Pennsylvania as the greatest producer of lumber. Conditions were favorable. On the slopes of the Adirondacks, Catskills, and Alleghenies grew fine stands of white pine suitable for most building and carpentry. Citizens in the large cities at the mouth of the Hudson, the Delaware, Susquehanna, and Genesee rivers kept demanding more lumber for their homes, stores, and factories. The steamboats and locomotives used up large amounts of wood for fuel.

At first, small sawmills sprang up along every stream. Operators piled boards, staves, and shingles on rafts which floated down to the cities. Of course, most sawmills also served the local farmers who needed lumber for barns, fences, and houses. As the years passed, sawmills became larger and used steam for power. Towns such as Glens Falls, Fort Edward, Watertown, and Ogdensburg had large mills. Lumberjacks (often farmers) cut logs during the fall and winter, and oxen dragged the logs to the banks of the river. During the spring floods, the logs were pushed into the river and floated downstream. Most of the lumber of the Adirondacks reached Albany, where thousands of men loaded it on ships bound for New York City and other ports.

The furniture industry also grew rapidly. German cabinetmakers in New York produced quality pieces, as well as cheap tables, chairs, and chests. They also made cases for pianos, for it was at this time that Henry Steinway began to make New York world-famous as the major center of piano manufacturing.

Wage Earners Organize

In colonial days the most important group of workers were craftsmen such as carpenters, hatters, bakers, and masons. Proud of their skill, these craftsmen refused to permit anyone to practice a craft within city limits without going through a long training period. A person undergoing this training was called an apprentice. There were also unskilled workers in the towns and cities and in New York a number of black slaves. But there were no factory workers like those of today.

The state gradually abolished slavery and the blacks went to work as free laborers. Even the craftsmen found the apprentice system breaking down. Many newcomers from the countryside or from Europe demanded the right to work at any occupation. Furthermore, employers tried to use unskilled labor in order to cut their costs. For example, businessmen bought sewing machines and then divided the task of making shoes into several simple operations. Instead of hiring skilled shoemakers they hired women and children to perform these simple jobs. The new factories put thousands of craftsmen out of business. Some of them found it necessary to work in the factories.

Most workers in the textile factories were women and children. Women had done the spinning and weaving in their own homes for a long time. They were willing to work for half the wages of men. Many factory jobs were done by children. To us, this practice seems cruel. But remember that most children on the farm or in town had to help the family as soon as they were strong enough. Much of the work was simple enough for even youngsters to perform. Besides, people in those days believed that idle children would get into mischief. It took quite a few years before they realized that factory work was bad for the health, education, and morals of children.

Workmen had to put in long hours six days a week. At first, textile mills required women to work 12 or more hours a day. During the 1830's the movement for a 10-hour day made headway and by 1860 this had become the usual thing in most lines of work.

Wage earners realized that they had certain problems in common. Consequently, they tried to organize unions and to secure reforms. By the 1830's they were demanding changes, such as free public schools, a 10-hour day, and repeal of the law sending people to jail for small debts. The various craftsmen were the first to organize unions. Printers, shoemakers, and tailors were the most successful in winning better wages and conditions of work. But these unions ran into many troubles. Bad times and the coming of thousands of immigrants created an oversupply of job hunters which, in turn, made it difficult for the unions to keep up their wages. Goods made by machinery operated by women or unskilled workers undersold handmade articles. During the early 1850's, however, good times returned. Existing trade unions became stronger, and new unions were organized.

Laboring conditions gradually improved from 1800 to 1860, although some families suffered severely from unemployment and low wages. Only a few workers were discontented enough to listen to radical leaders. After all, conditions in Europe were even worse. Furthermore, most working people had faith that they, or at least their children, would share in the opportunities provided by the growth of America.

Summary

The Empire State was taking the lead in almost every kind of business by the time of the Civil War. In trade, New York was far and away the champion, with hardly a serious competitor. The fine transportation system and the rise of New York City as a port were two of the main reasons for New York's position. Upstate, a number of important cities sprang up along the Erie Canal. The storekeepers in the small towns exchanged the wheat of the farmers for the manufactured goods and imports which the New York City merchants obtained.

Meanwhile, manufacturing grew rapidly as it moved from the home into the factory. The making of cotton and woolen cloth, originally a home operation, soon grew into the huge textile industry. Later the invention of the sewing machine laid the foundation for the large and important manufacture of clothing. Other factories and mills which produced a large variety of products were founded in many parts of the state. The growth of manufacturing caused important changes for working people. Many craftspeople were hit hard by the rise of the factory. Factories emphasized old labor problems, such as long hours, low wages, and child labor. Some workers began to organize labor unions to better their conditions.

Checking the high points

1. Why did New York City become the nation's largest city?

2. How did waterways affect the location of cities?

3. What effect did the Erie Canal have on the growth of upstate cities?

4. How did the country storekeeper help the growth of business?

5. In what ways did New Yorkers depend upon craftsmen in the early 1800's?

6. What caused the rise of factories?

7. Why did the making of cloth move from the home to the factory?

8. Why was New York a great leather-producing state?

9. How did New Yorkers get their lumber to market?

10. What factors harmed the status of the craftsman?

11. What problems arose as a result of the rise of factories?

12. How did workers attempt to solve some of their problems?

Think these over

1. Do individual craftsmen or factories make better goods?

2. Has the factory system helped or harmed the American people?

3. Is "child labor" a bad thing?

4. Should women workers receive less money than men for doing the same job?

Checking locations

Troy
Hudson
Nantucket
Saratoga Springs
Ogdensburg
Cortland
Canandaigua
East River
Geneva
Rochester
Utica
Glens Falls
Cohoes
Elmira
Corning
Fort Edward
Watertown
Binghamton
Homer
Ithaca
Prattsville
Auburn

Vocabulary building

metropolitan
auction
broker
capital
portage
junction
textiles
tannery
leased
apprentice
radical
ford

Chapter Objectives

To learn about

- pre-Civil War immigration to New York
- the urbanization of New York City
- the rise of reform and religious movements in pre-Civil War New York
- New York's leadership role in the arts and literature

chapter 15

NEW YORKERS MAKE SOCIAL PROGRESS

European Immigrants

Fairly few immigrants came to the United States from Europe in the period between the opening of the Revolution and the end of the War of 1812. During most of these years Europe was at war, and crossing the ocean in wartime was very dangerous. After 1820 the number of immigrants began to rise, and after 1845 the number became very large. By 1855 people born in Europe made up over one-fourth of the population of the state and nearly one-half of the people of New York City.

Almost all of the immigrants before the Civil War came from western and northern Europe. Most emigrated from Ireland and the German states, but English, Scots, and Welsh also came in good numbers. Most of these people were fleeing hard times and bad government. When they heard about the fertile land, the good jobs, and the political freedom in America, they wanted to come here.

A few immigrants were political refugees driven out by the wars and revolutions in Europe. Napoleon's brother, Joseph Bonaparte, who had been King of Spain, was one of these. He lived in a home near the St. Lawrence River.

The Irish came to America because conditions at that time in their lovely homeland were unbearable. In the land of tiny farms and large estates owned by English landlords, the rapidly increasing population could find no outlet. The tenant farmers and the farm laborers hated the landlords because they were English, and because they charged high rents. Furthermore, the Catholic Irish wanted independence from the English, who forced them to support the Church of England.

After 1815 increasing numbers of Irish sailed across the Atlantic, because they heard of liberty and decent living in America. Then, in 1845, a potato blight hit Ireland. This was a disease which killed the potato plants, the chief source of food for

Irish immigrants land at the Battery in New York City in 1855. The round building at the left is Castle Garden, a harbor fort, later used as a theater, and still later as an aquarium.

many Irish. Thousands starved to death, but many more fled to England and to America. By 1860 over 200,000 Irish lived in New York City, which was second only to Dublin as the greatest Irish community in the world.

Many Irish made their way in the New World, and some won wealth and honors. Watch the career of a typical Irishman who settled in New York. We will call him Patrick Kelly.

Pat was an 18-year-old lad who grew up on a farm in Galway. He wanted to become a farmer like his father, but he had no money to buy expensive land. He heard stories about America, where even the poorest man could rise to the top. Saving a few pennies, Pat walked to Dublin, where he took a boat to Liverpool. At Liverpool he wandered down to the docks where the cotton ships were tied up. He learned that he could go to America for a few dollars. The two-month trip was a terrible experience, since hundreds of men, women, and children were crowded into the dark hold of the ship. An epidemic ran through the ship, and several passengers died. The crew simply tossed the bodies overboard.

When Pat landed in New York, he ran into some petty criminals, who wanted to swindle him of his few possessions. Fortunately, a society of Irish-Americans came to his aid by finding him a job swinging a pick.

Pat soon found a better job in a grocery store. Within a few years he had saved enough money to bring over his childhood sweetheart, Katie O'Connell. After they were married, they opened a little store and waited on the customers for long hours each day. Pat, however, did take off time for other matters. He attended St. Mary's Church faithfully. He marched in the St. Patrick's Day parade. He joined the Democratic party, in which he became a local leader. He kept informed of civic affairs.

By 1860 Pat was a prosperous and influential citizen. Every Sunday he, Katie, and their five children attended Mass in the family pew. People asked his advice about candidates to put up for public office. He built a large brick house with a fine garden behind it. America, for Pat, and for thousands more, proved to be the land of opportunity.

Many Irish settled in the cities along the canals and railroads which they helped

Rochester from the west in 1853. Note the canalboats and the many bridges linking the parts of the city.

build. Irishmen often went to work in the new factories springing up throughout the state. The Irish became the backbone of the Democratic party, especially in the cities.

Second only to the Irish in number were immigrants from the various German states. Although many settled in New York and Brooklyn, most of them headed north and west. In both Buffalo and Rochester the Germans were more numerous than the Irish.

Many things were causing unrest among the German people during the first half of the 1800's. Poor crops and low prices ruined the farmers. Germany was divided into many provinces, ruled by petty kings and princes who laid heavy taxes and permitted no political freedom. The population was growing rapidly because of large families. For the young men, there were few jobs and no more land. Attempts to improve their government failed, and many had to flee the country. Throughout Germany people were repeating the famous line by the poet Goethe, "Amerika Du Hast Es Besser," (America you have it better). They began to read travel accounts of America and to receive letters from friends who had gone to the New World. These early settlers had good news: jobs for everyone, high wages, cheap and good land, freedom to do what they liked.

Many German immigrants were skilled craftsmen who turned out fine furniture and pianos. German mechanics helped operate machines in the new factories. The breweries were almost always operated by Germans. Other Germans became contractors. Some brought new industries to America. For example, John Jacob Bausch, a lens grinder, started the Bausch & Lomb Optical Company in Rochester. The Germans set up many different kinds of churches. Because they enjoyed dancing and singing, they organized bands and singing societies.

The Irish and the Germans tried to become "American" as quickly as possible. When the Civil War came, thousands of immigrants and their children fought in the New York regiments for the defense of the Union.

New Yorkers Become City Dwellers

The growth of cities and towns was fully as spectacular as the settlement of the upstate frontier. Before the Civil War almost half the people of the Empire State lived in cities and towns. Over one million lived in metropolitan New York, that is, New York City and its surrounding communities.

We often admire the courage and resourcefulness of the pioneers. But remember that the people in our early cities also faced danger and hardships. The lady needleworker feeding her children on her tiny earnings was as heroic as the pioneer housewife carrying out her household chores in the wilderness. The laborers on the docks, the workers in the factory or on construction jobs faced just as many dangers as the frontiersmen.

More city dwellers died at a younger age than those living in the country. The reasons were many: bad housing, poor sanitation, epidemics, poor food, and little medical care. Health conditions were very bad. Streets and alleys were not only muddy, but also ankle deep in garbage and filth. The hogs, dogs, and rats which nosed around the garbage spread disease. Clean and wholesome milk could not be bought. Most people drank water from wells into which sewage drained. New York City in the 1840's built Croton Dam in order to create a supply of clean country water. The other cities, however, did very little to get pure country water until after the Civil War.

People came to the cities so fast that it was impossible to build enough houses. The poor herded together in old rat-infested buildings or in tenements. Some houses had six persons to every room. Thousands had to live in cellars, attics, or shanties on the outskirts of town. Only the rich had inside bathrooms.

Fire was always a threat. Every city ex-

Until the 1820's, the Tea Water Pump in New York City supplied 10 to 12 thousand people with fresh water for their favorite beverage, and for other purposes. "Carmen" filled their casks and delivered water to those who lived too far from the pump to fetch water themselves. Obviously, the supply was hardly adequate for fire fighting.

perienced great fires in which whole city blocks became blackened ruins. The volunteer fire companies tried their best, but they could do little more than keep the fires from spreading. City dwellers feared criminals as much as frontiersmen feared the Indians. The lack of street lamps made it easy for criminals to sneak into buildings or to rob people on the streets at night. The police were unable to give proper protection. In fact, New York City did not have around-the-clock police protection until 1844.

By 1879 the Roman Catholic Church had grown sufficiently to have built St. Patrick's Cathedral on New York City's Fifth Avenue. Its 17 marble side altars and 70 stained glass windows make it one of the most beautiful Gothic-style churches in America. This picture was taken from the RCA Building.

Mayors and city leaders did not provide honest and efficient government for several reasons. All too often ordinary citizens were so busy with their own affairs that they did not bother to vote or hold office. The government fell into the hands of bosses, who built up political machines. These bosses did not tackle the problems of slums, fire and police protection, and schools. The reformers of the time were more interested in checking the spread of slavery and closing the saloons than they were in cleaning up the dishonesty in their city governments.

Nevertheless, some progress was made toward solving the worst problems of city life. The cities of New York by 1860 were providing free public elementary schools. Some had opened high schools for ambitious youths. Church groups and kindhearted people did much to help the poor and the sick. Some towns and cities forced saloons to close at midnight, and to stop serving young people. Some citizens worked hard to secure honest government, and some political leaders served the people well. For example, the City Council of New York set aside Central Park in the 1850's as a recreation spot for its citizens. Slowly New Yorkers were learning how to improve living conditions and government in our cities.

Churches

The first half of the nineteenth century was an exciting time in which to live. New Yorkers tried to build a richer life of the spirit and mind which would equal their gains in democratic government. Progress was made in many ways.

More people in New York began to join

churches. The passing of the rugged frontier gave farmers and their families more time for such matters as church and school. Furthermore, many newcomers from New England or from Ireland were loyal Christians who naturally wanted to join a church. Able young men began to preach to people in all parts of the state about the importance of worshiping God. As a result, churches grew in number and in strength.

The Roman Catholic Church grew very rapidly and by 1855 it was the largest single group in the Empire State. The Catholic Church gained many members after 1845 when tens of thousands of Irish and Germans arrived in New York City. Bishop John Hughes and his priests had to work hard to build enough churches and schools to handle the increase in membership. They were very successful, especially in the larger cities.

In the period before the Civil War most New Yorkers were Protestants. There were dozens of different church groups, but most Protestants belonged to one of seven churches: Methodist Episcopal, Baptist, Presbyterian, Congregational, Protestant Episcopal, Dutch Reformed, or Lutheran.

The Methodists made the most striking gains. Not far behind them were the Baptists. The leaders of these two groups preached at every crossroads and street corner. As a result, thousands of people joined the Methodist and the Baptist churches.

The Presbyterians and Congregationalists made gains in the cities and towns, as well as among the prosperous farmers. Newcomers from New England usually joined one of these groups. The Episcopal Church grew steadily. Most of its churches were located in the larger cities. The Dutch Reformed Church grew slowly since it built few churches outside the Hudson Valley. Lutheran churches sprang up wherever the German people settled.

An impressive statue of the Angel Moroni tops Hill Cumorah near Palmyra. This is the place Mormons believe the angel left the tablets which are the basis of the religion Joseph Smith founded.

Several thousand Jews settled in New York City before the Civil War. The first congregation had been founded in 1654. The synagogue was the center of religious activities and of Jewish community affairs as well. New York now has the largest Jewish population in the world.

New York was also the birthplace of several new religions. Joseph Smith of Palmyra founded the Church of Jesus Christ of the Latter-Day Saints, which is known as the Mormon Church. Eventually the Mormons, under Brigham Young, set up a community near Salt Lake in Utah. Today there are over three million Mormons in this country. Every August thousands visit Palmyra where Smith founded the Mormon religion.

Another new religion was that founded by William Miller of Hampton in Washington County. He preached the idea that the world was coming to an end. After careful study of the Bible, Miller fixed the date in 1843. Thousands of people believed Miller and waited in prayerful attitude for the final day. Nothing happened! Despite this disappointment, Miller's followers organized the Adventist Church which today carries on a very active missionary program throughout the world.

Scarcely had the excitement over Miller's prediction died away when the news spread through upstate New York that two young girls, Margaret and Kate Fox of Hydeville (near Rochester), were speaking with the spirits of the dead. The Fox sisters heard noises at night, especially in the cellar of their house. The younger girl began to make contact with the spirit. "Here, Mr. Splitfoot, do as I do," she said, snapping her fingers. The spirit answered by rapping twice. Later, the girls admitted that they had been fooling everyone. They made the rapping noises by throwing their big toes in and out of joint. Meanwhile, thousands of Americans and foreigners believed that people could talk with the dead. Today, at Lily Dale near Lake Chautauqua, the followers of the Fox sisters, called the Spiritualists, hold their meetings at the site of the Fox house which burned after being moved there.

Other religious groups tried to set up communities in which all the members lived together as one big happy family. The community owned all the property and a council of adults made all the important decisions. The most successful of these communities were those founded by the Shakers. Shaker men and women lived in separate dormitories. They were not allowed to marry and to have children. The men worked in the fields while the women did weaving, spinning, and basketmaking. The Shakers became famous for the excellence of their products: garden seeds, furniture, baskets, and chairs. The Shaker communities declined after the Civil War since they were not able to get many new members.

Reform

A great reform movement swept across the country in the first half of the nineteenth century. New York became the center of it. Many New Yorkers not only tried to live better lives, but they also tried to help their neighbors. Wherever they saw something that was wrong, they tried to do something about it. For example, they tried to stop slavery from spreading, and a few people called for the end of slavery everywhere. Some citizens tried to stop such evils of city life as slums, crime, poverty, drunkenness. Still others wanted more democracy both for men and women. Free public schools got their strong support.

New York women took a leading part in the fight for women's rights. Elizabeth Cady Stanton of Seneca Falls and Susan B. Anthony of Rochester were world famous for their crusade for equal rights for women. Few of us realize that less than 100 years ago women had few legal rights, and could not vote or hold public office. In fact, a married woman could not hold property in her own name. Her husband could take whatever she earned. In practice, many husbands treated their wives with love and respect but if they did not, wives had to suffer in silence.

Mrs. Stanton, a woman with great leadership ability, joined the antislavery movement. In 1840 she attended a world convention in London, but the men would not allow her or other women delegates an official seat at the convention. Mrs. Stanton decided to devote her life to securing equal

A cartoonist's view of the women's rights movement. Does the cartoon favor more rights for women?

rights for women. She was joined in this cause by other concerned women.

Mrs. Stanton gained her ablest follower in 1851 when Susan B. Anthony joined the drive. The two women became close friends and worked together for over 50 years. At first they had to face insult and ridicule. Gradually they won important rights. Women got the right to speak at antislavery and temperance meetings. Finally, the legislature gave women full control over their property and earnings. The same law made them equal to their husbands in the control of their children. After the Civil War the two leaders crusaded for the right to vote. In 1872 Miss Anthony actually voted. She was arrested and fined by a judge. Miss Anthony got up in court and said, "May

Seneca Falls Convention

In 1848 Lucretia Mott, the Quaker reformer, was traveling near Seneca Falls. There she called on Elizabeth Cady Stanton, another reformer who opposed slavery and whiskey. The two women decided to call a meeting of men and women to discuss the rights of women. Appealing to the example of the Declaration of Independence, the delegates drew up a long list of grievances against men. They charged them with trying to establish "an absolute tyranny" over women.

Editors, politicians, and clergy ridiculed the Seneca Falls convention as a threat to family, church, and state. But the delegates kept writing letters to the newspapers, preparing petitions, and organizing more conventions. Soon they enlisted the support of Susan B. Anthony, a Rochester schoolteacher, who spoke with eloquence. As one observer noted, "Mrs. Stanton forged the thunderbolts and Miss Anthony hurled them."

Opponents took special delight in poking fun at women interested in dress reform. Mrs. Elizabeth Smith Miller designed and then wore a new costume which had a knee-length skirt with loose trousers gathered at the ankle. When Amelia Bloomer sallied forth in this garb, she won everlasting fame. Catcalls and jeers greeted Amelia and other women who dared to wear the "bloomer." After seven years of struggle Mrs. Miller went back to skirts; the champions of women's rights, however, never gave up.

it please your honor, I will never pay a dollar of your unjust penalty." And she never did! The judge decided not to send her to jail.

Women first got the right to vote in local elections. After a long battle they won the right to vote in state elections in New York in 1917. Shortly thereafter, the nineteenth amendment to the Constitution of the United States gave women the right to vote in national elections.

Meanwhile, women were making gains in education. In 1821 Emma Willard opened a school for girls in Troy. Colleges for women opened their doors: Elmira in 1855 and Vassar in 1865. Cornell University was the first in New York State to admit both men and women as students in the same college. Other women went into medicine. Elizabeth Blackwell applied for admission to the small medical college at Geneva. At first, her fellow students jeered and played jokes on her. But Elizabeth Blackwell graduated at the head of her class in 1849, and became the first woman to practice medicine in the United States.

The Criminals, the Mentally Ill, and the Poor

Under Governor John Jay, laws setting up the punishment for crimes were made less cruel. Criminals no longer were whipped in public, placed in stocks, or had their ears clipped. However, conditions in the jails remained very bad. Men and women, young and old, drunkards and mentally ill, hardened criminals and youthful offenders lived together in a single room. Prisoners had to beg for food or pay the jailer for food and drink. The prisoners had nothing to do all day long. Some spent the time learning the tricks of crime from expert criminals.

A leader in reforming the prisons was Thomas Eddy, a Philadelphia Quaker, who settled in New York City and became a prosperous business man. He also took an active part in such good work as freeing the slaves, promoting free schools, and caring for the poor. His chief interest, however, was prisons. As warden of the Newgate Prison after 1797 he had prisoners placed in separate cells. Eddy believed in reforming the prisoners, not merely in punishing them.

In 1816 New York built Auburn Prison on a new plan. Each prisoner had a separate cell at night. During the daytime he worked in the prison shops with the other men. One unusual feature was the rule that prisoners could not speak with one another. The "Auburn System" attracted wide attention in Europe and the rest of the United States.

A few years later a group of Auburn prisoners was taken to Ossining on the Hudson River where Sing Sing Prison was built on the Auburn cell-block plan. Reformers tried to put an end to the harsh methods often used by the jail keepers. Such punishments as solitary confinement and bread-and-water diet were substituted for whipping. Another great reform was the separation of youngsters from old criminals. In 1824 the New York House of Refuge was set up, the first reformatory in the United States. People saw the importance of reforming criminals so that they could become useful members of society. Much remains to be done in this regard, however, even today.

People who were mentally ill received poor treatment. Families and officials had to send dangerous cases to the public jails and poorhouses. Sometimes jailers would place them in cages in order to get them out of the way. Few people realized at that time that mental illness is a condition requiring expert care and that in many cases patients can greatly improve and some can be cured.

Reformers demanded a separate institution to take care of these people. As a result the first "lunatic asylum" was built at Utica. The doctors in charge restored many patients to normal and useful lives. Some patients were permitted to work on the asylum farm instead of being locked up in cells.

The poor were taken care of by relatives, church groups, and the local town. In some cases the town officials would "auction" off the poor to the lowest bidder. Farmers who "bought" the poor became expert in getting work out of them without giving them too much to eat. After much criticism, the state decided to use the county poorhouse as the main way of helping these people. Each poorhouse was to have a farm. Each person in the poorhouse was to help earn the cost of his keep. The system did not work well, partly because of overcrowding in the poorhouses, partly because of bad direction by officials. The poorhouses had all kinds of people in them: children and old folk, feebleminded and mentally ill, criminal and drunkard, men and women. Some improvement came when the state set up asylums for the mentally ill, and religious groups established children's homes.

Heavy drinking was a serious problem leading to the ruin of many people's health and homes. The temperance movement was aimed at the evil of liquor. Reformers tried to get people to sign a pledge that they would no longer drink intoxicating beverages. At Hector, New York, the secretary of the local society put the letter "T" beside the names of those who agreed not to drink at all. The story goes that this is the origin of the word "tee-totaler," (T-total) which means a person who drinks no intoxicating beverages.

The temperance leaders began to demand the prohibition of the sale of alcoholic beverages within the state. Many people opposed prohibition because it interfered with their habits. Thus the prohibition movement at this time failed to win out, although the temperance movement accomplished a great deal in cutting down heavy drinking.

The Fight Against Slavery

In the colonial period New York had more slaves than any other northern state. A few people, especially Quakers, or Friends, questioned the rightness of owning slaves. When the Declaration of Independence, which says that all men are created equal, was signed, many New Yorkers attacked the institution of slavery, because it was based on the inequality of men. By 1799 reformers, including Governor John Jay, passed a law providing for the freeing of New York's slave children when they reached adulthood.

Meanwhile, some citizens were beginning to take a stand against slavery in the country as a whole. At first they favored the American Colonization Society, which planned to send freed slaves back to Africa. After 1830 the movement against slavery won much wider support, especially among church groups. At first most people regarded the abolitionists (those who wished to abolish slavery) as dangerous radicals. In Troy a mob stoned Theodore Weld, the leading antislavery organizer. In Utica another mob drove an Abolitionist convention out of the city.

New Yorkers showed their hatred of slavery in many ways. Some joined antislavery societies. Some urged their Congressmen to vote to keep slavery from moving into new

Gerrit Smith, leader in many reform movements of his day, was a man of principle and good deeds.

territories. Quite a few people actually risked jail to help runaway slaves trying to reach Canada. These people organized an "Underground Railroad" over which slaves were moved from "station to station" during the dark of the night. Owners of some old houses still point out the secret closets and attics in which their ancestors hid fleeing slaves. Hundreds of slaves reached Canada and freedom over the Underground Railroad. Congress in 1850 passed a strict law laying heavy fines and jail sentences for persons found guilty of aiding runaways. This law failed to stop the enemies of slavery.

Gerrit Smith's home in Peterboro was an important station on the Underground Railroad. Smith had inherited a large fortune, which he dedicated to reform. He wrote pamphlets and letters urging people to follow his ideas. Among his interests were the distribution of Bibles, the spread of Sunday Schools, temperance, world peace, women's rights, and abolition.

"Aunt Harriet" Tubman

The United States government often named Liberty ships in World Wars I and II after heroes in the fight for liberty and freedom. One ship had the name of Harriet Tubman, the famous black woman who made her home in Auburn, New York.

Harriet Tubman was born a slave in Maryland. In 1849 she escaped to the North. During the next ten years she became a "conductor" on the Underground Railroad, leading over 300 slaves to freedom. At one

time a reward of $40,000 in gold was offered for her capture. "Aunt Harriet" also led, in Troy, a band of abolitionists who took a runaway slave away from the police.

During the Civil War, Miss Tubman put on the blue uniform and bore arms for the Union army in South Carolina. She became a spy and directed U.S. gunboats where to go. On one raid Union forces freed over 700 slaves. After the war, Aunt Harriet's admirers, including Secretary of State William Seward, gave her a house in Auburn where she lived until she was over 90 years of age.

A typical one-room schoolhouse built in 1847. Do you think you could get a good education with one teacher having to teach all grades?

Smith took personal risks for his beliefs. In 1851 he helped organize the mob which rescued Jerry McHenry, a runaway slave, from the hands of the federal marshal in Syracuse, who was taking Jerry back to slavery. The mob freed Jerry, who escaped to Canada. Later, Smith gave help to the abolitionist, John Brown.

Let us remember that abolitionists never numbered more than a few thousand people. Their activity, however, awakened many more thousands to the need to do something about stopping slavery from spreading. By 1860 most New Yorkers disliked slavery and wanted to see it kept out of the western territories of the United States.

Free Public Schools

In colonial New York, the school system was poor. More than half of all the children never saw the inside of a schoolroom. Some children attended private schools, where their parents had to pay fees. To attend church schools, students usually had to belong to the church which ran the school. Public education was unheard of.

The Revolutionary War disorganized many of the schools that existed, but after the war, people turned their attention to establishing a better school system. Governor George Clinton and the legislature set up the Board of Regents of the University of the State of New York, with the right to establish schools and colleges. The movement for more and better schools was a part of the drive for more democracy. Workingmen joined the drive because they wanted their children to have an equal chance to get an education. Certain reformers—Thomas Eddy and De Witt Clinton in New York City and Jedediah Peck of Otsego County—came out for free public schools. In 1805 the Free School Society opened several schools in various sections of New York City. Public spirited citizens contributed to this society, which also got help from the city and the state. The Yankee newcomers, who were from a region where each town had a public school, usually backed public schools.

The district school law of 1812 helped New York to catch up with the New England states. Citizens in a neighborhood could elect three trustees who would build a school, hire a teacher, and collect taxes. To encourage them, the state granted each district a certain amount of money. Gideon Hawley, the first superintendent of common schools, was a brilliant and hard-working man. He traveled up and down New York helping citizens to organize school districts. By the time he left office, New York schools were probably the best in the country.

District schools were not free since tax money and state money paid only part of the costs. The parents of each child had to make up the difference. If parents could not pay the fee, they had to sign a pauper's oath, that is, a statement that they had no money. Some people were too proud to sign such an oath. Other parents preferred or needed to have their children work rather than go to school. As a result, many children did not attend any school.

The backers of free schools fought hard in every district to win their battle. They had to convince some parents that education was the best thing for their children. Some wealthy taxpayers did not want to pay taxes to educate the children of their neighbors. Some private schools did not want to compete against free public schools. Gradually, the free school reformers won out. Finally,

Eight-Sided Houses

Today, few of us have heard of Orson Fowler although his name was a household word a hundred years ago. Fowler became famous as a phrenologist, that is, a man who claims he can tell people's character by feeling the bumps on their heads.

After making a fortune explaining this new theory, Fowler worked out the idea of an octagonal dwelling. He claimed that an eight-sided building was the most efficient way of building a house. It got rid of corners and saved steps. Fowler took ten years to build a five-story residence just north of Fishkill, which neighbors called Fowler's Folly. Hundreds of people throughout the northeast read Fowler's book on houses and decided to build octagonal houses, with rooms shaped like pieces of pie. The traveler can still see many of these houses in upstate villages. Is there one in your neighborhood?

in 1867 the state ruled that all public schools should be free to all students.

A district school was usually a shabby building without blackboards, maps, or even toilets. One teacher had to handle all the students of every age and grade. Each pupil had a textbook in reading, writing, and arithmetic. The teacher would call two or three students to his desk to recite. The others sat at their benches and studied.

The district school had many faults. The teachers, poorly trained and underpaid, sometimes knew little more than their pupils. The textbooks were poorly written and worn out. Nevertheless, the little red schoolhouse won a place in the hearts of the people. The ambitious youngster was able, if he so desired, to learn history and other subjects in addition to reading, writing, and arithmetic. Many graduates of these schools made great names for themselves in government, business, and the professions.

Only a handful of students continued their education beyond the elementary school. In many towns, citizens set up academies which operated under the direction of the Board of Regents. The students had to pay tuition although both the local and state governments gave the academies some help. The academies taught Latin and Greek for those who wanted to prepare for college. They also gave courses in English composition and literature, modern languages, natural sciences, and practical business subjects.

During the 1840's and 1850's a growing number of people demanded free education on the secondary or high school level. The legislature in 1835 permitted enlarged school districts to set up free public high schools. The larger cities soon established high schools, often taking over the academies. After the Civil War, the drive for high schools speeded up and soon there were more high schools than academies. In several cases high schools took over the academies but kept the old academy name.

By 1860 New York State had 15 colleges. Columbia was the oldest. Upstate, the various church groups supported colleges to educate men for the ministry. In addition, professional schools began to teach students to become lawyers, doctors, and ministers. At West Point (1802) and Rensselaer Polytechnic Institute (1825) engineers were instructed. Of course, the construction of the Erie Canal trained dozens of men as engineers. These men later built canals and railroads all over the United States.

Newspapers also helped to educate the citizens of New York. At first, papers were dull political party journals and far too costly for the average citizen. In the 1830's the penny press came to New York. James Gordon Bennett built up a large circulation by cutting the price of his paper to one cent and by using pictures and sensational stories. Horace Greeley, the editor of the *New York Tribune*, was the outstanding editor in the country. A loyal Whig and Republican, Greeley also attacked evils such as slums and low wages. In 1851 *The New York Times* was founded and it soon became famous for its honest and accurate reporting of the news. New York City became the news capital of the United States.

Literature and the Arts

By the time of the Civil War, New York was clearly the leader in music, arts, and the theater. It was a close rival of New England in literature. Washington Irving was the first American writer to attract a nationwide audience and to gain European recognition. His first success came in 1809 when he published a humorous *History of New York.* He acquired more fame with the *Sketch Book,* which contained the "Legend of Sleepy Hollow" and "Rip Van Winkle." No doubt you have read these two stories about the Hudson Valley and its early Dutch settlers. Irving made his home near Tarrytown. You can visit it today.

James Fenimore Cooper is a New York novelist widely read in all parts of the world. Even comic books have told the story of Leatherstocking, the frontier scout. Cooper's boyhood was spent in the frontier town of Cooperstown, which had been founded by his father. His first successful novel, *The Spy,* told the story of Harvey Birch, a spy for George Washington. Cooper's *Leatherstocking Tales,* which are stories about the frontier, won him the most fame.

Walt Whitman in his younger years.

New England writers—Longfellow, Emerson, Hawthorne, and others—dominated American literature from 1825 to 1850. But during the 1850's two New York writers rose to the front ranks—Herman Melville and Walt Whitman. Melville was brought up in Albany and Troy, but he left home for the sea. During his voyages he visited the islands of the South Pacific. His greatest book was *Moby Dick,* published in 1851. This novel tells about Captain Ahab who tried to hunt down the great white whale.

Walt Whitman grew up on Long Island. He worked as a carpenter, then became a teacher, and an editor. During the Civil War he helped to nurse the wounded soldiers in the hospitals of Washington. When Lincoln died, Whitman wrote "O Captain! My Captain!" Whitman's poems are written in a fresh style, distinctively his. They usually describe and praise the pioneer, the worker, the common man. Most of all, he gloried in American democracy. *Leaves of Grass* is his greatest work, one of the finest in American literature.

New Yorkers took the lead in painting. In Albany, Ezra Ames painted portraits of many businessmen and officials. Samuel Morse, as a young man, did some remarkable landscapes of Cooperstown. Later he gave up painting for invention, and is famous for inventing the telegraph. William Sidney Mount of Setauket, Long Island, has left us some warm and exciting pictures of life on Long Island. We can see the people playing games, hunting eels, and holding barn dances.

During the 1830's and 1840's so many artists concentrated their talents on the

"In the Catskills," by Thomas Cole. Painted in 1837, this picture shows the kind of work the early Hudson River artists did.

beauties of the Hudson River and the Catskills that they became known as the Hudson River School of Painting. Among the better known artists in this group were Thomas Cole and Frederick Church.

New York City became the leading musical center in the nation. Almost all trained musicians were immigrants from Italy or Germany. When Jenny Lind, the "Swedish Nightingale", gave a concert in 1850, over 7,000 listeners thronged the Castle Garden Hall in Battery Park at the tip of Manhattan. In 1842 the Philharmonic Society of New York was founded and began giving symphony concerts. Today, under the name of the New York Philharmonic Symphony Orchestra, it is one of the most famous orchestras in the world.

New York City took the lead in drama. Upstate cities also had theaters in which traveling companies gave performances. The two most popular plays written by Americans were *Uncle Tom's Cabin* and *Rip Van Winkle.*

Summary

Church membership increased in New York. Protestants had the greatest number of church-goers during the period before the Civil War. But the Roman Catholic Church became the largest single church. New religions arose, such as the Mormons, the Adventists, and the Spiritualists.

New York furnished many leaders for the reform movements which swept across the United States in the first half of the 1800's. Elizabeth Cady Stanton and Susan B. Anthony led the women's rights movement. In these years reformers improved conditions in prisons, asylums, and poorhouses. The temperance movement made some progress in cutting down the amount of drinking.

New York eliminated slavery within its own boundaries and many New Yorkers tried to prevent the spread of slavery in the country. Some, like Gerrit Smith, broke the law by "working on the Underground Railroad."

The fight for free public schools was a long one, but by 1867 a district school system operated schools that were free to everyone. Public high schools were growing rapidly in the cities of the state. Colleges, too, were increasing in number.

By the time of the Civil War, New York was the leader of the nation in music, art, and the theater. The Empire State also made important contributions to literature. Outstanding writers were Washington Irving, James Fenimore Cooper, Herman Melville, and Walt Whitman.

Checking the high points

1. Why did so many Irish and Germans come to New York?

2. What contributions did the Irish and Germans make to life in New York?

3. What was done about solving the problems of city life before the Civil War?

4. Why did church membership grow before the Civil War?

5. Name two religions that started in New York State. Describe the main beliefs of one of these religions.

6. How did Gerrit Smith contribute to reform?

7. Compare the legal, social, and economic positions of women in 1880 with those of today.

8. What changes were made in treating criminals? The mentally ill?

9. What steps did New Yorkers take against slavery? Drunkenness?

10. What groups fought for and against free schools?

11. How did New Yorkers contribute to literature, education, and art?

12. Identify: Thomas Eddy, Elizabeth Cady Stanton, Susan B. Anthony, Washington Irving, James Fenimore Cooper, Harriet Tubman, Walt Whitman.

Think these over

1. Life in the city required as much bravery and resourcefulness as that on the frontier. Do you agree?

2. Women today have equal rights with men. Is this true? Explain.

3. Reformers are the conscience of society. They are praised more often after their death than in life. If so, why?

Vocabulary building

academy
asylum
phrenologist
temperance
prohibition
spiritualism
epidemic
sanitation
tenements
political machine

Checking locations

Auburn
Lake Chautauqua
Palmyra
Tarrytown
Ossining
Cooperstown

Chapter Objectives

To learn about

- the growth of new political parties in New York
- New York's involvement in the Civil War

chapter 16

ISSUES DIVIDE NEW YORKERS

New Parties

The formation of many new political parties was a sign that more people were becoming interested in political questions. Usually, people do not take the trouble to form new parties unless they feel strongly. Politicians do not leave an old party unless they think a new group has a better chance of winning elections.

Some parties had strange names. In 1826 the Anti-Masonic party swept through western New York like a hurricane. The rumor had spread that some members of the Free and Accepted Order of Masons had killed a printer, William Morgan, in order to stop him from telling the secrets of the organization. This group is important because many of its leaders later helped form a more important party, the Whigs.

The Workingmen's Party was a small group of men in New York City who wanted free public education and the end of jail sentences for people in debt. It did not last long.

More important were the political parties which arose because of the flood of immigration to America in the 1840's and 1850's. People born in the United States, were often suspicious of the newcomers because of their different religion, speech, and habits. Workingmen said that the immigrants took away their jobs or forced down wages. As a result, several political parties sprang up with the aim of cutting down immigration and keeping Americans who were born here in political control. This "nativist" feeling gradually died away because the slavery question became more important to Americans. Also, the good sense and spirit of fair play of New Yorkers led them to turn against the nativist movement.

As Americans became more worried about the question of slavery, new parties arose. Their members came from the old parties.

A curious movement which spilled over into politics was the antirent uprising of the 1840's. In 1846 the *antirenters* supported John Young, a Whig, who defeated Governor Silas Wright. Wright had sent troops against the antirenters of Delaware County. The term antirenter had been coined ear-

Presidential Candidates of the Major Parties

(Bold type indicates men who were born in New York or were residents of New York at time of candidacy. White boxes show the winners of the elections.)

YEAR	DEMOCRAT	WHIG-REPUBLICAN
1828	Jackson	Adams, J. Q.
1832	Jackson	Clay
1836	**Van Buren**	Harrison, W.
1840	**Van Buren**	Harrison, W. *(Tyler became President in 1841.)
1844	Polk	Clay
1848	Cass	Taylor *(**Fillmore** became President in 1850.)
1852	Pierce	Scott
1856	Buchanan	Fremont
1860	Douglas	Lincoln
1864	McClellan	Lincoln *(Johnson, A. became President in 1865.)
1868	**Seymour**	Grant
1872	**Greeley**	Grant
1876	**Tilden**	Hayes
1880	Hancock	Garfield *(**Arthur** became President in 1881.)
1884	**Cleveland**	Blaine
1888	**Cleveland**	Harrison, B.
1892	**Cleveland**	Harrison, B.
1896	Bryan	McKinley
1900	Bryan	McKinley *(**Roosevelt, T.** became President in 1901.)
1904	**Parker**	**Roosevelt, T.**
1908	Bryan	Taft
1912	Wilson	Taft
1916	Wilson	**Hughes**
1920	Cox	Harding
1924	**Davis**	Coolidge
1928	**Smith**	Hoover
1932	**Roosevelt, F.**	Hoover
1936	**Roosevelt, F.**	Hoover
1940	**Roosevelt, F.**	**Willkie**
1944	**Roosevelt, F.** *(Truman became President in 1945.)	**Dewey**
1948	Truman	**Dewey**
1952	Stevenson	**Eisenhower**
1956	Stevenson	**Eisenhower**
1960	Kennedy *(Johnson, L. became President in 1963.)	Nixon
1964	Johnson, L.	Goldwater
1968	Humphrey	**Nixon**
1972	McGovern	Nixon *(**Ford, G.** became President in 1974.)
1976	Carter	**Ford**

Vice Presidents who filled out Presidential terms.

lier, after Stephen Van Rensselaer died in 1839. His will said that all unpaid rents should be collected and used to pay off his debts. The tenants were short of money, organized a committee and offered to pay about one-half of their debts. The Van Rensselaer family, however, turned down this offer. Thereupon, the tenants got together and refused to pay their rents at all. Governor William Seward sent out the militia into the Helderberg region in order to put down the tenants, or antirenters. Order was restored but the tenants still refused to pay the rents. By 1844 most of the other tenant farmers in eastern New York had joined the movement.

The antirenters disguised themselves as Indians or wore calico gowns. Some sported a fox or raccoon tail in their hats as they rode up and down the country roads. Whenever they met a land agent or a sheriff, they shouted "Down Rent" and drove them out. Their leaders often took the names of Indian chiefs, such as Big Thunder. Unfortunately violence broke out. In Delaware County an undersheriff lost his life, and Governor Silas Wright had to place the county under martial law.

The antirenters won several victories. In fact, they became so powerful that leaders of both political parties sought their support. Sheriffs refused to go up into the hills be-

William H. Seward

William Seward came from a well-to-do family in Orange County. He attended Union College, settled at Auburn, and entered the law. As a lawyer he became famous for defending some poor people. Like Thurlow Weed, he supported the Anti-Masonic party and then joined the Whig party. Short, slender, and rather plain looking, Seward attracted attention by his fine speech, keen mind, and friendly manner. As governor he showed much courage. He favored legal reforms, sympathized with the antirenters, and promoted public education. When the governor of Virginia asked for the return of runaway slaves, Seward refused. Soon he became known as the leading

antislavery figure in the Whig party. He opposed the annexation of the land taken from Mexico in the Mexican War unless slavery were prohibited there.

In 1860 Senator Seward was the leading candidate for the Republican nomination for President. But Abraham Lincoln won the prize. He immediately made Seward his Secretary of State. Secretary Seward managed to keep European nations from helping the Confederacy. After the Civil War, he arranged for the purchase of Alaska from Russia for $7,200,000. Many people of that time thought we were foolish to buy Alaska. They referred to the new territory as "Seward's Icebox." Today, we know that it was a splendid bargain. Alaska is now the largest state in the Union and has many rich resources.

If you are ever in Auburn, you can visit Seward's home and see his desk and library, just as they were when he was alive.

cause they feared they might be shot or tarred and feathered. Landlords, finding it impossible to collect rents, finally decided to make the best deal possible. Many of them sold their land to the tenants for a low price. Public opinion supported the antirenters in their argument that leaseholds were bad for the country. In 1846 the State Constitutional Convention prohibited the leasing of agricultural land for periods of more than 12 years, but it did not touch existing leases. The story of the antirent wars is still remembered in the folk songs of the farming regions of eastern New York.

A major source of unrest and strong feeling in America was the problem of slavery. New parties were formed, their members coming from the ranks of old parties, to express differing points of view. The Liberty party called for the abolition, or ending, of slavery. It received few votes. In 1848, however, some Democrats formed the more successful Free Soil party. They believed that slavery should not be allowed to spread to any part of the country where it did not already exist.

Whigs, Democrats, and Republicans

Between 1834 and 1855 the two most important political parties in the United States were the Whigs and the Democrats. In New York State these two groups had battled for political control. Each side had outstanding leaders. Martin Van Buren, a Democrat, became governor in 1828. He resigned in order to become Secretary of State under President Andrew Jackson. In 1832 he was elected Vice-President of the United States, and in 1836 President. He was the first New Yorker to live in the White House. He came from Kinderhook, and Democrats used to refer to him as "Old Kinderhook." The Democrats used O.K. as the secret name of their political clubs in New York

Thurlow Weed

There are few examples of two men who worked together so closely for so many years as Thurlow Weed and William Seward. Weed was the party boss while Seward was the statesman. The story of their lives tells a great deal about the state and the nation.

Weed, the son of a poor carter, was born in Cairo near Catskill. He spent only one year in school, but he set about to learn the printer's trade. After knocking about for several years, Weed settled in Rochester, where he edited a paper. He helped organize the Anti-Masonic party. In 1830 he moved to Albany, where his paper, the *Evening Journal*, became one of the leading Whig and, later, one of the leading Republican papers. Friendly and tactful, Weed liked to get people to do what he wanted. He showed great ability in getting laws he favored through the legislature. His enemies called him the "Wizard of the Lobby." Weed became wealthy, but never held high office.

in 1840. Today, O.K. is a part of our language, but few people know that it once meant the home of Martin Van Buren.

From 1820 to 1962 New York had the largest population of any state and for that reason had the most electoral votes. The political party carrying New York almost always wins the Presidency. Consequently, the major parties since 1828 have often picked New York men for their candidates. See the chart, "Presidential Candidates of the Major Parties" on page 224. In every election from 1928 through 1956 a New Yorker ran on one of the major party tickets. Whenever party conventions have selected the Presidential candidate from outside New York, they have often chosen a New Yorker as his running mate. Seven New Yorkers served as Vice-President. Three of them—Millard Fillmore, Chester A. Arthur, and Theodore Roosevelt—moved up to the post of Chief Executive.

One of the important Whig leaders in these years was William Seward. He reached the governorship in 1838. A strong governor, Seward made enemies by his actions. For example, he spent a great deal of money deepening the Erie Canal. The Democrats opposed this and demanded that government spending be cut.

Differences over slavery affected the political parties. Both the Whigs and the Democrats had members who tried to avoid the slavery question, and members who felt that the party should oppose slavery. Sometimes groups split from the major parties and formed their own parties. That is the way the Free Soil party started in 1848. Free Soilers campaigned under the slogan "Free soil, free speech, free labor, free men." Their candidate was Martin Van Buren, the former President of the United States.

In 1854 Congress passed a law called the Kansas-Nebraska Act. This law allowed slavery in the Kansas and Nebraska territories where it had been banned after 1820. This aroused all the antislavery people of the north, whether they were Whigs or Democrats. Many of them left their old parties and joined a new group called the Republican party.

The Republican party was willing to let slavery continue in the sections of the nation where it already existed, but did not want it to expand to other areas. The Republicans had several good leaders in New York. Their outstanding man was the former Whig, William Seward. He was one of the leading antislavery men in the country. In a famous speech he said, about the struggle over slavery, "It is an irrepressible conflict between opposing and enduring forces, and it means that the United States must and will, sooner or later, become either entirely a slaveholding nation or entirely a free labor nation." When Abraham Lincoln was elected President, he recognized Seward's ability and made him Secretary of State.

New York Helps Preserve the Union

Shortly after the election of Abraham Lincoln, the southern states seceded from the Union and formed the Confederate States of America. This posed a problem for all Americans. Did the southern states have the right to leave the Union? Should they be forced to remain in the United States?

During the winter of 1860–1861, most New Yorkers were not sure what should be done. Some men, like Horace Greeley of the *New York Tribune,* wanted to let the

Frederick Douglass

"My free life began on the third of September 1838. . . . I found myself in the big city of New York, a free man. . . . No man now had the right to call me his slave or assert mastery over me."

Those were the feelings of Frederick Douglass as he stepped off the ferryboat to New York City. He was leaving behind a life of brutality and cruelty. As a boy he had suffered several beatings, but at age sixteen he thrashed a cruel overseer who never touched him again. He also taught himself to read by studying the Bible and a book of famous speeches.

But life in the North was not easy for Douglass, who had married and had a small family. He settled in New Bedford, Massachusetts, where he did odd jobs. But in his spare time he was reading and mastering the English language. One night he attended an antislavery meeting and got up and described his life as a slave. His moving talk stirred his listeners. Soon friends, including William Lloyd Garrison, the famous abolitionist, asked him to join the antislavery crusade. Douglass was in great demand because of his skill as an orator and because of his true life experiences. In 1844 he wrote *The Life and Times of Frederick Douglass, Written by Himself.* The book sold well and brought him a good income. Fearing recapture, he spent the next two years lecturing in England, Scotland, and Ireland. In 1847 he settled in Rochester, where he started an abolition newspaper called the *North Star.*

Douglass fought slavery with all his might. He helped dozens of fugitive slaves to escape to Canada. In the Civil War he helped form the all-Negro Union regiment—the Fifty-fourth Massachusetts Regiment. His two sons were wounded in battle. Douglass called at the White House several times to urge President Lincoln to free the slaves.

After the war he kept fighting for the right of freedman to vote. President Harrison appointed Douglass Ambassador to Haiti in 1889. Today a statue of Douglass stands in a Rochester park.

southern states leave the Union. Others, like Mayor Fernando Wood of New York City, wanted his city to avoid taking sides in a civil war. Many Democrats did not believe that the government had the right to stop a state from leaving the Union. A small but growing number called for the defense of the country against those rebelling against its officers and laws. They said that secession would destroy the Union for which the early leaders of our country had fought so hard and so long.

The shots of Confederate soldiers at Fort Sumter in Charleston, South Carolina, awakened most New Yorkers to the dangers of disunion. They felt that the rebels must be put down. Horace Greeley called for the capture of the Confederate capital, shouting "Forward to Richmond!" Young men by the thousands volunteered for the army. In 1862 one-fifth of all Union soldiers came from the Empire State. New York also gave money and valuable supplies to help win the war. The cost to the state was very great, not only in money but also in life. More than one out of every ten of the 464,701 New Yorkers who served in the Union armies lost his life. Colonel Elmer Ellsworth of Mechanicville was the first northern officer to die. A Virginian shot Ellsworth when he tried to pull down a Confederate flag from the roof of a hotel. Thereafter, New York regiments often went into battle shouting "Remember Ellsworth."

New York's Governor Edwin D. Morgan worked hard to collect men and supplies for the Union army. The day after Fort Sumter surrendered, Morgan decided to send 30,000 troops to Washington. Later it became harder to find soldiers. In order to encourage enlistment, the states, counties, and towns offered money to those who volunteered for the army.

Horace Greeley, editor of the *New York Tribune,* was a very influential person.

During the war, Congress passed a draft law which forced all men between the ages of 20 and 45 to register for service in the armed forces. The law worked badly. For one thing, a rich man could avoid the draft by hiring a substitute or by paying $300. The federal officials treated New York City unfairly by giving it a high quota of men. They refused to give New York City credit for all the volunteers who had rushed to fight in 1861. Furthermore, some workingmen saw no point in fighting to free the slaves. Would not the freed slaves come north and push them out of their jobs?

All these reasons made the workingmen fearful and angry. In July 1863 they formed a mob to oppose the draft. For three days this mob roamed the streets, burning down the homes of the abolitionists. Governor Horatio Seymour put down the disorder as soon as he could. Some Republicans blamed Seymour for the riots because he had criticized the draft.

The union armies needed a tremendous amount of equipment such as uniforms,

Winter quarters of Company C, 35th Regiment, New York S. V. This crayon drawing was made in the winter of 1861–1862 by a soldier in the regiment.

Philip Henry Sheridan (1831–1888)

The next time you visit the State Capitol in Albany, take a look at the statue of General Philip Sheridan, the famous cavalry leader in the Civil War.

Sheridan was a New Yorker who was a fierce fighter. He became famous in 1863 during the Battle of Chattanooga. The Union forces had occupied the city of Chattanooga, but the Confederates held the crest of the hills on both sides of the city. Confederate guns on top of Missionary Ridge kept pounding the Union lines.

Sheridan sat on his horse looking up at the hill. He drew a silver flask from his pocket to take a drink. "Here's to you," shouted Sheridan and waved to a Confederate battery. Far above him a Confederate commander signaled to his gun crews to fire at Sheridan. The shot came close, kicking up dirt on Sheridan's uniform. The fiery officer growled, "I'll take those guns for that!" and he spurred his horse forward. The Union soldiers climbed up the steep hillside in a rush. Sheridan had his horse shot from under him so he joined the men clambering up the steep slopes. Finally, he and his men captured the top of Missionary Ridge. The Confederates were astonished. They thought the Ridge could not be taken.

When Ulysses S. Grant took command of the Union Army in Virginia, he called for Sheridan to command his cavalry corps. Sheridan won many famous victories in the Shenandoah Valley. His victory at Cedar Run was made famous by the poet, Thomas B. Read, who wrote "Sheridan's Ride." Have you read it?

blankets, shoes, guns, rifles, cannons, horses, and mules. The woolen mills ran night and day, turning out yards of blue cloth. Thousands of tailors and women made this cloth into uniforms. The shoe factories operated at top speed and hired thousands of new workers. War orders kept the flour mills and packing houses busy. On the other hand, cotton mills had to let some workers go because they could not get enough cotton.

The iron and steel industry grew and prospered. In Ilion the Remington plant made guns, while in Watervliet the United States Arsenal made cannon. In nearby Troy, factories turned out shells and bullets. One factory made the iron plates for the Union warship, the *Monitor.* Everyone was thrilled when Lieutenant John Worden, a New Yorker, took the *Monitor* into Chesapeake Bay and fought the dangerous Confederate ironclad, *Merrimac.*

New York's farmers had to produce more food at a time when they were losing their sons and hired men to the armies and factories. By working harder and by using more machinery—reapers, harvesters, and mowing machines—the farm families raised more wheat, wool, dairy and meat products. Since farm prices rose rapidly, most farmers were prosperous.

Canals and railroads had to take care of a great increase in traffic and travel. The Erie Canal carried more freight than ever, even though the New York Central and the Erie railroads also handled a great deal. The shipowners of New York City lost money because the Confederates sent out raiders, who seized American ships. Some owners decided to place their ships under the British flag in order to protect them from the raiders. When the war was over, the British

Mathew Brady

"Brady and the Cooper Institute (speech) made me President of the United States," So said Abraham Lincoln of Mathew Brady, the most famous photographer in American history.

Brady grew up in the shadow of the Adirondacks. One day he met Samuel F. B. Morse, the inventor of the telegraph. Morse

was also a fine painter who had learned about the first experiments in photography in France. Brady learned all he could from Morse and began to experiment on his own. In 1842 he opened his studio on Broadway. There thousands came to have their pictures taken, because Brady had the knack of taking pictures that looked as well as painted portraits.

When the Civil War began, Brady got permission to follow the Union soldiers. He and his assistants wandered into camps and on to battlefields with their cameras. Our finest pictures of the war were sometimes taken under gunfire. He took the pictures of great generals but also of common soldiers.

Brady returned to New York after the war. His reputation spread across the Atlantic and important visitors stopped at his Broadway studio to be photographed.

Here is the famous Brady photograph of Lincoln.

merchant fleet was growing much faster than the American.

The Civil War hurt the laboring men and women. Prices kept rising faster than their wages. Some workers tried to strike for higher pay, but they won few strikes. The war was especially hard on the families of soldiers, who received very small allowances from the government. Fortunately, many New Yorkers rushed to help wounded soldiers and their families.

The economic effects were mixed. Although some industries boomed, the rate of industrial growth slowed. The shipping interests suffered while rail and canal traffic expanded. Farmers enjoyed good prices, but rural communities lost population—in some cases permanently.

The Civil War helped to crush the spirit of reform which had been so strong in the years before that war. After the war, citizens seemed more interested in making money than in reforming themselves or their neighbors. However, one good result of the war was the growth of good will toward Irish and German immigrants. Their courage and patriotism in the war had proved them to be fine Americans.

Summary

In the years before the Civil War a number of new political parties appeared in New York. Some of them arose because of the suspicions that Americans had of the many new immigrants who were coming to America.

Diary of a New Yorker in 1865

April 3. Petersburg and Richmond captured. *Gloria in excelsis Deo.* New York has seen no such day in our time nor in the old time before us. . . . An enormous crowd soon blocked . . . part of Wall Street, and speeches began. . . . Never before did I hear cheering that came straight from the heart, that was given because people felt relieved by cheering and halloing. . . . I walked about on the outskirts of the crowd, shaking hands with everybody. . . . Men embraced and hugged each other, kissed each other, retreated into doorways to dry their eyes and came out again to flourish their hats and hurrah. . . .

April 10. (after news of surrender of Confederate Army) . . . It has rained hard all day, too hard for jubilant demonstrations out of doors. We should have made this Monday something like the 3rd of April, 1865, I think, had the sun shone. . . . Guns have been firing all day in spite of foul weather.

April 15. Nine o'clock in the morning. LINCOLN AND SEWARD ASSASSINATED LAST NIGHT!!!! . . . Up with the Black Flag now! Ten P.M. What a day it has been! Excitement and suspension of business even more general than on the 3rd instant. Tone of feeling very like that of four years ago when the news came to Sumter. . . . No business was done today. Most shops are closed and draped with black and white muslin. Broadway is clad in "weepers" from Wall Street to Union Square.

April 28. . . . Little business has been done in town these ten days. Never, I think, has sorrow for a leader been displayed on so great a scale and so profoundly felt. It is very noteworthy that the number of arrests for drunkenness and disorder during the week that followed Lincoln's murder was less than in any week for very many years! The city is still swathed in crape and black muslin.—*George T. Strong*

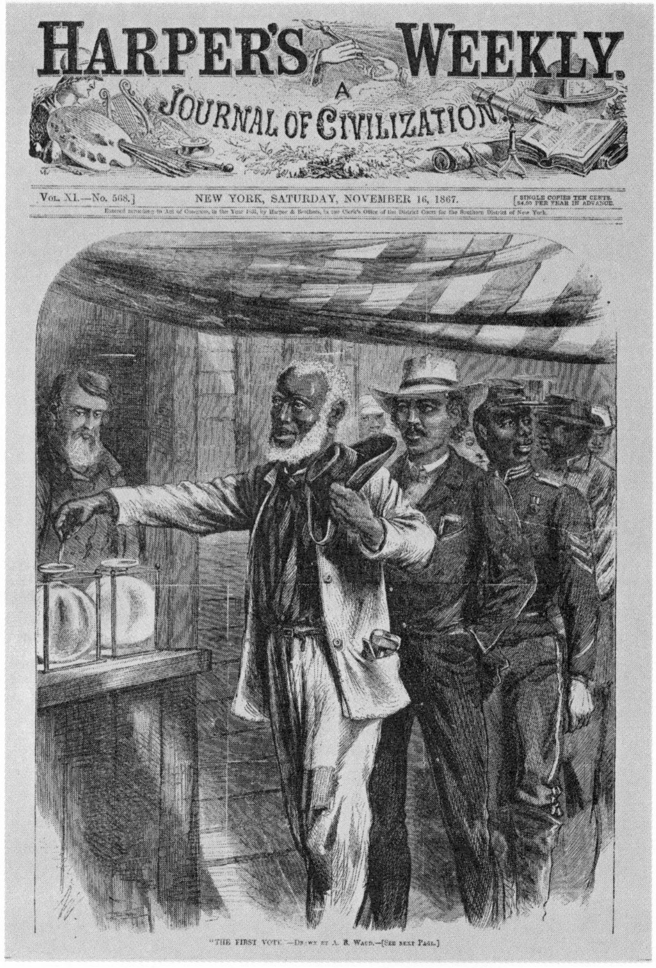

HARPER'S WEEKLY.
A JOURNAL OF CIVILIZATION.

Vol. XI.—No. 568.] NEW YORK, SATURDAY, NOVEMBER 16, 1867. [SINGLE COPIES TEN CENTS. $4.00 PER YEAR IN ADVANCE.

"THE FIRST VOTE."—Drawn by A. R. Waud.—[See next Page.]

This picture from *Harper's Weekly* dated November 16, 1867, was called "The First Vote." At that time newspapers did not have the equipment to print photographs, and all such news pictures had to be drawn. This one shows freed men proudly casting their first ballots in the South at the close of the Civil War. Note the man in uniform. There were many black soldiers in the Civil War on both sides.

As the slavery question became more important, it divided both major political parties, the Democrats and the Whigs. After the passage of the Kansas-Nebraska Act in 1854, a significant new party arose—the Republican party. It opposed the spread of slavery in the territories of the United States.

New York played an important part in the Civil War. It contributed men, money, and supplies to the Union cause. It also manufactured great quantities of uniforms and weapons. The war slowed the pace of industrial growth and led to social unrest that caused the bloody draft riots of 1863. The burdens and costs of the war fell unevenly on New Yorkers. All were overjoyed at the news of victory in 1865. Joy turned to sorrow when New Yorkers heard that Abraham Lincoln had been murdered.

Checking the high points

1. What did these political parties stand for: Liberty party? Free Soil party? Anti-Masonic party? Workingmen's party?

2. Why did some New Yorkers favor cutting down immigration?

3. How did the slavery question affect the major political parties?

4. Why was the Republican party able to rise to power so rapidly? Did the Republican party seek to abolish slavery?

5. How did New Yorkers feel about the secession of the southern states?

6. Why were there draft riots in New York?

7. In what ways did New York help win the Civil War?

8. How did the Civil War affect farmers? laboring men? manufacturers?

9. What were the major contributions of (a) Thurlow Weed, (b) William Seward, (c) Edwin Morgan?

Think these over

1. True or false: To postpone burning issues is sometimes the mark of a great political leader. Give an example to prove your answer.

2. Do minor political parties serve any useful purpose? Explain.

3. Were the New Yorkers who opposed the draft laws justified in rioting?

Vocabulary building

nativist	draft
tolerant	quota
ban	strike
secede	reform

chapter 17: TRANSPORTATION, TRADE, and AGRICULTURE

chapter 18: INDUSTRY and LABOR

chapter 19: URBAN PROBLEMS

unit six

The Gilded Age

New York state history dates are shown in color.

1852 New Yorker Elisha Otis invents the elevator

1868 New Yorker Ulysses S. Grant elected President

1876 Alexander Graham Bell invents telephone

1884 First skyscraper built in Chicago

1886 Statue of Liberty dedicated

1888 New Yorker George Eastman markets the Kodak camera

1892 General Electric established in Schenectady

1898 Five boroughs of New York join to form present-day New York City

1901 New Yorker Theodore Roosevelt succeeds to the presidency

1909 New York State flag adopted

1916 Congress restricts child labor

1920 19th Amendment grants women the right to vote

First modern radio broadcast in Pittsburgh

1927 Charles Lindbergh takes off from New York to complete first solo non-stop transatlantic flight

Each generation of New Yorkers has faced a special challenge. Colonists rebelled against royal governors and finally won independence. Their children and grandchildren had to conquer the wilderness, build canals and railroads, and create democratic institutions. The post-Civil War generation faced many problems—industrial expansion, absorption of immigrants, and the improvement of working conditions. In addition, New Yorkers in a period known as the Gilded Age had to make government work more effectively and more honestly.

Good progress was made in tackling these problems. By 1900, New York produced about one sixth of the nation's manufactured goods. A new generation of leaders—Grover Cleveland, Theodore Roosevelt, Alfred E. Smith—was trying to secure conservation of resources, better housing, and more popular control of the government. No doubt many of New York's mistakes lay in dealing with its cities. Corruption and boss rule brought disgrace to both state and city governments.

In general, gains outweighed shortcomings. Millions of people from every nation and state settled here. Did not New York provide a good living for those willing to work hard? Were not the opportunities greater here than in almost any other region in the world?

Chapter Objectives

To learn about

- changes in transportation and communication and their effects on the economy
- the rise of modern business and financial practices
- changes in farming

chapter 17

TRANSPORTATION, TRADE, and AGRICULTURE

The Age of Railroads

Today we take for granted our modern transportation network, upon which our trade rests. It was not always so. One hundred years ago only the railroads offered reasonably fast service the year around. Ice closed the rivers and canals to ships during the winter months. Most roads were only packed earth and gravel. Stagecoaches and freighting wagons moved slowly over them. In the winter, sleighs were used. No wonder the railroads were so important to the people of the times. They referred to locomotives as iron horses and eagerly sought to have railroads run through their towns.

Cornelius Vanderbilt was the greatest figure in New York's railroad history. In Chapter 13 we learned how the "Commodore" started in the sailing business and built up a fortune of over 20 million dollars. You would think that, with his fortune made, the gruff old sailor would settle down to a life of leisure. But at the age of 67, Vanderbilt, who lived to be 85, was just starting his career. He got control of the New York and Harlem and the Hudson River Railroads which connected New York City with Greenbush across the Hudson River from Albany. Then he gained control of the New York Central running from Albany to Buffalo. Before long, the New York Central secured connections with many cities.

William Vanderbilt, the "Commodore's" son, fought hard against the West Shore Railroad, built along the west bank of the Hudson River to the Albany region and then across the state to Buffalo. Because they were losing money, the men who had built the West Shore Railroad sold it to Vanderbilt, who made it a part of his system. The New York Central Railroad also secured a route from Utica northward through the Adirondacks to Montreal. In 1968 it merged with the Pennsylvania Railroad to become the Penn Central, which soon fell into bankruptcy. This railroad line is now part of ConRail.

The New York and Erie Railroad had reached Dunkirk (on Lake Erie) in 1851 and later was extended to Buffalo. It ran across the Southern Tier of counties and served such cities as Binghamton and Elmira. Many farmers and townsmen who lived in the area between the Erie and the New York Central hoped to connect the two lines. Would not railroads push up land values, encourage the growth of industry, and open up markets for farmers? They were so eager for railroads that they were willing to offer money to rail companies, even as today some cities and counties provide free airports. The 2,682 miles of track in 1860 increased to 8,100 by 1900, much of it supported by government funds.

The Lehigh Valley and the Delaware, Lackawanna and Western railroads pushed northward from Pennsylvania to Buffalo. These lines helped citizens in the Allegheny Plateau but did not seriously compete with the New York Central and the Erie. The third-largest railroad in the state began as a canal company. You may remember that the Delaware and Hudson Canal ran from

Horse Cars

In the early 1800's you walked to church or work. If you had enough money you owned or hired a carriage. Then Europeans introduced local stagecoaches in Paris and London. In 1827 Abraham Brower of New York decided to try out the idea, and he started one coach on Broadway. The people liked it so much that he was able to add another coach in two years.

A few years later John Mason, a New York banker, laid some iron rails down the center of the street. He had some special stagecoaches built with iron wheels. The first trip also had the first streetcar accident in America. Two coaches were rolling down the track, one after the other. The first one came to a halt but the driver of the second forgot to put on the brakes. There was a crash but fortunately no one was hurt.

Operating streetcars became a big business. The larger companies owned several thousand horses, since each car needed several shifts. During the Civil War the government took so many horses that the companies had to reduce their service. Streetcars employed several thousand people on the cars, in the barns, and on the tracks. Various kinds of cars were introduced: open car, half and half (one section closed and one open), and double deckers. Gradually the electric trolley replaced the horse car.

The trolley, in turn, gave way to the bus and the automobile. The last horse car was seen in the lower part of Manhattan Island in the 1920's.

A trolley car in Brooklyn in 1899. This one is powered by electricity.

Kingston to Port Jervis. Not long after the Civil War, the canal company acquired the tracks that ran from Binghamton to Albany. Later the line ran northward from Albany along the west shore of Lake Champlain and on to Montreal. This railroad carried a good deal of coal from Pennsylvania.

As the population of Long Island grew, the people of that region demanded rail service. The Long Island Railroad was formed to meet this need. In 1899 it secured a bridge across the East River, enabling it to run trains to the heart of New York City. This railroad was important to the economic growth of Long Island. A great many suburban dwellers still use it to travel to work.

Transportation changes were taking place in the cities also. The streetcar, drawn at first by horses and later by cable, or electric power, became popular. New York City needed better transportation because of its large population and its shape. Since only a few avenues ran north and south on Manhattan Island, there was much congestion. In 1860 horse cars carried 50,000,000 passengers a year. Forty years later this figure had risen to 12 times that number. Meanwhile, the horse car had given way to the cable car. Cable cars were pulled forward by an underground cable. Cable cars, in turn, gave way to electric trolleys.

The electric streetcar was very popular between 1890 and 1925. Trolley lines reached out to the suburbs and even to other cities miles away. For example, in 1914, passengers could travel by trolley all the way from Little Falls to Buffalo, a distance of 220 miles. Businessmen built parks on the outskirts of town, and on warm summer evenings open cars carried hundreds of pleasure-seekers to the parks. By 1912 the streetcar had reached its greatest development. After that date, the automobile and the bus began to take away the business. Today, most of the trolley tracks have been torn up.

In most cities trolley cars were able to handle the passenger traffic, but in New York City they were unable to take care of the huge crowds going to and from work. Men began to plan other means for passenger transportation. The elevated railway came first. People, however, complained not only about the clanging cars, but also about the soot, cinders, and the live coals that dropped from the steam locomotives. In 1902 electric engines replaced the steam locomotives on elevated structures.

Very early some people suggested subways that would travel underground, but subway builders had to fight the opposition of both trolley and elevated companies. In 1900 a private company began digging the first subway near City Hall in Manhattan. By 1920 a person could travel underground most of the way to the outskirts of Brooklyn and the Bronx. On hot summer days, thousands of people took the subway and trolleys to Coney Island. The subway was fast and convenient, and all sections of the city wanted a line. In 1932 the City of New York opened its own subway. Before long, people demanded one unified system so that they could travel over both the private and public lines on one fare. Mayor La Guardia, in 1940, effected such a merger.

After World War II, New York found that the subway system was losing money each year. Wages, materials, and power kept costing more. As a result, the fare rose from five cents to fifty cents. Under the law, the subway system is required to pay its way. The city, however, pays for new subway construction out of tax money. In 1965 the subways and bus lines were placed under the Transit Authority and in 1968 became part of the Metropolitan Transportation Authority.

Loading machinery aboard ocean-going ships at a Port Authority pier in Brooklyn. Manhattan piers and skyscrapers are in the background.

Waterborne Commerce

The ocean continued to be the main waterway for New York. Each decade after the Civil War the amount of goods coming into and passing out of New York Harbor grew in value. Steam gradually replaced sailing vessels, and steel ships proved more useful than wooden ones. Meanwhile, the number of American-owned ships became smaller, especially in the overseas trade routes. British and German shipowners paid lower wages and bought ships at lower prices than American shipowners. Americans could not compete. When World War I began, the United States did not have enough ships to carry troops and war supplies. The federal government built hundreds of ships during the war years. In 1920 most of these ships were turned over to private companies. Once more, the American firms found it difficult to compete with the foreigners. When World War II started, the United States again raced to build ships. When the war ended, a great number were no longer needed. Scores of them were left anchored in the Hudson River near West Point where they form a "mothball fleet."

Have you seen the large ships that carry wheat or iron ore to Buffalo? The history of shipping on the Great Lakes is somewhat like that on the high seas. One hundred years ago only small sailing vessels were used. Then steam power drove side-wheelers similar to those used on the Mississippi River. The side-wheelers, with their paddle wheels exposed, were not safe in rough water. For this reason, owners changed to the propeller-driven ship. Meanwhile, in the 1870's the railroads began to haul wheat directly from Chicago to New York. To fight these competitors, the ship companies built larger ships, and after 1890 they made them out of steel.

The canal system lost importance in the years following the Civil War. The New York Central and the Erie railroads took away from the Erie Canal its remaining wheat and lumber traffic. The railroads had many advantages: speed, year-round service, better-located terminals, and more connections with other kinds of transportation. In 1874 an overwhelming majority of the people voted to abandon most of the feeder canals, such as the Chenango, the Genesee Valley, and the Black River. These canals had never paid their way.

The canals, however, had many supporters who argued that a new canal was needed to make sure that New York City would keep its position as the leading business center in the United States. They gradually won public support and in 1903 the voters backed a bond issue of $101,000,000 for the purpose of building a barge canal across the state.

The Barge Canal was an entirely new canal, which used only a few parts of the old Erie Canal. It used rivers and lakes wherever possible. For example, the Mohawk River was canalized to a point near Herkimer. Unlike the Erie Canal, the new Barge Canal passed through Oneida Lake. This canal has not been as successful as its backers had predicted. Traffic has not reached the level the Erie enjoyed in its heyday. Furthermore, the Barge Canal cost twice as much as the voters had expected. Since no tolls are charged, the State of New York is really providing a free transportation route for the companies using the canal. Oil and gasoline are the most important cargoes.

Pioneers in Communication

Merchants and manufacturers depend as much on new ways of communicating information as they do on the rapid transport of goods and people. The telegraph, cable, telephone, television, and radio have linked together the markets of the world and greatly speeded business transactions.

New Yorkers were among the first to use the telegraph. Businessmen used it to buy and sell goods hundreds of miles away. Hardly had the people overcome their wonder at this new mechanical miracle when another invention—the telephone—came into use. In 1876 Alexander Graham Bell, a Scottish immigrant who had taught deaf children for many years, showed that a human voice could be sent over a wire. Soon wires were strung over the countryside between the larger cities. Today nearly every home in New York State has a telephone.

The Italian scientist M. Guglielmo Marconi, in 1895, found a way of sending signals through the air without wires. From Marconi's wireless was developed the radio. Dr. Lee De Forest of New York made some of the basic discoveries in the development of the radio. In 1909 he arranged for the famous tenor, Enrico Caruso, to sing over the air from the Metropolitan Opera House. The first modern radio broadcast took place in Pittsburgh in 1920, but New Yorkers were soon in the forefront of those who were developing the invention. A New York station was the first to send a program by wire to a Chicago station, and thus to make the first successful "chain" broadcast. A station in New York City was the first to advertise products. Station WGY in Schenectady was the first to put plays over the air. By the end of the 1920's several radio chains had grown up, with headquarters in New York. In fact, Rockefeller Center included a "Radio City."

Television developed from radio. Once again, New York City became headquarters for companies sending telecasts across the nation. The importance of television is clear to all the people of New York. Not only does it provide the public with entertainment, but it also has proved to be a good way to educate people. The manufacture of television and other electrical equipment is a major industry in this state. The General Electric Company, with large plants in Schenectady, Utica, Syracuse, Ithaca, and other cities, is the largest manufacturer of electrical equipment in the world.

Almost everyone has heard of George Eastman, the Rochester genius who made a fortune in the photography business. Eastman was a young bank clerk who began to experiment with photography in his spare time. People had been taking and developing pictures for many years. But cameras were big and heavy, and photographers had to use "wet" plates made out of glass. As a result, only a few persons in large cities had the proper skill and equipment to make a good picture. Eastman began to read and experiment. His aim was to find some way to take pictures by means of a dry plate. He developed a dry plate and eventually was able to print film on paper rolls. In 1888 he offered a camera to the public for 25 dollars. It was called a Kodak. Eastman sold the camera with the slogan, "You press the button, we do the rest."

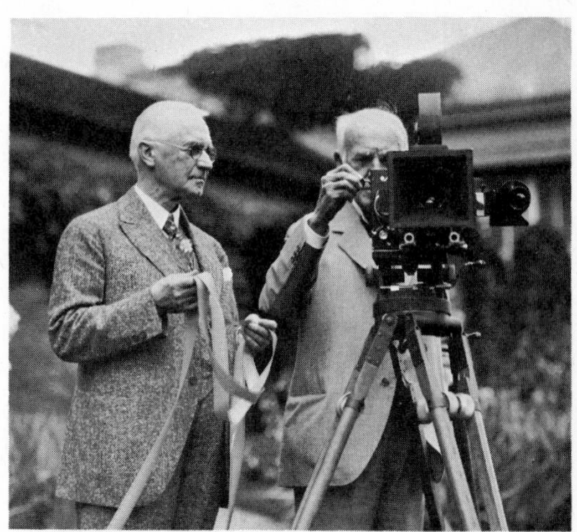

George Eastman (left) and Thomas Alva Edison at the first showing of a Kodak color motion picture process in 1928.

Eastman's business flourished and made him a rich man. He gave much of his fortune to educational and charitable institutions. The Eastman School of Music and the University of Rochester's Medical School rose to top rank because of Eastman's support. Today, people can trace the main events in the history of photography by visiting the Eastman Museum in Rochester.

Thomas Alva Edison and others saw the possibility of combining photography with motion. Edison developed a Kinetoscope, a device whereby a person could look through a peephole at a series of pictures in motion. If you have ever visited a penny arcade, you have probably looked into a similar machine. Various people developed projectors which would throw the moving pictures on a screen. In 1896 a vaudeville theater in New York gave the first motion picture show—some waves, a dancer, and part of a boxing match. The public showed a lot of interest and rushed to pay a nickel to visit the small "movie" halls with a screen

A bargain counter of a busy department store in the early 1900's.

at one end. These became known as nickelodeons. By the opening of World War I in 1914, several huge theatres were being built to show motion pictures. One of the most famous was the Roxy in New York City.

At first, many movies were made on Long Island, and in New York, Ithaca, and other cities. Most companies, however, moved their studios to Hollywood, where the climate and the weather were more favorable for outdoor photography.

Marketing Goods

The revolution in transportation made it easier to get goods to the stores. The rise of the daily penny newspaper and the development of advertising made it easier to tell people about various products. As a result, changes in the method of selling goods came about. New Yorkers were to keep the lead in the field of mass selling.

R. H. Macy of New England founded his famous store in New York just before the Civil War. He popularized the selling of goods at one fixed price. Before this, customers used to bargain with the storekeeper over the price of each product. The idea of the modern department store probably began in New York, although Pennsylvanians claim the honor for John Wanamaker. Macy was the first to establish book, china, and silverware departments in addition to dry goods, but Lord and Taylor was the first to add furniture and shoe departments. An Irish immigrant, Alexander T. Stewart, established one of the largest dry goods stores in the world. A British visitor in 1864 wrote:

> He is, I suppose, next to the President, the best known man in America. . . . His white marble stores, one for the wholesale, the other for the retail trade, would dwarf British stores into pigmies. We went over one of them ascending by the lift which carries up the goods, through the successive tiers of show-rooms and down the

> magnificent staircases which connect the several flats, in utter amazement at the extent of the area enclosed by the walls, and the business transacted within them.

New Yorkers had much to do with developing the chain store, especially the five-and-ten cent stores. Frank W. Woolworth of Watertown dreamed of a store in which every article would sell for five or ten cents. He opened his first store in Utica in 1879, but it failed. Woolworth refused to give up his dream and moved to Pennsylvania, where he was successful. By 1910 he had over a thousand stores in his chain. Chain stores selling drugs, candy, tobacco, hardware, dry goods, clothing, hats, shoes were found in New York cities at an early date. Most of these chains have established their headquarters in New York City.

The marketing techniques of Macy, Wanamaker, Stewart, and Woolworth were well suited to the developing cities. These merchants realized that the growing population of the region made it possible to attract many customers by charging low prices. They knew that much money could be obtained by making a small profit on each of many sales.

Finance

The Civil War caused a sharp rise in prices and wild speculation in stocks and bonds. Those brokers or dealers in securities (stocks and bonds) who were not members of the New York Stock Exchange met and traded on the sidewalk. Thus was the origin of the New York Curb Exchange, which eventually became the American Exchange.

Ups and downs, and sometimes boom and bust, have marked the history of these stock exchanges. Speculation led to panics in 1873 and 1893, followed by long depressions. During the 1920's the prices of shares spiraled upward as stockholders made more and more money. Then came black Friday in October 1929 when the bottom fell out of the market. Billions were lost by the end of the year and the price of shares fell downward until 1933. More careful regulation by the stock exchanges and by the federal government have stopped the wild speculation of the past.

Bankers of New York played an important role in serving not only the businessmen of the Empire State but also the needs of companies throughout the nation and the world. Manhattan bankers financed much of the railroad network and the expansion of big business. For example, the banking firm of J. P. Morgan in 1900 organized the United States Steel Company, the first billion-dollar corporation. Many Republicans and Democrats in the federal government became alarmed about the power of the "money trust" and in 1914 set up the Federal Reserve System in order to secure closer public control.

The business boom after World War II meant prosperous times for most banks. In addition, many banks increased their assets by merging together. They also set up branches, following the people who moved to the suburbs.

Savings banks and saving and loan associations have lent billions of dollars to individuals who built new homes since World War II. This financing of homes has contributed to the growth of the suburbs.

New York City has remained the insurance capital of the nation. Its three leading companies—Metropolitan, New York Life, and Equitable—write about one-fourth of

In 1869 member brokers of the New York Stock Exchange made their bids as the president called the roll of stocks listed. A few years later, continuous bidding was begun, as exists now.

all the life insurance in this country. Unfortunately, some unscrupulous and crooked men were attracted to the growing business in its early days. But Governor Charles Evans Hughes in 1907 secured careful regulation and since that time the companies have enjoyed able and successful administration.

Farmers Adjust to Modern Ways

A hundred years ago a majority of New Yorkers lived on farms. Every member of the family worked long hours each day. Farm families stayed close to their homes, and only once in a while would they see their neighbors. Children walked to the district school. The head of the family drove his team to town once a week or so over the muddy or snow-clogged roads. There was no mail service to his door, no telephones, radio, television, or automobiles.

Fortunately, a number of changes have taken place since the Civil War and, as a result, the lives of people who live in the country are much more pleasant. Many changes were painful at first. Farmers who failed to keep pace with new developments often lost their money and their farms. Sometimes whole communities disappeared and families were scattered. Let us look at the things that caused these changes.

A most important factor was the great growth of population and the gradual appearance of urban communities. New York farmers had to produce more and more food to feed the increasing number of people. Whereas city markets, and later suburban ones, meant a profit for farmers, the cities drew many able young people from the countryside. In the cities they sought fame and fortune. Many found success and a few became very wealthy. John D. Rockefeller, Jay Gould, George Eastman—all young men from rural New York—became millionaires.

We saw earlier that the suburbs have taken up much farm land. At the same time many who work in the cities have taken homes in rural areas. As a result, there has been both a decline in farm population and a decline in the number of acres planted. The greatest amount of New York land under cultivation was in 1880. Since that time, one-third of the cultivated land has been returned to forest, to brush, or to pasture. Fewer than one in fifty New Yorkers belong to farm families.

The rich farms of the western states probably have affected New York farmers almost as much as the growth of population. The western farms produced foods cheaply, making it difficult for New Yorkers to compete. Before the Civil War, western wheat growing forced the farmers of the Empire State to shift from wheat to fruit and dairy products. More recently, the western manufacture of butter and cheese has made it necessary for New Yorkers to concentrate

The Abandoned Farm

Who has not wondered why the owners of an abandoned farm left their home? A writer in 1893 described one farm:

"The shingles and the clapboards loosen and the roof sags, and within, damp, mossy decay has fastened itself to walls, floor, and ceiling of every room. Gaps have broken in the stone walls along the roadway, and the brambles are thick."

Thousands of farms have been abandoned in this state. Since 1880 over one-half of the cultivated land has gone back to forest, brush, or pasture.

There are several reasons why this has happened. Many farmers went west to find cheaper, more fertile land. Some farms had poor soil that was soon worn out. Others were located too far from railroads or highways. Finally, many young people left the farm for careers in the city.

Today, a great number of old farm houses have become attractive homes or summer places for city dwellers. Much of the once productive land around them, however, is still abandoned.

on the sale of fluid milk for drinking purposes.

Another factor has been the increase of government help and control. At first, farmers turned to the government for information, fairs, and agricultural schools. In 1865 the state chartered Cornell University with a small agricultural department, which became the state college of agriculture in 1904. The state opened two-year agricultural institutes in such places as Morrisville, Canton, Delhi, and Cobleskill. Congress set up an experiment station at Geneva, the first in the country. It is associated with the Cornell Agricultural College. Here experts study better ways to grow crops and develop new varieties of fruit. Since 1914 most counties have had agricultural experts called "agents." Their job is to show farmers how to keep better records, raise more crops, and use machinery. During the depression of the 1930's farmers could not sell their milk, except at very low prices. As a result, the state government, and then the federal government, fixed the selling price for milk at a level that would permit the farmer a reasonable profit.

Important changes also took place on the farms. Farmers bought more machinery in order to increase their production of food. Between 1865 and 1910 they tried to substitute horsepower for man's muscles. A rake drawn by a horse could rake a field of hay faster than several men with hand rakes. More important still was the coming of the gasoline engine. With tractors, farmers could plow fields deeper and faster and reap their crop more quickly. With trucks, farmers could haul goods to the creamery or market in a hurry. In the old days, a farmer spent a whole day taking his wagon load to market. Today goods can be taken to market before breakfast. Machines have lightened the hard work of farming.

Electric power brought almost as many changes as the gasoline motor. In 1929 not even one-third of our farmers had electricity. Each year, however, the wires were

Operation Sail, 1976

July 4, 1976, the two hundredth anniversary of the signing of the Declaration of Independence, was a great day for Americans. Foreign governments helped us celebrate by sending naval ships which steamed into New York harbor on July 3.

Impressive as this display was, the real show took place on the Fourth. Sailing ships, about 225 in all, joined in Operation Sail. At 11 A.M. the celebration began with the sixteen tallest ships leading the procession. When they reached the giant aircraft carrier *Forrestal* near Verrazano Bridge, they spread their sails and moved upriver in single file north of the George Washington Bridge. Over six million New Yorkers and visitors watched in awe.

As night fell a 200-gun salute from the ships signalled the start of a magnificent fireworks display. *Operation Sail* was an exciting event—the world's way of saying "Happy Birthday America."

strung farther into the countryside, until today almost all farms have electric power. What a change it has made! Electricity lights barns, cools milk, and runs machinery. It has lifted a big load off the backs of farm women. The modern kitchen, with its gleaming refrigerator, stove, and washing machine, is very different from the old farm kitchen with a black wood stove, hand pump for water, and kerosene lamp. Almost all farm families have radios and television as evidenced by the television antennae on practically every farmhouse roof.

Machines do many different kinds of work: blow chopped corn into silos, milk cows, dig potatoes. Because of these machines, our farmers produce much more than their fathers did, and with less manpower.

Farmers learn about new methods in many ways. They read farm magazines and study pamphlets put out by the agricultural colleges. They listen to radio programs and talk with county agents and teachers in schools and colleges. All members of the farm family can join farm clubs, such as the Four-H Clubs, the Farm Bureau, and the Grange. The first local Grange unit was organized at Fredonia. Farmers also watch what their neighbors are doing. If Farmer Jones seems to be doing well, other farmers along his road will copy his methods.

Dairying has been the most important kind of farming in New York. At the time of the Civil War, most people made butter and cheese in their own homes. About this time, however, cheese factories began to make cheese of better quality than that made by individual farmers. New York has always been famous for its cheese. Herkimer County cheese, in particular, has had a fine name in this country and in England. New York butter is also of excellent quality. To protect the buttermaker, the state legislature passed a law that made it a crime to sell margarine colored as butter. This law was repealed in 1950, and today more margarine than butter is eaten.

Fortunately, as urban regions grew in population, the demand for fresh milk kept rising. Railroads sent tank cars into the rural regions and took the milk to the cities. During the 1920's milk dealers began to use tank trucks, which often travel all night in order to have the milk in the city by morning. To protect the dairy farmer against extremely low prices for milk, the federal government continues to set the price of milk coming to New York City.

During World War II, New York farmers produced vast quantities of badly needed food, despite shortages of gasoline, feed, machinery, and labor. It was a time of hard work, fine growing weather, and good profits. Many farmers paid off debts which they had acquired during the depression. After the war, good times continued, although farm income fell off when milk prices dropped. New technology has helped farmers since 1920 to increase output more than one third. In the same period the number of farms fell to less than a quarter and land in cultivation to less than half.

Summary

Changes in transportation since the Civil War have revolutionized the economic life of New York. The number of miles of railroad track in the state tripled between 1860 and 1900. In the cities, horsecars gave way to electric trolley cars. In New York City, elevated railways and subways were introduced.

The ocean has remained the main waterway for New York. The state canal system lost importance after the Civil War even though the Barge Canal was built across the state early in this century.

New Yorkers were prominent in developing and improving new methods of communication. Lee De Forest and George Eastman were important figures. Improved transportation and communication were reflected in the growth of the chain store and the department store. New York took a top place in finance after the Civil War, the Stock Exchanges, banks, and insurance companies lending strength and credit to the expansion of business. The competition of western farms led New York farmers to concentrate on fruit and dairy products, particularly the production of milk. The use of farm machinery has led to greatly increased production with fewer farmers.

Checking the high points

1. What important railroads were built in New York after the completion of the New York Central and the Erie railroads?

2. How did cities try to solve their transportation problems?

3. Why did the number of American-owned merchant ships decline after 1855?

4. Why did the New York State canal system become less important after the Civil War? Has the Barge Canal been successful?

5. What contribution did these people make in the field of communications?

Alexander Graham Bell
Guglielmo Marconi
Lee De Forest
George Eastman
Thomas Edison

6. Why was R. H. Macy important in the retail selling business?

7. What is a department store? A chain store?

8. In what ways does the government help the New York farmer?

9. How have the gasoline engine and electric power influenced farming in New York?

10. What effect has finance in New York had on the nation as a whole?

Think these over

1. Are chain stores good or bad?

2. Is it a good idea for the government to fix the lowest price at which milk can be sold in New York?

3. How does government regulation check speculation in the stock market?

Vocabulary building

bankruptcy
canalized
transactions
subsidize
boom and bust
dry plate
penny arcade
fluid milk
securities
speculation

Checking locations

Port Jervis
Binghamton
Lake Champlain Valley
St. Lawrence Valley
Montreal
Utica
Watertown
Dunkirk
Ogdensburg
Blue Mountain Lake
Malone
North Country
Herkimer
Oneida Lake
Ithaca

Chapter Objectives

To learn about

- **reasons for industrial growth in New York**
- **important industries in late 19th century New York**
- **the growth of the labor movement**
- **late 19th century European immigration to New York**

chapter 18

INDUSTRY and LABOR

Causes and Effects of Industrial Development

We have seen that four things encourage industry: the wealth to build manufacturing plants, the presence of skilled workers, a great market for manufactured goods, and excellent transportation. These four factors can be found in the cities. They have enabled the Empire State to win and hold industrial leadership.

Millions of European immigrants, many of them highly skilled in their trades and willing to work hard, arrived from overseas. To these were added large numbers of Americans who came to the cities to work in the factories. Many of the newcomers had the money to start their own businesses. The great banking houses on Manhattan and the smaller banks in other communities had money to lend to businessmen who wished to establish factories or to expand existing plants.

Our state does not have all the natural resources needed for large-scale industrial development. It has waterpower and iron ore. There are large forests, but we haven't enough timber for the expanding construction industry. There are other important resources, such as gypsum and salt. The nearest fuels are in Pennsylvania and Ohio.

The transportation network has not only brought in the needed raw materials; it has enabled New York manufacturers to sell their products all over the world. No wonder New York State has been the leader in almost every transportation development! The Erie Canal, the New York Central Railroad, and the state highways (especially the Thruway) have made New York one of the busiest thoroughfares in the world. In addition, New York is the largest port in the country, for both ships and airliners. New York State, with its large population and its high standard of living, provides the greatest market in this country.

Another reason for New York's industrial development has been the willingness of businessmen to adopt new methods of making things. In addition, the state has helped business by making it easy for persons to organize *corporations.* A corporation is a business company owned by its stockholders. It can own property, conduct a

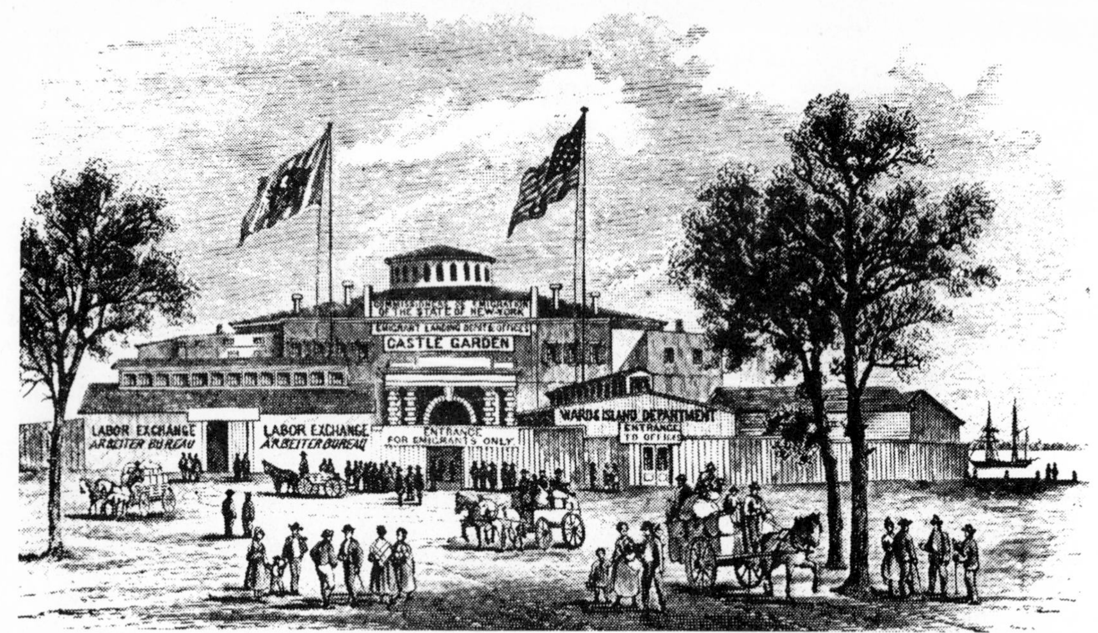

Castle Garden at the Battery in Manhattan was the landing depot for immigrants for many years after the Civil War. The door at the left led the newcomer immediately to the labor exchange.

business, and even sue in the courts. Corporations are controlled by a board of directors elected by stockholders. We can see corporations in almost all parts of the Empire State. Some are huge businesses, such as General Electric; some are small, such as a local automobile sales agency or, perhaps, the company that delivers milk to your door.

The Industrial Revolution has changed the lives of all of us. It has brought better pay for workers, many of whom have joined unions. It has made our country rich. Our factories have attracted millions of immigrants. Cities, large and small, have grown up around the factories. Large corporations have sprung up, controlling important parts of the nation's wealth. Both New York and the United States have had to regulate railroads and other large corporations. Expansion of industries has caused problems of air and water pollution. The Industrial Revolution made a difference in the lives of our farmers and brought many changes to the industries of New York. Some industries have become less important. Other industries have boomed.

How do you compare the size and importance of one industry with another? One way is to count the number of people employed in a certain industry. But some industries are hard to compare by number of employees. For example, a cannery may hire many people for only a few months of the year. Their salaries may be low, and the profits for the company may also be low. On the other hand, a small factory making scientific instruments may employ only a few people. But their salaries may be high, and the company profits may be even higher.

Another way to compare industries is to count the total number of things they produce. But how do you compare tons of steel with hi-fi sets or women's hats?

A third way to compare one industry with another is to check the total cost of production for each industry. However, some industries buy expensive parts and put them together quickly and cheaply. Other industries buy raw materials and go through many expensive processes before turning out the final product.

According to many experts, the best way to measure one industry against another, is to compare the *value added* to one industry's product through manufacturing with that added to another industry's product. Value added is expressed in dollars and cents. It is obtained by subtracting from the price the manufacturer charges for his product the cost of raw materials, supplies, power, heat, and light. These are things that are needed in the manufacture of the product but that are produced by someone else. For example, subtract from the manufacturer's price for a coat the cost of the cloth, buttons, and lining that go into it and the cost of the gas, electricity, and fuel needed to run the plant. What is left is the value added by the manufacturer. This includes the salaries of all employees, for it is their skill that shapes the raw material into the finished product. Value added also includes the profit made by the industry.

One hundred years ago, the 10 most important industries in New York State were flour, men's clothing, sugar refining, leather, liquors, lumber, printing, boots and shoes, machinery, and oil. In the past 10 years, New York's leading industries have been clothing, printing and publishing, food, transportation equipment, machinery, electrical machinery, chemicals, instruments, fabricated metals, and primary metals (steel, etc.).

Compare these lists and you will see that the Industrial Revolution has brought many changes to the industries in New York State.

Clothing and Allied Industries

The clothing industry has outranked all others since the Civil War. Three things changed the manufacture of clothing by hand in homes or in small tailor shops to the manufacture of clothes by machines in factories. First, the invention of the sewing machine greatly speeded up the process of sewing. Isaac Singer of Oswego, a pioneer in the improvement of the sewing machine, built up a large business making sewing machines. Second, the Civil War created a big demand for uniforms and shoes. The army had uniforms made according to standard sizes. If you look at pictures of Civil War soldiers, you will see that many men did not receive a perfect fit. Nevertheless, veterans bought ready-made clothing willingly after the war because it was inexpensive and because it could be had in a hurry. Third, labor was plentiful and cheap. Immigrants were glad to work in the clothing industry, even though the wages were low. Many women and children were employed.

Before 1860 practically all women made their own clothes at home. Thereafter businessmen began to make ladies' coats and dresses in factories. The women's clothing branch of the industry grew very rapidly and, just before World War I, became more important than the men's clothing branch. Since 1965 the clothing industry has employed fewer workers because many firms have migrated from high costs in Manhattan to smaller cities. Business has declined with the shift to more informal apparel, such as levis and sportswear. New York is also the leading state in preparing furs for market and in making women's hats.

The boot and shoe industry is closely

connected with the clothing industry. Shoes had long been handmade by men called shoemakers or cobblers. The sewing machine revolutionized this industry too. It permitted shoes to be made in factories by semiskilled workers.

The textile, or cloth-making industry, was important in the nineteenth century. About 1900, manufacturers of textiles in southern states began to sell cloth more cheaply than the mill owners of New York and New England. Some owners moved their plants south or abroad where they could hire workers for low wages. Important knitting mills have been located in the Mohawk Valley and in New York City. The Bigelow Sanford carpet mills got started in Amsterdam before the Civil War, and Alexander Smith set up a mill in Yonkers in 1865. The carpet industry grew and expanded for many years.

Printing, Food, and Transportation Equipment

Printing and publishing recently became the largest industry measured by the added value of the product. New York City has been the center of publishing newspapers, books, and magazines ever since the Civil War. New inventions and methods speeded up the process of setting type and running off pages.

Advertising is an important business in New York because so many ads appear in New York's newspapers, magazines, and on

Immigrants from about 1885 to 1910 did piecework in their homes. The whole family, even the children, worked long hours trying to turn out as much as they could, but earned very little.

radio and television. Many of the largest advertising concerns are located in New York City, especially on Madison Avenue.

The processing of food products has always been important. Actually, it includes several branches, such as flour milling, baking, sugar refining, meat packing, candy manufacture, and canning and freezing.

Flour milling was the largest industry in New York in 1860. When the center of wheat growing moved westward toward the Great Plains, the milling companies followed. Minneapolis and Kansas City became the largest flour-milling cities. But flour milling in New York gained a new life in 1903, when the first of several Minneapolis companies moved back to New York. By 1930 Buffalo had become the largest milling center in the country. It handled millions of bushels of wheat from the Middle West and Canada.

The baking industry did not operate on a large scale until after 1900, although small bakery shops continue to the present day. The industry has two main branches: the manufacture of crackers, and the manufacture of bread and pastries. Fifty years ago most housewives made their own bread. Today they buy their bread and pastries. The refining of most cane sugar sold in the United States has centered in Brooklyn for over a hundred years.

Meat packing has changed a good deal in the last century. Formerly, each town and city had several small packing houses. After the Civil War, the center of cattle raising shifted to the Middle West, and the meatpacking industry followed the cattle, hogs, and sheep westward. The development of refrigeration and refrigerator cars permitted western packers to ship meat to eastern cities. Furthermore, a few large companies came to control the industry. Since World War II, the big packers have declined. More efficient firms, including several in New York State, have grown, some providing special products, such as kosher meat.

The canning of vegetables and fruit has become a principal part of the food processing industry. Even before the Civil War several men had experimented with canning fish, corn, and milk. Probably the most successful was Gail Borden, who opened up the first factory for making condensed milk in Dutchess County. Canning took another step forward in 1885, when machines to make cans were developed. Improvements continued to be made as the canners tried to meet the demand of the growing city population. After World War II many canners turned their efforts to freezing vegetables and fruits. The development of home freezers and large store freezers greatly stimulated this branch of the industry.

New York has taken a leading part in the making of beer, but only a minor part in the distilling of whiskey. Breweries had sprung up before the Civil War in most cities. During the 1920's the Eighteenth Amendment to the United States Constitution prohibited the manufacture of alcoholic beverages. Upon its repeal in 1933, brewing companies resumed operations. The soft-drink industry, with several plants in the state, does a thriving business.

Along the Erie shore and around the Finger Lakes, the soil and climate are ideal for vineyards. In 1893 Dr. Thomas Welch gave up dentistry for the business of bottling grape juice in Westfield, Chautauqua County. His company has since passed into a farm cooperative owned by the grape growers. The wineries in the Finger Lakes

New York's great port has always attracted ships bearing foods from all over the world. Some of the fresh food is consumed by New Yorkers; other food is processed and shipped inland. Here tropical fruits are being unloaded and bought as they come off the ships.

region produce domestic wines of excellent quality.

Transportation equipment is a newcomer to the top 10 industries. During the great days of the railroads, New York shared in the business of making railroad coaches and steam locomotives. The declining importance of the railroads has meant a drop in the manufacture of railroad equipment. The automobile industry became important, especially after 1910. Although most of the industry is located in Michigan, there are several assembly plants in New York. Near Farmingdale on Long Island and in Buffalo are large factories making aircraft and supplies for airlines and the armed services.

Machinery, Chemicals, Instruments, Metals

One of the largest industries in New York has been the making of machines. A good example is the Otis Elevator Company in Yonkers. Elisha Otis developed the first passenger elevator in 1857. This invention permitted the construction of skyscrapers and paved the way for the growth of cities. Other factories make machines used in textile mills, canneries, laundries, printing shops, bakeries. Almost as important as machinery is the manufacture of electrical equipment and supplies. Before 1880 this industry hardly existed. But the discoveries of Edison, Westinghouse, and others brought electricity to the home, factory, street, and farm. The General Electric Company, in 1892, started to make electrical equipment. It hired Charles Steinmetz, a German immigrant, to work out complicated problems in research. Steinmetz was one of the first to produce artificial lightning. The General Electric Company, with its headquarters in Schenectady, became the largest industry in the state. During and after World War II this company built large plants in Syracuse, Utica, and Auburn. Before 1914 the General Electric Company concentrated on making turbines, light bulbs, and equipment for the transmission of electricity. In the 1920's it added radios to its line. After World War II, its managers built several plants near Syracuse, which produce television and other electrical equipment. Today the company has moved into the field of atomic research.

Chemicals have become steadily more important among the products of the Empire State. The Solvay process made use of the minerals in the Syracuse area. The manufacture of drugs increased very rapidly, especially following World War II. New York and Syracuse have important drug manufacturers in their communities. Since 1940 many firms have manufactured articles out of plastic.

New York produces one-third of the scientific and engineering instruments in the United States. Among New York companies making these things is the Sperry plant at Great Neck, Long Island, which makes delicate instruments for airplanes and ships.

Each of us should be particularly interested in the optical industry since the chances are better than even that some day each of us will wear glasses. Interestingly enough, New York State makes over half of the optical lenses and instruments in this country.

John Bausch, the owner of a small store in Rochester, made the first hard rubber frame for spectacles in 1860. Before that time, people who did not see well generally used a hand glass. Obviously, it was much better to have glasses attached to the head, thus freeing the hands for other work. Business grew rapidly, and Bausch formed a company with his friend, Henry Lomb.

Thomas Edison and Charles Steinmetz discuss an experiment.

Before World War I all the optical glass and most lenses were imported from Europe, particularly from Germany. The outbreak of war cut off this supply. The government appealed to Bausch & Lomb for help. Working under heavy pressure, their scientists were able to produce optical glass in a short time. Today they make over 100 kinds of optical glass.

At Corning, both optical and industrial glass are made at the Corning Glass Center. The famous Steuben crystal is made there also.

Metals and products made of metals are among the top 10 New York industries. Most New York steel is made in the Buffalo region. The steel industry made rapid headway, especially in the 1870's when railroads carried in coal from Pennsylvania, and lake

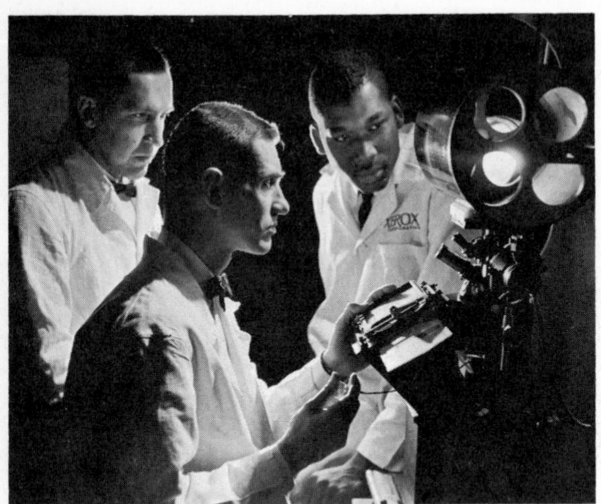

Making computers and electronic equipment requires highly skilled labor.

ships brought iron ore from Minnesota. Because of its cheap water power, New York has become a large producer of aluminum. Large plants for its manufacture grew up at Niagara Falls and Massena. The St. Lawrence Project means more cheap power in the Massena region.

Trade Unions

The rise of industry brought many benefits to working men and women. It opened up thousands of jobs and freed people from a good deal of back-breaking work.

At first, industrialization brought serious problems to workers. It often reduced or eliminated the need for skilled labor. Tailors had once taken pride in producing a good suit of clothes. Machines eliminated much of the work requiring a tailor's skill and knowledge. Few tailors found satisfaction in doing a routine and simple job, such as sewing on hundreds of buttons a day. Worse yet, they lost some of their power to bargain with employers because unskilled women and children could perform many of the operations required in the manufacture of clothing.

The rise of the corporation made relations between employer and worker less close. In small mills the owners had often worked side by side with their workers, whom they called by their first names. But in the large factory, the boss could not know personally the hundreds of workers under him. In fact, the owner might live hundreds of miles away. If goods were not selling, he would order the factory closed. If costs were too high, he might lower wages. The workers felt helpless.

Machinery tended to become more important than the people who operated it. The employer invested thousands of dollars in machinery and would hire and fire a worker at will. If the employer could make a profit by operating a machine 24 hours a day for seven days a week, he had men and women work nights and Sundays. Long hours in confined quarters wore out many workers. When they could not keep up with the machines, they lost their jobs.

Faced with these problems the factory workers organized unions, believing that, by acting as a group, they could get more money and better working conditions. Their representatives met with the employer to discuss problems and work out their differences.

This practice is called *collective bargaining.* A few unions of skilled craftsmen started in the 1830's, and more unions had developed in the 1850's. These early unions, however, found it hard to bargain with their employers. Employers were afraid that unions would cause wages to rise to the point that their competitors might undersell them.

The American Federation of Labor was started in 1886 as a federation of *craft unions.* Craft unions are unions of skilled workers such as carpenters or electricians. Its first president and guiding genius until 1924 was Samuel Gompers of New York.

Practically all the craft unions—those representing carpenters, plumbers, electricians, printers, machinists, and other skilled workers—joined the A. F. of L. In general, the federation made little effort to form unions for the unskilled workers.

Two unions—the International Ladies' Garment Workers' Union and the Amalgamated Clothing Workers—deserve special mention. These unions grew strong and powerful after 1910, despite many obstacles. They were *industrial unions,* that is, they included all the workers in the industry and not just members of one craft. They succeeded in bringing good working conditions into the clothing industry. These two unions have done some unusual things for their members. They have offered lectures and concerts, set up health clinics, run summer camps, and even financed apartment houses. To help their industry they have loaned money to employers, carried on research, and brought in new machinery.

The International Ladies' Garment

Samuel Gompers

Imagine an upstairs room in which there are about 20 men sitting at tables. Each is swiftly rolling cigars. Most of them are Jewish immigrants. In front of the room is a young man who, in a loud voice, is reading novels and serious books to the workers. The cigar workers have paid the man to read to them while they work.

This young man was Samuel Gompers, who was to become the leading man in American labor. Born in a London tenement, he began work at the age of ten. Times were hard, so his father sailed for America. The boy soon learned how to roll cigars. Before long, he joined the cigarmakers union and became its president in 1877.

Meanwhile, Gompers was trying to learn as much as possible by attending lectures at Cooper Union in New York City, and engaging in debates. Gradually he worked out his ideas of what the trade unions should do for their members. He believed that each group of skilled craftsmen (cigarmakers, carpenters, etc.) should form its own union. Gompers was a very practical man. He did not want workingmen to form a political party, but he wanted them to concentrate on getting better wages and working conditions. He did recommend that laboring men help elect their friends to office and punish their enemies by not voting for them.

Gompers helped form the American Federation of Labor in 1886. He served as president of this organization until 1924, except for one year. Under his leadership the Federation grew until it had over four million members. Gompers won the respect of government officials and businessmen. They admired his courage and drive and devotion to his cause.

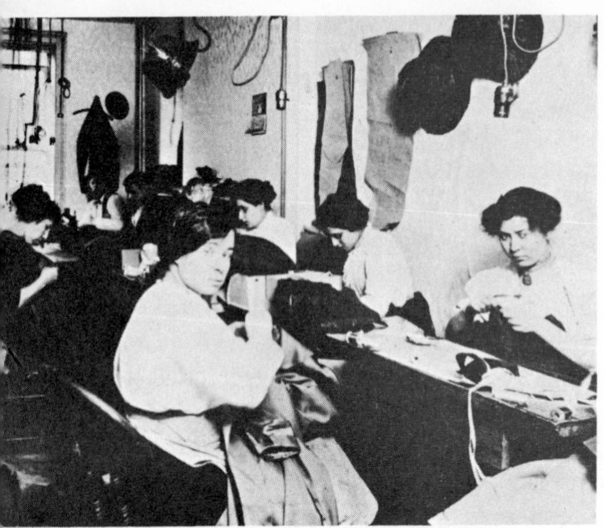

In 1910 when this photograph was taken, there were over 4,000 such "sweatshops" for clothing manufacturing in New York City. Girls worked in dark, unhealthful lofts 12 to 18 hours a day, 6 days a week, for an average of $6.34 per week.

Workers' Union won its first important victory in 1909 when it won the 50-hour week, the end of work in the home, and the *closed shop.* In a business having a closed shop, all the workers must belong to the union. If they do not belong when they are first hired, they must join to keep their jobs. About the same time, Sidney Hillman, an immigrant from Russia, was winning a good agreement or contract for his Amalgamated Clothing Workers Union. During the 1920's both unions faced and overcame serious problems. They threw out the Communists who tried to get control of the unions. They also fought the racketeers who were invading the clothing industry. David Dubinsky led the ILGWU from 1932 to 1966.

When Franklin Roosevelt became President, he supported many laws which helped unions. Labor leaders such as Hillman and Dubinsky tried hard to strengthen their bargaining power by getting more members. Millions of New Yorkers became members of various unions.

Labor Laws

The employment of women and children in factories caused many people to demand laws to protect them. These reformers were especially interested in abolishing the sweatshops, which were small shops, usually located in tenements, where people worked for long hours at low pay under bad conditions. They also wanted to reduce the number of hours which a person could work each day. All these things interfered with family life and sometimes harmed the health of children.

Several laws were passed to protect children and workers. The legislature required all children to attend school. It also took steps toward the eight-hour day. In 1886 the legislature passed a strong labor law. No children under 13 could work in factories, and no person under 21 could work more than 60 hours a week. A factory inspector was appointed to visit all factories and to enforce this law.

Each year thereafter New York added to these laws until today it has the most complete set of labor laws of any state. Along with the new laws have come a small army of officials to carry out the provisions of the laws.

In 1911 there took place in New York City one of the most important events in our labor history. It was the fire that broke out in the factory of the Triangle Shirt Waist Company. Robert F. Wagner, Sr., and Alfred E. Smith were members of the investigating committee which looked into this fire. Their experience on this committee made them champions of labor reform. When Wagner became a United States senator he fought for a law which protected labor unions.

Accidents and disease were other problems. In early factories there were no safety guards on fast-moving machines. In the quarries the rock dust got into the lungs of the workers and caused diseases. If workers got ill they had to look out for themselves. Each year tens of thousands of workers lost their health or ability to work. Their families suffered, and the cities had to support them with relief money. To remedy this situation, the legislature did two things. First of all, it set higher standards of safety. Factories had to erect guards around machinery. Secondly, it passed the Workmen's Compensation Law. Employers were forced to take out insurance for their workers against job-connected accidents and disease. Today, if a worker cannot work because of such accident or illness, a part of the weekly salary is received and medical bills are paid.

Waves of Immigration

More immigrants settled in New York state during the Gilded Age than in any other period. By 1910 a majority of our city dwellers had either been born abroad or had parents of foreign birth.

Before 1840 the New England states had provided the largest number of immigrants to the Empire State. Energetic and educated, the Yankees came to dominate the business, professional, and political life. During the late 1840's the potato blight struck Ireland, driving thousands of Irish poor to New York. The Irish kept coming in large numbers right up to World War I. They worked hard in construction and manufacturing, supported hundreds of Roman Catholic churches and schools, and dominated the Democratic party. The Germans, who were second in numbers to the Irish in the 1850's, became the most numerous immigrants in the period between 1865 and 1900. Because they brought with them many skills, some education, and even small amounts of money the Germans were fairly successful in business, farming, and industry. Two more groups—the British and the Scandinavians (Norwegians, Swedes, Danes)—arrived in large numbers and adapted fairly easily to American ways.

During the 1890's the tide of immigration began to flow from southern and eastern Europe. It brought waves of Italians, especially from the poverty-stricken region south of Rome. In 1917 over 700,000 persons in New York City alone were of Italian birth or parentage. Because the governments of Austria-Hungary and Russia did not treat their minorities fairly, millions of these people—Jews, Poles, Ukranians, Czechs, Lithuanians—chose America for their home. The great majority of immigrants passed through Ellis Island in New York harbor, and the Empire State became the home for more of them than any other state.

Their fight against poverty, disease, and miserable working conditions is a fascinating story of courage and hard work. Most immigrants settled in the cities, where they found jobs in construction, factories (especially clothing and textile), railroads, and various services. Some opened shops—grocery, barber, tailor, shoemaking. Among these newcomers were a few professional men: lawyers, doctors, priests, and musicians. Yet, thousands of immigrants failed to "make it" and ended up in poorhouses, cheap lodging houses, or early graves.

Big city life was difficult for many immigrants who grew up on farms or in small villages. Add to that change the shock of moving to a foreign country where the language was strange and the customs unusual. Most children quickly learned how to speak English, play American games, and to look for better jobs. Some of them rebelled against their parents, who spoke broken English and clung to Old World clothing and customs. Native-born Americans who were chiefly British in background and Protestant in religion showed suspicion, sometimes hatred, of the Roman Catholic Church and Jewish traditions.

Immigrants therefore tended to band together in neighborhoods where they could find protection against the outside world. In "Little Italy" or "Dutchtown" they could trade with merchants speaking their language, they could worship God in the language of their fathers, and they could find the food and drink of their homeland. Clubs sprang up where they played cards, held dances, and sang the old folksongs. New York City naturally had more of these ethnic neighborhoods than any other city in the United States.

Summary

New York has led the nation in manufacturing since the Civil War. Its business leaders were able to take advantage of the supply of labor and capital, the natural resources in and outside the state, and the fine transportation network. The industry of the Empire State is the largest and most varied in the country. Before 1965 the clothing industry outranked all others. Now the first-ranking industry by value of product is the combination of printing and publishing. Other important industries include the processing of food, the manufacture of transportation equipment, and the making of machinery, electrical equipment, chemicals, and scientific instruments. Some industries, such as lumbering and textiles, became less important after the Civil War.

In the long run, the rise of industry brought many benefits to working people. At first it led to serious problems. Machines reduced the need for skilled labor. Workers felt helpless in bargaining for wages and better working conditions. Unions were organized to help achieve these things. Gradually New York passed laws to help its workers. Today this state has the most complete set of labor laws of any state, although other problems of air and water pollution have arisen.

The Gilded Age was the greatest period of European emigration to New York State. Irish, German, English, and Scandinavian immigrants continued to come up to World War I, but in the 1890's peoples from southern and eastern Europe (Italians, Jews, Poles, etc.) began to outnumber the earlier groups. Immigrants banded together in ethnic neighborhoods, hoping in this way to cushion the difficulties of adjusting to the life of urban and industrial America.

Checking the high points

1. What things are needed to develop manufacturing? Does New York have all of these things?

2. How has the Industrial Revolution affected the lives of Americans?

3. How can we compare the importance of one industry with another?

4. How do you explain the fact that the manufacture of clothing moved from the home and tailor shop to factories?

5. What kinds of food processing take place in New York? How important are they to the state?

6. What do these New York companies make?

Otis
General Electric
Sperry
Bausch & Lomb

7. How did the use of machinery in factories help workingmen and women? How did it hurt them?

8. How did the rise of big corporations affect the relations between the employer and the worker?

9. Why did workingmen organize unions?

10. Why were clothing workers' unions unusual?

11. How does New York State try to help its workers?

12. Why was the Triangle Shirt Waist Company fire important?

13. What were the main groups of immigrants?

14. What problems faced immigrants?

Think these over

1. Does the increasing use of machines in factories help or harm the worker?

2. Do you think a closed shop is a good thing?

3. True or false: Brains are more important to New York industry than natural resources. Explain your answer.

Vocabulary building

capital
corporation
stockholder
sue
board of directors
prohibition
fabricated metals
repeal
professional
sweatshop
federation
craft union
closed shop
social security
relief money
pension
unemployment
insurance
ethnic

Checking locations

Oswego
Massena
Chautauqua County
Yonkers
Great Neck

Chapter Objectives

To learn about

- the effects of industrial urbanization
- political reform in late 19th century New York
- New York in World War I

chapter 19

URBAN PROBLEMS

Urban Living

Most New Yorkers, upstaters as well as citizens of the great metropolis, lived in cities in 1900. Indeed, about half lived in the five boroughs of Greater New York.

Urban living, especially in New York City, differed strikingly from that of the rural-village society described in the Age of Homespun. Probably the best way to understand these differences is to read the descriptions found in newspapers and in the writings of other observers of that era.

Change—constant and continual—was the main feature of life. The population kept increasing and the great city kept expanding in every direction with the appearance of new stores, office buildings, and apartments. Because of the traffic tie-ups and congestion, the city and some leaders promoted subways, elevated lines, tunnels, and bridges. Each year thousands of immigrants from almost every country and state flocked to New York. Where else were there better opportunities to make money or to win fame? After businesses formed great trusts, they often set up their headquarters on Manhattan Island, close to the banks, the stock market, and shipping.

Neighborhoods in New York

New York City was actually a collection of hundreds and hundreds of neighborhoods. Within a block or two an individual family could find several kinds of stores (bakery, grocery, butcher), all kinds of shops providing services (barber, dry cleaner, restaurant, saloon), and perhaps a school, a church, and a theater. Some neighborhoods were composed of persons of one nationality or race. For example, there were places such as Harlem, Chinatown, and Little Italy. Other neighborhoods attracted working-class families who found it easier to live near their work at the docks or the clothing lofts. Some neighborhoods had an unusual range of groups: rich and poor; foreign-born and United States-born; old and young; blacks and whites.

Jacob Riis, an immigrant from Denmark, was a reporter who wrote a famous book

Mulberry Bend about 1889. This was New York's lower West Side where thousands of immigrants came to start life in America.

called *How the Other Half Lives.* His description of the population of New York City gives a vivid picture of how neighborhoods changed as new waves of immigrants swept into the city.

> A map of the city, colored to designate nationalities, would show more stripes than on the skin of a zebra, and more colors than any rainbow. The city on such a map would fall into two great halves, green for the Irish prevailing in the West Side tenement districts, and blue for the Germans on the East Side.

Riis goes on to point out islands of Italians, French, and blacks. In addition Russian and Polish Jews were challenging the Italians for many sections of New York.

About 15 years later, L. B. More made a study of Greenwich Village in lower New York City where he found many changes taking place.

> The old two- and three-story houses, with their quaint doorways and gabled roofs, are rapidly being torn down to make way for large tenements, or are being altered for the use of three or four or even more families. It is a district of extremes in housing conditions. The crowded Italian tenements on Macdougal, Thompson, and Sullivan Streets are almost neighbors to fashionable Washington Square and lower Fifth Avenue. . . The old houses now occupied by several families are somewhat rundown, but dignified even in their decay. At the other extreme are cheap tenements of the "double-decker", "dumbbell" type, tumbledown

rear houses, and several very disreputable "courts" and short streets, sometimes containing tenements hardly fit for human habitation. The very poor frequently live in houses whose sanitary conditions and general character are as bad as can be found anywhere in New York. The whole neighborhood is in a state of transition, and its rapidly increasing population is changing the external features of the district.

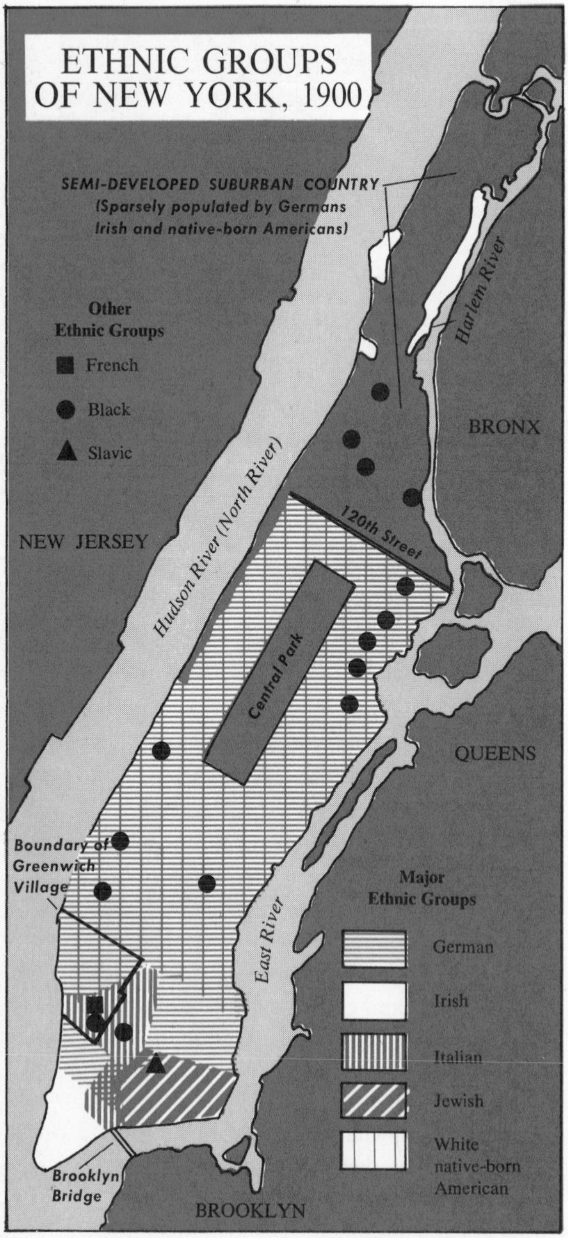

ETHNIC GROUPS OF NEW YORK, 1900

Map 23

Nationalities and Families in Greenwich Village

The mixed character of New York's population obviously was continuing. Was the so-called "melting pot" working at full blast? (This term, if you recall, means the combination of various nationality and religious groups into a new blend.) Or were the various races and nationality groups keeping to themselves? Read More's comments on this subject, the result of a study of some 200 families.

> The population is changing rapidly. It includes native-born Americans as well as immigrant Irish, German and French.
>
> Until recently, these nationalities largely predominated in the district. There was also a large colored quantity. Within the last few years the population has become much more cosmopolitan[1], and now has representatives of almost every nationality to be found in New York. For several years the Italians have come in steadily increasing numbers until now it is one of the most important Italian quarters in the city. Other nationalities in the district include Swedish, English, Scotch, Norwegian, Swiss, and Austrian.

More found that more than half of the 300 families married persons of their own race or nationality. Nevertheless many individuals married outside their group: black and white, immigrant and native white, and

[1] Mixed, not of one nationality

many with people whose nationalities differed from their own. Thus, while many persons in each group chose to remain distinct, others did begin new families that combined different customs and beliefs.

Housing

Governor Theodore Roosevelt, in 1900, urged the state legislature to create the New York State Tenement Commission. Its secretary was Lawrence Veiller, who drew up a report highly critical of the tenements of New York City. He paid particular attention to the so-called "dumbbell tenement" which had been built by the thousands. Here is a description:

> The tall tenement house, accommodating as many as 100 to 150 persons in one building, extending up six or seven stories into the air, with dark, unventilated rooms, is unknown in London or in any other city of Great Britain. It was first constructed in New York about the year 1879, and with slight modifications has been practically the sole type of building erected since, and is the type of the present day. It is a building usually five or six or even seven stories high, about 25 feet wide, and built upon a lot of land of the same width and about 100 feet deep. The building as a rule extends back 90 feet, leaving the small space of 10 feet unoccupied at the rear, so that the back rooms may obtain some light and air. This space has continued to be left open only because the law has compelled it. Upon the entrance floor there are generally two stores, one on each side of the building, and these sometimes have two or three living rooms back of them. In the centre is the entrance hallway, a long corridor less than three feet wide and extending back 60 feet in length. This hallway is nearly always totally dark, receiving no light except that from the street door and a faint light that comes from the small windows opening upon the stairs, which are placed at one side of the hallway. Each floor above is generally divided into four sets of apartments, there being seven rooms on each side of the hall, extending back from the street to the rear of the building. The front apartments generally consist of four rooms each and the rear apartments of three rooms, making altogether 14 upon each floor, or in a seven-story house 84 rooms exclusive of the stores and rooms back of them. Of these 14 rooms on each floor, only four receive direct light and air from the street or from the small yard at the back of the building.

Like the upstate pioneers a century earlier, the city dwellers tried hard to make their homes neat and comfortable. Here L. B. More describes a worker's home in Greenwich Village about 1905.

> The typical home of the wage-earners in this district is quite well furnished and fairly neat and clean. . . . The bedroom is only large enough for a white iron bed, generally covered by a white spread, and is quite clean. The kitchen, which is also the dining room, is just large enough for a cupboard, a few chairs, and the table covered with white oilcloth. . . . On the whole, however, it is quite a comfortable home.

Work and Pleasure in Greenwich Village

More's study tells us a good deal about how the people of one small neighborhood made a living.

> It is a district largely given over to candy, paper box, and artificial flower fac-

tories, and to wholesale houses. Its proximity to the North (Hudson) River and the docks of the great steamship lines gives occupation to many long shoremen, or dock laborers, and to truck drivers. Probably these occupations give employment to a larger number of men than does any other one industry. A great many clerks live here, as well as porters, waiters, carpenters, painters, plumbers, factory workers, foremen in factories, bakers, boot-blacks, bookkeepers, letter carriers, policemen, and petty shopkeepers. All kinds of skilled and unskilled labor are represented. There is probably a larger proportion of unskilled than of skilled laborers in the district.

Although life was hard for these people, they relaxed in many ways.

Their social life consists of the usual diversions*—the public halls (dances), cheap theatres, christening parties, and the clambakes and free excursions given by local politicians in summer. The Italians have their fetes and church festivals.

The men have the saloons, political clubs, trade unions, or lodges for their recreation, the young people have an occasional ball (dance) or go to a cheap theatre, and in the evenings congregate on the streets and in the small parks for their

* Entertainment

William Marcy Tweed was a political boss who organized his associates into the *Tweed Ring.* He and his friends swindled New York City out of millions of dollars. Thomas Nast brought attention to Tweed's corrupt practices through cartoons such as this one.

> pleasure, while the mothers have almost no recreation, only a dreary round of work, day after day, with occasionally a door step gossip to vary the monotony of their lives. The Settlements and institutional churches are giving more social opportunity for the mothers and young people.

In general, the immigrant groups were hardworking people who made the best of the difficult conditions under which they lived.

Corruption

After the Civil War corruption and dishonesty marred business and political activities. Many citizens were so busy as soldiers or workers that they paid little attention to what some politicians were doing. The national and state governments spent a lot of money for guns, uniforms, and supplies. Dishonest officials in league with dishonest businessmen stole some of this money. Furthermore many elected state officials were not under the control of the governor, who could do little to police their activities. New York City had an unworkable government partly because the state legislature had taken away much of its power.

The growth of big business also encouraged corruption in both state and local governments. Businessmen wanted favors such as the right (franchise) to operate trolleys or to install phones or gas and electric lines. Railroads, fearing that the government would regulate their fares, gave money to politicians who agreed to oppose such laws.

The growth of political machines was both the cause and the result of the increase in corruption. A political machine is an organization that runs a political party. It is usually controlled by a boss. Some bosses were able, honest, and responsible leaders who got things done. Others were dishonest.

One of the most powerful bosses was Boss Tweed, the leader of Tammany Hall. William Marcy Tweed became well known in his neighborhood when he organized a volunteer fire department. Then he entered politics. By 1863 he was in charge of the streets of New York City. Every time a contract was given for the paving of the streets, Tweed and his friends collected 10 percent of the amount of the contract.

Tammany Hall was careful to help the poor, the friendless, and recent immigrants. Tammany workers distributed coal in the winter, gave picnics in the summer, and provided jobs for people who needed them. Naturally, these people supported Tammany Hall. To make sure they stayed in power, Tweed's gang stuffed the ballot boxes at election time by putting in extra ballots for their candidates. In one election, Tweed's friends stuffed the ballot boxes with over 25,000 fake votes. There were many more votes in the ballot boxes than there were voters! Incidentally, less important bosses were doing the same thing upstate.

Boss Tweed grew rich and proud. When reformers attacked him, he said, "What are you going to do about it?" Fortunately, a few people were willing to do something. Thomas Nast, a cartoonist for *Harper's Weekly* magazine, drew cartoons of Tweed and his supporters. His cartoons worried the gang so much that they offered him a half-million dollars to stop. He refused. *The New York Times* also printed proof of Tweed's thefts. Finally, leading citizens under an outstanding lawyer, Samuel J. Tilden, joined to put Tweed in jail. Tweed was brought to trial and was convicted of stealing $6,000,000. He was sent to prison and died there.

Governors Bring Reform

Gradually New Yorkers went about the job of getting rid of corruption. Under the leadership of a number of good governors, democracy in New York again began to move forward.

The Democrats picked Tilden to run for governor in 1874. He won easily and pushed through several laws making it harder for officials to escape punishment for corruption. Meanwhile, Tilden was secretly collecting evidence about the dishonest activities of the "Canal Ring." This group of politicians plotted with contractors to overcharge the state for work done on the canals. With this evidence, Governor Tilden broke up this corrupt practice.

In 1882 Grover Cleveland was elected governor. As a young lawyer in Buffalo, he decided to enter politics. Soon he won the positions of sheriff of Erie County and mayor of Buffalo. His reputation for honesty earned him the nomination of governor. In this office he cut down on spending and appointed competent men to state jobs. He later served two terms as president, 1885-1889 and 1893-1897.

Tom Platt was the leading Republican boss during the later 1890's. Because he shunned publicity he was known as the "Easy Boss." Strangely enough, Platt was partly responsible for bringing Theodore Roosevelt to public attention.

Roosevelt, who was sickly as a boy, made himself into a strong athlete and sportsman by constant training. He even took boxing lessons. He bought a ranch in the Dakota Territory and lived the life of a cowboy for a time. Young Roosevelt decided to go into politics as a young man because he wanted "to join the ruling class." He served in the State Assembly and then, as police commissioner of New York City, he fought graft and corruption. Finding a desk job too dull, Roosevelt rounded up his old cowboy friends in 1898 and formed the Rough Riders, a cavalry troop. He led this group against the Spanish in Cuba during the Spanish-American War.

Tom Platt recognized Roosevelt's popularity and helped him win the Republican nomination for governor. Winning easily, Roosevelt soon showed that he would not take orders from Platt or anyone else. He tried to improve conditions in tenement houses and to end sweatshops where women and children worked long hours for low pay. In 1900 Roosevelt became the candidate for Vice-President on the Republican ticket. When President McKinley was killed by an assassin in the fall of 1901, the former Rough Rider became President. He was the fifth New Yorker to become President.

Roosevelt became one of the most famous Presidents in our history. He started the building of the Panama Canal, and he established many forest reserves. He fought big business. When Roosevelt left the White House in 1908, he was loved by the American people.

Charles Evans Hughes, another fine governor, was also a reformer. He became famous when he headed investigations of gas and insurance companies in New York City. This investigation won him the Republican nomination and, because of his efforts, the election.

As governor, Hughes gave the state honest and efficient government. He created a public service commission to regulate the rates that gas and electric companies could charge the people. He favored laws to help working people.

Women's Rights

Women had demanded equal rights from the time of the Woman's Rights Convention in Seneca Falls, New York in 1848, but changes came very slowly. Nevertheless, Elizabeth Cady Stanton and Susan B. Anthony kept making speeches and writing articles in favor of women's suffrage. The state legislators and political leaders avoided the issue, however. In the years between 1900 and 1914 another drive for women's rights got under way with Carrie Chapman Catt as the leader.

The state legislature proposed the right to vote in 1913 and again in 1915 but the voters (male) refused to approve such an amendment to the state constitution. Finally, in 1917, the proposal was accepted by the voters. Two years later the Nineteenth Amendment to the United States Constitution passed. It declared that no state could discriminate against anyone's right to vote on the basis of sex. At long last women had won at least partial equality.

The Empire State in World War I

World War I broke out in the summer of 1914. France, England, and Russia became allies against Germany and Austria-Hungary. Soon the war spread to other countries. More than half the people of New York were immigrants or the children of immigrants. Some few favored their mother countries, and a small number who were not citizens of the United States went back to fight. By far the great majority regarded the United States as their first and only loyalty.

Congress declared war on Germany after German submarines sank several American ships. Congress drafted all able-bodied men between 18 and 45, and over 500,000 New Yorkers entered the armed forces. They served in every division that fought in France. Over 14,000 lost their lives.

The 27th Division marching in a homecoming parade in New York City on March 25, 1919.

The industries of the Empire State led all other states in furnishing goods for the war. The shipyards turned out many Liberty ships and other vessels to carry men and materiel to Europe. Factories produced an amazing amount of goods. The General Electric Company in Schenectady made searchlights, submarine detectors, compasses for airplanes, radios, and radio parts. In Rochester, Eastman Kodak made cameras, lenses, plates, and films. The Bausch and Lomb Optical Company made telescopes, binoculars, and gunsights. Other factories near Utica made rifles and machine guns. The steel mills of Buffalo worked overtime, and the textile mills in the Mohawk Valley cities made blankets, tent cloth, sweaters, and uniforms.

The end of the war on November 11, 1918 caused great rejoicing. The grateful citizens of New York City gave each homecoming division a rousing welcome as it marched up Broadway. The state gave the veterans a bonus for their service.

The war had brought about several changes in the state. Immigration had declined during the war, and when peace led to another wave of immigrants, Congress placed restrictions on the number of people who could enter the nation. Some industries, especially the electrical, received a great stimulus during the war years. As a result of wartime bond drives to raise money, citizens learned how to cooperate in raising peacetime funds, known at first as Community Chests or United Funds.

Summary

The typical New Yorker in the Gilded Age lived in either upstate cities or Greater New York, the latter in 1900 containing about half the population. Urban living kept changing because of the expansion of transportation and business, the arrival of immigrants, and the growth of cities. City dwellers lived in neighborhoods often composed of separate nationalities or races. Most people lived in families which survived the pressures of poor housing, shifting neighborhoods, and economic troubles. The people made brave efforts to adjust by finding jobs, furnishing their homes comfortably, and enjoying various kinds of recreation.

Corruption appeared in American business and political life after the Civil War. Political bosses, such as Boss Tweed of New York City, dominated politics and stole large amounts of money. Under the leadership of able governors, good government was restored to the state. Samuel Tilden, Grover Cleveland, Theodore Roosevelt, and Charles Evans Hughes all contributed to improving life in the Empire State. Furthermore, women fought hard and successfully for more rights, winning the right to vote by World War I. New York State contributed the most soldiers, manufactured the most supplies, and furnished the most money to the nation in World War I.

Checking the high points

1. What were the main features of urban living?

2. What purposes did neighborhoods serve?

3. What was the influence of immigrants on neighborhoods and family life?

4. What kind of housing was available?

5. What kind of jobs did the people have in Greenwich Village?

6. What was the entertainment of workers and their families?

7. Why was there so much corruption after the Civil War?

8. How did the people get rid of Boss Tweed?

9. What did Samuel Tilden, Grover Cleveland, and Theodore Roosevelt do to improve government in New York State?

10. What contributions did New York State make toward winning World War I?

Think these over

1. Do people get as good government as they deserve? Explain.

2. Which term best describes the population mixture in New York City in 1900: "melting pot" or "salad bowl?"

3. Slum dwellers showed as much bravery as frontiersmen.

Vocabulary building

political machine
boss
stuff the ballot box
tenement
dumbbell tenement
sweatshop

Liberty ships
metropolis
nationality
reformer
bonus
materiel

chapter 20: MEGALOPOLIS and ITS SOCIETY

chapter 21: BOOM, DEPRESSION, and WARS

chapter 22: CULTURAL GROWTH

unit seven

Megalopolitan Society

New York state history dates are shown in color.

1901 Pan American Exposition opens in Buffalo
1906 Theodore Roosevelt wins the Nobel Peace Prize
1914 World War I begins
1918 World War I ends
1921 Port Authority of New York established
1925 New Yorker Edna Ferber wins a Pulitzer Prize
1926 First scheduled air line service begins in Pasco, Washington
1929 Stock market crash
1932 New Yorker Franklin D. Roosevelt elected President
1941 United States enters World War II
1945 World War II ends
1946 United Nations headquarters established in New York
1948 State University of New York established
1958 Nelson Rockefeller elected governor of New York
1959 St. Lawrence Seaway opens
1971 John F. Kennedy Center for the Performing Arts opens in Washington, D.C.
1974 Nelson Rockefeller appointed Vice President of the U.S.

Megalopolis is a Greek term meaning "very large city." The ancient Greeks planned such a city and actually called it Megalopolis, but their bold scheme did not succeed. About the time of Christ, more than 350 years later, Philo, a Jewish philosopher living in Alexandria, Egypt, used the name Megalopolis to describe what he called a city of ideas that would rule the world.

Professor Jean Gottmann writing in 1961 used the term Megalopolis to include the urbanized northeastern seaboard of the United States. This Megalopolis is truly a supercity—extending from Portsmouth, New Hampshire, to northern Virginia and reaching westward into the foothills of the Appalachian Mountains. Both the headquarters of the United Nations and the national capital are located in Megalopolis. Here dwell the men and women who exert great influence over the cultural, economic, and political life of our nation.

Today a large majority of New Yorkers are also citizens of Megalopolis, where some 40 million Americans live. Other millions of New Yorkers live in the 20-mile-wide belt linking Albany with New York and Buffalo. In this unit we shall describe the growth of our cities—the problems and opportunities resulting from Megalopolis—and how our people have adjusted to urban living.

Chapter Objectives

To learn about

- **the growth of Megalopolis**
- **population shifts in New York**
- **the relationship between modern transportation and urbanization**
- **the significance of business enterprise in New York**

chapter 20

MEGALOPOLIS and ITS SOCIETY

Megalopolis Appears

In 1784 American trade with China was opened by the sailing ship *Empress of China.* This famous vessel was built in Baltimore, managed by a Boston firm, and financed by Philadelphians; but its home port was New York City. Today these four cities, with Washington, D.C., form the core of our modern Megalopolis.

Washington grew largely because of governmental activities, whereas the other core cities had their beginnings in colonial times. All of them have good harbors and transportation routes to the interior. Wealth earned in commerce allowed these cities to build manufacturing plants and to establish businesses, including banks and insurance companies.

New York City is the hub of Megalopolis; it ranks first in foreign trade, wholesale and retail trade, and finance. Furthermore, it is the greatest manufacturing center of the nation as well as the headquarters of many of our largest corporations. More plays are staged here than in any other city. Its music, opera, and ballet companies are among the world's finest. Artists constantly strive to have their work exhibited in New York galleries or museums.

In addition to the city, New York Megalopolis embraces all of Long Island, and the counties of Putnam, Dutchess, Orange, Rockland, Sullivan, Ulster, and Westchester. Over 11 million people—nearly two-thirds of the state's population—live within Megalopolis.

One can divide the inhabitants of Megalopolis into three groups. First there are the *exurbanites* who live outside of both the city and suburbs. Second are the *suburbanites,* and third are the *urbanites,* or those living within a city.

Relatively few exurbanites are farmers. The majority of them work in the suburbs and core (central) cities and others provide services to farmers. The spreading highway network has made it possible for exurbanites to travel to shopping centers, doctors' offices, libraries, and theatres—either in the heart of the cities or in the suburbs.

Suburbanites are drawn largely from the

Megalopolis means heavy concentrations of buildings, vehicles, and people. This is rush hour in mid-Manhattan.

middle class, which seeks trees, grass, good schools, and clean air for its families. Suburbanites hope to escape the crowds, crime, noise, traffic, and tensions of city life.

In the mid-1970s the migration to suburbia slowed as suburbs, too, began to face many troubles. City lights also seemed to sparkle more brightly. Young couples and singles liked the excitement, fine restaurants, and wide choice of entertainment found in downtown areas. High paying and important jobs were also located in the cities. Furthermore, young couples found they could afford older houses, whereas suburban properties had become very expensive. Best of all, a home in the city freed people from long hours of commuting and the expense of two cars.

By 1978 New York City and many other cities had a shortage of apartments and houses. Meanwhile some corporations that had thought of moving their headquarters to open spaces found downtown areas still the best place to manage their business. Americans were falling in love with their cities—again.

Earning a Living in Megalopolis

The growth of Megalopolis changed the life of the farmer, usually for the better. As the demand for suburban building lots rose, the value of farm lands increased. Today these lands are worth more per acre than those in most other parts of the United States; many farmers were able to retire on the money made from selling their farms this way.

The megalopolitan farmer lives in the world's best market for agricultural products. Nearby is a large population with money to spend. To take full advantage of this situation, most farmers specialize in highvalue products for direct human consumption. Among the most profitable agricultural enterprises are poultry and egg production, dairying, and the raising of beef cattle.

The farmers of Megalopolis also produce fruits and vegetables for the table, and

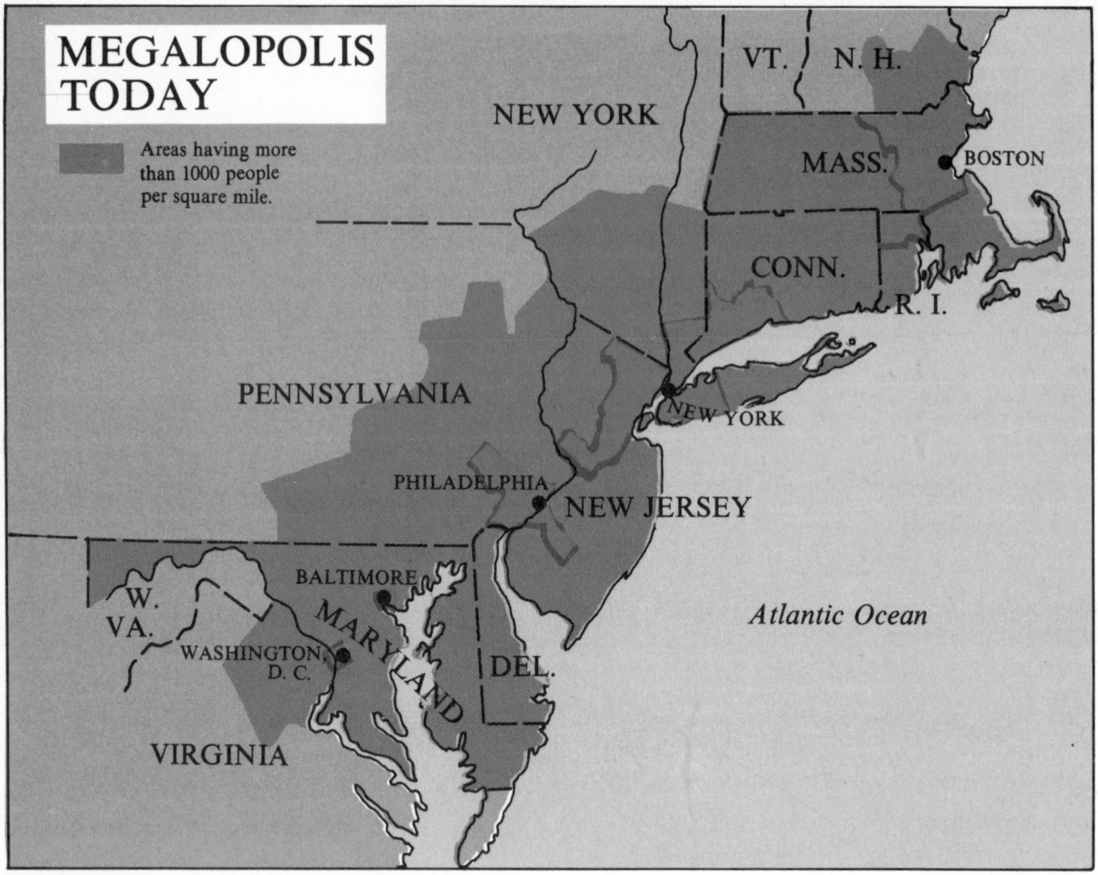

MEGALOPOLIS TODAY

Areas having more than 1000 people per square mile.

NEW YORK
VT.
N. H.
MASS.
BOSTON
CONN.
R. I.
PENNSYLVANIA
NEW YORK
PHILADELPHIA
NEW JERSEY
BALTIMORE
W. VA.
MARYLAND
WASHINGTON, D. C.
DEL.
VIRGINIA
Atlantic Ocean

Map 24

More than 70 stores are in this suburban shopping center in Yonkers. Such complexes require good planning of roads and parking facilities to accomodate the heavy traffic.

shrubbery and greenhouse plants for decorating purposes. Ten of the nation's twenty counties leading in the production of greenhouse and nursery plants lie within the boundaries of Megalopolis.

Commerce also was affected by the developments with Megalopolis. Stores soon followed their customers to the suburbs and huge shopping centers appeared in the countryside. Among the first to establish branches in the suburbs were New York City's great department stores. This brought more convenience to suburban living and also provided many local jobs. The movement of retail stores had a serious impact upon the "downtown" areas. To offset this, many megalopolitan merchants increased the attractiveness of their mother stores. They have added parking garages and have begun programs of beautification.

With the exception of Washington, the core cities of Megalopolis have maintained leadership in the wholesaling field. Forty percent of the nation's ocean trade is handled by Megalopolis' fine harbors; and importers have found it convenient to establish wholesaling headquarters nearby. Furthermore, buyers for retail firms flock to New York and other core cities seeking merchandise. The wholesaler who is in Megalopolis, therefore, often finds his customer coming to him.

Wholesaling and retailing require large amounts of credit. Usually wholesalers borrow money to buy the goods they sell the retailer. Similarly, retailers borrow to buy the goods they sell the public. This demand for credit is met by the great banking houses of Megalopolis.

Shippers wish to insure their cargoes; merchants, both wholesale and retail, desire to insure their goods. This has led to the development of great insurance companies within Megalopolis.

Finally, merchants' buying and selling shares in various business ventures led to the establishment of stock exchanges early in the history of the core cities. Today, the New York Stock Exchange is easily the most important exchange in the world.

In the world of finance—banks, insurance companies, and stock exchanges—Megalopolis leads the nation and the world. The financial firms of this area provide many jobs.

Megalopolis contains practically every kind of manufacturing conducted within the United States. Among the more important products made and processed are clothing, food products, electronic devices, printed materials, drugs and medicines, shoes, and household furniture.

Modern shopping centers now mass scores of stores under one roof, such as this one in Colonie, near Albany.

Service industries include wholesale and retail selling, public utilities such as electric power and telephone companies, government jobs, the work of financial concerns, automobile and television repair, hotel and restaurant employees, and all professional work: education, medicine, law, and art. These service jobs have grown remarkably over the past quarter century. While many services employ various white-collar office workers and professional people, others, such as those in automobile repair, hire blue-collar workers. Often the blue-collar worker has more skill and earns more money than a white-collar employee.

Within the boundaries of Megalopolis lives the best-paid, most highly skilled, and best-educated populace in the world. This concentration of wealth and education has enabled it to take the lead in cultural affairs. Boston organized a Philharmonic Society in 1810. Other core cities followed suit, and both Philadelphia and New York have outstanding orchestras. In addition, New York

Facilities for transportation and trade in New York Harbor are among the finest in the world. Here freight cars meet cargo ships with the New York City skyline in the background. Docks and a passenger ship can also be seen.

The John F. Kennedy Center for the Performing Arts in Washington, D.C. was opened in 1971. It contains four separate theatres.

City has the world-famous Metropolitan Opera Company as well as excellent ballet and many fine theaters. Washington was slow in musical progress, but in 1971 the John F. Kennedy Center for the Performing Arts was opened with a gala celebration.

Washington's Smithsonian Institution is only one of several excellent museums in Megalopolis. Probably the finest art museum in the nation is the Metropolitan Museum of Art in New York. Megalopolis has 12 of the 16 foremost art museums in the United States. The Museum of Natural History in New York and the Franklin Institute in Philadelphia are outstanding in the sciences.

No area of similar size can approach Megalopolis in the field of higher education. Among the famous universities known for their excellence are Harvard, Columbia, Massachusetts Institute of Technology, Yale, Princeton, and Johns Hopkins.

The libraries of Megalopolis hold over 100 million volumes—one third of the total library holdings in the country. The four largest libraries in the United States are located here: Library of Congress, New York Public Library, Yale University Library, and Harvard University Library. More than one-half of the nation's book publishers are located in Megalopolis as well as the major magazines. For example, the Time-Life empire and the *Reader's Digest* are located in Greater New York. Several of the nation's most important newspapers are *The New York Times,* the *Washington Post,* and the *Christian Science Monitor* (Boston).

Spectator sports, particularly baseball and football, enjoy much popularity. In New York, Yankee Stadium is "the house that Babe Ruth built." In addition the Mets play in Shea Stadium. Madison Square Garden has been rebuilt three times, each time larger, to accommodate professional and college sports events, ice shows, large meetings, and even the circus. Other core cities have similar facilities.

The Population Belt

Most of the cities of the Empire State lie in a narrow strip called the Population Belt. This belt takes in Long Island and New York City, runs up the Hudson Valley to the Capital District, through the Mohawk Valley, and along the route of the canal and railroad to Buffalo and its suburbs. More than eight out of ten New Yorkers live in the Population Belt.

The most striking feature of city life since World War II has been the expansion of suburban areas around the central cities. At the same time almost all core cities have lost residents during the past thirty years. Buffalo, for example, has lost one third of its former population. In 1960 the Census Bureau drew up a new definition of the 212 large urban districts in the country and called them Standard Metropolitan Statistical Areas.

Three of the four largest cities in the Empire State are located on the Great Lakes Plain: Buffalo, the second largest city, Rochester, and Syracuse. Excellent highways connect these cities with the Midwest, Canada, and New York City. Many railroads serve Buffalo. Over 20 million tons of freight pass over the Great Lakes with huge quantities of wheat, iron ore, and coal reaching such lake ports as Buffalo, Chicago, and Cleveland. Airlines carry many times as many passengers as railroads; buses also carry millions of passengers a year.

The Metropolitan Museum of Art, the largest museum in New York City, has more than three million works of art representing almost every culture of the world for the past five centuries.

Buffalo is also a major center of foreign trade. About one-fifth of the trade between the United States and Canada is handled by the Buffalo Customs District. Niagara Falls is an important tourist attraction and is also the largest hydroelectric power source in the free world.

Standard Metropolitan Statistical Areas Estimates for 1976

Area	Population
New York City (plus Rockland, Westchester, and Putnam counties)	8,657,000
Buffalo	1,320,000
Rochester	972,000
Albany-Troy-Schenectady	793,000
Syracuse	651,000
Utica-Rome	332,000
Binghamton	269,000

Population figures from U.S. Census Bureau.

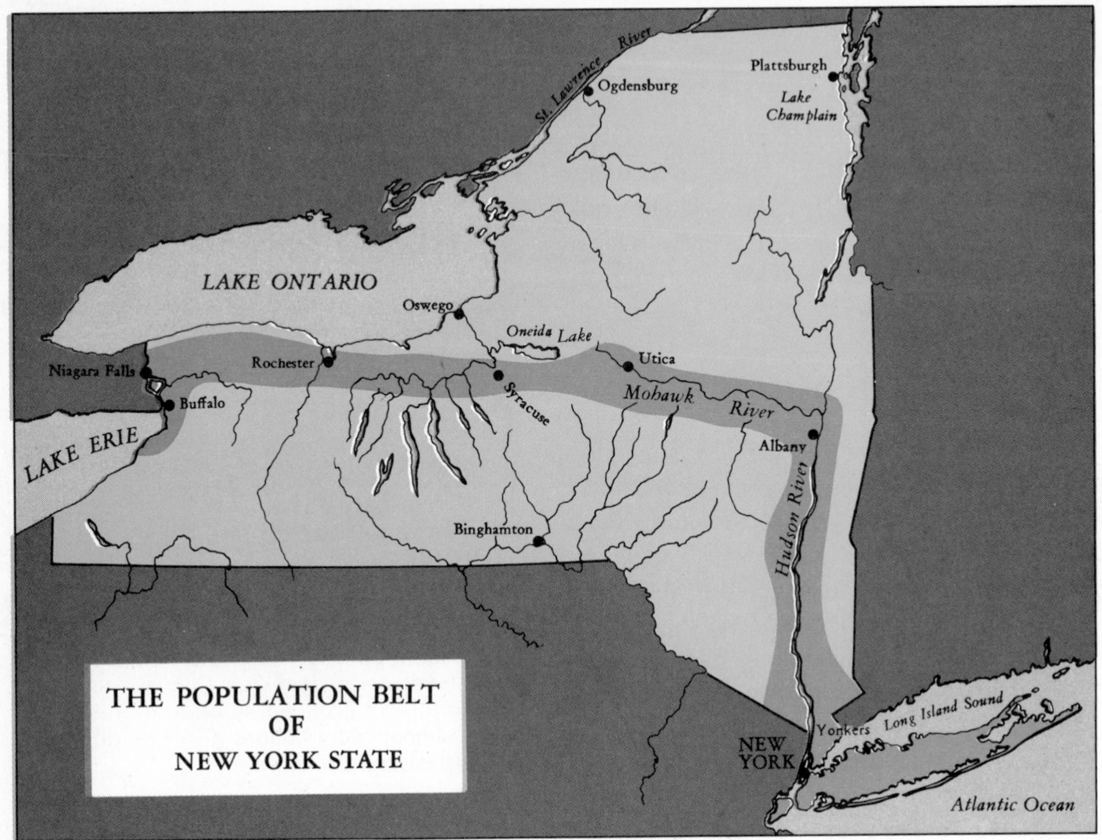

Map 25

Two factors—excellent transportation and cheap electric power—have caused the Niagara Frontier to become one of the most important manufacturing areas in the nation. Here large quantities of steel, flour, chemicals, electrical goods, and abrasives for grinding and polishing are produced.

Rochester and Syracuse also are important transportation centers. Rochester benefits by being close to Lake Ontario. It is the world's greatest producer of cameras, photographic supplies, and optical goods. Syracuse has many industries and is best known for television sets, typewriters, and machinery.

About four out of every ten workers living in the cities of the Great Lakes Plain earn their living from manufacturing. About two out of every ten earn their living from trade.

The oldest city in eastern New York is Albany, which was founded by the Dutch as a fur-trading post. Most of the cities in this region lie along the Mohawk River and the Barge Canal; the westernmost is Rome, close to the Great Lakes Plain. The cities of the region all make use of the railroads, highways, and waterways of the Hudson-Mohawk Route. The Capital District is especially well located for transportation. Over 10,000,000 tons of goods are imported through or exported from Albany by sea each year. Utica is a north-south transfer point along the Mohawk. While the remaining Hudson-Mohawk cities are important in local trade, only Albany is a center of world commerce. About one out of every five workers in these cities is engaged in trade.

Another third or more of the workers in each of these cities (with the exception of

Albany) is employed in manufacturing. In Amsterdam and Schenectady one out of every two workers earns his living in industry. Rome is noted for the manufacture of copper goods. Utica, once noted as a textile center, today has many different types of factories, especially those making electronics equipment. Schenectady has the world's largest factory for the production of electrical goods. Gloversville and Johnstown are major producers of gloves. Watervliet is an important center for the production of stainless steel.

Cities of the Allegheny Plateau and North Country

The cities of this region are much smaller and farther apart than those found in the Population Belt. The largest city is Binghamton, with a population of about 55,000. Nearby are Endicott and Johnson City. Taken together, these three cities are called the Triple Cities, where over a quarter of a million people live. Besides Binghamton,

The Penn Central railroad yard in Buffalo is automated. Radar and other electronic devices can sort hundreds of freight cars into trains bound for many different places. Only a few men are needed to handle the huge yard. Automation has created problems as well as benefits in Megalopolis.

A view of the General Electric Company in Schenectady in 1886. The manufacture of electrical goods has come a long way since then and is now a major industry in the state.

only Elmira, Jamestown, and Ithaca have over 25,000 inhabitants.

The Triple Cities are known for the production of shoes, business machines, and aviation training devices. Jamestown makes office furniture of high quality. Corning, with its famous Glass Museum, makes a wide variety of glass products. The famous 200-inch telescope mirror used in the Mt. Palomar Observatory in California was made there. Write the number 6 and follow it with 21 zeros—that is the number of miles scientists have been able to look into space with this remarkable telescope.

In the cities of the Allegheny Plateau, about two out of every ten workers are employed in trade and four out of ten in manufacturing. The sole exception is Ithaca, where large numbers of people are employed by Cornell University and Ithaca College.

The northern cities are those lying within the St. Lawrence and the Lake Champlain Valleys. The whole northern area of New York is thinly populated, and the cities there are smaller than those in any other section of the state. The largest city in this region is Watertown, which has a population of about 30,000. Plattsburgh and Ogdensburg are about half the size of Watertown.

The northern cities are in the middle of several vacationlands: the St. Lawrence valley, with its Thousand Islands; the Lake Champlain area; and the Adirondack Mountains. All these regions provide excellent swimming, fishing, and boating. In the winter, skiers, bobsledders, and skaters flock to the Adirondacks.

The northern region is rich in forests and minerals. All three of the largest cities manufacture paper products from pulp wood. But only two out of every ten workers here are engaged in manufacturing. Trade and services employ considerably more people. Plattsburgh, which has a population of just under 20,000, is a shopping center for nearly 140,000 people. In fact, thousands of Canadians drive to Plattsburgh and other centers for trade and recreation. On the other hand, many people in the north country look upon Montreal as their main metropolitan center.

Population Shifts

New Yorkers, like most Americans, have always been a migratory people. No other state has experienced the movement of so many different kinds of people as the Empire State. During the past 30 years New York State has been influenced by several major shifts in our population. A listing is useful.

1. flight from farm to city
2. westward movement
3. interchange of northern and southern populations
4. immigration of Caribbean peoples, especially from Puerto Rico
5. decline of the inner city
6. growth of the suburbs

Over 25 million Americans have left the farm during the past 30 years. Among them are black ex-sharecroppers, Appalachian whites, plainsmen, and farm youth. Clearly the young are the ones who are most likely to move. The westward movement of population continued at a rapid clip after World War II. By 1964 New York had lost the first place position to California, which had doubled its numbers since the war.

Another striking migration is that of blacks from Southern United States and Puerto Ricans and other islanders from the Caribbean to the cities of the north. As large plantations began using mechanical cotton pickers, they no longer needed the black sharecroppers, who picked the crop by hand. The economic boom after World War II opened up many jobs to these workers, who left for the large urban centers in the north. What is sometimes overlooked is that an even greater number of whites—Appalachian farmers and miners, sharecroppers, and college graduates—also migrated from the south, where opportunities were fairly limited until the last decade. In addition, New York City has attracted a Latin-American community of over two million, most coming since World War II. Close to 1,300,000 persons of Puerto Rican descent live in Greater New York. But there are also great numbers of Cubans, Dominicans, and other Latin-Americans. Spanish is now the second language of New York City, a fact which is clearly seen in restaurant signs and is evident in radio programs and motion picture offerings. Several prominent blacks—for instance, Shirley Chisholm, the first black congresswoman—are from families which migrated from the former British islands of Jamaica and Barbados.

Balancing this northward movement is the flight of thousands of Northerners to the beaches of the Sun Belt in the South or toward the dry regions of Arizona, New Mexico, and California. Other thousands have found jobs in the aerospace industries located in Texas, Alabama, and Florida.

The central city, or inner city, has stopped growing since 1950. Most New York cities of 100,000 or more persons have lost population since that date. For example, Rochester fell from 332,000 to 279,000, while its suburbs had an explosive growth. In fact, Rochester, as defined in the Standard Metropolitan Statistical Area (Monroe, Livingston, Wayne, and Orleans counties), had an increase of 20 percent in the 1960's.

Actually this trend outward is not new. Today as in the past, newcomers migrate to a central city; then they or their children move outward if they prosper. For example, New Yorkers originally lived on the southern tip of Manhattan Island. Gradually the city center moved northward and people set up homes in Greenwich Village and later Harlem. As the population grew and moved outward, the city fathers annexed the surrounding areas. Perhaps the best example was the move by New York City (Manhattan) in 1898 to annex Brooklyn, Staten Island, Queens, and the Bronx. Suburbs existed long before the automobile. Before 1914 citizens followed trolley tracks and railroad lines (later subways and buses) to find homes.

When the Census of 1960 and again that of 1970 came out showing declines in the inner city, many persons declared our cities were decaying and about to collapse. What they forgot was that large cities no longer annex the suburbs. New York City today extends up to Yonkers, with an estimated population of 202,000 in 1975; and east to Nassau County, which has over 1,420,000 inhabitants. Neither the city nor these suburbs want to join each other.

Suburbs since 1945 have grown spectacularly, while the inner cities and the rural areas have declined in population. As a result more people live in suburbs than in the other two areas.

Motor Vehicles

In 1900 practically all roads were in poor condition. They received little attention because town officials had neither the money nor the skill to construct good highways.

A growing number of people demanded better roads. The riders of bicyles wanted smoother paths so they could ride into the countryside. The early purchasers of automobiles urged better roads because the dusty and bumpy highways took all the pleasure out of driving. Some farmers also wanted to transport their milk and other products more rapidly to market. All these pressures caused towns and counties to make improvements. Furthermore, by 1910, New York State had taken its first steps in constructing major highways between the larger cities.

Good roads, however, were and are costly to build. Who should pay for them? Gradually the principle was established that the user must pay for part of the cost of transporting himself and goods. As a result the politicians worked out a system whereby the towns and counties took care of the local roads while the state built and maintained the major highways. The state taxed the user by license fees and gasoline taxes. Federal grants for highways in the 1920's were small but became huge during the 1930's when the government employed thousands of jobless people on public works.

World War II brought most road building to a halt because the government needed labor and materials for defense projects. After the war Governor Thomas E. Dewey pushed the construction of a superhighway (the Thruway) from New York City to Albany, then west to Buffalo and on to the Pennsylvania line. In 1956 Congress passed the important act which has financed the building of thousands of miles of interstate highways. The states receive 90 percent of the cost of these roads, provided they charge no tolls and meet other conditions. As a result of this act the Northway extends from Albany to the Canadian border, while Route 81 stretches from the Pennsylvania border to Binghamton, Syracuse, and Watertown. Route 17 is another beautiful highway which passes through the Southern Tier of counties.

The automobile has revolutionized every aspect of life and is fantastically popular in America and lately in Europe and Japan. Americans love their cars beyond reason. Every youth dreams of the day when he or she will pass the test and can drive a car.

The automobile industry, one of the largest in the nation, has plants to make parts in Buffalo, Syracuse, and other cities. Furthermore, hundreds of thousands of New Yorkers work in gas stations, motels, restaurants, repair shops, salesrooms, contracting companies, trucking firms, and insurance companies that serve this industry. The motor vehicle has not only changed the life of urban dwellers but has also revolutionized the way farm families live. Yellow buses carry rural children to centralized schools. Farm women shop in distant cities, while the farmer sends milk to the creamery daily. The automobile and truck have made farm families part of the urban culture and economy.

Automobiles and Urban Growth

Our cities, especially, have felt the impact of the motor vehicle. Within the central business district the parking problem seems almost hopeless. Cities and private companies have constructed huge parking garages to store the cars of commuters. Old buildings are torn down to create parking lots. But still the demand for parking is not satisfied. Despite the new federal regula-

The New York State Thruway follows the valley of the Mohawk for many miles.

tions limiting the amount of pollutants which new cars can emit, air pollution remains a serious problem in New York and other large centers. Another problem is the abandoned car. Every major city has to drag away thousands of abandoned vehicles each year.

Because of traffic jams, officials have built arterials (through roads) from downtown to the outskirts, and ring roads around the center city. These highways help tens of thousands of commuters to get to work more rapidly and enable tourists to bypass the traffic congestion downtown. New shopping centers, offices, and even factories have located near or along the new routes, especially where two arterials intersect. But many people and some neighborhoods are harmed by the new routes. For example, earthmoving machines have torn down perfectly good buildings thus uprooting thousands of families. Quite often these families are blacks who find it difficult to secure new apartments or houses. Moreover the highways have divided old neighborhoods, thus hastening the decline of churches, marketing areas, and social clubs. In many cities—Albany, for example—stores have left the downtown area for the outskirts where parking is available. The arterials have encouraged the flight of city people to new homes in the countryside.

Arterials are frightfully costly to build and to maintain. Who should pay this cost? The commuter? The city? The state? City officials complain that they have to spend great sums on roads, police, and other services for commuters who pay taxes in the suburbs.

The term "sprawl" is sometimes used to describe the way our population has spread out from the inner city. Developers have bought up land along old roads and near new highways, laid out lots, and put up houses. New developments sometimes surround and even gobble up old communities, whose residents resent the newcomers while welcoming their trade. Individuals have bought lots along country roads, providing a hit-or-miss development of the land. Fairly dense settlements are often separated by farms where a few stubborn individualists refuse to sell. All too often no one has done any adequate planning for sewers, water lines, and schools.

Who are the people who live in the suburbs? In the main they are families with good incomes, and their children tend to stay in school longer. They are likely to have and keep a white-collar job. Residents in suburbia generally own their own homes, whereas the majority of city dwellers do not. Suburban homes are newer and have more appliances. There are comparatively few nonwhites in the suburbs, while the center cities have now become the main home for blacks. Recently blacks have joined the march toward the suburbs. For example, White Plains and New Rochelle have large numbers of black residents.

People still move toward suburbs and beyond for the same reasons as before: fresh air, more space, and a smaller community. In addition, they want to escape the problems of our center cities: high taxes, crime, pollution, declining neighborhoods, poor schools, and unfamiliar neighbors. For most, the move probably has meant a more pleasant life, but no one can entirely escape the pressing problems of megalopolitan life. Taxes in the suburbs skyrocket because the people want services: excellent schools, streetpaving and snow removal, sewage lines, and so forth. As more people move in, they overload the drainage and water systems. They congest the streets and highways. Lately the rates of crime and drug use have gone up faster in the suburbs than in the center cities, which still have the worst rates.

Railroads and Rapid Transit

Every day throughout Megalopolis millions of business people, factory and office workers, shoppers, students, and sightseers crowd the highways, rail lines, and airways. Each day over two million commuters—that is, people who travel regularly from home to work—enter the central business district of lower Manhattan Island. Highway and air traffic between Boston and New York and between New York and Washington is heavier than that of any other area of similar size in the world.

Greater New York, the core of Megalopolis, provides the best but most puzzling example of the transportation needs and problems of our sprawling cities. Not only does New York City have the largest number of people and the heaviest amount of freight traffic, but it must also get these people and goods through bottlenecks caused by the water barriers. The Bronx is the only part of New York which is not located on an island. Of course we must not forget that the Hudson and East rivers, Long Island Sound, and the Atlantic Ocean served as highways throughout most of the history and growth of the metropolis.

By 1900 the railroads brought an overwhelming volume of goods from the interior to New York harbor. Goods arrived in tramp steamers and liners, although a handful of sailing vessels were still in operation. After World War I trucks began to challenge the supremacy of the railroads. Since World War II airplanes have been carrying increasing amounts of freight, especially perishable goods from distant places.

In 1921 the states of New York and New Jersey established the Port of New York Authority to deal with transportation problems. The Authority has the responsibility of providing transportation and terminal facilities and also of promoting international trade. It can build, rent, and operate any facility within the Port of New York District. The District includes the sections of New York and New Jersey lying within 25 miles of the Statue of Liberty.

Today the Authority operates most of the transportation facilities in Greater New York. This includes the three major airports and heliports, many of the bridges, the Holland and Lincoln tunnels, several piers and truck terminals in the harbor, as well as major bus stations in Manhattan. In addition it operates the rapid transit system (PATH) under the Hudson River between Manhattan and New Jersey. It has constructed the mammoth World Trade Center in twin towers at the foot of Manhattan. The Port Authority has its critics, who charge that it has concentrated on transportation by automobile so completely that it has neglected the railroads and subways. As a result, the rapid transit system—subways, bus lines, commuter railroads—is in very poor condition.

Railroad cars and ships still carry the bulk of freight into New York harbor, although over 10,000 long-haul trucks enter the Port District daily. Nine railroads connect the area with all parts of the United States and Canada. More than 25,000 ships arrive and depart each year—an average of one ship entering or leaving every twenty minutes. More than 38,000,000 passengers use the three airports each year.

The George Washington Bridge spans the Hudson River, connecting Manhattan with Fort Lee, New Jersey. It is a major route for New Jersey commuters who work in Manhattan and for trucks carrying goods in and out of the New York City area.

The water barriers made transportation much more difficult. Before World War I, four bridges were built across the East River, joining Manhattan to Brooklyn and Queens. The Hudson proved a greater obstacle, although a tunnel for the Pennsylvania Railroad had been dug as early as 1904. Next came the Holland Tunnel of 1927, which carried cars and trucks. Four years later the Port Authority constructed the magnificent George Washington Bridge. Still the number of motor vehicles kept rising so the Authority built the Lincoln Tunnel in 1938. In 1962 it added another deck to the George Washington Bridge to take care of the traffic.

During the 1930's the Triborough Bridge and Tunnel Authority was created to improve transportation within the city. Led by Robert E. Moses, the Authority built the Triborough Bridge (1934), which connected Manhattan with the Bronx and Queens. Moses built superhighways along the east and west sides of Manhattan and through the other boroughs. No doubt the most spectacular venture was spanning the Narrows between Brooklyn and Staten Island.

The Verrazano Bridge, which opened in 1964, stimulated the growth of population on Staten Island.

Automobiles and buses took away passengers from the commuter railroads serving Long Island, Connecticut, Westchester, and New Jersey. When the railroads raised fares and cut out unprofitable trains, the highways became even more crowded. The governors of New York, New Jersey, and Connecticut set up a Tri-State Transportation Commission to plan for the improvement of transportation. It received the power to assign the funds for mass transit

Industrial Growth of New York

Our industrial development is a complicated story because New York has had so many different kinds of manufacturing. It may help if we point out the main trends in several periods of time.

Period I, 1865–1900
- Railroads were supreme.
- Most manufacturing was in small mills and factories. There were few large companies.
- Manufacturers used the products of farm and forest. For example, they turned wheat to flour, cotton to cloth, and lumber to paper.

Period II, 1900–1929
- Automobiles and trucks challenged the railroads.
- Factories grew in number and size.
- New industries arose, especially those making electrical equipment.
- The rising standards of living and education helped the clothing, food processing, and printing industries.

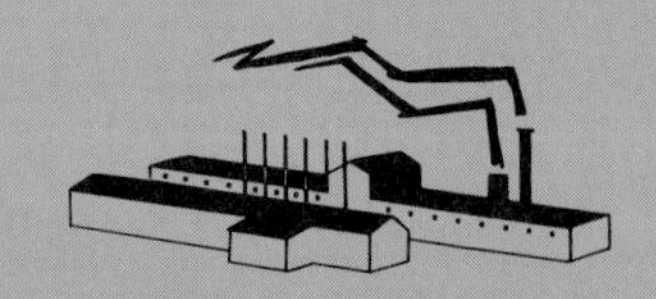

Period III, 1929–1940
- Industrial growth slowed down because of the business depression.
- The government hired many of the unemployed to build bridges, tunnels, highways, and parks. Labor unions spread rapidly.
- Much social legislation, such as that providing pensions and unemployment insurance, was passed by the state and federal governments.

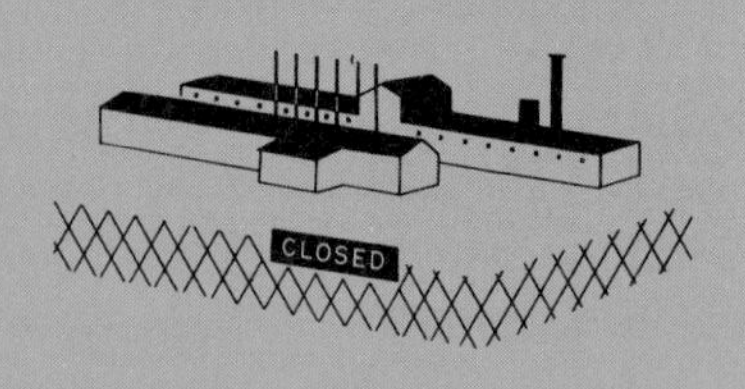

Period IV, 1940–1979
- Prosperity returned. Cities grew and spread.
- The government spent heavily for war and defense.
- Industries making hard goods (machinery, instruments, steel) made the greatest gains.
- Electrical equipment and aircraft industries also expanded.
- Construction boomed. Many skyscrapers, highways, houses, and factories were built.
- Transportation by air and superhighways increased.
- Industrial expansion caused air and water pollution.
- Economic slowdown in 1970s.

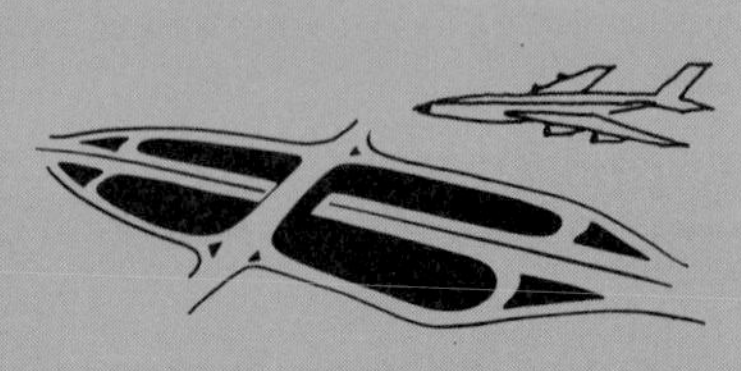

which the federal government had begun to grant to cities.

When the Long Island Railroad was near bankruptcy, Governor Rockefeller and the state legislature set up the Metropolitan Transportation Authority in 1968 to coordinate the facilities of the area. A board of 11 people and 58,000 employees run the world's largest subway system (720 miles of track, 7,000 passenger cars), 4,200 buses, two airports, the Penn Central's Harlem and Hudson Divisions, the New Haven and the Erie-Lackawanna Railroad's commuter services, and several bridges and tunnels. In fact the MTA also took over the Triborough Bridge and Tunnel Authority.

Each day in 1978 the MTA moved over 5,500,000 riders. Perhaps the most important task is to transport some 2,000,000 people in and out of the central business district of Manhattan, an area about the size of Kennedy Airport. Because of the construction of many new skyscrapers, bringing in many more office workers, the MTA must handle additional persons employed in the financial and commercial district of Manhattan.

Airline Passengers
Port of New York Authority Airports

Year	Domestic	Overseas
1954	7,871,458	1,098,906
1960	12,931,000	2,736,000
1966	22,584,000	5,683,000
1971	27,463,000	9,635,000
1976	30,339,000	10,159,000

Source: New York State Department of Commerce

Air Traffic

Passenger air traffic, of minor importance during the first quarter of this century, began to grow steadily. As late as 1951 domestic air traffic that originated within the state totaled only 2,000,000 passengers and a scant 34,000 tons of cargo per year.

Greater New York became the terminal for the leading airlines of the world. When Newark Airport could no longer handle the increasing traffic, the Port of New York Authority opened La Guardia Airport in 1939. Increasing air traffic forced the construction of Idlewild (renamed John F. Kennedy) Airport in 1948. Congestion at the three airports caused Governor Rockefeller to propose Stewart Air Base near Newburgh as an additional airport.

C. S. Robinson in 1945 made frequent trips from Ithaca to New York in his private plane. When his friends and business associates began to ask for rides, he organized an airline. Robinson Airlines in 1952 became Mohawk Airline and rapidly expanded its routes to over 100 cities within and beyond New York's borders. A costly strike by pilots in 1971 caused the collapse of Mohawk Airline, which was taken over by Allegheny Airlines.

Concentration of Corporate Power

The concentration of power and wealth among a few supercorporations is a trend which has alarmed many Americans. The formation of large corporate giants seemed to come in three waves. The first, 1895–1903, saw the creation of such giants as United States Steel by the famous Wall Street banker, J. P. Morgan. During the 1920's, promoters put together huge holding companies, especially in the field of

John F. Kennedy International Airport on Long Island. The airport covers almost 5,000 acres, an area as big as all of Manhattan south of 42nd Street. About 35,000 people are employed here handling passengers, cargo, and mail.

public utilities. Later, during the 1960's, mergers took the form of *conglomerates,* that is, combinations of corporations which often had no logical connection. (One conglomerate included a steel company, a rent-a-car agency, a chain of hotels, and a greeting card company.)

In 1958 some 268 corporations owned about two-thirds of all manufacturing plants and assets in the United States. Many important industries—automobile, aluminum, tires, meat products, and copper refining—were dominated by three or four large producers. Such a situation is called *oligopoly.*

But competition has remained a powerful force in the American economy. Powerful combinations of retailers, such as chain stores, have forced manufacturers to offer better goods at lower prices. Furthermore, imports have undersold some American products, notably automobiles, television sets, and cameras. The federal government has brought antitrust suits against some combinations which have fixed prices and eliminated competition.

Most of the 500 largest corporations have located their headquarters in Megalopolis. A large number have taken advantage of Delaware's laws and secured corporate charters in that state. Other companies in Massachusetts and Pennsylvania have become nationally known and operate under the charters of those states. But New York State far surpasses all other states as headquarters for companies. Of the top 500 industrial corporations, about 100 have headquarters in New York City. In addition, upstate New York is home for such giants as Eastman Kodak, General Electric, International Business Machine, and General Foods.

By the mid-1970s California displaced New York as the leader in manufacturing. Like most northeastern states, New York in the last decade has lost many factories, and its rate of unemployment has stood above the national average. (Although manufacturing jobs have dropped by almost one third during the past twenty years, services, finance, and government agencies have hired more employees.)

Competitors in foreign countries and in the southern and western states have undersold New York firms. These rivals usually have lower taxes, cheaper power, and weaker unions. Nevertheless New York retains some advantages: skilled labor, plenty of capital, good transportation, a large home market, and many services. More than one thousand research laboratories aid New York business. Since 1945 electronics and the making of electrical machinery have become the chief employer in many cities.

By the end of the 1970s there were many signs of economic recovery. Foreign investors placed billions of dollars in New York City. Lower air fares set off a boom in tourism and hotel construction. Corporations such as I.B.M. and A.T.&T. planned new headquarters. People were once again ready to chant, "I love New York, I love New York."

Summary

Megalopolis is the name given to the urbanized area extending from Portsmouth, New Hampshire, to northern Virginia and reaching westward into the foothills of the Appalachians. It contains five core cities: Boston, New York, Philadelphia, Baltimore, and Washington. Two out of every three New Yorkers live in Megalopolis, whose hub is New York City. The main street of America, Megalopolis dominates foreign and wholesale trade, finance and insurance, manufacturing and services. In addition its inhabitants enjoy the greatest range of cultural activities: museums, libraries, and universities.

Eight out of ten New Yorkers live within a 20-mile-wide strip running from Buffalo to Albany, south to New York, then eastward into Long Island. This Population Belt contains all cities having a population of over 90,000.

The Empire State has experienced many types of population movements: the flight from the farm, the westward movement, the interexchange of northern and southern population, the arrival of Puerto Ricans, and the desertion of the city for the suburbs. No doubt the growth of suburbia is the most important change of all. Its expansion was both a result and a cause of the automobile revolution, which has transformed the lives of farmers, suburbanites, and city dwellers.

New York City illustrates to the extreme the problems of the core cities. The Port of New York Authority and the Metropolitan Transportation Authority have struggled to handle the millions of commuters and visitors who must pass through bottlenecks over and under the Hudson and East Rivers. Megalopolis is the management center of the country because a majority of the largest corporations have set up their headquarters here. Although New York City and New York State have lost many jobs in manufacturing, at the same time, they have added more white collar employees. Tourism, finance, and corporate headquarters have continued to employ many New Yorkers.

Checking the high points

1. What is Megalopolis?

2. What is the range of economic and cultural activity within Megalopolis?

3. What are the main centers in the Population Belt? Outside the belt?

4. What are the major shifts in population since 1914 and how have they affected Megalopolis and New York State?

5. Why have people moved to the suburbs?

6. How have our roads been built and financed?

7. What effects have automobiles had upon city and countryside?

8. Do suburbanites differ from residents of center cities? If so, how?

9. What have been the problems facing the Port of New York Authority?

10. How has New York adjusted to loss of manufacturing jobs in the 1970s?

Think these over

1. The automobile and the city cannot coexist. Give reasons.

2. True or false: The current problems of inner cities are not very different from those of one hundred years ago. Explain.

3. One expert asserts that there is more competition and less monopoly today than 50 years ago. Is this true? Explain.

4. Megalopolis has been a success. Why else would millions of people decide to settle there?

Vocabulary building

Use these words correctly.

core city
culture
urban
suburban
exurban
rapid transit
arterial
developer
commuter
Megalopolis
wholesaling
oligopoly
retailing
broker
automation
sprawl

Checking locations

Check your ability to locate the five core cities in Megalopolis.

Boston
New York
Baltimore
Philadelphia
Washington

Check your ability to locate these urban communities of New York State.

Yonkers
Utica
Schenectady
Troy
Capital District
Poughkeepsie
Amsterdam
Newburgh
Kingston
Buffalo
Rochester
Bronx
Staten Island
Syracuse
Niagara Falls
Binghamton
Elmira
Massena
Niagara Frontier
Jamestown
Ithaca
Corning
Watertown
Plattsburgh
Ogdensburg

Chapter Objectives

To learn about

- New York politics and government after World War I
- the Depression and New Deal in New York
- New York in World War II
- political leadership in New York after World War II

chapter 21

BOOM, DEPRESSION, and WARS

The Legacy of World War I

When the victorious soldiers marched up Broadway in 1919, they came back to a country where people were worried about their jobs and the nation's problems. People were complaining about shortages, high prices, strikes, and radicals. When the government canceled war contracts, thousands lost their jobs, and soon thousands of veterans joined the search for work. Actually most did find employment in industries which were turning to peacetime activities. Millions of people spent their war savings on cars, new houses, and appliances, even though prices seemed very high.

But neither the economy nor the social situation was stable. Prices kept soaring because of the high demand and the end of government price-fixing. Union leaders, claiming that prices were outracing wage raises, demanded new contracts with higher wages. Employers, however, took a stiffer line against the unions, which they felt had already received too many benefits during the war. As a result strikes took place in many industries.

Meanwhile the public shifted the hatred it felt for the Germans to strikers and radicals. Although there was only a handful of radicals in the United States, many people thought that Communists and anarchists were hiding behind every union demand. Who else but radicals were sending bombs to government officials and business leaders? Were not strikes proof of a conspiracy by radicals to take over this country? The Communist revolution had taken place in Russia in 1917. Had not a tiny minority of Communists captured that huge country? The strike of the Boston Police sent shivers of fear up and down the spines of most Americans. Hoping to win popularity and thus office in 1920, many politicians called for the expulsion of alien radicals and the jailing of dangerous citizens. As a result, federal, state, and local officials began a witchhunt against radicals, which soon spread to anyone suspected of being radical. In New York the Assembly refused to allow five elected Socialists to take their seats. Unfortunately the right of free speech and free press was often violated during this Red Scare. Charles Evans Hughes and Alfred E. Smith warned the people that individual rights were being trampled upon. Although the Red Scare largely ended in late 1920, the feeling against aliens continued, causing Congress to place restrictions upon European immigration.

Farmers, who had secured high prices during the war, were shocked in 1920 when prices fell sharply. Some asked the government to fix prices. Others tried to help themselves by forming cooperatives and farm organizations. For example, New York farmers in 1920 organized GLF, named after the Grange, the Dairymen's League, and the American Farm Bureau Federation. GLF was a cooperative which sold feed and other supplies at cost. At least half the farm children—millions all told during the 1920's—silently left the farms in search of better jobs in the cities.

Alfred E. Smith Reorganizes the State Government

Alfred E. Smith was one of New York's greatest governors. He was born in a slum section on the east side of Manhattan Island. At an early age he had to sell papers and work in the Fulton Fish Market in order to help his widowed mother. He joined the Democratic party, where his abilities were soon recognized. In 1903 the people of his district elected him to the State Assembly. Ten years later he became Speaker of the Assembly, that is, he became its presiding officer. Although Smith had little schooling, he was very intelligent, and he observed carefully how the state government worked. In 1915 a convention met to consider ways of improving the state government. The chairman of the convention called Al Smith the best-informed man on state government at the convention.

Our government was very complicated in 1915. As the state took on new jobs such as road building, conservation, park management, and factory inspection, new government agencies were set up to run these things. As a result, the state government was a hodgepodge of more than 150 separate boards, agencies, and commissions. The governor had little control over many of them. The convention that met in 1915 recommended that these agencies be combined into a much smaller number of state departments. It also recommended that the governor be given the power to appoint the heads of most of these departments. At first, the people of the state voted against a revision of the constitution.

Al Smith was first elected governor in 1918. He served from 1918 to 1920, and from 1922 to 1928. During all this time he kept up a fight for better government. The people finally changed the constitution so as to give the governor most of what he wanted. Before he left the governorship, Smith combined the various agencies of the state government into 18 separate departments.

Smith fought for many things. He got new buildings for the insane, better prisons, more money for education. The salaries of teachers were raised and women teachers received the same salary as men teachers for doing the same work. He pushed through a law which called for a 48-hour week for workers in New York State, and more money for workers who were injured. Smith urged the state to build and operate generating plants for electricity, and to see that private companies sold electricity at fair prices. New York City received more power to govern itself without state interference.

Prosperity and Depression

Prosperity returned to New York by 1922 and continued with a few dips throughout the 1920's. The construction industry, building highways, houses, skyscrapers, and factories, led the economic boom. Tens of thousands found work in the service industries, especially in secondary and higher education, recreation, and financial institutions. Promoters made millions putting together supercorporations and then selling the stock. Investors grabbed this stock because they hoped it would go up. And it did—for a time.

The wild rise of the stock market could not hide the weaknesses in the economy. Farmers were in trouble because of declining markets and falling prices. The buying power of the people did not go up fast enough to buy all the goods that were produced. To get rid of surplus goods businessmen permitted customers to buy cars, furniture, and appliances on credit. Meanwhile too large a share of the national income was going into the hands of the rich, who put more of their funds into the stock market. Other countries never recovered their losses in property, manpower, and assets from World War I. The United States did not help world recovery when it raised tariffs, which cut down on foreign imports.

By 1928–1929 Wall Street was a madhouse of speculation. Finally, in October 1929 the bubble burst. The crash in stock prices was the signal for the worst depression in American history. Persons who had borrowed money to buy stock sold their securities for whatever price they could get. Many people, some already owing money for goods bought on credit, stopped buying, and this in turn caused manufacturers to lay off workers. The jobless could no longer pay for their cars and mortgages, which hit the automobile and construction industries. The banks were afraid to lend money because they needed their funds to pay off depositors. By 1933 several banks closed their doors when thousands of depositors demanded their savings.

Two master politicians—Alfred E. Smith (right) and Franklin D. Roosevelt—study a problem in 1930.

Miss Agnes Hamilton, a British Member of Parliament, found New York City a dreary place in December 1931. Here is her account.

Friends met me at the dock. "I'm afraid you won't have much of a trip," said the first. . . . "These bank failures . . . The clubs are all going bust."

"Things are just appalling," said the other. "A million and a half unemployed in the city alone."

I looked about me, as we moved out. Yes, those grey-faced, shambling men, standing about in serried[1] rows and groups, had never been there, looking like that, before. More of them: masses, indeed, as we drove along and across the high-numbered avenues: listlessly parked against the walls, blocking the sidewalks. . . .

Every day one sees the degrading misery of the bread lines. Every day one is told that this great industry and that, from railroads to publishing, is collapsing. The building slump spreads. In New York, for

[1]Crowded together

Rockefeller Center

Most visitors to Manhattan want to see Rockefeller Center. This magnificent "city" of 19 buildings has more than 30 restaurants, a broadcasting company, a garage, a security force and fire department, and a post office. It has eight gardens, the world's largest indoor theater, and an outdoor skating pond. Here about 60,000 people come to work each day. In addition, more than 175,000 people visit the center daily. The 70-story RCA Building (center) towers above the other structures.

Rockefeller Center was really an accident. John D. Rockefeller, Jr. and some of his friends planned to construct a building for the Metropolitan Opera Company. They decided to use an area between 48th and 51st streets for this purpose, and rented it from Columbia University for many years. Then bad times struck in 1929, and the whole project was abandoned. Rockefeller, however, decided to get some income from the area by putting up office buildings. He poured over a hundred million dollars into the new project at a time when it was hard to find tenants to fill the offices. In the summer time, when the "city" was being built, Rockefeller cut special openings in the board fences so that people could watch the construction. Each observer received a card saying he was a member of the Sidewalk Superintendents' Club. After World War II there was a shortage of office space in New York. As a result, Rockefeller Center built additional skyscrapers.

Christmas is a good time to visit the Center. Inside, on the stage of the Radio City Music Hall, there is always a special holiday show featuring the famous precision dancers, the Rockettes. Outside, visiting choruses sing carols in front of the Christmas tree that is erected every year near the skating rink. The tree ranges from 65 to 85 feet high and is decorated with thousands of lights and ornaments.

example, the most salient[2] new structure, the magnificent Empire State Building, stands unlet and can only pay its taxes by collecting dollars from sightseers who ascend to its eyrie[3] for the stupendous view to be got thence, . . .

At every street corner, and wherever taxi or car has to pause, men try to sell one apples, oranges, or picture papers. . . . On a fine day, men will press on one gardenias at 15 cents apiece; on any day, rows of them line every relatively open space, eager to shine one's shoes.*

In the hard times of the 1930's, prices were low but people had little money. Compare some of these 1935 prices with what we pay today. The picture was taken in New York City but the situation was the same all over the country.

These desperate conditions led to big drives for private charities such as United Funds. Rochester created jobs for its unemployed, but most cities found the task far too large for their resources. By 1931 the State of New York had to come to the rescue. The Temporary Relief Emergency Committee gave groceries to many families and hired others on various projects. These costly steps threatened the state's credit, and New York State had trouble selling its bonds. Soon the federal government had to help out, which it did under President Franklin D. Roosevelt in 1933. Able-bodied men were given jobs building schools, fixing roads, and cleaning parks.

Meanwhile, New York was taking the lead in social security. This term describes the system whereby money is granted to people when they are old, unemployed, or have certain mental or physical handicaps. New York passed a law providing assistance to old people as early as 1930. Then, in 1935, the national government passed the Social Security Act, which encouraged states to set up their own unemployment insurance plans. (Persons under these plans who lose their jobs receive a check for a certain number of weeks.) Furthermore, persons can retire and receive a pension from the age of 62, the amount depending upon the money that was paid in. The Social Security Act also provides for payments to dependents in certain cases, and to survivors after a worker's death. This law has been amended many times in order to increase the number of people covered and to give greater benefits.

New York and the country crawled out of the depression rather slowly. After striking rock bottom in 1932 and again in March of 1933, the economy gradually recovered. But unemployment remained fairly high all through the 1930's and especially in 1937–1938 when another recession hit the country.

[2] Outstanding
[3] Topmost place

**America Today*, Hamish Hamilton Ltd, London, 1932, pp. 20–24.

The Franklin D. Roosevelt library at Hyde Park. Built in the Dutch colonial style, the library contains Roosevelt's papers and other items of interest from his presidency.

A New Deal in State and Nation

Franklin D. Roosevelt followed Al Smith as governor. A distant cousin of Theodore Roosevelt, the new governor was born in Hyde Park in 1882. After graduating from Harvard and practicing law, the young Democrat won a seat in the state senate. By 1920 his reputation was such that the Democrats made Franklin Roosevelt their candidate for Vice-President. Shortly after the Democratic defeat, poliomyelitis struck him down. He fought his way back to health, although he always had to wear heavy braces on his legs. In 1928 Al Smith asked Roosevelt to run for governor, an office which he won by a narrow margin.

As governor, Roosevelt carried out Al Smith's policies. He stood for conservation of natural resources, laws to help workers, better prisons, and more help to the poor. He believed that the state should develop electric power on land owned by the state, and he favored a stricter regulation of public utility rates.

New York City proved troublesome for Roosevelt because Mayor James Walker allowed dishonest men to have a free hand. Smart, dapper, and flip, Walker had won the hearts of New Yorkers with his wisecracks. After an investigation showed a good deal of graft in the city government, the public turned against Walker. What would Governor Roosevelt do about Walker? If he fired Walker, he would lose the support of New York City politicians in the Democratic convention of 1932. If he did not touch Walker, Roosevelt would lose the support of progressive and decent citizens throughout the country. After some delay, Roosevelt called Walker before him and questioned him. As the evidence of wrongdoing piled up, Walker quit his office and left the country.

When Roosevelt moved to the White House in 1933, he left behind in Albany his able lieutenant governor, Herbert H. Lehman. Lehman was a wealthy banker who gave a great deal of money to charity. One of the outstanding governors in New York's history, Lehman was re-elected three times. He appointed experts to state jobs. He saved every penny he could. When he became governor, the state had a debt of over 100 million dollars. Before he left the governorship, New York had paid back the debt. Lehman encouraged the building of low-rent housing projects. Working people were grateful to him because he favored many laws that helped them. School teachers received better salaries and better working conditions. Companies producing electricity were closely regulated. Lehman and the legislature helped dairy farmers by setting the bottom price that farmers could receive for milk.

As President, Roosevelt was making many changes in the United States government. People called Roosevelt's government the "New Deal." Since Lehman was doing many of the same things in New York State, his administration was sometimes called the "Little New Deal."

New York in World War II

World War II required a tremendous effort on the part of all citizens. Even before the Japanese attack on Pearl Harbor in 1941, the Empire State was feeling the effects of the war. The first shock came in 1939 when Adolf Hitler sent the German Army into Poland. As a result, France and Britain placed many orders in New York for supplies for their armed forces. When Hitler overran most of Europe, New Yorkers felt the war moving closer to them. The United States government began to rearm as fast as it could. The Brooklyn Navy Yard received orders for many new ships. Young men in New York and the other states were drafted and sent to army camps, such as Camp Upton on Long Island. In the spring of 1941, millions of dollars worth of tanks, trucks, guns, planes, and ammunition were loaded on ships in New York Harbor. These supplies were sent to Great Britain, China, and other countries resisting Germany, Italy, and Japan.

The Empire State out-produced all other states in World War II, as it had in World War I. Two-thirds of all the war goods produced in the state came from factories in New York City and Buffalo. Almost every city in New York, however, helped to defeat our enemies by turning out goods of various kinds.

How did New York increase its output at the same time that it was sending more than one million men and women into uniform? Businesses brought about this miracle of production in several ways. First of all, they hired thousands of men who had lost their jobs in the depression. Then, they hired older men, and boys over 16 years of age. An even greater source of labor was provided by women. By the end of the war, over a million women—more than one third of the war labor force—had left their homes to work in factories and offices. Many war workers worked harder and for longer hours. Some factories ran seven days a week with three eight-hour shifts every day. A million workers became more skilled during the war and thus were able to turn out more goods. Thousands of farm folk went to work in factories in nearby towns. The many Jewish and other refugees from Hitler who had been admitted to New York gratefully gave their talent and energy to the war effort. Finally, thousands of blacks came to New York from the southern states as well as newcomers from Puerto Rico and other West Indian Islands. The factories of New York were thus able to set new records for the production of goods.

Dewey Leads the Empire State

New York has always attracted many of the ablest and most ambitious young men of both the United States and Europe. Among the bright young men who came to New York in the 1930's was Thomas E. Dewey, a native of Michigan. Governor Lehman appointed him special prosecutor to investigate racketeering in New York City. Racketeers were gangsters who took money from merchants by threatening to beat up their workers, break their windows, or throw bombs into their stores.

Dewey did a brilliant job cleaning up the rackets. Swiftly and systematically, he and his team of young lawyers collected evidence. Soon, dozens of gangsters were in jail. In 1937 the public rewarded Dewey

Thomas E. Dewey served three terms (1943–1955) as governor of the Empire State.

by electing him District Attorney of New York County. In that office he continued his crusade against crime. The Republicans were looking for a strong and vigorous candidate to run for governor, and they selected Dewey in 1938 and again in 1942. The second time Dewey won and became the first Republican governor of New York in over 20 years. he held the office for the next 12 years. In 1944, and again in 1948, Dewey ran unsuccessfully for President of the United States.

New York's leaders took steps to fight discrimination against certain of its citizens because of their race, religion, or color. The Ives-Quinn Act of 1945 was a pioneering act which several other states copied. It set up a commission of five men whose job was to prevent and to eliminate discrimination against individuals seeking work. Under this law, a person can complain to the commission if he or she feels that a job was denied because of race or religion. The commission then makes an investigation. If it finds the complaint is true, it will ask the employer to stop discrimination in hiring of new workers. Usually, this suggestion is all that is needed. If the employer refuses to act, the commission can go to court and force a stop to unfair practices. The commission has proved quite successful in educating both employers and the public to treat all Americans fairly.

No doubt many people will remember Thomas Dewey for the construction of the Thruway. In 1950 the legislature established the New York State Thruway Authority to construct and operate a 550-mile highway between New York City and the western boundaries of the state. Late in 1955 the Tappan Zee Bridge, crossing the Hudson near Yonkers, opened. The entire highway was renamed the Thomas E. Dewey Thruway in 1964.

The Dewey government attacked other problems. It granted more money for education. It set up the State University. Labor laws were improved. The state spent more money on medical research, especially in the fight against tuberculosis, cancer, and cerebral palsy.

In 1954 Averell Harriman defeated Senator Irving Ives for the governorship by the paper-thin margin of 11,000 votes. Harriman was a wealthy businessman, who had turned to a political career in the 1930's. President Franklin D. Roosevelt appointed Harriman to many important positions. During World War II he was in charge of aid to our allies and he also served as Ambassador to Russia. As governor, Harriman took steps to help the aged and the consumer. He greatly expanded the amount of state aid for education. State employees received higher salaries and health benefits and more highways were built.

Rockefeller as Governor

Nelson A. Rockefeller won a smashing victory over Averell Harriman while most other Republican candidates were losing in 1958. A hard-working campaigner with millions of dollars in his campaign chest, Rockefeller won reelection three times. He failed, however, to secure the nomination for President, although he made strong efforts in 1960, 1964, and 1968.

New York politics has always been known for its complexity and quarrels among rival factions. The recent history of both Democratic and Republican parties is only another chapter in party bickering. A "reform" faction of Democrats, which opposed American participation in the Vietnam War and favored a strong civil rights program, fought the old leaders, who were more interested in jobs and preferred to avoid troublesome issues. Although Arthur Goldberg, the Democratic candidate for governor in 1970, had a distinguished career as Justice of the United States Supreme Court, he ran poorly against Rockefeller.

The Republicans also had many quarrels: Rockefeller against Nixon for the presidential nominations in 1960 and 1968; Rockefeller against Mayor John Lindsay of New York City over state aid to cities; conservatives such as James Buckley versus Senator Charles Goodell, a critic of President Nixon. Meanwhile Lindsay and several liberal Republicans switched to the Democratic party in 1971 because of the administration's policy in Vietnam.

The legislature and Rockefeller faced a multitude of problems, almost all of which cost money. As a result Rockefeller found it necessary to raise taxes on incomes, cigarettes, gasoline, liquor, and sales. Further-

The Governor Nelson A. Rockefeller Empire State Plaza in Albany is the seat of New York state government. The plaza includes a cultural center and shopping areas, as well as office buildings.

more, the state gave up its pay-as-you-go policy and kept borrowing more money. In 1971 Controller Arthur Levitt found that the state's direct debt had tripled to over three billion dollars. In addition the state was responsible for paying back another two billion dollars in socalled "indirect" debt. For example, the state guarantees rentals (much higher than ordinary rates) in the Albany Mall, the new complex of buildings which is actually financed by Albany County.

The rise in spending, debt, and taxes has set off a taxpayer revolt, and some legislators have cut back the state budgets. In 1971 the people soundly defeated a bond issue called for spending two and a half billion dollars more on transportation.

Conservation was a favorite goal of Rockefeller, and the voters approved several bond issues for the purchase of more parks and forests. When a state commission declared that two-thirds of the state's waters were polluted, Rockefeller backed a program for sewage disposal plants to be financed by state, federal, and local governments. He also set up special commissions to protect the scenic and historic features of the Hudson valley and the Adirondacks. The Council on the Arts has encouraged the growth of many arts centers, libraries, museums, opera companies, and drama organizations with financial grants.

After the federal government, in 1965, provided health insurance (Medicare) for persons over 65, Rockefeller took advantage of another provision in the law which stated that the federal government would pay half the cost of medical benefits for "needy" persons of any age. The state defined "needy" to cover about 40 percent of all families. This program, called *Medicaid,* served many people. Costs shot upward forcing many counties to levy sales taxes in order to pay the 25 percent share required of them. By 1975, a monthly average of 1,450,000 citizens, roughly one-twelfth of the state population, received some form of public assistance. It cost the state almost two billion dollars, while many counties complained that welfare, including Medicaid, took over half of their budgets.

Governor Carey was first elected to office in 1974. He was re-elected in 1978.

Unfortunately a national recession started in 1973, and it struck the northeastern states particularly hard. In the Empire State many business firms closed their doors or cut their work force. They did so because of rising costs, such as soaring oil prices and high taxes. Some firms could not compete with companies located in the southern states. Between 1970 and 1977, New York State lost over 600,000 jobs, most of them in manufacturing. During the same period the state also lost population.

In 1975 New York State and some of its largest cities faced bankruptcy. This was largely because the economic slowdown cut revenues and at the same time raised welfare costs. Clearly New Yorkers had spent too much money and piled up too much debt during the previous decade. Officials of New York City had mismanaged city finances, added thousands of people to the city payroll, and granted employees large increases in salaries and pensions. Meanwhile, the number of people on welfare climbed over one million. When the banks refused to lend the metropolis any more money, Mayor Abraham Beame appealed to Washington, D.C. and Albany for help. After much criticism of New York City's extravagance, President Ford agreed to support Congress in lending money to head off bankruptcy.

Meanwhile, Governor Rockefeller resigned his office to become Vice President, leaving Malcolm Wilson as governor. In 1974 Wilson lost his office to Hugh Carey, a Democratic congressman. Faced with the collapse of several state agencies as well as New York City, Carey had to take strong measures. He worked out a plan for a Municipal Assistance Corporation that would permit New York City to reorganize its debts, postpone some payments, and secure more state aid. "Big Mac," as newsmen quickly called his agency, required Mayor Beame to fire thousands of employees, cut back on services such as free tuition at CUNY, and bring order into city finances. These steps naturally angered city employees, some of whom threatened to strike. Union officials, realizing the danger of bankruptcy, helped out by buying city bonds for their pension funds.

Carey and the legislature had to cut the budget of the state government. They raised taxes to achieve a balanced budget and stopped hiring. These measures worked out well, but the upturn in the national economy helped even more by bringing in more revenues. By 1978 New York State bonds were selling at the highest credit rating. Although New York City made some progress in straightening out its finances, in 1978 it had to ask Congress for an extension of the federal loan.

In 1978 Carey ran for reelection as Democratic candidate for governor and won. The Republicans selected Perry Duryea as their candidate. Both parties vied for voter support in promising a cut in taxes. Other campaign issues dealt with unemployment and inflation, the migration of residents from New York City to the suburbs, and problems related to public education. Politicians, business leaders, and labor officials realized the need to nourish and stimulate business. The decline in population, the near collapse of New York City, the loss of jobs in manufacturing, and the state's high taxes convinced New Yorkers that they had to cooperate to regain economic health.

Summary

World War I left many problems: inflation, labor unrest, and fear of radicals. The postwar boom was short, ending in 1920 when farm prices fell and unemployment rose.

Alfred E. Smith rated high among New York governors, especially for his reorganization of the state government. The prosperous 1920's ended in the Wall Street crash of 1929, which ushered in a decade of depression. The state and federal government helped the jobless by relief and work projects. Governors Franklin D. Roosevelt and Herbert H. Lehman carried out many reforms, including labor legislation and the regulation of utility rates. The factories of the Empire State out-produced all others in World War II by the skillful use of manpower.

Thomas E. Dewey left three major legacies: the Thruway, the State University, and the law banning discrimination in employment. Nelson Rockefeller won the office of governor four times. Rockefeller expanded state services, especially the State University, mental health, medical care, conservation, and the arts. All these projects forced an increase in taxes and state debt. By 1975 New York City and New York State faced bankruptcy due to excessive spending and a national recession. Governor Hugh Carey and the legislature rushed to help New York City and to restore state credit by cutting spending. Business and labor leaders joined Carey in trying to bring back prosperity to the state.

Checking the high points

1. Why was there economic and social instability in 1919–1920?

2. Alfred E. Smith is often called New York's greatest governor. Do you agree?

3. What stimulated the prosperity of the 1920's? Why did it end?

4. How did the government combat the depression?

5. What problems faced Governors Roosevelt and Lehman?

6. How did New York increase production during World War II?

7. Compare the achievements of Thomas E. Dewey before and after he became governor.

8. Why is New York politics so complicated? Give examples.

9. What were the main achievements of Governor Rockefeller? Main problems?

10. Why did New York experience such hard times in the 1970s?

11. What steps did Governor Carey take to solve the financial crisis?

Think these over

1. Outsiders and aliens are often blamed—usually unfairly—in every country for troubles. Why?

2. The city has been a bigger safety valve than the frontier.

3. Welfare should be a local rather than a national responsibility. Explain your reasoning.

4. New York politics are complex because of the diversity of nationalities, economic interests, and ambitious personalities.

Vocabulary building

radicals	pollution
anarchists	racketeering
witchhunt	seaway
Medicaid	discrimination
graft	turbines
crusade	social security

Chapter Objectives

To learn about

- cultural developments in New York
- the expansion of higher education
- religious activities in New York

chapter 22

CULTURAL GROWTH

The Cities and Culture

Throughout history it has been the wealth of the cities that has made possible most intellectual and cultural advances. Sometimes great universities have been created in small communities, but these have usually been supported by state or church funds. Nearly always the cities themselves have been centers of intellectual and cultural activity. Not only do the cities have the wealth to support scholars and artists but they have a wide variety of human talents in their large populations. These talented people tend to spur each other to greater efforts, and to attract still others.

As we have seen, New York State has become highly urbanized. The entire Population Belt has taken on the characteristics of Megalopolis. This development has brought a new interest in intellectual and cultural affairs, with New York City serving as the leading center of Megalopolis. Most other such centers in New York are found within the Population Belt, but, as we shall see, there are important exceptions.

In the years following the Civil War, New York City pushed ahead of Boston as the main center of intellectual activity in this country. Many of the large publishing houses had their offices in New York, and authors sent their writings to them for publication. To be near the publishers, a number of writers came to live in the metropolis.

An extremely popular writer was O. Henry, whose real name was William Sidney Porter. Writing about 1900, O. Henry described the joys and sorrows of the little people—policemen, department store salesgirls, shopkeepers. His short stories often had unexpected endings.

Meanwhile, John Burroughs—who had known Walt Whitman as a young man—popularized the study of nature. Born in Roxbury, Burroughs spent most of his life in the Catskills observing the trees, birds, and flowers. His books had a lot to do with the growing interest in outdoor life and camping. Theodore Roosevelt, a friend of Burroughs's, also wrote several books on American history and the western frontier.

Rural and small town New York was the

Greenwich Village has long been the center of creative activity in writing and art. It is a combination of the old, such as Washington Mews shown here (once the carriage houses of the aristocratic families of Washington Square North) and the most avant-garde, such as the "bohemians" of the 1920's and the hippies of the 1960's. Note the modern apartment buildings in the background.

scene of hundreds of novels and stories. *David Harum,* by Edward Westcott, was a best seller around 1900.

One of the most amusing and accurate descriptions of small town life in nineteenth-century New York is given by Samuel Hopkins Adams. No one should miss his book *The Erie Canal* or his delightful *Grandfather Stories.*

The rich history of New York, especially that of the Revolutionary War and the frontier, has attracted many novelists. Harold Frederic's *In the Valley* is one of the first important historical novels. It described the stirring events in the Mohawk Valley during the Revolution. Compare it with the novels of Kenneth Roberts, whose *Rabble at Arms* gives us a vivid description of the Saratoga campaign, in which the British invasion led by General Burgoyne was defeated. Some of you may have seen the motion picture *Drums Along the Mohawk,* which was based on a fine novel by Walter Edmonds. Edmonds has also written several novels about the Erie Canal.

One of America's greatest writers, Henry James, was born in New York City. James wrote novels which were studies of people's characters. The action of his book *Washington Square* takes place in lower Manhattan. Edith Wharton was also born in New York City. Most of her books, written around the turn of the century, are studies of New Yorkers living in high society.

The Industrial Revolution, new scientific discoveries, and World War I completely changed American life and the things American writers wrote about. Some writers criticized small-town life. Some writers wrote of social and economic problems. Others wrote of the city. F. Scott Fitzgerald, Theodore Dreiser, John Dos Passos, and Thomas Wolfe used Manhattan as a background for some of their stories.

Many of the books of the 1940's were about World War II as seen by American writers who fought in it. Two New York novelists, Norman Mailer and Herman Wouk, did some of their best work during the war period.

Since then the trend has been to tell of unhappy and confused individuals who feel beaten by life's pressures. These people think more and act less. They are critical of themselves and the world. New York City is often the background for this kind of story. In recent years, fewer of these stories are published as novels but they do appear as short stories in New York magazines.

In 1953 a brilliant new author appeared

in the person of James Baldwin. His novels and essays gave a clear-cut view of relations between blacks and whites. Alex Haley, who was born in Ithaca, New York, helped edit the *Autobiography of Malcolm X.* Malcolm X was a militant black leader. Haley's search for his African ancestors became the basis of the book *Roots*. When this bestseller was dramatized for television, it attracted one of the largest television audiences in history.

Women authors have seemed particularly interested in regional history and folklore. Oriana Atkinson's *Big Eyes* (1949) was a novel set in the Catskill country. In western New York, Taylor Caldwell wrote bestsellers such as *The Earth is the Lord's,* which earned her popular acclaim. In Brooklyn, Marianne Moore won literary prizes for her poems. Lillian Hellman's play *The Little Foxes* (1939) is often revived for the current stage.

In journalism New York City also showed the way. Its newspapers and magazines set the pattern for the rest of the state and the country. Joseph Pulitzer, an immigrant from Hungary, got control of the *World* in 1883. He appealed to a large audience by stressing crime stories. His paper, however, provided a great deal of news and advocated reform. Ten years later, William Randolph Hearst, a young millionaire from California, battled Pulitzer for first place in circulation. Hearst followed even more sensational tactics and built up the largest chain of papers in the country. In 1896 Adolph Ochs of Chattanooga saved *The New York Times* from collapse. He built *The Times* into a great newspaper with a fair and complete coverage of the news. During the 1920's the tabloids, such as the New York *News* and *Mirror,* became popular because they were easy to read on the subway and because they used many pictures to illustrate their stories.

In 1910 there were 13 major newspapers being published in New York City. To overcome high production costs, several papers combined. In 1960 there were seven papers, and in 1969, there remained only the

Founder of the Westerns

Everyone likes the "westerns"—stories about Indian scouts and cowboys. Few know that a New Yorker by the name of Edward Zane Judson had a great deal to do with starting the thousands of stories about the Wild West.

Judson wrote under the name of Ned Buntline. He lived a wild life, as colorful as those of his heroes. As a boy he ran away to sea, where he served as a midshipman. He began to write and founded a magazine. In 1846 he was lynched for a murder and was left for dead by the crowd. However, he recovered. Ned could not stay out of trouble, and before long he was arrested for leading a mob in New York City against an English actor by the name of Macready. The next few years he was an organizer for the Know Nothings—a group of native Americans who opposed foreigners. He served in the Civil War, but was not a good soldier and was dishonorably discharged. For many years he kept a home in the heart of the Adirondack Mountains.

After the war, Judson went west and ran into William Cody. Ned made Cody famous under the name of Buffalo Bill. Cody was a brave Indian scout but Ned described him as almost a superman.

The public liked to read about cowboys and Indian scouts. Ned wrote dozens of novels telling about their adventures and thus helped to create the modern story known as the "western."

New York Post (established in 1801), *The Times* (1851), and the *News* (1919).

This was due in part to rising production costs and long strikes by printers, but also to lack of advertising, competition from suburban, trade, and specialty papers, and from radio and television stations.

The upstate papers have followed the features of the press in New York City: lively reporting, comics, "scare" headlines. Frank Gannett of Rochester built up a chain of papers in such cities as Utica, Rochester, Binghamton, Ithaca, Elmira.

In the years after the Civil War, New York City shared with Boston and Philadelphia the leadership in publishing magazines. *Harper's Weekly* was especially important in the 1860's, when it carried the cartoons of Thomas Nast. You will recall that we read in an earlier chapter how Nast attacked Boss Tweed.

In 1865 Edwin L. Godkin founded and published *The Nation,* which stood for honesty in politics. It is still being published.

One of the most important events in magazine history in the years after 1900 was the appearance of articles calling for reform in politics and business. An Irish immigrant, Samuel McClure, published many articles attacking political bosses and certain big businesses. As a result, Congress, under the prodding of President Theodore Roosevelt, pushed through the Pure Food and Drug Act, and laws to regulate railroads.

In the 1920's Henry Luce rose as a magazine publisher. Born of missionary parents in China, Luce came to the United States for his education at Yale. He and two friends created a weekly news magazine called *Time.* Luce founded several publications: *Life,* the picture magazine; *Fortune,* a journal for businessmen; *Sports Illustrated,* and *Architectural Forum.*

Equally successful was DeWitt Wallace. Wallace had lost his health. While sitting

Nellie Bly

Have you ever heard of Nellie Bly, one of the first women reporters? Actually, her real name was Elizabeth Cochrane but she took the name of Nellie Bly because people were singing about Nellie in one of Stephen Foster's popular songs of that era.

Her first big story came in 1887 when she pretended that she was insane so that doctors would put her in Blackwell Island Asylum, where conditions were very bad. Ten days later Nellie came out and wrote the story of her experiences. The public was shocked at the way the patients were treated and demanded better care.

Nellie loved to disguise herself and go to work in factories or stores. Once she even had herself arrested so that she could see how prisons were run. Her stories made interesting reading and led to many improvements.

Her most famous stunt came in 1889 when everybody was reading the book *Around the World in 80 Days,* by Jules Verne. Nellie's assignment was to beat the record set by the hero of the novel. Each day Nellie sent back reports on her progress around the world. The whole city turned out to greet her when she arrived home in 72 days, 6 hours, and 11 minutes.

At 28 Nellie gave up writing and married a rich industrialist. When he died, Nellie ran the corporation. She was thus one of the first women to enter both the newspaper and the industrial worlds.

at home, he decided to keep his busy friends better informed by summarizing for them important articles in various magazines. The idea proved so helpful that he started a magazine, the *Reader's Digest,* which today has the largest circulation of any magazine in the world. It is published in Pleasantville in 13 foreign languages. There is also a "talking record" edition for the blind and it is published in Braille in five languages.

Between 1925 and 1951 Harold Ross was probably the most important editor of American fiction. His magazine, *The New Yorker,* contained stories and essays by James Thurber, Dorothy Parker, Robert Benchley, and E. B. White. Today, *The New Yorker* and *Harper's Magazine* publish the writing of John Updike, John Cheever, Mary McCarthy, and many other well-known, popular authors.

Painting and Sculpture

New York produced three outstanding artists after the Civil War. Among them was John La Farge (1835–1910). La Farge began his career as a painter but later devoted much of his effort to making stained glass windows. For his work in stained glass, the French government awarded him the insignia of the Legion of Honor. La Farge used his position and his skill as a lecturer and writer to arouse his countrymen to a greater interest in art.

Augustus Saint-Gaudens (1848–1907) is generally considered a great sculptor of the United States. His work established standards of excellence against which later artists could measure their skill. Saint-Gaudens was born in Ireland. As a youth he became an apprentice in cameo cutting. His statues of Admiral David Farragut at Madison Square and of General William T. Sherman

"Dempsey Through the Ropes" by George Bellows. Compare the subject matter of this picture with that of Thomas Coles's painting on page 221.

at Fifth Avenue and 59th Street in New York City are examples of his work.

Albert P. Ryder (1847–1917) was a strange man. Much of his life was spent in a small room in New York City, where he devoted all his time to painting. He frequently worked over one picture for years, changing and improving it. During his entire life he produced only about 150 paintings. His pictures have the power to cast a spell, creating a lonely and poetic mood in the viewer. Moonlight, the sea, ghostlike figures, and shadowy masses frequently are found in his pictures.

In spite of the work of these three gifted men, sculpture and painting developed slowly in New York. Many of our artists went abroad to study. Most of them followed the styles of the various *schools* of art developed in Europe. As used here, the word *school* means a group of artists whose work is similar in nature. The Hudson River School of painting, which developed in New York before the Civil War, lasted until about 1875. The painters of this school greatly admired the beauty of the rivers and mountains of the Empire State. They painted landscapes, using views of the rivers and mountains as subjects. The picture by Thomas Cole entitled *In the Catskills* on page 221 is typical of the Hudson River School.

Gradually, artists turned to what is called French impressionism. They became less interested in making exact copies of what they saw, and tried to capture the mood of the scene and the play of light over form.

After 1900 another group of artists began to paint urban life as they saw it. Among their subjects were prize fights, elevated railroads, back alleys, and pool rooms. The work of these artists shocked many people. Critics labeled their work the Ashcan School. A good example of this school is George Bellows' famous drawing *Dempsey Through the Ropes* (p. 311). A leader in this school was Arthur B. Davies, a Utica-born artist who had won a good reputation both in this country and in Europe. Davies determined to introduce the American public to modern art. He organized the International Exhibition of Modern Art in 1913 at the armory of the Sixty-ninth Regiment in New York City. The exhibit promptly became known as the Armory Show. Sixteen hundred works of painting and sculpture by American and European artists were displayed to thousands of people. Probably the Armory Show did more to arouse the interest of Americans in modern art than any other single event.

American painters have eagerly experimented with the various phases of modern art. For the first time in art history, America is the leader of a new art movement, abstract expressionism. The capital of this movement is New York City. This style of painting grew out of the work of artists who were cubists, surrealists, and futurists in Europe. Abstract expressionism has also been influenced by the art of Africa and Asia. Sometimes objects such as houses, people, and animals can be seen in these paintings. More often, the paintings are big areas of color and free forms on large canvasses. Some of these paintings express definite feelings such as fear, hate, joy, or calm. Jackson Pollock was a famous artist of this movement.

Quite different from the abstract expressionists was Anna Mary Moses, known as Grandma Moses. Born in 1860 near the Vermont border, Grandma Moses taught herself to paint in her 70's. Her pictures are simple gay scenes of farm life, which have often been reproduced on Christmas cards.

During the 1930's the public began to show a greater interest in art. This interest has grown rapidly since World War II. For example, attendance at the world-famous Metropolitan Museum of Art increased from one and one-half million people in 1945 to over six and one-half million in 1970. Many people have also studied painting and sculpture during their spare time.

The Museum of Modern Art on West 53rd Street is devoted to the study, practice, and display of modern art. It offers a variety of activities. Twice a day there are showings of famous old motion pictures. Classes are giving in painting, sculpture, woodworking, and crafts of all kinds. The museum lends exhibits to colleges and to other museums. In this way, it makes fine examples of modern art available to people who live outside New York City. In 1959 the Guggenheim Museum was opened. It has attracted thou-

Designed by Frank Lloyd Wright, the Guggenheim Museum has six stories with a continuous ramp that spirals around a central court, as seen here. In effect, it is one corridor, a quarter of a mile long, from which art can be seen from many points.

sands of visitors who wish to see modern art in a building of striking architecture.

The Whitney Museum of American Art is devoted to American painting, sculpture, and graphic arts of the twentieth century. It also has a permanent collection of important historical works but its major presentations are of contemporary art.

Besides these and other museums, New York City has over 300 galleries, which show every kind of art from all over the world.

The Performing Arts

Music. New York City also took the leadership from Boston in the field of music in the years after the Civil War. One reason for New York's supremacy was that most of Europe's outstanding performers arrived at this great port. Furthermore, there were enough people to support opera and symphony concerts. The Metropolitan Opera Association, founded in 1883, soon ranked with the finest in Europe. Enrico Caruso began his famous career at the Metropolitan in 1903. Five years later another artist of Italian birth, Arturo Toscanini, became the conductor of the Metropolitan Opera orchestra. Later he conducted the New York Philharmonic. Starting in 1958, Leonard Bernstein brought this orchestra to new heights of excellence and popularity by his playing, conducting, composing, and TV programs. The Juilliard School of Music, founded in 1926, has trained many hundreds of musicians.

Dance. The American dance world is centered in New York City, which boasts of four internationally-known ballet companies. The New York City Ballet has as its permanent home, Lincoln Center's New York State Theater—the only theater in the world specifically designed for the ballet. Two of the greatest dancers in the United States have been produced by New York's ballet companies: Edward Villella (New York City Ballet) and Lupe Serrano (American Ballet Theatre). Other major companies are the Joffrey, City Center, and Harkness ballets, but smaller groups such as the Manhattan Festival Ballet perform regularly for enthusiastic audiences. Modern dance also makes New York City its base of operation; the Martha Graham and Merce Cunningham companies are leaders in this field.

Popular Music. Tin-pan Alley is not a definite place, as you might suppose, but the name given to New York City's song-writing industry. It turns out most of the popular tunes that you hear on radio, on television, in Broadway theaters, and on records. An outstanding composer is Richard Rodgers, who wrote the music for *Oklahoma!*, *The King and I,* and *South Pacific.* George Gershwin won international fame for his symphonic interpretation of jazz. *Porgy and Bess,* a folk opera by Gershwin, has received praise all over the world. Irving Berlin, who wrote dozens of hit songs, is among the best known of popular song writers.

Jazz is said to be the only original American contribution to world music. Jazz began with blacks in New Orleans, spent the 1920's in Chicago, and came to New York in the 30's for the swing era.

Many of the "big bands" went out from New York engagements to tour the country and the world. These included bands of Tommy Dorsey, Benny Goodman, Guy Lombardo, and many of the fine Negro bands such as those of Duke Ellington, Cab Calloway, and Louis Armstrong.

In the 1940's a group of musicians in New York City began to try out new musical ideas. They developed a style of playing called bebop or bop.

In the 1950's the bop musicians began playing a more relaxed style called cool jazz. They were joined by musicians who had studied in music schools after World War II. The style of music became slower but more complicated.

In the 1960's a different style of jazz became popular. This style had been influenced by blues singers and the heavy beat of "rock and roll." By the late 1960's the field of popular music was dominated by the Motown (the Supremes) and Mersey (the Beatles) sounds and finally by Far Eastern instruments and arrangements. "Pop" music included music from many sources—folk songs, ballads, and protest songs against the war in South Vietnam and problems concerned with race and social conditions.

Since the swing era, many jazz musicians have lived, worked, and made records in New York. Today, especially in New York City, jazz is treated as serious art, and can be heard not only in night clubs, but in concert halls as well. It is even used for religious services.

The Theater. Broadway has long set the pace for the entire American theater. In the 1890's the three Shubert brothers from Syracuse organized chains of theaters across the nation. They featured the best and most popular actors of their day. Broadway hits were presented throughout the nation in the playhouses of the Shubert chain by traveling companies of players. Other theaters followed.

Motion pictures, especially the "talkies," ended the old theater everywhere but in New York City. Even here it caused a drop in the number of playhouses. The depression of the 1930's hit the theater business a hard blow, although the government helped jobless actors by hiring them to put on plays.

The theater again became a big business in the 1950's. People flocked to see the plays of Tennessee Williams, Arthur Miller and Eugene O'Neill. They went not only to established theaters but also to playhouses in the state's many summer resorts and to "off-Broadway" theaters, which presented less expensive productions of plays and musicals in parts of New York City outside the theatrical district.

Movies. Movies themselves became important to New York. Many of the largest motion picture theaters were built in the Broadway area; among them were Radio City Music Hall, the Roxy, and the Paramount. There were numerous neighborhood houses as well.

Although most studios center around Hollywood, many movies have been filmed on location in New York, and the main sales offices of most companies are in New York City.

In recent years foreign films have become very popular and a film festival is held each year at Lincoln Center.

Edison showed his first movie in New York City in 1896. It consisted of scenes from a prizefight, showed a dancer, and a sequence of ocean waves. Seeing it was an exciting experience. People fled to the back of the theater to avoid being drenched by the realistic-looking water.

Radio. Radio reached the public directly after World War I. In 1922 companies began to sponsor programs. Soon independent stations formed networks which carried the most popular programs across the continent. The most important radio networks were the Columbia Broadcasting System, the American Broadcasting Company, the National Broadcasting System, and the Mutual Broadcasting System. All had headquarters in New York City. Radio became more important each year for entertainment and for information. In the presidential election of 1932, Franklin D. Roosevelt showed how effective political campaigning by radio could be. The broadcasting companies usually spent most of their time presenting light entertainment. They also put on more serious programs such as those of the Metropolitan Opera and the various symphony orchestras.

One of the longest running hits on Broadway, "Hello, Dolly" represents many forms of theater. Originally a play, it was made into a musical and later into a movie. This is a location shot as it was actually being filmed in Garrison. The story takes place in Yonkers in the 1890's and Garrison even now looks much like the Yonkers of that time. The film company made a few changes in the present village, such as painting the street brick-red and stenciling on the "bricks."

Television. Television rapidly captured the public fancy after 1945. Today most homes have TV sets. It has changed the old methods of political campaigning. Its news reporters and commentators bring to viewers events as they are happening. The public feels itself to be experiencing, not merely observing, current history. It has brightened the lives of millions of shut-ins and retired people. Television is primarily devoted to light entertainment, but it also presents plays, concerts, and discussions of a more serious nature. Several stations give courses

The glamour of the Metropolitan Opera House at Lincoln Center is felt as an audience gathers for a performance. Gigantic paintings by Marc Chagall fill the windows of the two end arches. The interior decor is red, gold, and white—with thousands of lights in the starburst chandeliers. To the left is the New York State Theater; at right is Avery Fisher Hall, behind which is the Vivian Beaumont Theater and the library-museum of the performing arts.

in such subjects as physics, chemistry, foreign languages, and American history. Viewers are able to earn school credit by doing homework and taking examinations.

Architecture

During the nineteenth century, many of the architects of New York imitated some of the features of European styles. About 1850 the Gothic style, with its pointed arches and pinnacles, was introduced. St. Patrick's Cathedral in New York City is a fine example. One of the great architects was Henry Hobson Richardson, who was trained at Paris. Richardson helped design the State Capitol, with its famous "million dollar" staircase and its ornate Senate Chamber.

In the twentieth century, modern architecture has given new form to New York's skyline. Rockefeller Center in the heart of New York City is an example of this new form, with its buildings of various heights. New York has more than 100 skyscrapers of 30 stories or over. Several new buildings show taste and style. Citicorp Center, opened in 1977, has an indoor plaza ringed with shops. The World Trade Center's twin towers, 110 stories high, dominate the tip of Manhattan.

The Museum of Modern Art, designed in 1939, consists of large areas of stone as well as sheets of glass. In 1951 a team of 10 international architects designed the Secretariat building at the United Nations. This building is a thin rectangle with two walls of stone and two walls of glass.

In the past 20 years, architects and engineers have worked together to change the shapes of buildings. Using steel cables and concrete, they have made buildings with round, curved, and zig-zagging roofs and walls. Frank Lloyd Wright's Guggenheim Museum employed this technique. A leading architect of this movement was Eero Saarinen. The TWA Terminal, built in 1961 at New York's Kennedy International Airport, is a good example of his work.

The Cultural Explosion

By the mid 1950's music, art, and the theater were rivaling sports for the attention of New Yorkers. Averell Harriman, who was elected Governor in 1954, was a noted collector of art. When he moved into the governor's mansion in Albany, he took many of his favorite paintings with him. Harriman was succeeded in 1958 by Nelson A. Rockefeller, whose interest in art probably exceeded that of any other governor. Like Harriman, Rockefeller placed a number of his favorite works of art in the governor's mansion.

Under Governor Rockefeller's influence the Lincoln Center for the Performing Arts came into being in the heart of New York City. On a 14-acre tract of land that had been slums are buildings for drama, dance, opera, concerts, a music school, and a library-museum. Lincoln Center is now the home of four world-famous artistic organizations: the New York City Ballet, the Metropolitan Opera, the New York Philharmonic Orchestra, and the Juilliard School of Music. No other center of the performing arts can equal it.

Governor Rockefeller was also largely responsible for the establishment of the Saratoga Performing Arts Center at Saratoga Springs, 30 miles north of Albany. Here in an outdoor setting is a beautiful covered amphitheater that will seat over 5,000 people. An additional 10,000 can be seated on the surrounding lawns to listen to musical performances. The Saratoga Performing Arts Center is the permanent summer home of the New York City Ballet and the Philadelphia Orchestra.

At the urging of Rockefeller the legislature created the New York State Council on the Arts. The Council received funds which are used to bring performing artists of the highest talents to small communities, schools, and colleges. Often the Council employed young artists who had great ability but had not yet won fame. In this manner young artists were given experience and encouragement. At the same time the performances sponsored by the Council aroused the attention of ordinary citizens in the performing arts.

The Council also granted money to many local museums. Across the state, interest in the arts continued to rise. Hundreds of thousands flocked to art exhibits and to artistic performances. Scores of thousands became Sunday painters, joined local music organizations, or took part in community drama groups. This interest in the arts was further encouraged by the rapid growth of colleges and universities throughout the state. Not only did these educational institutions bring exhibitions and performers to local communities but they offered lectures on the arts and a wide variety of other subjects. Late in the 1960's educational television became available across the state.

Upstate Cultural Centers

New York City is unrivaled in its cultural and intellectual leadership. Yet upstate has many important centers for such activities, and a number of them are found in small communities or even in rural settings. We have already mentioned the Saratoga Performing Arts Center; and the Chautauqua Institute, one of the oldest organizations (1874), located in western New York on the shore of Lake Chautauqua. Every summer thousands of people gather not only to study and enjoy the arts, but also to work in the fields of science and social studies.

Most people know that Cooperstown is the location of the Baseball Hall of Fame. Fewer realize that it also has the headquarters of the New York State Historical Association and the Farmers' Museum operated by the Association. The museum shows what farm and village life was like in the

These young people are viewing art done by neighborhood creative art classes held in disadvantaged areas of Buffalo. The classes are sponsored by the Albright-Knox Art Gallery there.

1840's. At the headquarters are housed one of the nation's best collections of folk art, a library devoted to New York history, and collections of documents relating to folk tales, folk songs, and New York history.

At Ogdensburg is the Remington Art Memorial. It is named in honor of Frederick Remington, who was a well-known sculptor, painter, and writer. Cowboys and Indians were among his favorite subjects. The museum contains some of Remington's art work and the materials he collected in the West.

Ithaca is one of the smaller cities in our state but it has Cornell, one of the top universities in the United States. In the same city is Ithaca College, which has a growing reputation.

At Corning is the world's largest library devoted to glass. Here also is the internationally famous glass museum.

The Triple Cities area around Binghamton has shown a rapid increase in cultural and intellectual affairs. Here is the Triple Cities Opera, one of the excellent opera companies in the state outside New York City. The Roberson Center for the Arts and Sciences in Binghamton is busy. People gather at the center to see artistic and scientific exhibits and to try their own skills as artists. The State University of New York at Binghamton offers graduate and undergraduate courses to thousands of students.

Principal intellectual and cultural activities take place within the Population Belt. As we have seen, there is a growing concentration of population in the Capital District. Here are colleges and universities where one can study to become a lawyer, physician, druggist, teacher, engineer, or businessman. Three institutions of higher education located in the Capital District have nationwide reputations. Union University in Schenectady is one of the state's oldest. Rensselaer Polytechnic Institute at Troy is the oldest college of engineering and science in the United States. Its faculty has made many advances in these fields. In the capital city itself is the State University of New York at Albany, which has become noted for research as well as instruction.

The State Library in Albany has important holdings including many original documents. It is useful to scholars and to the students attending nearby colleges. The State Museum in the same city is especially noted for its materials concerning the Iroquois Indians. Best known in the field of performing arts are the Schenectady Symphony Orchestra and the Albany Civic Theater. Also of importance is the Albany Institute of Art and History where several art exhibits are held each year.

West of the Capital District is the Utica-Rome area. In recent years this region has reestablished its economic base and is now seeking to add new cultural and intellectual resources. The Munson-Williams-Proctor Art Museum in Utica has a magnificent building designed by Philip Johnson. At Clinton, near Utica, is Hamilton College, a fine college of liberal arts which attracts students and faculty members from all over the United States.

Moving still farther west the Population Belt broadens out as it leaves the Mohawk Valley and enters the Great Lakes Plain. Here are three major centers of intellectual and cultural activity: Syracuse, Rochester, and Buffalo in the Niagara Frontier. All three have excellent public libraries. The University of Rochester, Syracuse University, and the State University of New York at Buffalo enroll thousands of students and are among our nation's finest universities.

The Syracuse Museum of Fine Arts has one of the best collections of *ceramics* in the country. Ceramics is a term used for articles made of baked clay, including china and pottery. The George Eastman House of Photography in Rochester is a nationally famous museum and study center dealing with photography. The Albright-Knox Art Gallery in Buffalo is noted for its collection of modern American and European paintings. The Buffalo Philharmonic Orchestra and the Rochester Philharmonic Symphony Orchestra are known by lovers of classical music throughout the nation. In the field of music education the Eastman School of Music of the University of Rochester ranks as one of the best.

Education

As we have seen, notwithstanding the slum areas with their hundreds of thousands of deprived persons, the people of Megalopolis have a higher level of education than the population of any other area of similar size in the world. Such persons demand educational opportunities for their children. At the same time the rapid changes in technology, new advances in fields such as medicine and engineering, and an increased interest in cultural affairs led to a demand for what has come to be called *continuing education.* Continuing education is that needed (1) to keep workers' knowledge of their jobs up to date and (2) to provide an opportunity to learn about matters that interest a person regardless of how old that person may be.

As the characteristics of Megalopolis began to appear throughout the Population Belt, the demand for higher education and continuing education became more and more widespread. Private colleges and universities increased their enrollments, sometimes aided financially by the state and federal governments. The State of New York increased the number of Regents Scholarships that are granted to able high school graduates. A Scholar Incentive Plan was established to pay part of the tuition costs for every New Yorker who enrolled in a New York college. The state and federal governments also established loan funds to aid needy students.

In 1948 the State University of New York was created. It now has over 38 two-year colleges, 14 colleges of arts and science, four universities, four medical centers, and specialized colleges of maritime science, forestry, ceramics, agriculture, home economics, veterinary science, and industrial and labor relations. City University of New York includes, in addition to other schools, four well-known colleges: Brooklyn College, City College, Hunter College, and Queens College. The private colleges and universities continue to provide educational leadership. For example, Cornell and Columbia Universities have law schools and medical colleges ranking among the top dozen. Vassar, Hamilton, and Rochester (a fine medical college and school of music) attract students of the highest calibre. The public university systems, however, are growing at a much more rapid rate than the private schools.

Both the public and private institutions of higher education have sought to provide continuing education in a variety of ways. For example, the State University has offered televised programs for lawyers dealing with changes in the law and changes in court procedures. It has also offered televised programs for physicians explaining advances in medical science and even a televised course on small-boat handling for weekend yachtsmen. Night classes and summer programs are offered by both public and private institutions to enable high school graduates to earn a college degree. Similar programs for college graduates enable them to undertake advanced studies.

Often continuing education is informal. It may consist of a series of classes given at an industrial plant to teach the workers new methods needed in their jobs. It may be a conference at which business, labor, and college leaders discuss common problems and seek a solution. It may even be a gathering of scientists called by a university to discuss the latest development in their field.

Religion

The driving demand for knowledge, skill, and understanding that exists in a megalopolitan society does not neglect religion. The seeming conflict between religion and science and the obvious gap between religious teachings and the treatment of blacks and other deprived persons led to many searching questions.

New Yorkers, after the Civil War, continued to worship in an ever-increasing number of churches. Difficult problems faced church leaders. What should they do about the shifting population? People were moving from the country to the city, forcing many rural churches to close. Immigrants were coming into cities, while other groups moved toward the suburbs.

The Roman Catholic Church has been New York's largest denomination since 1865. Largely composed of Irish and German immigrants before the Civil War, the Catholic Church later gathered in most of the Polish, Italian, and Slavic immigrants. After World War II the heavy immigration from Puerto Rico added to the number of Catholics. Generally the Catholic Church has been successful in building churches, schools, hospitals, and colleges. However, enrollments in nonpublic schools have fallen since 1967 by one third.

Jewish congregations grew rapidly, especially after 1890, when persecution in Russia and Poland drove thousands to America. Most Jews settled in New York City, although in the larger upstate cities there were strong congregations. When Hitler took control of Germany in 1933 and began his systematic persecution, he set in motion another wave of Jewish migration. Several thousands of these Jewish refugees found haven and employment in the Empire State, and became American citizens.

Protestant churches also increased in membership. The great majority of Protestants belonged to the Protestant Episcopal, Presbyterian, Baptist, Lutheran, and Methodist churches. Each of these faiths grew steadily. Some new groups sprang up, such as the Christian Scientists and Jehovah's Witnesses. The larger Protestant churches learned to cooperate with one another. In cities, they formed federations and cooperated in such things as radio programs, missions, and young people's programs. In 1908 they established the Federal Council of Churches of Christ in America, which had its headquarters in New York City.

The city posed problems for many Protestant churches. Some churches moved out to the suburbs, following their members. Others set up church houses with gymnasiums, classrooms, and playgrounds which the people could use for recreation and education during the week. Some ministers began to preach the "social gospel," in which they urged more help for the poor.

During the 1920's some young people made fun of religion because they felt it was old-fashioned. During the 1930's the depression hurt churches as it did most other groups. After World War II there took place a "return to religion." Church activity reached new highs as many new churches and synagogues were built, membership increased, and contributions went up. Many religious leaders and lay-people, both black and white, became involved in the civil rights and peace movements.

During the latter half of the 1960's the *ecumenical* movement made itself felt in New York State. The ecumenical movement is an effort on the part of all Christian sects to understand one another better, to stress common goals and bonds, and to cooperate on basic issues. The movement, encouraged by Pope John XXIII and Pope Paul VI, obtained support from many Protestant and Catholic leaders in New York State. This trend toward cooperation and mutual support among Christians led also to a greater willingness to work with Jewish leaders. The common desire of the religious leaders of the three faiths to help the poor and to encourage equal opportunity for blacks strengthened their determination to work together.

The Cathedral of St. John the Divine is the largest Gothic church in the world. It seats ten thousand. Under construction for over seventy years, it is still not completed.

Summary

Cities have made possible most intellectual and cultural advances because many of their inhabitants have considerable wealth and a great variety of talents. New York City is the greatest cultural and intellectual center of the state and of the northeastern region called Megalopolis. The Population Belt includes many other centers of cultural activity. Binghamton is one of the few centers outside the Population Belt.

New York has had several able authors. Among the best are O. Henry, John Burroughs, Henry James, and James Baldwin. In journalism New York City was the nation's leader. Its newspapers and magazines set the pattern for the rest of the country. At first New York artists followed European styles but slowly developed their own schools, including the Hudson River School, the Ash Can School, and abstract expressionism. Governor Rockefeller helped establish the New York Council on the Arts and the Lincoln and Saratoga Centers for the Performing Arts. Today New York City is the art capital of the world. It has also been the nation's leader in music, both classical and popular, and in theater, radio, and television.

The demand for higher education led to the rapid growth of the private colleges and universities and to the even more rapid growth of the City University of New York and State University of New York. There has also been a growing demand for continuing education which is offered by both public and private institutions.

By 1865 the Roman Catholic Church had more members than any other and it has maintained this position. After 1890 there was a rapid increase in the number of Jews. The ecumenical movement brought a new feeling of brotherhood among Christians and a more cooperative attitude toward Jews. Many Protestant, Catholic, and Jewish leaders became concerned over the social and economic problems of blacks and the plight of the poor.

Checking the high points

1. What subject did these New York authors write about?

O. Henry — Herman Wouk
Edith Wharton — Alex Haley
John Burroughs

2. What contributions have been made by black and women authors from New York?

3. What contributions to journalism did these men make?

William Randolph Hearst — Adolph Ochs
Henry Luce

4. What are two important magazines published in New York?

5. Describe the style of paintings of these "schools:"

Hudson River — Abstract-expressionist
Ashcan

6. Why does New York lead in the field of music?

7. What role has New York played in theater, motion pictures, radio, and television?

8. How have the latest developments in architecture taken form in New York?

9. Take a cultural tour of New York State pointing out an important museum or institute in each section.

10. Note important developments in education since 1940.

11. What has been the impact upon Roman Catholics, Jews, and Protestants of population changes, the rise of suburbia, modern science, and ecumenicism?

12. Why has art become more popular during the past two decades?

Think these over

1. A daily newspaper does not have room to print everything. What kind of news should it print?

2. Should paintings give realistic portrayals of people and landscapes? Should they give you an impression or feeling?

3. Genius is born. Therefore schools for art, music, drama are pleasant but basically unimportant. Debate.

Vocabulary

abstract expressionism
ecumenical

chapter 23: The STATE GOVERNMENT EXPANDS ITS SERVICES

chapter 24: LOCAL GOVERNMENTS and PARTY POLITICS

chapter 25: NEW YORK: The EMPIRE CITY

unit eight

The Government of New York

New York state history dates are shown in color.

1960 New York State Thruway completed

1964 U.S. Supreme Court calls for more equal representation in Congress

1969 United States astronauts land on moon

1971 26th Amendment lowers voting age to 18

New York State congressional districts reapportioned

1974 New York City suffers fiscal crisis

Hugh Carey elected New York's 55th governor

1975 Congress backs federal loans to aid New York City

1976 Jimmy Carter elected 39th President

1978 Hugh Carey re-elected governor of New York

Government. What does this word mean to you? Our fighting forces, ships, and planes? The President meeting foreign dignitaries at the White House, or in Paris? Congress making laws? Social security checks for retired and jobless people? Saluting the flag at ball games? Filling out income tax forms in April? The federal government does touch our pocketbooks, pull on our heart strings, and, at times, puts its citizens into uniform.

But state and local governments have always had an even greater impact upon our daily lives. We elect school board members to manage our schools. Cities, villages, towns, and counties provide police protection, while the state troopers patrol outlying areas. County governments with state and federal aid provide public assistance to the poor and medical care to the ill. Our highways are largely built, maintained, and supervised by city, town, county, and state governments. Local officials guard our water, put and keep criminals behind bars, and set the tax rates. To carry out these functions, each level of government requires money and many skilled officials.

We shall study state and local government in this unit. We shall examine how these governments are organized and how they serve us. Because New York City is so important, not only to its own residents but also to the nation, it receives special treatment.

Chapter Objectives

To learn about

- the organization and functions of New York state government
- New York's educational, social, and recreational systems

chapter 23

The STATE GOVERNMENT EXPANDS ITS SERVICES

New York is Related to Other Governments

Each of the 50 states is represented in the United States Senate by two senators, and each state is represented in the House of Representatives according to its population. As do all states, New York State has many important powers. These are limited, however, by two things. First, the national government also has certain powers. These are listed in the United States Constitution. Only the federal government can declare war, control foreign trade, control trade between the states, and make treaties with other nations. Second, the people have certain rights which cannot be taken away from them by any government. Powers not granted to the federal government remain in the hands of the people or the states. The constitution of the state also lists the rights of citizens. Thus our rights are protected by both the federal and the state constitutions.

The state and national governments work together in many ways. The Federal Bureau of Investigation makes available to the New York State Police and to city police departments its master fingerprint file. Perhaps the best example of cooperation is the grant of money which the national government makes to the states. Every year the United States government grants billions of dollars to New York State for highway construction, education, agriculture, public health, help to the aged, and aid to the blind.

Not only does New York have to cooperate with the United States government, but it must also work with its neighboring states. Can you imagine New York spending millions of dollars on a superhighway to the Pennsylvania border if Pennsylvania refused to connect the highway with its own system? Or think how important it is for New York to work with New Jersey in building tunnels under and bridges over the Hudson River. New York has recognized the need for cooperation among states, and a committee of the state legislature is set up to deal with this subject.

The State's Constitution

As the Constitution of the United States is the framework for the government of the United States, so the constitution of the state of New York is the basic law for our state government. Perhaps you have seen the Constitution of the United States. It is quite short. The state constitution, on the other hand, is very detailed and is over four times as long. One of the reasons for this is the great number of amendments that have been added to the state constitution—over 300 since 1800.

Since the first state constitution of 1777, eight special meetings or conventions have been held to rewrite it. During these years four important changes have taken place in our state constitution:

1. *Democracy has spread.* There are no longer property qualifications for voting or for office holding. Citizens who are 18 years old or more may vote and run for office. In the past, certain groups of people have undergone hardships because of their race, color, sex, or religion. Our constitution now says it is unlawful to *discriminate against* people in this way. To discriminate against means to treat people unfairly because of their race, color, sex, religion, or for other reasons.
2. *The governor's power has increased.* In our earliest constitutions the governor was weak and the legislature strong. Today, the Governor of New York is a very powerful official.
3. *Local governments have more home rule.* The state government still supervises cities, towns, villages, and counties. Nevertheless, these local governments now have much more freedom of action.
4. *The services provided by the state government have increased.* This is particularly true of such social services as furnishing public health nurses and providing care and hospitals for those who are mentally ill, and for those who suffer from tuberculosis and other diseases.

This is the New York State Capital in Albany. Begun in 1867, it took 30 years to complete. The governor's office and the rooms of the State Assembly and State Senate are here.

The first 10 amendments to the United States Constitution are known as the Bill of Rights. They protect certain rights of the people against the power of the national government. The New York Constitution also has a Bill of Rights. As a matter of fact, New Yorkers have made their Bill of Rights the very first article of the state constitution. Many of the rights listed in the two constitutions are the same. Both protect freedom of worship, freedom of speech, and freedom of press. Both give us the right to be free from having our homes searched without just cause; both guarantee us a trial by jury. The New York Constitution goes beyond the national constitution. It grants workers the right to organize unions. It further protects persons from discrimination because of race, color, or religion. In addition, the legislature of New York has the power to pass laws to protect the health and safety of workers.

The Legislature

Early in January each year 150 assemblymen and 60 senators meet in Albany to make the laws for about 18 million citizens. Their job is a huge one. They generally meet for only two to four months. In that time over 10,000 *bills* will be introduced and over 1200 will be passed. A bill is a proposed law. To become a law it must be passed by the legislature and signed by the governor.

The Senate and Assembly are quite different due to size. In the Assembly, party leaders have tighter control. In the Senate, committee heads have more power.

Former Governor Rockefeller addresses a joint session of the Senate and Assembly. The Governor annually addresses the first session of the legislature.

"There ought to be a law." Every one of us has thought from time to time that the government ought to do something concerning some problems we know about. Where do our laws come from? Bills (proposed laws) may come from several places. A senator or assembly member wants a new law. He or she draws up a bill and takes it to the legislature. A member of either house may be asked to introduce a bill by the representatives of some organized group. State workers may want higher wages. Farmers may want the state to do something about certain insects that are destroying crops. A labor union may desire better safety rules in factories. Government officials think up more bills than any other group. Sometimes they want to change old laws so the laws will be more useful. The governor himself can send recommendations to the legislature. Lastly, local governments make their own laws.

In order to find out how a bill becomes a law, let us follow a particular bill through the legislature. We will select a bill to raise the salary of certain state workers. An organization of state workers has persuaded a legislator to introduce this bill. Here are the steps it must follow. The procedure in both houses of the legislature is much the same.

1. An assembly member gives the bill to the clerk in the Assembly. Bills such as this are generally introduced in both houses about the same time. To avoid a last-minute rush, both houses set a deadline after which no more bills may be introduced without leadership approval.
2. The bill is given a number and a title. In this case, the bill is identified as *A500,*

State Income and Outgo 1978–1979

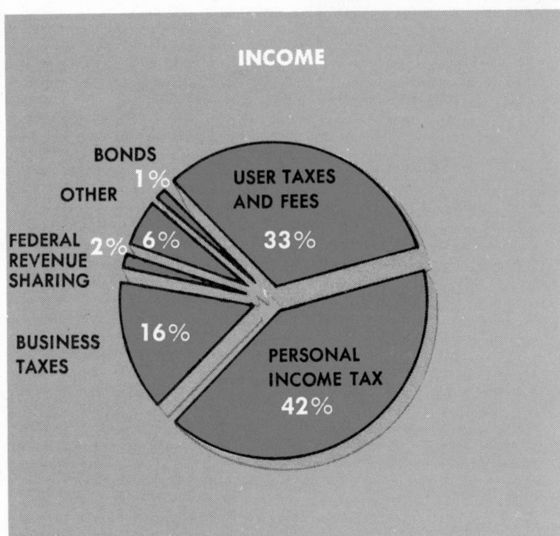

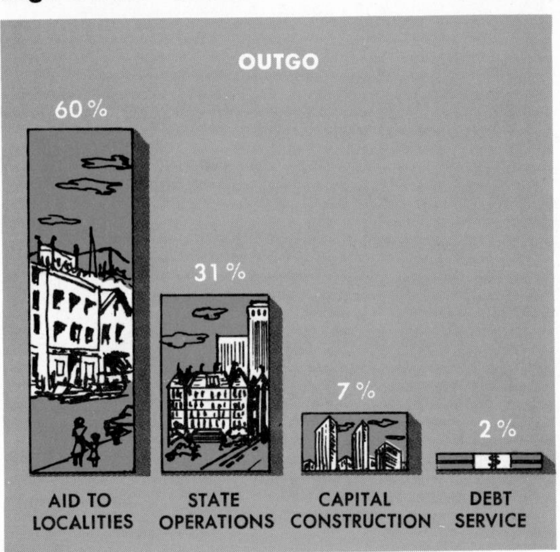

Source: State of New York Annual Budget Message 1978-1979. Hugh L. Carey, Governor.

"An Act to raise the salary of certain employees of the government of the State of New York." The "A" stands for Assembly. If it were a Senate bill, the letter "S" would be used. The bill is then turned over to one of the standing committees which handle topics from agriculture to public health. A500 is sent to the Committee on Civil Service.

3. The committee may accept the bill, change it, or let it "die in committee" [no action at all is taken on the bill]. The committee may call in experts to give their opinions on A500. The chairperson of the committee has a lot to say as to whether the bill will be approved or not. He or she has a committee member write a majority report if the bill wins approval. The committee members opposed to the bill can also write a report. In this case, A500 quickly wins approval by the Committee on Civil Service.

4. Our bill is placed on the calendar of business of the Assembly. A printed copy of the bill must be on the desks of each legislator three days before voting begins. This is to prevent a bill from being rushed through without warning.

5. A500 finally comes to a vote in the Assembly, and passes. Many bills pass unanimously and without any discussion.

A Bill Becomes Law

Organization of the Executive Branch*

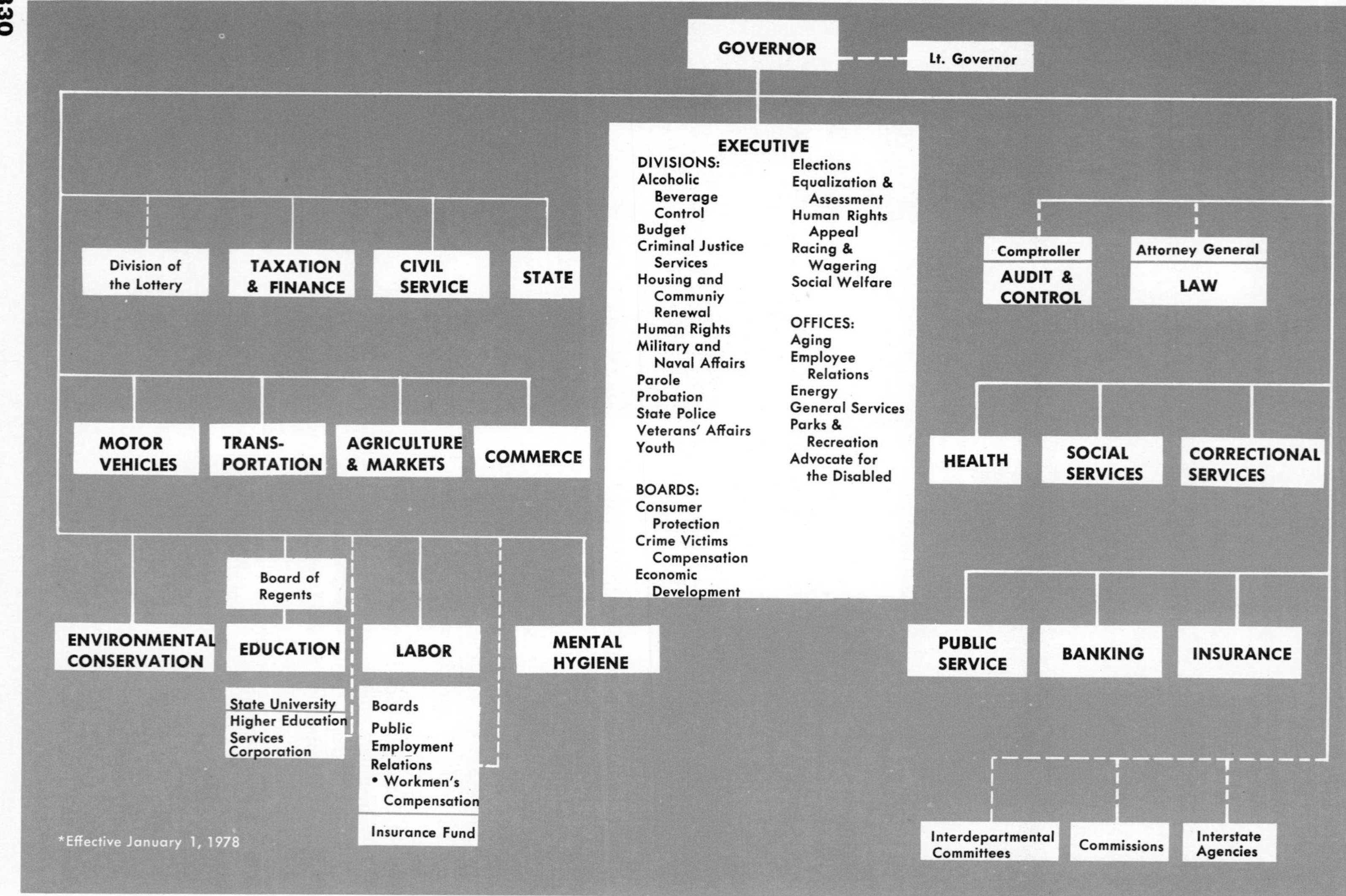

*Effective January 1, 1978

This surprises many visitors to the legislature. Normally, most bills do not deal with things about which people disagree. Besides, the real debating has already taken place in the committee meetings. Most legislators are willing to accept the recommendations of the various committees.

6. After the bill passes in the Assembly, it goes to the Senate. Here it goes through the same procedure. If there are any differences between the bills passed by the Assembly and the Senate, backers of the bills try to work out a compromise. Finally, A500 passes the Senate.

7. Next, the bill goes to the governor, who has several choices. He or she can sign the bill and make it a law. He or she can, however, veto the bill. It is then sent back to the legislature. A two-thirds vote of each house can override the veto, but this rarely happens. If the governor does not do anything about the bill for 10 days, it automatically becomes a law. There is one exception to this. The governor has 30 days to accept or veto all bills that are passed in the last 10 days of the meeting of the legislature. If he or she fails to do so, it is dead. Such a procedure is called a *pocket veto.* In this case, let us assume that the governor signs the bill.

Thus A500 is published as a law of the state of New York.

The Governor

The governor of the Empire State is an important national figure. In the twentieth century, five of our governors became candidates for the presidency: Theodore Roosevelt, Charles Evans Hughes, Alfred E. Smith, Franklin D. Roosevelt, and Thomas E. Dewey.

Once voted into office, a governor finds that the job is not an easy one. There are so many different things to do. Here are some of them:

1. *The Governor Represents the State.* He or she welcomes distinguished visitors, gives speeches to organizations, cuts ribbons to open bridges and highways. The governor also visits regions which have suffered disasters.

2. *The Governor Is the Chief Policy Maker.* He or she sends an annual message and several special messages to the legislature. One of these messages deals with the budget. It shows how the governor expects to get the money with which to run the government. It also shows how he expects to spend the money. The legislature has the right to change the budget. However, the governor can veto changes.

3. *The Governor Is an Important Legislator.* We have seen that the governor can recommend laws to the legislature. He or she can veto bills and prevent their becoming law.

4. *The Governor Defends the Public Interest.* The governor can investigate any office in both state and local governments and can put a stop to any wrong doing. He or she can even remove certain officials.

5. *The Governor Is the Leader of His Political Party.* The governor appoints many people to jobs within the state and can use these jobs to reward faithful party workers. Local political leaders listen carefully to his orders.

6. *The Governor Is Head of the Executive Department.* On page 330 is a chart that shows the 20 departments of the state government. One of these is known as the *Executive Department.* It is directly under the governor's control. The Division of the Budget, the State Police, Youth, and Human Rights are in this department. The

governor has the power to pardon prisoners. The Division of Parole in the Executive Department helps decide whether a person should be punished or pardoned.

7. *The Governor Oversees the Work of the State Departments.* The governor has considerable power over the other 19 departments as well. He or she appoints the heads of all but three of these departments. As the chart indicates, the governor has little direct control over the Department of Education. The Department of Law and the Department of Audit and Control are headed by the Attorney General and the Comptroller. Both of these officials are chosen directly in the state elections. The governor appoints the members of the Board of Public Employment Relations, chooses the head of the Department of Social Services, and appoints the commissioners who run the Departments of Civil Service and Public Service.

The Courts

Good laws are not worth much unless they are enforced and lawbreakers are punished. It is the job of the courts to see that justice is done. Most Americans go through life without ever being involved in a court case. Nevertheless, if it were not for our courts, our government could not operate.

Doubtless you have seen television plays that feature court trials. Generally, they are murder trials and are very dramatic. The work of the courts is rarely that exciting. What kinds of cases do our courts handle? Two neighbors may disagree as to where the boundary line between their property is located. Or John Smith owes Sam Jones money, but Sam cannot collect. Examples like these, in which no laws have been broken, are known as *civil cases.* Trials for violations of the law, such as murder and robbery, are *criminal cases.*

To handle the different kinds of court cases we have a number of courts with different powers. Local governments have courts of their own. Villages have a police justice, who can handle minor matters. Towns have justices of the peace, who are busy with traffic violations. Cities have city courts with varying degrees of authority. There is a county court in each of the counties outside of New York City. All of these courts operated by local governments are called *inferior courts.* Above the inferior courts are three levels of state courts. On the lowest level is the Supreme Court. The next higher court is the Appellate Division of the Supreme Court. The highest court in the state is the Court of Appeals.

The Supreme Court. Do not let the name of this court fool you. It is not the highest court in New York State, nor does it have any connection with the Supreme Court of the United States. The State Supreme Court does not meet in any one place. Actually, it is organized into eleven districts. Each district has a number of judges who are elected by the people of the district for 14 years. The sessions of the Supreme Court are usually held in the various county courthouses of the district.

The Supreme Court is the workhorse of the state court system. It generally considers cases for the first time, although sometimes it hears cases which were first tried in a lower court.

New York's System of Education

Shortly after the Revolutionary War, the legislature established the Board of Regents, which supervised colleges and private academies throughout the state. (A regent is a member of a governing board.) The legislature set up a school system which was divided into districts. Elementary schools were made free. After the Civil War, public high schools grew rapidly. Finally, early in the 1900's, the legislature placed the Board of Regents in charge of all public and private education in the state. The members of the Board of Regents appointed a Commissioner of Education to run the State Department of Education.

The Board of Regents is so powerful that it is sometimes called the fourth branch of the state government—equal to the governor, courts, and legislature. The regents have under their control over 3,000,000 students and 200,000 teachers. Its budget generally accounts for about 45 percent of all state expenses. It controls all institutions of higher education. It sets standards for over a dozen professions, such as nursing and medicine.

The Board is made up of 15 members called Regents. The Regents are chosen by the legislature for terms of 15 years. Their duties are to watch over the actions of the Commissioner of Education and to make educational plans. The Commissioner of Education helps the Board of Regents make these plans. He or she directs the work of the State Department of Education. Much

An aerial view of the State University of New York at Oneonta. The old campus is the area in the foreground. The new expansion is shown by the modern buildings in the center of the photograph.

of the work of the Education Department is supervising elementary and secondary education. This work is done by conferences, letters, and visits to schools. One office in the State Department of Education outlines social studies classwork.

The department also supervises colleges and universities besides those in the State University of New York. It gives permission for new schools to open and checks up on old ones. It also regulates most of the professions, except law. People who want to practice medicine, dentistry, nursing, pharmacy, architecture, engineering, and several other professions must pass an examination.

In 1948 the legislature put all the state schools of higher learning under a new Board of Trustees of the State University of New York. The State University included over 70 institutions which enrolled over 225,000 full-time students in 1976. It runs 14 State University Colleges—in Buffalo, Brockport, Cortland, Fredonia, Geneseo, New Paltz, Oneonta, Oswego, Plattsburgh, Old Westbury, Purchase, Empire State, Utica/Rome, and Potsdam.

The State University operates four university centers at Albany, Binghamton, Buffalo, and Stony Brook. Discovering that medical colleges were not training enough doctors, the state took over medical schools in Syracuse, Brooklyn, and Buffalo. Communities have set up about 40 community colleges where youth can study liberal arts, textiles, retail management, and other occupations. The state pays half of the construction costs and 40 percent of the operating costs of these colleges.

Almost every denomination and church have established colleges in New York. To mention a few: the Baptists founded Colgate and Rochester, while the Presbyterians sponsored Wells and Eisenhower. Over a score of Roman Catholic colleges and universities dot the state. In the Buffalo area are Niagara, Canisius, and D'Youville, and in Syracuse is LeMoyne. In the Albany area are Siena and the College of St. Rose. Manhattan, Fordham, and St. John's are perhaps the best known Catholic colleges in metropolitan New York.

The state has tried to keep independent higher education alive because of the shift of students to heavily subsidized state, city, and community colleges. In 1974 the legislature enlarged the "scholar incentive" program to provide annual grants on a sliding scale according to family income. By 1978 this amounted to a minimum of $200 to a maximum of $1,800 to approximately 350,000 students in both private and public institutions. Private colleges also get "Bundy" aid, that is a grant for each degree they award. The Regents also provided scholarships to 71,000 students with fine academic records. Private colleges have received low interest loans from the state for building dormitories.

New York City developed a fine system of free colleges. The major campuses are The University of the City of New York, Brooklyn College, Queens College, and Hunter College. These colleges have established graduate programs. The state government grants large amounts to these institutions for teacher training programs, graduate education, and other expenses. The Board of Higher Education runs two-year community colleges in each borough.

The Education Department gives general direction and supervision to our schools, but local boards of education actually run them in each district. The state also grants a great deal of money to the local school boards, which raise the rest of the school budget from local taxes. The state gives a certain minimum amount for each pupil. Poor districts get extra money for each pupil. All schools must stay open 180 days a year and must pay a certain minimum salary to each teacher.

Practically all of the old "country" one-room schoolhouses have been combined into centralized schools. There are a number of advantages to centralization: a greater variety of courses; a better program of student activities; superior buildings and equipment. Teachers can devote all their attention to one grade and to one or two subjects. The school bus makes it possible for children to attend a central school in nearly all kinds of weather.

Each city has a board of education. It is often elected by the voters, but is sometimes appointed by the mayor. The board builds and maintains school buildings, hires teachers, approves the courses taught, and buys books and equipment. It chooses a superintendent of schools, who carries out its orders. Centralized schools have a similar organization.

Emma H. Willard

"Why do girls need schooling? Their job is to raise children and do the household chores. Besides, they are not as smart as men." These views sound strange. But so many people believed them in the early 1800s that few girls could learn more than the simplest elements of reading and writing.

Emma Willard, a self-educated Connecticut schoolteacher, fought the prejudices of her day. She decided to teach "men's subjects" like mathematics, sciences, and philosophy to young women. After the New York legislature turned down her request for money, the City Council of Troy agreed in 1821 to provide her school with a building.

Troy Female Academy was different from most high schools. For example, it gave the students a large share of self-government. It encouraged young women to become teachers. Over two hundred graduates helped encourage education for women throughout the nation.

Mrs. Willard was a dynamic person looking after every detail. She wrote history and geography textbooks. She taught herself to teach science courses. She loaned thousands of dollars to needy students. She even wrote poetry. Have you ever heard her poem "Rocked in the Cradle of the Deep"?

Health, Welfare, and Correction

Perhaps the best way to understand the value of the State Department of Health is to describe one of its main activities, the fight against tuberculosis. Fifty years ago tuberculosis, called the "White Plague," was the number-one killer. It was particularly dangerous to young people, who died from it by the tens of thousands each year. In the late nineteenth century Dr. Edward Trudeau had discovered a method of treating tuberculosis. Following his lead, the State Department of Health looked for people who had tuberculosis and tried to cure them. It urged X-ray examinations for everyone. By looking at X-ray plates, doctors were able to discover the disease in its early stages. The Department of Health built seven tuberculosis hospitals. It encouraged the building of many others. The various tuberculosis hospitals offered free care to patients. Many were sent home well.

The Bronx State Hospital is for the mentally ill. The state provides many other health services for care, rehabilitation, prevention and control of disease.

Equally important was the fact that the ill people in the hospitals could no longer spread the disease to their friends and neighbors. Because of its successful programs, the state has closed all its tuberculosis hospitals.

New York's most important health problem is the care of the mentally ill and the mentally deficient. New York State has hospitals for the mentally ill, schools for the mentally deficient, and an institution for epileptics. (Epilepsy is a disease of the nervous system.)

Not until 1890 did New York State agree to take over the whole burden of the mentally-ill people who could not afford private treatment. Treatment is so costly that only a few families can afford the small private hospitals.

Since 1958, improved procedures, tranquilizing drugs, and community programs have reduced the number of patients in hospitals by over three-fourths. The state provides aid for constructing and operating community mental health centers which can offer part-time services close to the homes of mentally disabled persons.

New York has taken leadership in accepting responsibility for the care of unfortunates. The state does many things: (1) it assists people who are in need; (2) it provides services for special groups such as young people, the aged, veterans, and members of minority groups; and (3) it removes criminals from society and makes attempts to reform them.

The Department of Social Services has important duties. Its agents inspect over 1,500 institutions, including about 600 hospitals and clinics. They visit homes for children and for the aged to make sure basic standards of safety and sanitation are maintained. About 1,300,000 persons receive some kind of public assistance in New York State. Children and the mothers who care for them account for about three-fourths of this total, and about one-eighth are aged, blind, or disabled. Another small group consists of families unable to support themselves on the income they earn.

The Correctional Services Department (newly named in 1971) has redoubled its former but largely unsuccessful efforts to cut down the rate of reimprisonment. All of the 21 correctional institutions are placing emphasis on education and job training as a means of rehabilitating convicted offenders. The Attica prison riot of 1971, in which about 30 convicts were killed, shocked the public and called attention to the failure of the penal system.

New York tries to reform criminals in various ways. A judge will sometimes place a first offender on *probation* for a year or two. During that time he or she has to report to an official and keep out of trouble. It also separates youthful offenders from hardened criminals who might teach the young person dangerous habits and skills. Another method is to make the length of jail sentence depend in part on the behavior of the prisoner.

Ski jumping at Lake Placid and other Adirondack resort areas is an exciting part of the winter sports season.

The 4,000 troopers and other staff members of the State Police are responsible for patrolling the highways, investigating crimes, aiding local law enforcement officials, and operating an anti-crime system of communications.

Conservation and Recreation

During the second half of the nineteenth century a few citizens became worried about the destruction of our forests. They pointed out that roots and decaying leaves hold back rain water and thus help to prevent floods and soil erosion. They warned that New York would need trees in the future to keep alive the paper and pulp industry, not to mention the furniture industry.

In 1894 the State Constitutional Convention unanimously approved an amendment which stated that state forest preserves shall be forever kept as wild forest lands.

The state kept buying land over the years in order to enlarge the preserve. The area grew from 800,000 to over 2,270,000 acres in the Adirondacks, and from 50,000 to over 240,000 acres in the Catskills.

New York set up a College of Forestry (now at Syracuse University). The college supplies information on all kinds of forestry and forest products. It carries on research and it provides aid to woodland owners and the forest-products industries.

Forests are a natural resource which can be restored. New York has undertaken a great program of reforestation. Fire is the great enemy of the forests. New York has a fire-fighting service to protect its forests. Perhaps you have seen one of the 180 observation towers scattered throughout the forested areas.

Fish and game were hit hard by the destruction of forests, the pollution of streams, and the slaughter of wild life. Slowly the state set up agencies and passed laws designed to protect birds, fish, and game. Today nearly two million hunters, trappers, and fishermen secure licenses. The revenue from these licenses is spent improving hunting and fishing. For example, the state has 16 fish hatcheries which produce young fish for stocking various streams, rivers, and lakes.

Water pollution has become a serious problem in almost every section of the state. Under its Pure Waters Program, the state is developing plans for the protection and use of water, one of our most valuable re-

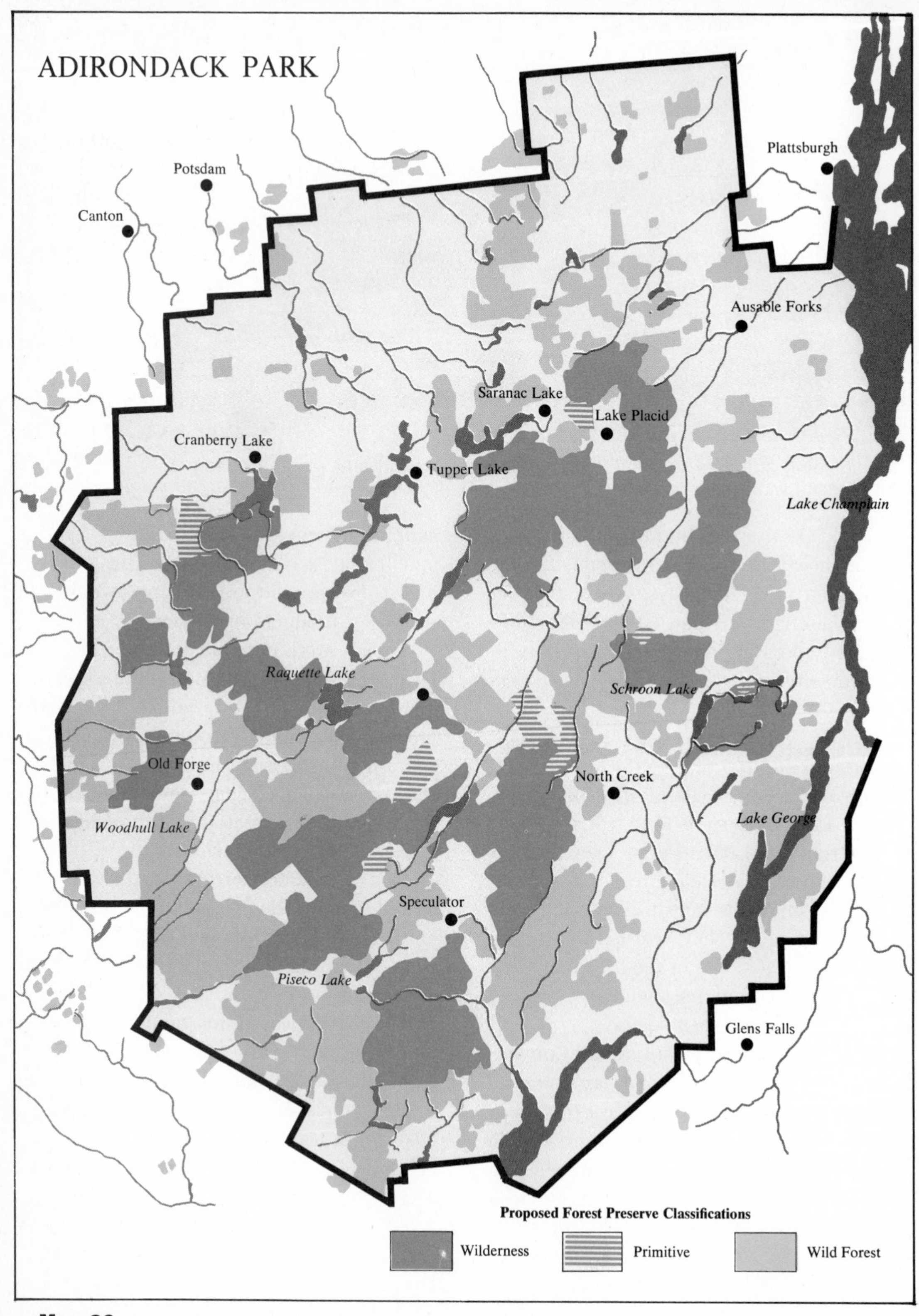
ADIRONDACK PARK
Plattsburgh
Potsdam
Canton
Ausable Forks
Saranac Lake
Lake Placid
Cranberry Lake
Tupper Lake
Lake Champlain
Raquette Lake
Schroon Lake
Old Forge
North Creek
Woodhull Lake
Lake George
Speculator
Piseco Lake
Glens Falls
Proposed Forest Preserve Classifications
Wilderness
Primitive
Wild Forest

Map 26

sources. By 1976 over 500 sewage treatment projects were completed or planned. The legislature has banned the dumping of oil and other chemical materials in the rivers. The federal clean water acts have helped to regulate discharges into navigable waters. Fish are returning to waterways such as the Hudson River and Lake Erie.

The state parks and forests of New York are almost as large as those of the other 49 states combined. The Office of Parks and Recreation, which comes under the Executive department, administers 145 state parks, including more than 238,000 acres. Adirondack Park (Map 26) is a large state-controlled forest preserve in the northeastern corner of the state. Over 50 million visitors annually enjoy camping, hiking, swimming, picnicking, tennis, golf, and winter sports. The state also gives localities up to 50 percent of the cost of developing land into city parks, historic sites, and playgrounds.

The tourist industry brings in over six billion dollars a year because of the attractions of New York City, Niagara Falls, historic sites, and scenic splendors. To promote tourism the Department of Commerce gives away more than 1,500,000 copies of *Vacation Lands —New York State.* Each New Yorker will find this booklet a wonderful introduction to the attractions of this state.

Adirondack Park

"The lands of the State, now owned or hereafter acquired, constituting the forest preserve as now fixed by law, shall be forever kept as wild forest lands. They shall not be leased, sold or exchanged, or be taken by any corporation, public or private, nor shall the timber thereon be sold, removed, or destroyed." That amendment to the State Constitution in 1894 has been called the most loved and the most hated provision in the whole document. On one side are lined the conservationists and many sports-lovers who want to keep the Adirondack and Catskill regions safe from destruction. On the other side, businesses, utilities, and other groups want to develop the resources.

In 1885 the conservationists secured a forest preserve in fifteen Adirondack and Catskill counties. At first the Adirondack preserve had about 800,000 acres, but the state kept buying more land until by 1977 the area contained 2,640,000 acres. The legislature set up the Adirondack Park Agency and in 1972 adopted a master plan for the state-owned lands.

The plan sets aside about one million acres as pure wilderness area, free from the lumbermen, developers, and other businessmen. A slightly larger area called wild forest, will permit camping, snowmobiling and other recreational activities in special areas. Corridors for utilities, highways, and other activities will be set up. The High Parks area around Mount Marcy is in the wilderness area, but hikers can follow hundreds of miles of well-kept trails.

Almost all the state lands are within the lines surrounding the Adirondack Park. About 3,400,000 acres are still owned by private individuals. The Adirondack Park Agency has the power to supervise the way these lands are developed. Does an owner have the right to mar a beautiful site with an ugly motel with neon lights flashing all night long? Will developers be allowed to buy tracts of land and erect thousands of summer homes? These are the kinds of questions the agency will have to answer.

Summary

New York's government is large and complex because over 18,000,000 citizens need many services. The constitution is long and detailed with many amendments, including a Bill of Rights that protects citizens from state and private misuse of power. It sets up three branches of government: legislative, executive, and judicial. The legislature, consisting of an Assembly and Senate, passes laws for the governor's approval or veto. The powers of the governor include the supervision of 20 departments. The court system enforces the laws and protects individual rights.

The Empire State has developed an outstanding system of education under the direction of the Board of Regents. Private agencies, notably churches, have also promoted education of excellent quality on every grade level. The state protects health through the work of the departments of Health and of Mental Hygiene. The Department of Social Services assists people in need—the aged, poor, youth, and disabled. Correctional Services is the department which tries to restore criminals to useful citizenship.

The state set up forest preserves and over 100 parks. It has begun a campaign against water pollution by forcing cities and private concerns to stop dumping sewage, oil, and chemicals into streams.

Checking the high points

1. Compare the powers granted and denied to the federal and state governments.

2. How does the state government cooperate with the federal and local governments and with other states?

3. How does the state government of this century compare with that of the first 50 years? of statehood?

4. Where do our laws originate?

5. Explain how a law is passed.

6. What are the chief duties of the governor of New York State?

7. What kinds of courts do we have in New York State?

8. What are the powers of the Board of Regents?

9. Compare public and private education in New York State.

10. How does New York aid the ill? The poor? Criminals?

11. How does New York protect its forest and water resources?

Think these over

1. Welfare is a national responsibility. Explain why you agree or disagree.

2. Control of the schools should be in the hands of the community. Why or why not?

3. The public concern over conservation should override the freedom of individuals and corporations to do as they please. Explain your answer.

4. Do you agree that it is to the state's interest to encourage private activity in education and on every level? Why?

Vocabulary building

bill
die in committee
pocket veto
calendar
civil case
criminal cases
inferior courts
regent
probation
offender
hatchery
rehabilitate

Chapter Objectives

To learn about

- the many types of local government in New York and how they operate
- the role and structure of present-day political parties in New York

chapter 24

LOCAL GOVERNMENTS and PARTY POLITICS

Role of Local Governments

In a small pioneer community the people did not need much government. They might establish a volunteer fire department and select a part-time police officer. They might donate their services to putting the main dirt road in shape in the springtime. As communities grew, the people demanded more services. They wanted paved streets, trained policemen, pure water, and other things. As a result, governments became more complicated—and more expensive to operate.

Often Americans look upon their local governments as unimportant. We may know more about the national government at Washington, D. C. than we do about our own town or city. We may know the names of New York's United States Senators, but we do not always know our town supervisors. This is unfortunate because our local governments—counties, cities, towns, and villages—affect our lives every day. It is local government that gives us our schools, regulates automobile traffic, provides police protection, and takes care of the poor. It is in local government that thousands of our citizens learn to take part in making democracy work.

Local governments are not completely independent. They are controlled by the state government and by the state constitution. However, New Yorkers believe that local communities should handle their own affairs as much as possible. For this reason the state constitution allows local communities a great deal of self-government. This self-government by local communities is called *home rule.*

One of the most important ways the state controls local governments is through the use of money. Every year the state gives hundreds of millions of dollars to local governments to help meet the cost of such things as schools and highways. To get this money, local communities must agree to meet requirements established by the state. For example, your school must be open 180 days a year to obtain state money.

Local governments are responsible for many services and activities which citizens depend upon. For example, local governments run our schools (top photograph) and provide police services (middle photograph). Citizens are given the opportunity to express their views to local government officials at public hearings as shown in the bottom photograph.

The County

In the Middle Ages the kings of England divided their realm into smaller units called counties. When the British seized New York, in 1664, they brought the county form of government with them. In 1683 the famous Charter of Liberties and Privileges divided the province into twelve counties. Ten of the original counties—Albany, Dutchess, New York, Kings, Queens, Orange, Richmond, Suffolk, Ulster, and Westchester—still exist, although their boundaries have changed in most cases. After 1777 New York set up new counties as fast as the growing state needed them.

Today, New York State has 62 counties. They vary a great deal in size and population. The largest county in area is St. Lawrence. It has 2,772 square miles and is more than twice the size of Rhode Island. Rockland County covers only 178 square miles. The five counties within New York City are even smaller than this. They can hardly be considered as real counties, however, as they have lost most of their powers to the city. Erie County, in 1970, had 1,113,491 people. Hamilton County had only 4,714.

The county government carries out state programs. For example, under the national government's social security program, the state is given the task of helping people who are over 65 years of age and who cannot take care of themselves. The state gets money for this purpose from the national government and turns it over to the counties. The counties then look after these needy people. Aid to children and help to the blind are parts of the county's job. Some health services paid for by state and national governments are administered by the county government. Several counties have established two-year colleges which are supported by taxes and from student tuition. County courts are an important part of the state court system. In addition, the counties see that the state election laws are carried out within their boundaries. Also, state law makes the county responsible for checking weights and measures. If you buy five gallons of gas, do you really get five gallons? It is the county's job to check each gasoline pump. The county is also a unit of self-government. It has its own lawmaking body, makes its own rules, and raises its own taxes.

The building and maintenance of county roads takes a good deal of money. Public health services, such as public health nurses and laboratories for identifying diseases, are becoming more important. More than two-thirds of the counties maintain mental health programs and clinics. Some of the heavily populated counties have county police forces. Some provide golf courses, swimming pools, and parks. Others have airports.

The Board of Supervisors (or Legislators) is the governing body in most New York counties. It used to be made up of one representative from each town in the county; cities were generally represented by one supervisor from each ward or district. This meant that the citizens of some towns with few people were better represented than were very populous towns. As a result of a Supreme Court decision in 1964 which called for more equal representation, many counties have changed their methods of choosing supervisors. Counties have drawn new district lines so that districts are equal in population.

Besides the board of supervisors, the voters of the county also pick certain other officials, such as county clerk, district attorney, sheriff, coroner, county judge, and treasurer. Some of these officials are not responsible to the board of supervisors, who, therefore, cannot control them.

What do these county officials do?

County Clerk. A very important official is the county clerk, whose office is filled with books of records of various kinds. Every time a house or piece of land is sold in the county, this is recorded in the clerk's office. The clerk also issues hunting and fishing licenses, marriage licenses, and automobile licenses.

District Attorney. As the most important law enforcement officer of each county, the D. A. investigates crimes or suspected crimes in the county. When cases come to trial, the D. A. *prosecutes* the accused persons in the county courts. To prosecute means to carry on a law case against someone in court. The district attorney tries to prove that the accused persons are guilty.

Sheriff. The sheriff has charge of the county jail and its prisoners. Orders that are given out by the judge of the county court are carried out by the sheriff.

Coroner. No murder mystery story would be complete without a coroner nor would a county government. The coroner's job is to investigate fatal accidents and unexplained deaths, and to decide whether a crime has been committed.

County Finance Officer. This officer collects certain taxes, pays the bills for the county, and makes up the budget.

Judges. The Surrogate's Court handles the estates of dead persons and the guardianship and property of orphans. Judges are elected in each county for 10-year terms except in New York City where the term is 14 years. The Family Court hears cases dealing with all aspects of family life except the dissolving of marriage by divorce, separation, or annulment. The Supreme Court has power to dissolve marriage. The Family Court also handles cases of juvenile delinquency. Voters elect these judges for 10-year terms except in New York City where the mayor appoints them.

Commissioner of Social Services. This is generally an elected office. The state and national governments give the county money for welfare purposes.

Health Officer. This officer provides medical clinics for persons in need of medical care. Restaurants and water systems are inspected.

County Reorganization. Erie, Oneida, Monroe, Onondaga, Schenectady, Suffolk, Nassau, and Westchester counties have reorganized their governments by establishing a single executive who is responsible for overseeing most of the county's work.

Town Government

If you do not live in a city, you are a citizen of a town. New York State has 931 towns. Some of them are near large cities and are very large themselves. For instance, Hempstead on Long Island had about 800,000 people in 1970. On the other hand, some towns in rural areas are small. Benson, in Hamilton County, had fewer than 100 residents in a recent census. Hempstead's pop-

Second-Class Town

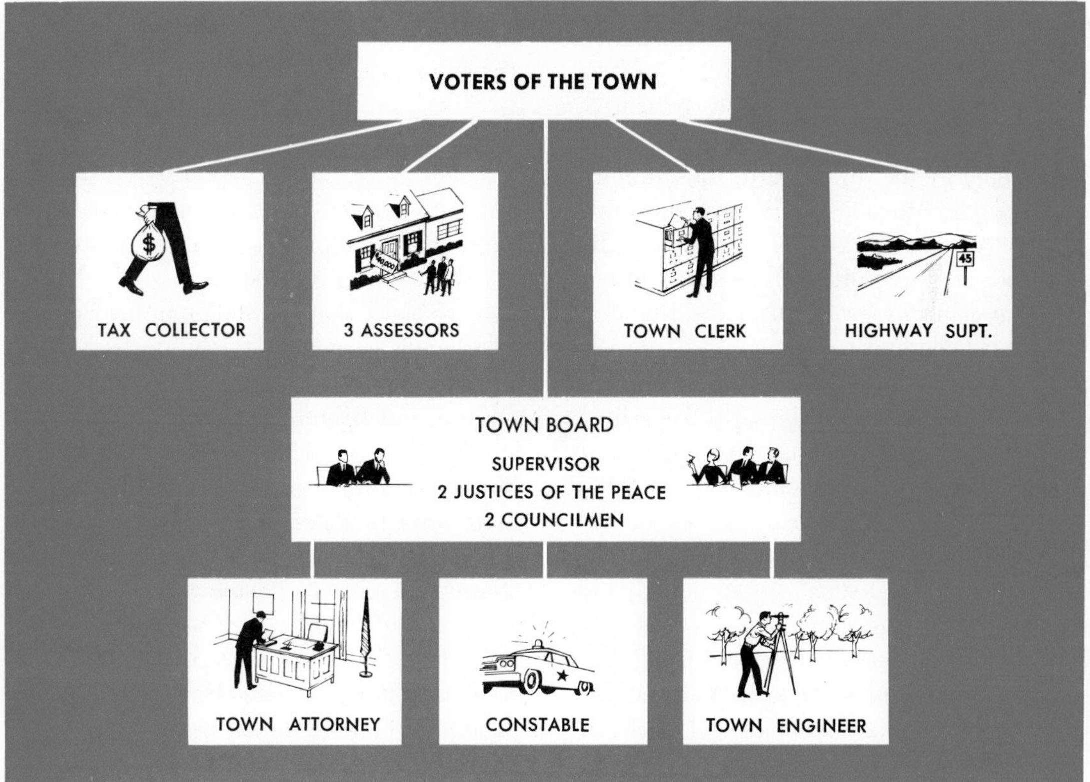

ulation was greater than those of 8 states in 1970.

New York State divides its towns into three classes—first, second, and suburban. With few exceptions, all towns over 10,000 in population are of the first class. When a town's population reaches 5,000, it may choose first class status, subject to popular referendum. In 1962 the legislature created suburban towns: any town of the first class having over 25,000 residents, or 7,500 residents within 15 miles of a city with over 100,000 people. As of 1976 all towns have the same powers.

The Town Board is the governing body. It consists of the supervisor and council members (usually two). A town clerk attends board meetings, but does not vote. In addition town voters also choose a number of other officials; a town tax collector, three assessors, and a highway superintendent.

Town governments do many things. In rural towns, building and maintaining roads is an important function. Such towns generally spend more than half their money doing these things. They may build drainage and flood control facilities. They may buy and install traffic control equipment, light the streets, provide health services, and *zone the town.* This means that the town board may set up districts or zones where only certain kinds of buildings can be constructed. In one part of town only homes can be built. In another part, stores and factories are permitted.

The *supervisor* is the key person who chairs the town board and is its most important member. When the board decides to do something, it is the supervisor who sees that it is done. He or she acts as treasurer, pays salaries, and sells town property when so directed by the town board. Close familiarity with day-to-day problems of the town helps supervisors guide the decisions of the town board. Quite often he or she is also a key figure in the local unit of the Republican or Democratic party.

The two *councilmen*, or *councilwomen*, are members of the town board. They help the board reach decisions. The *justices of the peace* serve on the board, but also take care of minor law cases. Justices of the peace find that most of their cases concern traffic violations, such as speeding and going through red lights.

The *town clerk* is a particularly important official, acting as secretary of the town board meetings and keeping all sorts of town records. Various kinds of licenses, such as marriage, hunting, and dog licenses are issued by the town clerk. The *superintendent of highways* has charge of the maintenance and construction of town roads. The *tax collector* receives town and county taxes which are paid over to the town supervisor and the county treasurer. The *assessors* have the very difficult job of putting a value on each piece of *real property* in the town. Real property includes buildings and land. It does not include such things as furniture, automobiles, and jewelry. These are known as personal property.

Sometimes people in one part of a town want special services which the town government does not provide. For example, they may want a water system, fire protection, sewers. If enough people want these things, they can ask the town board to set up a special district and arrange for the taxation of the people who will benefit by the improvement.

Village Government

Village governments are set up so people in smaller settlements can secure certain services. Generally, people organize a village because they want better fire, police, and health protection. They also may want a water system, a sewage system, paved streets, and street lighting. To obtain these things they ask the state to *incorporate* them as a village, that is, to put them under the state laws that deal with villages. When a village is established, the people living in it are still citizens of the town. They pay taxes to the town as well as to the village.

Villages in New York vary greatly in size and population. Dering Harbor on Shelter Island in Suffolk County had only 13 people in 1970. The village of Valley Stream in the town of Hempstead in Nassau County numbers over 40,000 citizens. The state law classifies villages according to their population. Larger communities may have better services but this does not determine class.

First class	5000 or more population
Second class	3000 or more
Third class	1000 or more
Fourth class	less than 1000 population

First-class villages have more powers than the rest. There are only minor differences among the other classes.

Every village has an elected *mayor* and a *board of trustees.* The board, numbering from two to six members, makes the laws. The mayor is the chief executive of the

"Justice's Court in the Backwoods" is a painting done in 1850.

village and carries out the laws, which are called ordinances. The board controls such things as the water system, public markets, parks, playgrounds, sewage system, street lighting, garbage disposal, and fire protection. The board of trustees appoints certain officials such as a *clerk, treasurer, street commissioner,* and *police.* The *police justice* who deals with minor misdeeds within the village is usually elected.

City Governments

Cities are very important in New York State, because one out of two of our citizens live in them. Most of New York's 62 cities are located in the belt stretching from New York to Albany, and then westward to Buffalo.

Cities must provide fire and police protection, streets, and street lighting. Water supply and sewage disposal are necessities. All cities regulate buses and some actually operate buses and airports. New York City owns and operates a subway system. Some have public parks and playgrounds, swimming pools, museums, libraries, colleges.

Within the last twenty years, many upstate cities have lost several functions—such as health, welfare, airports—to county government. City governments differ more than any other kind of local government. Cities are set up by the state legislature. In the early days of our state, each city was treated individually by the legislature, and many different kinds of city governments were permitted.

The most common type of city govern-

Mayor—Council

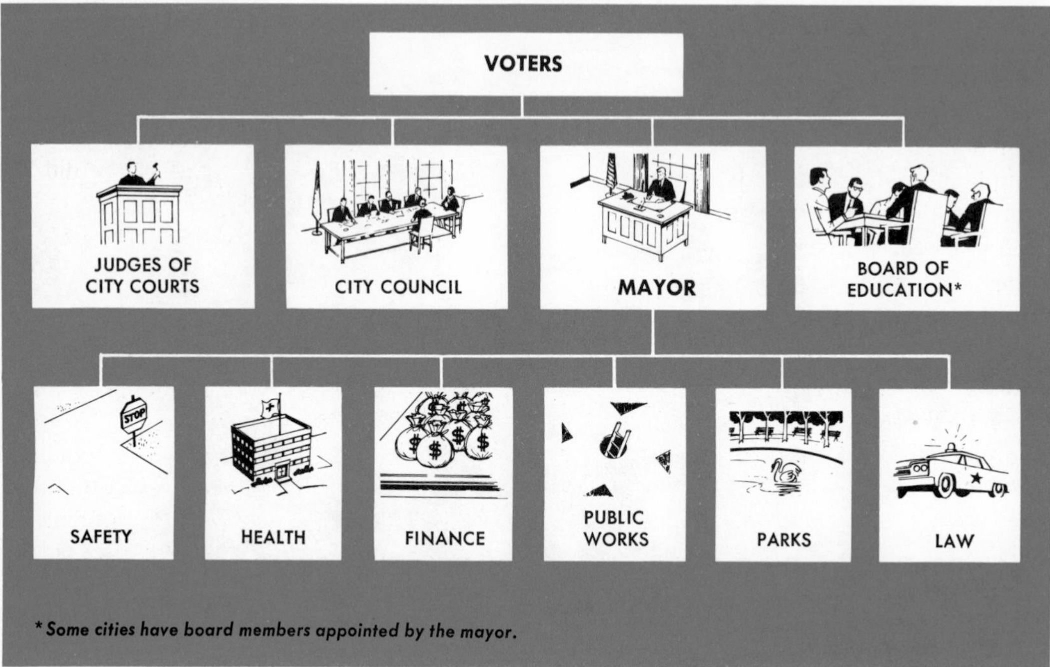

ment by far is the *mayor-council plan* of city government. Although the details will vary in different cities, this is about the way it operates: The city is divided into wards or districts. The voters in each ward elect a representative to the city council. These representatives are called either councilmen or councilwomen. The city council is the legislative body of the city and makes the laws. The mayor is chosen by the voters of the entire city and is the chief executive of the city. The mayor may or may not have the power to veto acts of the council, but has the responsibility to see that the various departments of the city, such as the police department, fire department, and the department of public works do their jobs. The mayor appoints the heads of the departments and holds them responsible for seeing that the work is done right.

In New York State our local governments get most of their money from a tax on real property—that is, buildings and land. Many cities and counties have a sales tax; they collect a few cents per dollar on articles sold

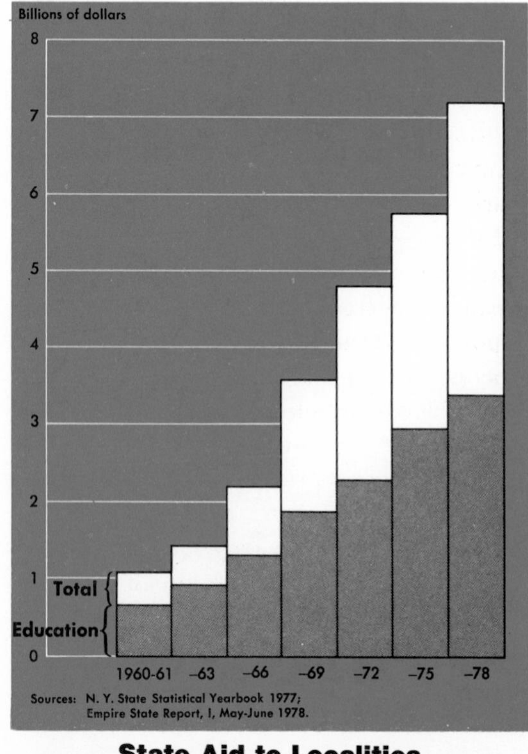

State Aid to Localities

within their area. The second largest source of income is money from the state. For example, the state pays each of the more than 9,000 local governments a certain amount for every person living within its borders. It grants money to support highways, schools, public health programs, and old age assistance. The federal government makes grants for law enforcement, community action programs, urban renewal, and unemployment programs.

Role of Political Parties

Early in our history we found that groups of people with the same interests naturally banded together to try to elect their candidates to office. These groups gradually became political parties.

In the United States today we have what is known as a *two-party* system, although we have many more than two political parties. We have Republican, Democratic, Liberal, Conservative, and other parties. But the Republican and Democratic parties are by far the largest. Their candidates win nearly all our elections.

In state-wide elections, New York State voters find on the voting machine the names of candidates from each political party—the Republican, Democratic, Conservative, and Liberal. Most Conservatives live upstate and party leaders sometimes endorse Republican candidates. Most Liberals live in New York City and this party often supports the Democratic ticket. New York City normally votes Democratic, while upstaters usually back Republicans. In order to get the names of its candidates printed in a voting machine, a political party must have received at least 50,000 votes in the last election for governor.

What do political parties do?

1. They provide a handy way for selecting candidates for public office. If we did not have political parties, how would we choose our candidates for the Presidency or for the governorship of the state—or for other offices?
2. Parties give the people a choice about how the government will be run. Each party draws up a program, called a *platform,* which it hopes will appeal to most of the voters. On some "planks" (points in platform) the parties may agree; on others they set forth widely different attitudes.
3. Parties keep a watchful eye on our government officials. The party which wins the election operates the government. The defeated party is on the alert to see that the administration gives us honest and efficient government.
4. Parties may help unite the community. If a party expects to win, it must appeal to different groups of people. It cannot offend any large group of voters. For example, it must have something to offer downstaters and upstaters. It must not overlook farm, labor, or business groups. If it does, they may vote for the other party's candidates. Frequently, party leaders "balance the ticket," that is, they put up as candidates for office members of different religious or racial groups. The idea is to convince each group that its interests are being considered.

Party Organization

It is easy to join one of the major political parties. You do not have to be initiated or pay dues. You do not get a membership card. At the time a person *registers* to be allowed to vote, a blank is signed indicating the choice of party. To vote, a person must register; but an eligible voter does not need to register very often in New York State.

At the proper time, the person appears at the local voting place and answers a few simple questions. A small card is then given which is proof of registration. The person can then vote in all general elections as long as he or she lives at the same address, or votes at least once in every two years. If the voter moves, or fails to vote once in two years, registration must be repeated.

About six out of ten voters enroll in—or join—a political party. Enrollment has one great advantage: party members may help choose the party's candidates for office and the officials who help run the party. Many of the candidates are chosen at party elections called *primaries,* at which only party members can vote. These are held in the fall before the regular election. An enrolled member goes to the regular voting place and receives a ballot of a color that represents the party. The voter marks the vote on the ballot and turns it in. The winners of the primary elections are the political party's candidates for office in the November election. Party officials are chosen at the primaries. To get one's name printed on a primary ballot, a candidate must obtain the signatures of a certain number of party members who want the person to run for office. The list of names for the candidate is known as a *petition.* The number of signatures needed varies according to the particular office the candidate is seeking. Independent candidates, not associated with any party, can place their names on a ballot by petition.

Only party members can help choose the people who run for office as party candidates. Only party members can select the officials who help run the political party. If political parties are to be strong, honest, and efficient, they need the active support of all their members.

A growing number of people, called independents, do not join parties. They feel they can do more good by supporting the best men put up by the various political parties. Sometimes they split their ticket by picking some candidates from one party and some from another.

To be able to vote in New York a person must

1. Be a citizen of the United States.
2. Be 18 years of age or older.
3. Be a resident of New York State for at least 30 days.
4. Be a resident of the county for at least 30 days.
5. Be properly registered.

How does a typical citizen, John Johnson, go about voting? First, he goes to the voting place in his neighborhood. Here an election official asks him his name and checks it against the Registration Book. John is then free to enter the voting booth and vote. Even though John may be registered or enrolled as a Republican, a Democrat, or an independent, he can vote any way he wishes.

Voters who have good reason to be absent on Election Day can receive a special absentee ballot. They can vote by mail.

When many Americans see the word "politician" they think of a fat, cigar-smoking, not-too-honest individual, who is shaking peoples' hands and kissing their babies. They probably have someone like Boss Tweed in mind. The politicians who fit this description are rare indeed. Most politicians are hardworking people who seek to improve the nation, state, and local community. They try to get good platforms, able candidates, and enough votes to carry

Cleaning Up the Hudson

Like most of the nation's waterways, the Hudson River had been growing dirtier and dirtier ever since towns and factories first appeared on its banks. In 1965 New York City alone discharged about 1.3 billion gallons of raw sewage into the river. Factories dumped wastes directly into the stream. The Hudson was becoming an open sewer.

Fish—striped bass, sturgeon, herring, white perch—became scarce. Shad, an important commercial fish, nearly disappeared. Few persons were foolhardy enough to go swimming in the Hudson.

In 1965 voters approved a one billion dollar bond issue intended to purify the state's waterways. A U.S. District Attorney began to enforce an old law prohibiting the dumping of wastes in navigable waters. The state legislators, hearing the complaints of citizens, required factories to clean up their wastes before passing them into the river. Cities and towns received state and federal loans enabling them to build sewage treatment plants.

Slowly the river water has been getting cleaner. The best evidence is the return of many varieties of fish. The state, however, regulates fishing strictly. No fish can be caught *except* shad and bait fish. The reason is the presence of a pollutant in the water called PCB, a chemical compound that can cause cancer in rats and possibly in humans.

An old fisherman declared, "I've seen this river die and now I'm seeing it come back." Let us hope he is right.

out their program. Boss Tweed was one kind of politician. Theodore Roosevelt, Al Smith, Thomas Dewey, and Franklin Roosevelt represented quite a different kind.

American political parties are not highly organized. They do have certain officers whose job it is to keep the party strong enough to win the next election. The most important organization in keeping a political party strong is the county committee.

The smallest political unit in the state is called an election district. It generally covers a fairly small area, yet large enough to include seven or eight hundred voters. Two members (usually a man and a woman) from each district are chosen in the primaries to represent the district on the county committee of the political party. These people are the foot soldiers of the party. They try to build up their party by helping the voters of their district. On Election Day they must try to get all of their party members to vote. These members of the county committee meet together and choose a chairperson. He or she is known as the *county chairperson* of the party and is usually the most important party official in the county. This person, more than anyone, is responsible for the strength of the political party in the county.

The cities of the state may have a more complicated system of organization than the counties. They generally have city committees to run the affairs of the party. In New

York City, however, the parties have clubs in every assembly district instead of a city committee.

At the state level, each party has a *state committee*, which is made up of two members (a man and a woman) from each of New York's assembly districts. This group names a state leader to run the party. He or she raises money for campaigns and helps choose candidates for office. This person also recommends people for jobs with the state government.

Elections for governor are apt to be exciting affairs. The parties do their best to win. Their candidates travel up and down the state, giving speeches and appearing on television and radio. They may eat yards of hot dogs at political party picnics. Sometimes, in the heat of a campaign, the candidates make bitter remarks about each other. It takes a strong man or woman to stand the strain of running for public office. It takes a lot of money, too, to support all this activity and required publicity.

Where does the money come from? The money comes from wealthy people, office-holders who want to keep their jobs, unions, corporations, and loyal party members. Do these people expect something in return for their money? Sometimes they do. There is a danger that campaign contributions might be used as bribes. For example, a gambling ring might give money to a party in return for loose enforcement of the laws against gambling. A state office holder might be forced to contribute on threat of losing his or her job.

To prevent this sort of thing, the state legislature requires all candidates to publish a list of their campaign expenses 10 days before the election. The state also sets a limit to the amount of money a person may spend in running for office. Unfortunately, these laws are poorly enforced. As a result rich people enjoy a great advantage in seeking high office.

Elections may be close. In 1954 Averell Harriman defeated Irving Ives for governor by only 11,000 votes out of a total of 5,000,000 votes. It was so close that election boards were required to go over their figures again.

Despite the importance of voting, many Americans do not take the trouble to secure information about political questions and to vote in party primaries and elections. Sometimes less than half of the eligible voters of the country cast their ballots in Presidential elections. No one has much

The Organization of Political Parties

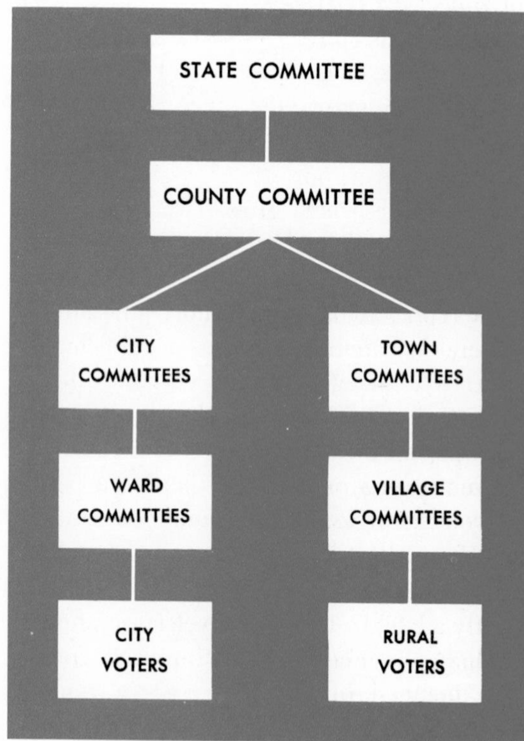

right to complain about the government, laws, or taxes if he or she does not vote regularly. Our form of government works best when all the people of the nation express their opinions at the polls.

Summary

Local government—county, town, village, city—affects each of us every day of our lives. Local governments are not completely independent because they are set up by the state.

All New Yorkers live in one of our 62 counties, although the five counties of New York City have lost almost all of their powers. The county has two functions: to carry out state programs and to govern itself. The most important governing body is the board of supervisors or legislators. A town board handles many duties, especially those concerning highways. Smaller settlements set up a village government with a mayor and a board of trustees. About one half of New Yorkers live in one of 62 cities where the mayor-council form of government is most commonly used.

The two-party system is the pattern in New York, although the Conservative and Liberal parties sometimes challenge the chief parties, the Republican and Democratic. Parties select candidates for office and perform many other functions. Most citizens join a party and thus have the right to vote in primaries. Parties have committees from the village to the state level. Campaigns are sometimes exciting but always costly affairs, a fact which gives rich people undue influence. In 1971 the voting age was lowered to 18. Each citizen has the obligation to vote in order to make our democracy truly representative of the wishes of the people.

Checking the high points

1. What are the relations between the state and local governments?

2. What are the chief functions of our counties?

3. List five county officials and the duties of each.

4. How does town government operate?

5. What are the main officials of city government?

6. What are the main sources of revenue for local governments?

7. How are political parties organized?

8. What steps does one take to vote in a primary? In an election?

9. What are the requirements for voting?

Think these over

1. Thomas Jefferson once said, "That government is best which governs least." Was he right for his time? For ours?

2. We get the kind of government we deserve. Comment.

3. We should fine people who fail to vote. Do you agree or disagree? Why?

4. True or false: Third parties do more harm than good. Explain your answer.

Vocabulary building

home rule
incorporate
ballot
zone
enrollment
candidate
election district
registration
two-party system
independent voter

Chapter Objectives

To learn about

- the importance of New York City as our nation's business, financial, and cultural center
- the organization of New York City government and the many services it provides

chapter 25

NEW YORK: The EMPIRE CITY

Economic and Cultural Capital

Few people can regard New York City with indifference. Each day thousands of its citizens complain about it but then come to its defense if an outsider starts to criticize their home city. Millions of visitors approach New York with a mixture of awe and disgust. Observers in almost every generation have declared the city unlivable and ungovernable. Somehow or other the metropolis has survived the sneers of its enemies and the fears of its friends.

One finds it hard to describe the city in terms other than "greatest" and other superlatives. Clearly it is the business, commercial, financial, and communication capital of America. Over a hundred supercorporations have made it their headquarters. Yet the city is also the home of more small industries and businesses than any other community. In 1975 the five largest industries which employed the most

Communities Joined to Form Greater New York City in 1898

Present Borough Name	*County Name*	*Location*
Manhattan	New York County	Manhattan Island
Brooklyn	Kings County	Long Island
Queens	Queens County	Long Island
Bronx	Bronx County	Mainland
Richmond	Richmond County	Staten Island

It is easy to confuse the names for various sections of Greater New York City. The city is made up of five boroughs. Each of the boroughs has the same boundary as a county. The Borough of Richmond includes all of Staten Island. The map of Greater New York City (Map 28) may help you to understand the meaning of the various names.

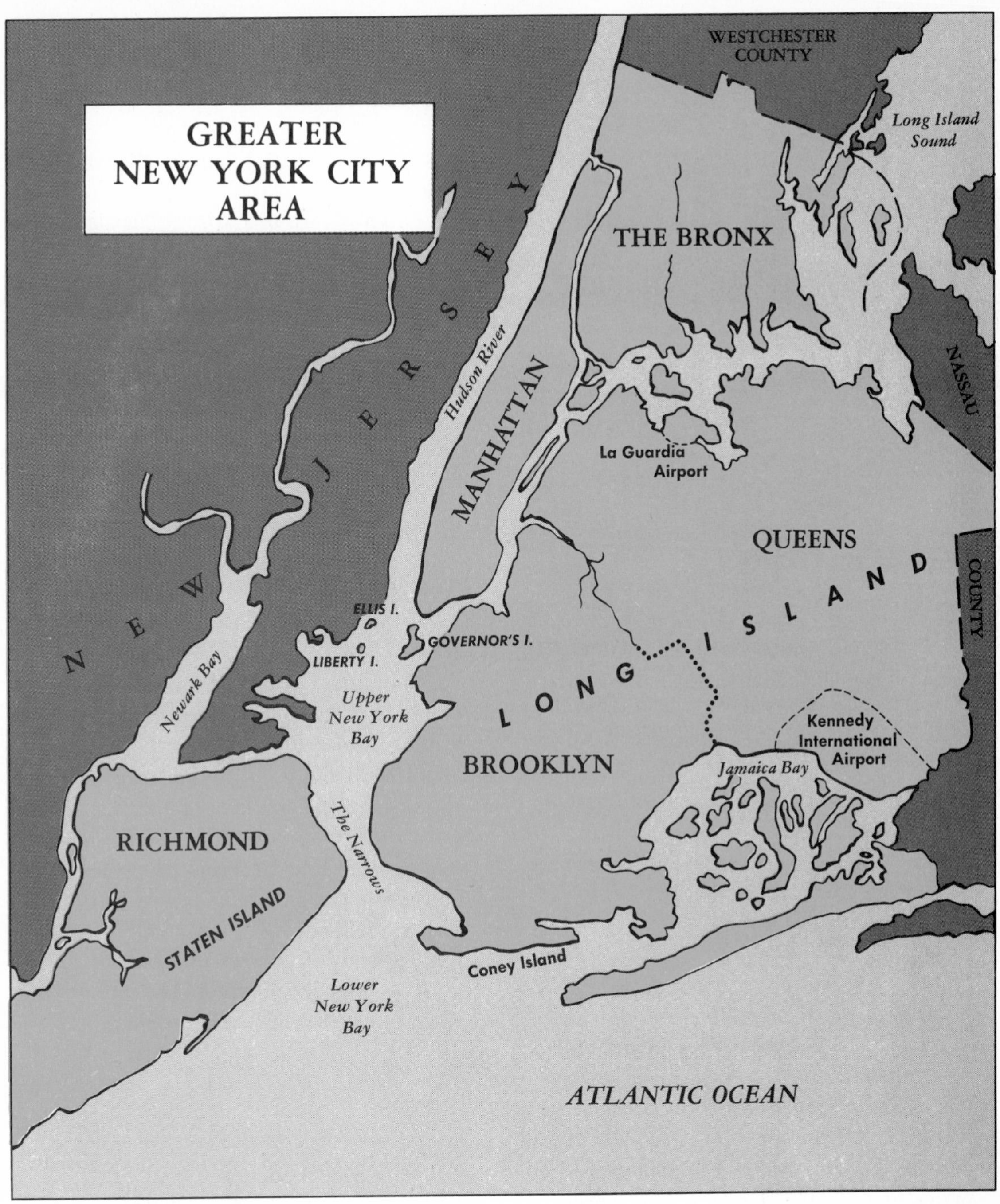

Map 27

workers were in order: printing and publishing, clothing, food processing, electrical machinery, and chemicals. In New York and its suburbs is the largest work force with the most varied skills in the country. Metropolitan New York with its high income is the top market in the country.

New York is a transportation turntable with air, sea, highway, and railroad connections with all parts of the country. It is also the cultural, entertainment, recreational, and sports center of the country. Few per-

Downtown Manhattan in 1883. The activity and crowds of people remain today. In what ways is this scene different now?

sons have ever visited even half the museums, music halls, theaters (about 75), night clubs, or sports arenas in New York.

Greater New York

Shots rang out on a day in 1903 while shoppers walked briskly up and down Park Avenue. A small group of shocked onlookers gathered round the slumped figure of an old man shot down by an insane gunman. On the ground lay Andrew Haswell Green, the civic leader who had earned the name of Father of Greater New York.

Since the Civil War, Green had dreamed about and worked for a better New York. He fought to secure and to protect Central Park, a splendid island of trees and grass in the heart of the city. As early as 1868 he called for a great metropolis that combined all the nearby urban centers. Green pushed the construction of the Brooklyn Bridge because it would link New York and Brooklyn. In 1890 the state legislature established a commission to study the question, and for a chairman they appointed Green. Four years later a small majority of the voters in the metropolitan region—Manhattan, Brooklyn, Queens, Staten Island, and parts of Westchester County—approved consolidation. For the next two years confusion marked the battle over consolidation, until Republican boss Tom Platt threw his weight behind the proposal. The legislature finally agreed to set up Greater New York on January 1, 1898.

Population

At the time Greater New York City was created, it had a population of over three million. Today this population has grown to about eight million. The table on this page shows how the number of inhabitants has grown over the years. The table shows us that in the 20-year period between 1910 and 1930 the city gained over two million people. After 1930 New York City grew more slowly. One reason for the slower increase was that Congress passed laws limiting immigration. During the 1950's the

Population of Greater New York City

Year	*Number of Inhabitants*
1910	4,766,883
1920	5,620,048
1930	6,930,446
1940	7,454,995
1950	7,891,957
1960	7,781,984
1970	7,895,563
1976	7,453,600*

*U.S. Census projections

The opening of the Brooklyn Bridge on the New York side. The opening of this bridge in 1883 linked Manhattan and Brooklyn for the first time.

city lost over 100,000 people. During the 1970s, declining birth rates and migration to the suburbs cut the city's population by about a half million.

As you read earlier, New York throughout its history has attracted a large number of foreign-born people. New Yorkers of European birth or parentage fell sharply in the 1960's, while those of foreign descent from the Caribbean and South America more than doubled. This latter group does not include the city's 870,000 Puerto Ricans, who are American citizens.

New York had in 1976 about 1,900,000 black residents, the largest concentration in the United States. About 26 percent of the city's population is black, a lower percentage than that of Newark, Baltimore, Washington, Philadelphia, Chicago, or Cleveland. Roughly one-fourth of the residents of Manhattan, the Bronx, and Brooklyn are black.

Some people claim that New York City life has been relatively good for black people, especially when compared with the life of a sharecropper in the South. Blacks can now earn higher wages and achieve a better health standard and, in some cases, better housing. For many the change has happened at a painfully slow rate. The recession and cutbacks in municipal jobs have led to high unemployment, especially among young blacks without strong education and skills.

Headquarters of the United Nations

In 1946 the United Nations decided to establish its headquarters on Manhattan Island. About 17 acres along the East River between 42nd and 48th Streets were set aside for this purpose. On this site where fierce fights took place between the British and Americans during the Revolutionary War and where the American patriot, Captain Nathan Hale, was hanged, the nations of the world have established a meeting place. Here is the glass-walled Secretariat building, where the employees of the United Nations work under the direction of the Secretary General. Here also is the assembly hall in which the delegates from the member countries discuss ways of keeping peace in the world and of helping poorer countries develop their resources.

The city is a convenient place for the representatives of all nations. It has excel-

The headquarters of the United Nations. The 39-story Secretariat, the Library in the foreground, and the General Assembly comprise in effect the capital of most of the world.

lent communications, which enable delegates to keep in touch with their home countries. Transportation connections are good, making it possible for delegates to travel to and from their homelands swiftly and comfortably. It is fitting that New York City should have been chosen as the home of the United Nations, because here millions of people of all races and creeds have learned to live together.

Mayor and the Council

In 1963 New York City received a revised charter which continued the former mayor-council type of city government. The mayor, whose powers were increased, remains the chief officer directing the many departments of city government.

The 37-member City Council passes local laws, checks budget items, and investigates matters affecting the city. Each councilmember is concerned with the improvement of his district: paved streets, better sewer systems, adequate street lighting, and more police protection.

National Origins in New York City, 1970

National Origin	*Foreign Born*	*Born in U.S. of Foreign-born Parentage*
Italy	212,000	470,500
Caribbean, Central and South America (except Cuba)	258,400	109,000
Soviet Union	117,400	277,000
Poland	119,600	173,000
Ireland	68,800	151,800
Germany	98,300	111,700
Austria	48,000	98,000
United Kingdom	48,800	67,500
Cuba	63,000	21,000
Hungary	31,700	40,400
Greece	35,000	28,500
China	37,300	18,900

Local Officials Elected Within the Boundaries of New York City

COUNTY OFFICIALS	
District Attorney Surrogate Court Judge	Elected on a county-wide basis. Counties have the same geographical limits as boroughs in the City of New York.
CITY OFFICIALS	
Mayor President of City Council Comptroller	Elected on a city-wide basis.
Borough Presidents	Elected on a borough-wide basis.
City Council Members	Each borough elects two members-at-large. Each state senatorial district elects one city council member. There are the following senatorial districts: Manhattan 6 Bronx 5 Brooklyn 9 Queens 6 Richmond 1

The Board of Estimate, a body not found in many cities, helps make the budget and plans for the development of the metropolis. Its members include three city officials (each with four votes) who are elected on a city-wide basis. They are the mayor, the controller, and the president of the City Council. The five borough presidents are also members but have only two votes each.

The counties or boroughs have lost almost all their functions. Citizens do vote for a Borough President who works with a board made up of the city councilmembers elected in that borough. This board discusses matters in its borough which require some agreement before taking them to the City Council. The district attorney, whose main task is to protect the public from criminals, is the most important remaining county official. Probably the busiest law office in the country is that of the district attorney of New York county. The responsibilities are immense, and several men—for example, Thomas E. Dewey—have won a national reputation holding this position.

Being mayor of New York is probably the toughest job in the country with the exception of the Presidency. The mayor appoints the heads of the Fire, Police, Health, Parks, Sanitation, and other departments. In addition he or she shares with the Council the power to appoint hundreds of officials, such as the judges of the criminal courts. He or she can veto or approve the acts passed by the City Council. The mayor is almost always an important party leader who must keep in touch with other party leaders. Because of its importance as a business and cultural center, New York City expects its mayor to welcome distinguished visitors. During the past 10 years the mayor has spent much time in Albany and Washington seeking funds to carry out city programs.

Money shortage is a constant problem for city officials. The city budget has climbed even faster and higher than the state budget. The bulk of the money goes into salaries for teachers, police, firemen, and other civil servants, who now have strong unions. The city has about one-eighth of its people on welfare and spends well over a billion dollars a year for their care. These rising costs have forced city fathers to levy taxes wherever they can find money. The Council collects a sales tax; and a tax on amusements, cigarettes, and liquor. A wage tax is placed on salaries, even of people who work in the city but live outside. The city has tried to raise money by operating a system of off-track betting. In the past 100 years, mayors of New York City have complained that the state government has taken much more out of the city through the state income, corpo-

Fiorello H. LaGuardia (1882–1947)

Cowboys, Indians, and soldiers were everyday sights to young La Guardia. Although he was born in New York City, his family soon moved to Prescott, Arizona, where the boy grew up on a frontier army post. Fiorello La Guardia was a gifted person. He was skilled in music and spoke several languages. In 1907 he became an interpreter at Ellis Island in New York Harbor. Here he helped immigrants by translating their speech into English. At night he studied law, and in 1912 he became a lawyer. Four years later he ran for the United States House of Representatives on the Republican ticket. Political bigwigs were surprised when he won the election in a district which usually gave the Democrats a large majority.

The new congressman quickly demonstrated his willingness to fight for what he believed to be right. He urged that women be given the right to vote. He called for the entrance of the United States into World War I and supported the draft law. He enlisted in the armed forces and was made commander of a bomber squadron. His plane was hit by gunfire on several occasions. Twice he was injured when his aircraft crash-landed after bombing the enemy.

When the war ended, La Guardia returned to Congress. Here he fought for the League of Nations and for laws protecting the rights of laboring men. Always a fierce fighter, he quarreled with the Republican leaders in New York City and became a political independent. From 1934 through 1945 La Guardia was Mayor of New York City. Able men were appointed to high office without regard to their political party. The finances of the city were put in order. A vast program of slum clearance and park building began. The people's confidence in the city government returned.

New Yorkers loved their mayor, whom they often called "The Little Flower" or "Butch." La Guardia, whose background was Jewish and Italian, was of the Episcopal faith. He knew what it was like to be poor, and he forcefully defended the rights of ordinary citizens without regard to race, creed, or color. Often his actions delighted the people. He expertly conducted the combined Police and Sanitation Department bands at Carnegie Hall before a packed house. He raced to fires wearing a fireman's hat. When a strike halted the printing of newspapers, he read the comics over the radio to the children of the city.

La Guardia is generally regarded as the best mayor New York ever had. He appealed to the vast majority of the citizens of the entire area.

ration, and sales taxes than it gave back in the form of state aid. Recently the state government has returned more money to the city budget by paying for part of the cost of the City University.

City Services

The public schools, with over a million students and more than 50,000 teachers, are a good example of a city service. The schools carry out the century-old task of teaching the basic skills of reading, writing, and arithmetic. In 1977 over 60 percent of New York City's students were blacks or Puerto Ricans. To make easier the task of helping Puerto Ricans adjust to city life, the Board of Education has hired hundreds of Spanish-speaking teachers. Black teachers, too, are becoming more numerous in the teaching profession. Some tension has arisen in the school system because the great majority of teachers are white, and some blacks have demanded more control of the schools in black communities.

Private schools educate tens of thousands of students at practically no expense to the taxpayer. During the last few years the number of students in parochial schools has declined for a variety of reasons, including steeply rising costs. The state of New York has granted these schools some aid for buses, health care, and textbooks.

The papers are full of the problems of the schools: crime, drugs, dropouts, and vandalism. What is sometimes forgotten is that New York schools produce students who consistently win a higher-than-average number of awards and scholarships. The Bronx High School of Science, for example, has hundreds of graduates in *Who's Who in America.*

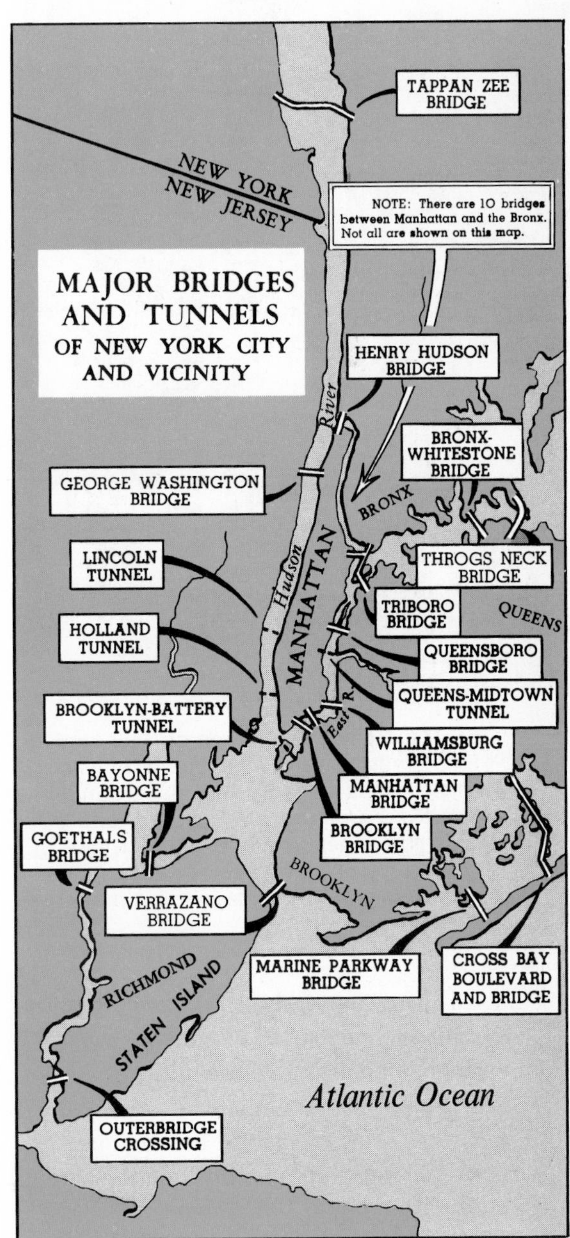

Map 28

Graduates of the City University of New York (City College of New York, Brooklyn, Queens, Hunter, and other units) have provided an exceptionally high percentage of the nation's university professors and scien-

One of the enjoyable duties of New York's Finest. The Official Directory lists over 21 pages of parks and playgrounds in the five boroughs, but children tend to play in the streets close to home. Play streets, supervised by PAL, help keep children safe and provide wholesome activities.

tists. During the early 1970s City University offered "open admissions," whereby any high school graduate could attend one of its units. Then the financial crisis forced CUNY in 1976 to charge tuition. This reduced the upsurge in enrollments among blacks and whites.

New York City has a good health record, not an easy achievement considering that thousands of strangers pass through the city each day and dozens of ships enter the port each week. At its best, medical care in the city is superb. The city hospitals, however, suffer from lack of skilled staff, overcrowding, and inefficiency. Mayor Lindsay in 1965 called the conditions in the 20 municipal hospitals a "disgrace."

The Department of Health watches over the city's food by inspecting restaurants, stores, dairies, and markets. A department of Air Pollution Control has taken only the first steps to fight smog. It has banned the burning of certain fuels, such as oil with a high sulphur content, and it has required the owners of buildings to install more efficient incinerators.

The Fire Department has a fine record in fighting fires. Most of its work is not the spectacular heroics of rescuing people from burning buildings but the dull task of fire prevention. Each year hundreds of thousands of inspections are made of basements, attics, and elevator shafts in order to prevent dangerous conditions.

The 32,000 men and women of the Police Department form an army larger than that of many countries. The department has scores of duties, including the regulation of traffic. Police patrol the city day and night, on foot, on horseback, on motorcycles, in automobiles, and even in boats and airplanes. Every cop on a beat now has a two-way radio.

Crime is a growing problem, although New York ranked seventh in 1970 in the total crime index of the nation's largest cities. However, corruption existed even within the police department. An investigation in 1972 showed that many police had taken bribes in order to protect drug pushers and other criminals.

All citizens must work to promote law and order since crime hurts everyone, especially the weak and poor. Although the police have been accused of brutality on occasion, the dangers and tensions of police work are seldom taken into consideration. The Police Department has itself recognized the necessity of bridging the gap between the men on the force and citizens, especially the minorities who have accused them of bias and rough treatment. It gives new recruits "sensitivity" training in understanding all kinds of people. The Department recruits young blacks and other minority groups. It has its own John Jay College, where trainees can learn more about psychology and the newest methods of crime detection.

Summary

New York City is the nation's capital of business, finance, and culture. Greater New York began in 1898 when the state combined the five boroughs or counties (New York, Brooklyn, Queens, Staten Island, and Bronx). Since 1946 the United Nations has made its headquarters on Manhattan.

The cosmopolitan population of New York rose from 3,437,000 in 1900 to almost eight million in 1970. It fell to about 7,500,000 by 1978. The number of New Yorkers of European birth or parentage fell in the 1960s, while those from Latin America and especially from Puerto Rico rose sharply.

New York City's government follows the mayor-council form, with the unusual addition of the Board of Estimate. The mayor has many duties and powers. His or her actions are limited, however, by a money shortage. Despite many problems, the school system does a creditable or, in some cases, even an excellent job. The regular functions of the Police, Fire, and Health Departments are usually well handled. Considering the many difficulties, the government of New York City works fairly well.

Checking the high points

1. In what fields does New York City lead all other American cities?

2. What were the achievements of Andrew H. Green?

3. How has the population of New York City changed?

4. What are the main officials and agencies of New York City government?

5. Why is the mayor's job so difficult?

6. How well does the school system perform?

7. What are some of the functions of the Police, Fire, and Health departments which the public seldom sees?

Think these over

1. New York City is ungovernable. Comment.

2. New York City should become the 51st state. Why or why not?

3. True or false: Government would work better if the city turned most functions back to communities or private companies. Explain.

Vocabulary building

superlatives	brutality
militants	sensitivity
open admissions	incinerator
pollution	administrative officer

glossary

anthropologist a scientist who studies people and the way they live

archaeologist a scientist who studies ancient peoples by digging for and examining their cultural remains

ballot a written or printed list of candidates used in a secret vote

bankruptcy state of complete financial ruin

Bill of Rights the first ten amendments to the U.S. Constitution protecting specific freedoms

closed shop a business where all workers must be union members

collective bargaining formal talks between employers and union members to set wages and working conditions

constitution a set of basic rules and principles for a government

corporation a company owned by many stockholders

culture the ideas, customs, skills, and arts of a people

delegate a person who has the power to act and speak for others

democracy a form of government in which the people decide, either directly or through representatives, how to run the government

depression economic condition of widespread unemployment, business slowdown, and falling prices

extended family a household that has three or more generations living together

federal a government in which power is divided between a central government and smaller regional governments

geology a science that studies the history and composition of the earth

home rule self-government by local communities

immigrant a person who moves from one country to settle in another

Industrial Revolution the changes which resulted from the development of large-scale machine production in factories in the late 1700s and early 1800s

legislature the body of government that enacts laws

megalopolis a very large city or urban area

mercantilism a system based on a nation expecting its colonies to supply raw materials and to buy all finished products made by the mother country

metropolitan a city and the suburbs around it

migrate to move from one place to another

nuclear family a household of a mother, father, and their children

Patriot a colonist who supported independence from Britain during the American Revolution

patroon a person to whom the Dutch government gave a portion of land in New Amsterdam in exchange for the patroon bringing people to settle the land

primary an election in which members of a political party choose people to run in the general election

ratify to approve a law

reform to improve or correct

suffrage the right to vote

Tory a colonist who supported Britain during the American Revolution

union an organization of workers joined together to improve and protect their wages and working conditions

urban having to do with the city

veto constitutional right of one branch of government to reject a bill passed by another branch

Index

D

E

F

G

H

I

J

N

S

T